Peggy Palo Boyles
Oklahoma City, OK

Myriam Met
Rockville, MD

Richard S. Sayers
Longmont, CO

Carol Eubanks Wargin

Boston, Massachusetts
Upper Saddle River, New Jersey

Inset image, front cover: Visitors in the Caribbean National Forest (El Yunque), Puerto Rico
Front cover (background) and back cover: El Morro Fortress, San Juan, Puerto Rico

ISBN 0-13-134090-5
3 4 5 6 7 8 9 10 11 10 09 08

PRENTICE HALL

Realidades B

Realidades Authors

Peggy Palo Boyles

During her foreign language career of over thirty years, Peggy Palo Boyles has taught elementary, secondary, and university students in both private and public schools. She is currently an independent consultant who provides assistance to schools, districts, universities, and other organizations of foreign language education in the areas of curriculum, assessment, professional development, and program evaluation. She is also a part-time instructor at Oklahoma State University. She was a member of the ACTFL Performance Guidelines for the K–12 Learners task force and served as a Senior Editor for the project. She currently serves on the Advisory Committee for the ACTFL Assessment for Performance and Proficiency of Languages (AAPPL). Ms. Boyles is the Past-President of the National Association of District Supervisors of Foreign Language (NADSFL) and is the Advocacy Chair for the National Network of Early Language Learners (NNELL).

Myriam Met

For most of her professional life, Myriam (Mimi) Met has worked in the public schools, first as a high school teacher in New York, then as K–12 supervisor of language programs in the Cincinnati Public Schools, and finally as a Coordinator of Foreign Language in Montgomery County (MD) Public Schools. She is currently a Senior Research Associate at the National Foreign Language Center, University of Maryland, where she works on K–12 language policy and infrastructure development. Mimi Met has served on the Advisory Board for the National Standards for Foreign Language Learning, on the Executive Council of ACTFL, and as President of the National Association of District Supervisors of Foreign Languages (NADSFL). She has been honored by ACTFL with the Steiner Award for Leadership in K–12 Foreign Language Education and the Papalia Award for Excellence in Teacher Education.

Richard S. Sayers

Rich Sayers has been an educator in world languages for 28 years. He taught Spanish at Niwot High School in Longmont, CO for 18 years, where he taught levels 1 through AP Spanish. While at Niwot High School, Rich served as department chair, district foreign language coordinator, and board member of the Colorado Congress of Foreign Language Teachers. Rich has also served on the Board of the Southwest Conference on Language Teaching. In 1991, Rich was selected as one of the Disney Company's Foreign Language Teacher Honorees for the American Teacher Awards. Rich serves as National Consultant Training Manager for Prentice Hall. He has been a national consultant for modern and classical languages for Scott Foresman/Addison Wesley and Prentice Hall since 1996. He is also one of the co-authors of the PASO A PASO and REALIDADES Spanish series. Rich lives in Longmont, CO with his wife, Debbie. Their two sons, Todd and Scott, attend college in southern California.

Carol Eubanks Wargin

Carol Eubanks Wargin taught Spanish for 20 years at Glen Crest Middle School, Glen Ellyn, IL, and also served as Foreign Languages department chair. In 1997, Ms. Wargin's presentation "From Text to Test: How to Land Where You Planned" was honored as the best presentation at the Illinois Conference on the Teaching of Foreign Languages (ICTFL) and at the Central States Conference on the Teaching of Foreign Languages (CSC). She was twice named Outstanding Young Educator by the Jaycees.

Contributing Writers

Eduardo Aparicio
Chicago, IL

Daniel J. Bender
New Trier High School
Winnetka, IL

Marie Deer
Bloomington, IN

Leslie M. Grahn
Howard County Public Schools
Ellicott City, MD

Thomasina Hannum
Albuquerque, NM

Nancy S. Hernández
World Languages Supervisor
Simsbury (CT) Public Schools

Patricia J. Kule
Fountain Valley School of Colorado
Colorado Springs, CO

Jacqueline Hall Minet
Upper Montclair, NJ

Alex Paredes
Simi Valley, CA

Martha Singer Semmer
Breckenridge, CO

Dee Dee Drisdale Stafford
Putnam City Schools
Oklahoma City, OK

Christine S. Wells
Cheyenne Mountain Junior High School
Colorado Springs, CO

Michael Werner
University of Chicago
Chicago, IL

National Consultants

María R. Hubbard
Braintree, MA

Jan Polumbus
Tulsa, OK

Patrick T. Raven
Milwaukee, WI

Joseph Wieczorek
Baltimore, MD

Tabla de materias

For: Online Table of Contents
Web Code: jbk-0001

Tema 5
Fiesta en familia

Capítulo 5A
Una fiesta de cumpleaños

Objectives
- **Describe families**
- **Talk about celebrations and parties**
- **Ask and tell ages**
- **Express possession**
- **Understand cultural perspectives on family and celebrations**

Video Highlights
- **A primera vista:** *¡Feliz cumpleaños!*
- **GramActiva Videos:** the verb *tener;* possessive adjectives
- **Videomisterio:** ***¿Eres tú, María?,*** Episodio 1

Capítulo 5B
¡Vamos a un restaurante!

Objectives
- **Talk about family celebrations**
- **Describe family members and friends**
- **Ask politely to have something brought to you**
- **Order a meal in a restaurant**
- **Understand cultural perspectives on family celebrations**

Video Highlights
- **A primera vista:** *En el restaurante Casa Río*
- **GramActiva Videos:** the verb *venir;* the verbs *ser* and *estar*
- **Videomisterio:** ***¿Eres tú, María?,*** Episodio 2

Tema 6

La casa

Capítulo 6A
En mi dormitorio

Objectives

- **Talk about your bedroom**
- **Describe bedroom items and electronic equipment**
- **Make comparisons**
- **Understand cultural perspectives on homes**

Video Highlights

- **A primera vista:** *El cuarto de Ignacio*
- **GramActiva Videos:** making comparisons; the superlative; stem-changing verbs: *poder* and *dormir*
- **Videomisterio:** ***¿Eres tú, María?,*** Episodio 3

Capítulo 6B
¿Cómo es tu casa?

Objectives

- **Identify rooms in a house**
- **Name household chores**
- **Tell where you live**
- **Understand cultural perspectives on different types of housing**

Video Highlights

- **A primera vista:** *Los quehaceres de Elena*
- **GramActiva Videos:** affirmative *tú* commands; the present progressive tense
- **Videomisterio:** ***¿Eres tú, María?,*** Episodio 4

Tema 7

De compras

Capítulo 7A

¿Cuánto cuesta?

Objectives

- **Talk about clothes, shopping, and prices**
- **Describe your plans**
- **Talk about what you want and what you prefer**
- **Point out specific items**
- **Understand cultural perspectives on shopping**

Video Highlights

- **A primera vista:** *Una noche especial*
- **GramActiva Videos:** stem-changing verbs: *pensar, querer,* and *preferir;* demonstrative adjectives
- **Videomisterio:** ***¿Eres tú, María?,*** Episodio 5

Capítulo 7B

¡Qué regalo!

Objectives

- **Talk about buying gifts**
- **Tell what happened in the past**
- **Use direct object pronouns**
- **Understand cultural perspectives on gift-giving**

Video Highlights

- **A primera vista:** *Un regalo especial*
- **GramActiva Videos:** the preterite of *-ar* verbs; verbs ending in *-car* and *-gar;* direct object pronouns
- **Videomisterio:** ***¿Eres tú, María?,*** Episodio 6

Tema 8 Experiencias

Capítulo 8A
De vacaciones

Objectives

- Talk about things to do on vacation
- Describe places to visit while on vacation
- Talk about events in the past
- Understand cultural perspectives on travel and vacations

Video Highlights

- **A primera vista:** *¿Qué te pasó?*
- **GramActiva Videos:** the preterite of *-er* and *-ir* verbs; the preterite of *ir;* the personal *a*
- **Videomisterio:** ***¿Eres tú, María?,*** Episodio 7

Capítulo 8B
Ayudando en la comunidad

Objectives

- Discuss volunteer work and ways to protect the environment
- Talk about what people say
- Talk about what people did for others
- Understand cultural perspectives on volunteer work

Video Highlights

- **A primera vista:** *Cómo ayudamos a los demás*
- **GramActiva Videos:** the present tense of *decir;* indirect object pronouns; the preterite of *hacer* and *dar*
- **Videomisterio:** ***¿Eres tú, María?,*** Episodio 8

Tema 9 Medios de comunicación

Capítulo 9A
El cine y la televisión

Objectives

- Describe movies and television programs
- Express opinions about media entertainment
- Talk about things you have done recently
- Understand cultural perspectives on common gestures

Video Highlights

- **A primera vista:** *¿Qué dan en la tele?*
- **GramActiva Videos:** *acabar de* + infinitive; *gustar* and similar verbs
- **Videomisterio:** ***¿Eres tú, María?,*** Episodio 9

Capítulo 9B
La tecnología

Objectives

- Talk about computers and the Internet
- Learn to ask for something and to tell what something is used for
- Talk about knowing people or knowing how to do things
- Understand cultural perspectives on using technology

Video Highlights

- **A primera vista:** *¿Cómo se comunica?*
- **GramActiva Videos:** the present tense of *pedir* and *servir; saber* and *conocer*
- **Videomisterio:** ***¿Eres tú, María?,*** Episodio 10

Apéndices

México

Ciudad de Guanajuato, México

El Zócalo, México, D.F.

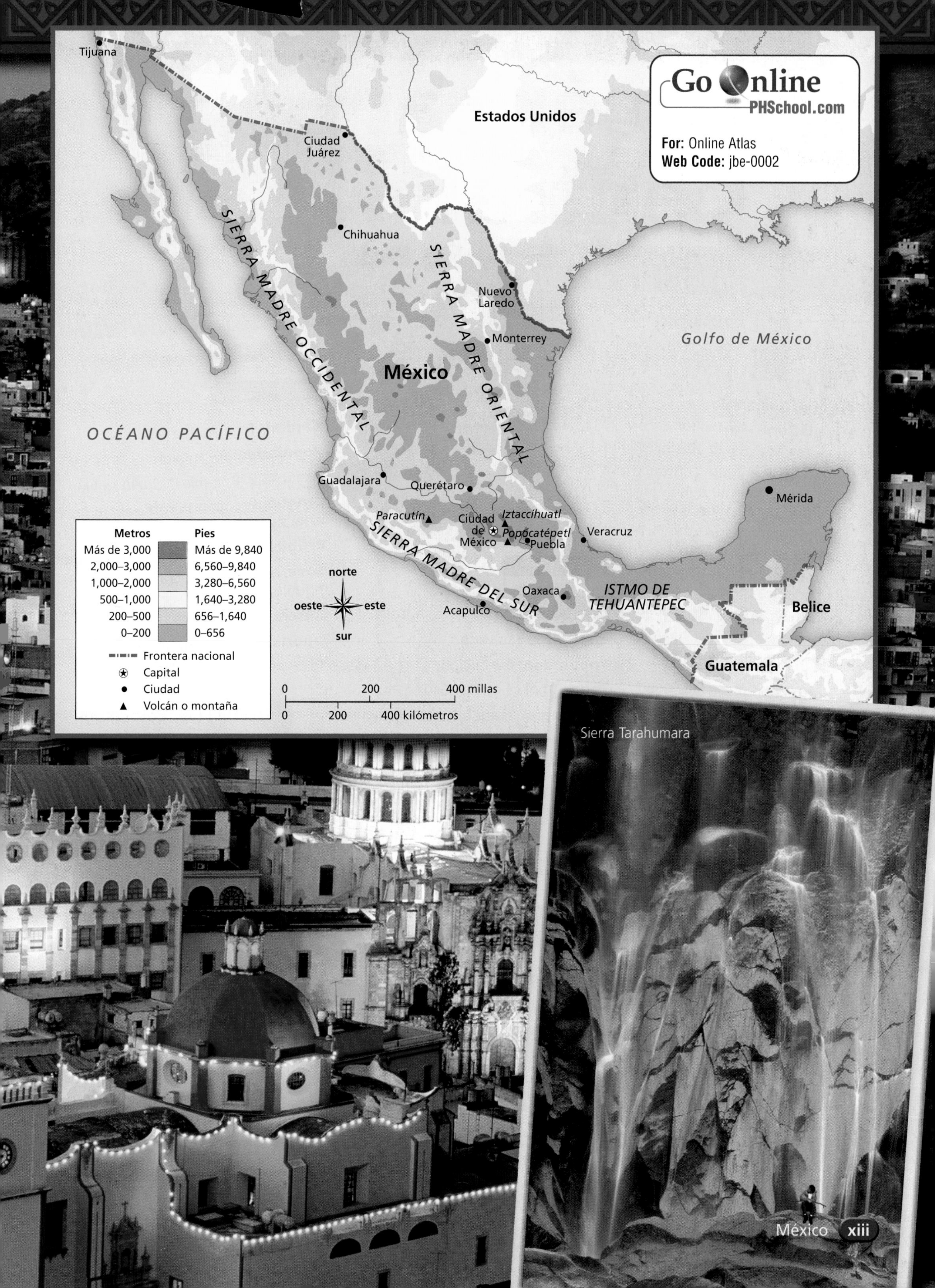
Go Online
PHSchool.com
For: Online Atlas
Web Code: jbe-0002
Tijuana
Estados Unidos
Ciudad Juárez
Chihuahua
SIERRA MADRE OCCIDENTAL
SIERRA MADRE ORIENTAL
Nuevo Laredo
Monterrey
Golfo de México
México
OCÉANO PACÍFICO
Guadalajara
Querétaro
Mérida
Paracutín
Ciudad de México
Iztaccíhuatl
Popocatépetl
Puebla
Veracruz
SIERRA MADRE DEL SUR
Oaxaca
Acapulco
ISTMO DE TEHUANTEPEC
Belice
Guatemala
norte
oeste
este
sur
Metros
Pies
Más de 3,000 — Más de 9,840
2,000–3,000 — 6,560–9,840
1,000–2,000 — 3,280–6,560
500–1,000 — 1,640–3,280
200–500 — 656–1,640
0–200 — 0–656
Frontera nacional
Capital
Ciudad
Volcán o montaña
0 200 400 millas
0 200 400 kilómetros
Sierra Tarahumara

América Central

Guatemala

Capital: Guatemala

Population: 14.7 million

Area: 42,043 sq mi / 108,890 sq km

Languages: Spanish (official), Quiche, Cakchiquel, Kekchi, Mam, Garifuna, Xinca, and other indigenous languages

Religions: Roman Catholic, Protestant, traditional Mayan beliefs

Government: constitutional democratic republic

Currency: *quetzal,* U.S. dollar *(dólar)*

Exports: fuels, machinery and transport equipment, construction materials, grain

El Salvador

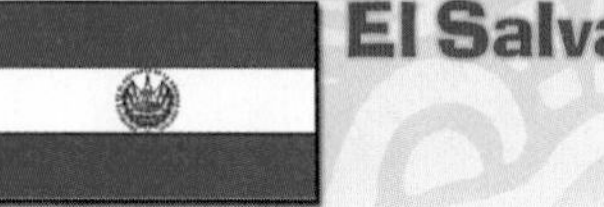

Capital: San Salvador

Population: 6.7 million

Area: 8,124 sq mi / 21,040 sq km

Languages: Spanish (official), Nahua

Religions: Roman Catholic, Protestant

Government: republic

Currency: U.S. dollar *(dólar)*

Exports: offshore assembly parts, equipment, coffee, sugar, shrimp, textiles, chemicals, electricity

Honduras

Capital: Tegucigalpa

Population: 6.7 million

Area: 43,278 sq mi / 112,090 sq km

Languages: Spanish (official), indigenous languages

Religions: Roman Catholic, Protestant

Government: democratic, constitutional republic

Currency: *lempira*

Exports: coffee, bananas, shrimp, lobster, meat, zinc, wood

Canal de Panamá

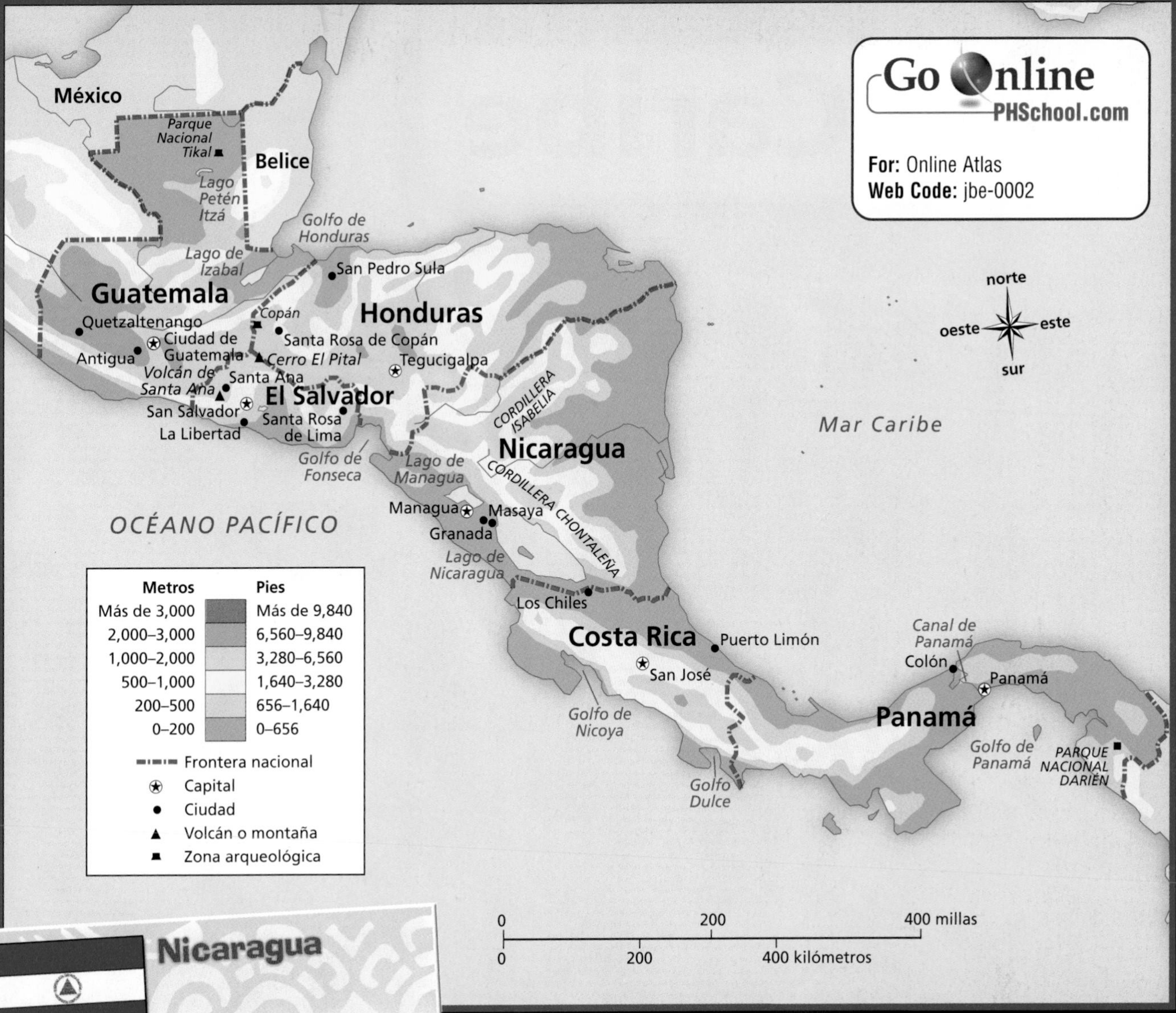

Go Online
PHSchool.com

For: Online Atlas
Web Code: jbe-0002

Metros		Pies
Más de 3,000		Más de 9,840
2,000–3,000		6,560–9,840
1,000–2,000		3,280–6,560
500–1,000		1,640–3,280
200–500		656–1,640
0–200		0–656

Frontera nacional
Capital
Ciudad
Volcán o montaña
Zona arqueológica

0 — 200 — 400 millas
0 — 200 — 400 kilómetros

Nicaragua

Capital: Managua
Population: 5.5 million
Area: 49,998 sq mi / 129,494 sq km
Languages: Spanish (official), English, Miskito, other indigenous languages
Religions: Roman Catholic, Protestant
Government: republic
Currency: *córdoba oro*
Exports: coffee, shrimp, lobster, cotton, tobacco, meat, sugar, bananas, gold

Costa Rica

Capital: San José
Population: 4 million
Area: 19,730 sq mi / 51,100 sq km
Languages: Spanish (official), English
Religions: Roman Catholic, Protestant
Government: democratic republic
Currency: *colón de Costa Rica*
Exports: coffee, bananas, sugar, textiles, electronic components

Panamá

Capital: Ciudad de Panamá
Population: 3 million
Area: 30,193 sq mi / 78,200 sq km
Languages: Spanish (official), English
Religions: Roman Catholic, Protestant
Government: constitutional democracy
Currency: *balboa,* U.S. dollar *(dólar)*
Exports: bananas, sugar, shrimp, coffee

El Caribe

El Morro, San Juan, Puerto Rico

El arrecife de coral, República Dominicana

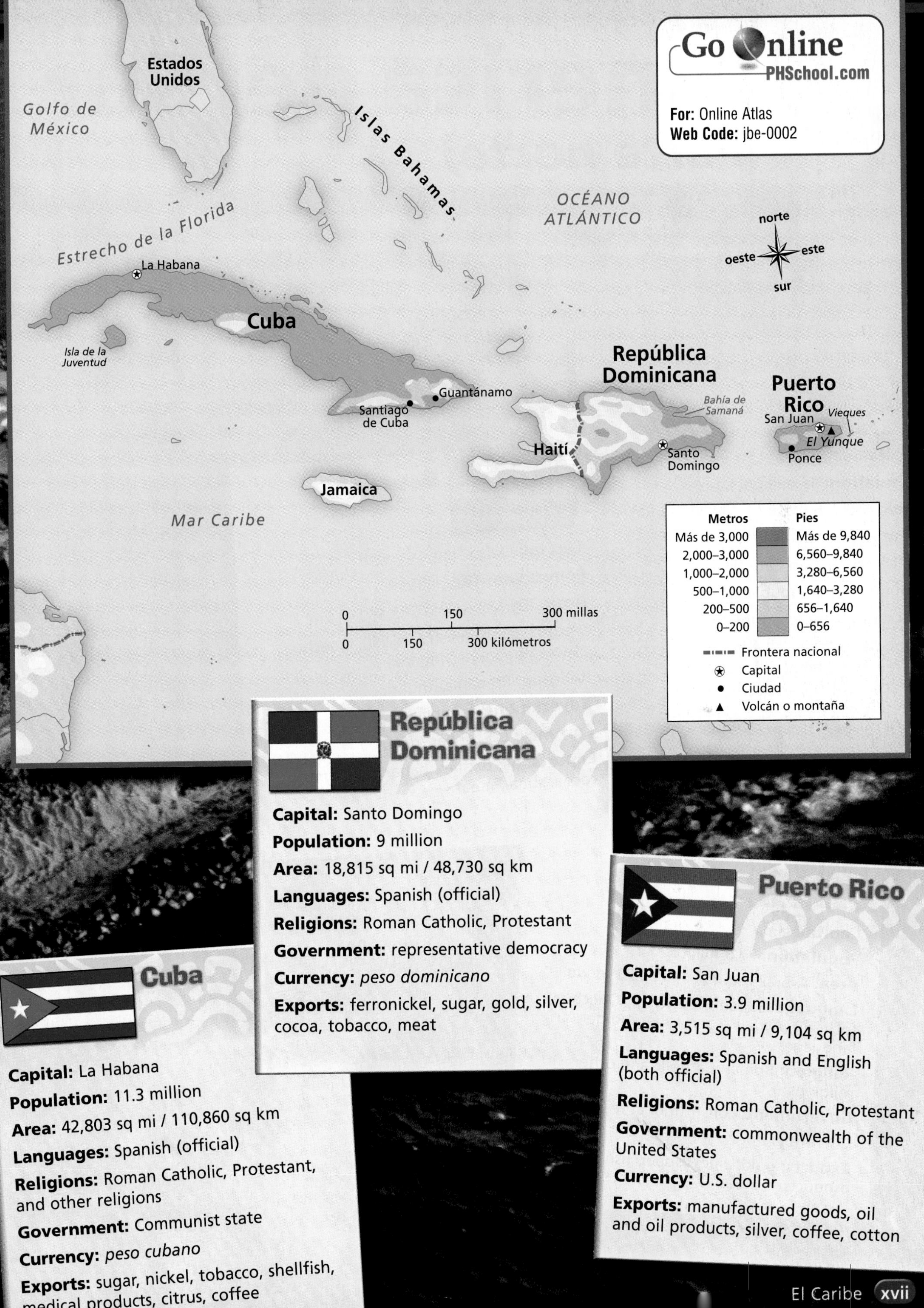

República Dominicana

Capital: Santo Domingo
Population: 9 million
Area: 18,815 sq mi / 48,730 sq km
Languages: Spanish (official)
Religions: Roman Catholic, Protestant
Government: representative democracy
Currency: *peso dominicano*
Exports: ferronickel, sugar, gold, silver, cocoa, tobacco, meat

Cuba

Capital: La Habana
Population: 11.3 million
Area: 42,803 sq mi / 110,860 sq km
Languages: Spanish (official)
Religions: Roman Catholic, Protestant, and other religions
Government: Communist state
Currency: *peso cubano*
Exports: sugar, nickel, tobacco, shellfish, medical products, citrus, coffee

Puerto Rico

Capital: San Juan
Population: 3.9 million
Area: 3,515 sq mi / 9,104 sq km
Languages: Spanish and English (both official)
Religions: Roman Catholic, Protestant
Government: commonwealth of the United States
Currency: U.S. dollar
Exports: manufactured goods, oil and oil products, silver, coffee, cotton

América del Sur
(Parte norte)

Colombia

Capital: Bogotá
Population: 43 million
Area: 439,736 sq mi / 1,138,910 sq km
Languages: Spanish (official)
Religion: Roman Catholic
Government: republic
Currency: *peso colombiano*
Exports: textiles, oil and oil products, coffee, gold, emeralds, bananas, tobacco, cotton, wood, hydroelectricity

Ecuador

Capital: Quito
Population: 13.4 million
Area: 109,483 sq mi / 283,560 sq km
Languages: Spanish (official), Quechua, other indigenous languages
Religion: Roman Catholic
Government: republic
Currency: U.S. dollar *(dólar)*
Exports: oil, textiles, bananas, shrimp, cocoa, sugar, meat

Perú

Capital: Lima
Population: 27.9 million
Area: 496,226 sq mi / 1,285,220 sq km
Languages: Spanish (official), Quechua, (official), Aymara, and other indigenous languages
Religion: Roman Catholic and other religions
Government: constitutional republic
Currency: *nuevo sol*
Exports: gold, zinc, copper, fish and fish products, textiles

Las ruinas de Machu Picchu, Perú

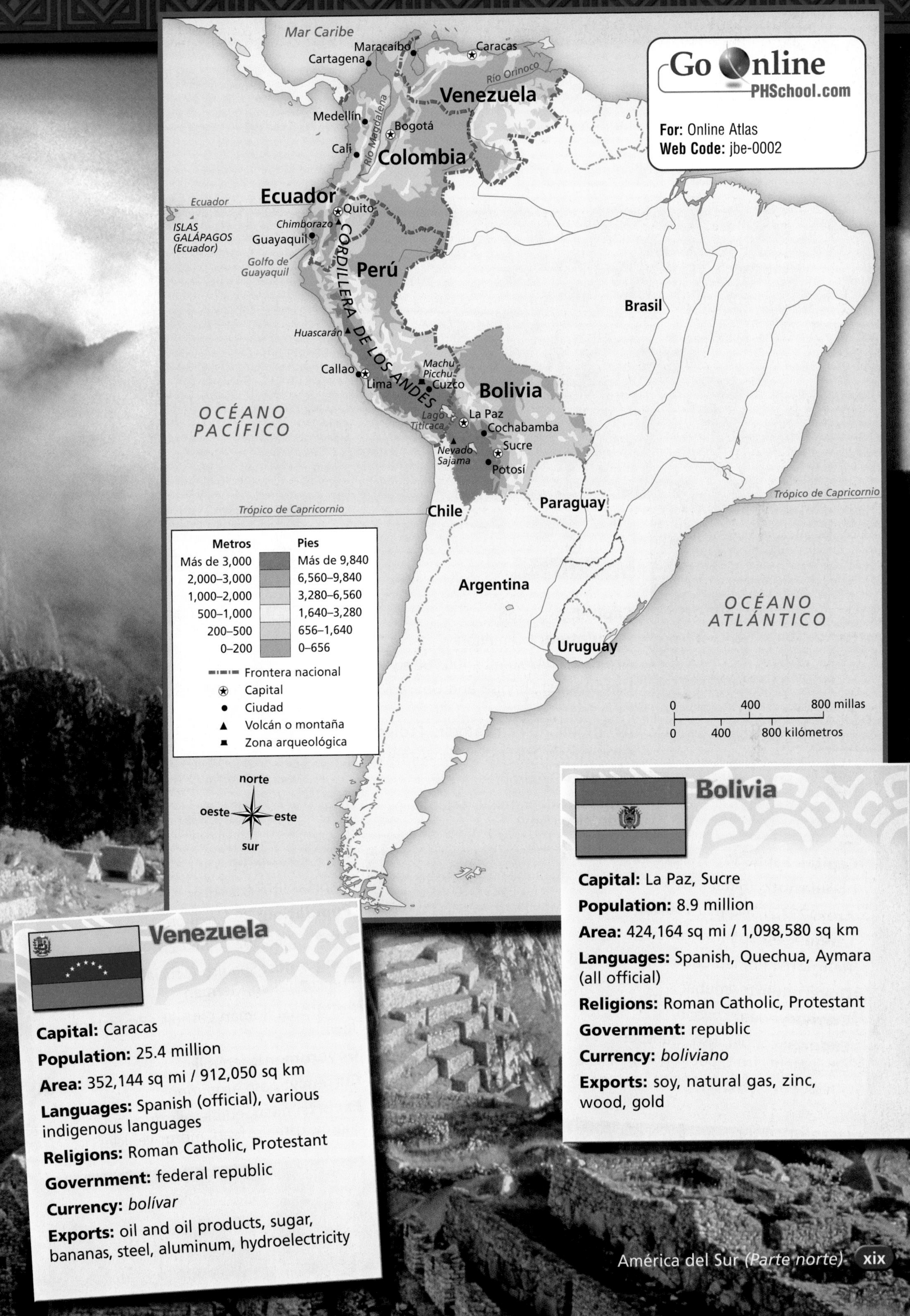

Bolivia

Capital: La Paz, Sucre
Population: 8.9 million
Area: 424,164 sq mi / 1,098,580 sq km
Languages: Spanish, Quechua, Aymara (all official)
Religions: Roman Catholic, Protestant
Government: republic
Currency: *boliviano*
Exports: soy, natural gas, zinc, wood, gold

Venezuela

Capital: Caracas
Population: 25.4 million
Area: 352,144 sq mi / 912,050 sq km
Languages: Spanish (official), various indigenous languages
Religions: Roman Catholic, Protestant
Government: federal republic
Currency: *bolívar*
Exports: oil and oil products, sugar, bananas, steel, aluminum, hydroelectricity

América del Sur
(Parte sur)

Monte Fitz Roy, Patagonia, Argentina

Paraguay

Capital: Asunción

Population: 6.3 million

Area: 157,047 sq mi / 406,750 sq km

Languages: Spanish and Guaraní (both official)

Religions: Roman Catholic, Protestant

Government: constitutional republic

Currency: *guaraní*

Exports: sugar, meat, tapioca, hydroelectricity

Chile

Capital: Santiago

Population: 16 million

Area: 292,260 sq mi / 756,950 sq km

Languages: Spanish (official)

Religions: Roman Catholic, Protestant

Government: republic

Currency: *peso chileno*

Exports: copper, fish, transport equipment, fruit, paper and pulp, chemicals, hydroelectricity

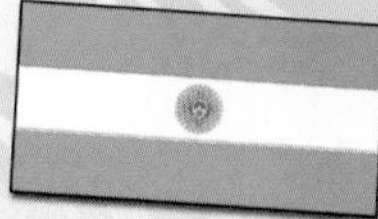

Argentina

Capital: Buenos Aires

Population: 39.5 million

Area: 1,068,302 sq mi / 2,766,890 sq km

Languages: Spanish (official), English, French, Italian, German

Religions: Roman Catholic, Protestant, Jewish

Government: republic

Currency: *peso argentino*

Exports: meat, edible oils, fuels and energy, cereals, feed, motor vehicles

Go Online
PHSchool.com
For: Online Atlas
Web Code: jbe-0002
Venezuela
Colombia
Ecuador
Ecuador
Perú
OCÉANO PACÍFICO
Lago Titicaca
Bolivia
ALTIPLANO
CORDILLERA DE LOS ANDES
GRAN CHACO
Paraguay
Río Paraguay
Trópico de Capricornio
Trópico de Capricornio
Cataratas del Iguazú
Asunción
OCÉANO ATLÁNTICO
Chile
Río Paraná
Argentina
Uruguay
Viña del Mar
Valparaíso
Santiago
Cerro Aconcagua
Rosario
Buenos Aires
Montevideo
Punta del Este
PAMPAS
Río de la Plata
Mar del Plata
norte
oeste
este
sur
PATAGONIA
Cerro de San Valentín
Torres del Paine
TIERRA DEL FUEGO
Estrecho de Magallanes
Cabo de Hornos
0 400 800 millas
0 400 800 kilómetros
Metros
Pies
Más de 3,000 | Más de 9,840
2,000–3,000 | 6,560–9,840
1,000–2,000 | 3,280–6,560
500–1,000 | 1,640–3,280
200–500 | 656–1,640
0–200 | 0–656
Frontera nacional
Capital
Ciudad
Volcán o montaña
Uruguay
Capital: Montevideo
Population: 3.4 million
Area: 68,039 sq mi / 176,220 sq km
Languages: Spanish (official), Portunol/Brazilero
Religions: Roman Catholic, Protestant, and other religions
Government: constitutional republic
Currency: peso uruguayo
Exports: foods, vehicles, meat, rice, timber

España
Guinea Ecuatorial

España

Capital: Madrid
Population: 40.3 million
Area: 194,897 sq mi / 504,782 sq km
Languages: Castilian Spanish (official), Catalan, Galician, Basque
Religion: Roman Catholic
Government: parliamentary monarchy
Currency: *euro*
Exports: food, machinery, motor vehicles

El Alcázar de Segovia, Segovia, España

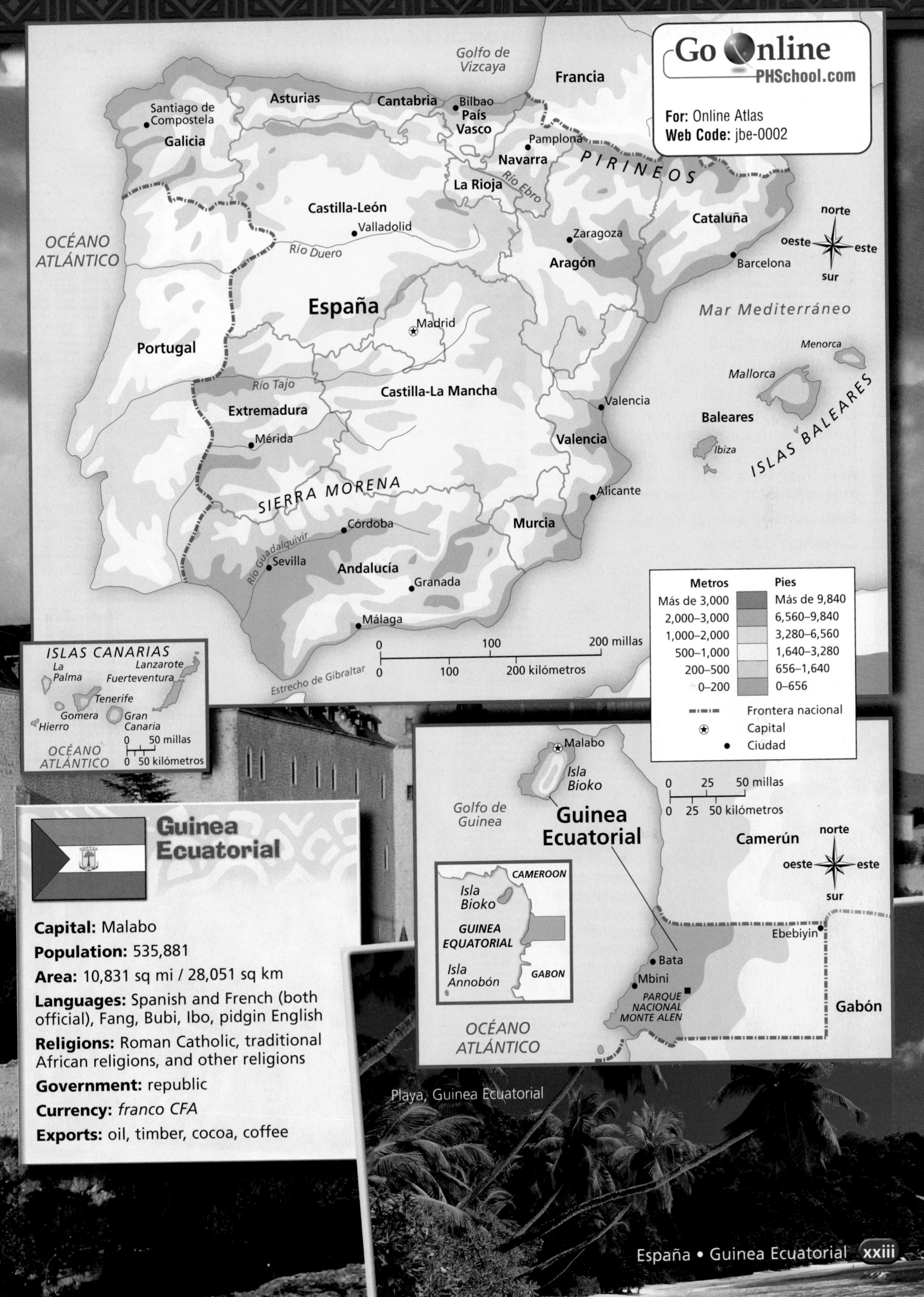

Guinea Ecuatorial

Capital: Malabo

Population: 535,881

Area: 10,831 sq mi / 28,051 sq km

Languages: Spanish and French (both official), Fang, Bubi, Ibo, pidgin English

Religions: Roman Catholic, traditional African religions, and other religions

Government: republic

Currency: *franco CFA*

Exports: oil, timber, cocoa, coffee

Playa, Guinea Ecuatorial

Estados Unidos

Estados Unidos

Capital: Washington, D.C.

Population: 296 million

Area: 3,717,813 sq mi / 9,631,418 sq km

Languages: English, Spanish, other Indo-European languages, Asian and Pacific Islander languages, other languages

Religions: Protestant, Roman Catholic, Jewish, Muslim, and other religions

Government: federal republic

Currency: U.S. dollar

Exports: motor vehicles, aerospace equipment, telecommunications, electronics, consumer goods, chemicals, food, wheat, corn

Las grandes llanuras

Caras estadounidenses

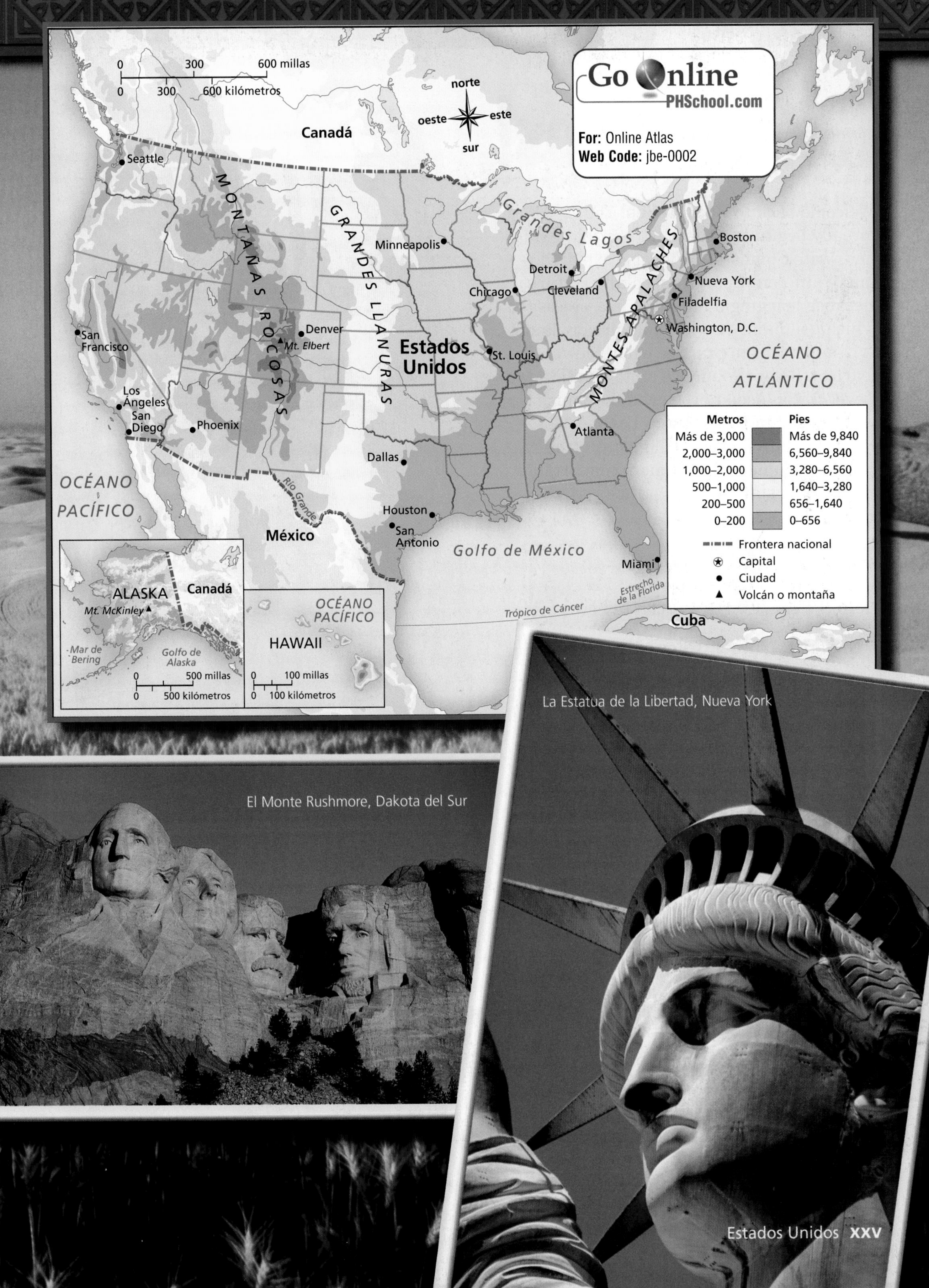

La Estatua de la Libertad, Nueva York

El Monte Rushmore, Dakota del Sur

¡Bienvenidos!

Welcome back to **Realidades!** You've already begun to understand, speak, read and write Spanish. You've also explored many different Spanish-speaking cultures. Because learning a language is a process in which you build on what you already know, it is important to practice what you've learned. Before you move on to **Realidades** Level B, you need to review the Spanish you learned in **Realidades** Level A. The *Para empezar* chapter will give you the practice you need to feel more comfortable. So, let's get started!

Tips for Reviewing

Here are some ways you can review.

- **Organize your information.** It's easier to remember a word if you think about the category it belongs to. The material you learned in Level A was organized into four *Temas:* friends, school, foods and beverages, and leisure activities. Brainstorm a list of words and expressions you remember that relate to each of these categories. How many can you think of?
- **Make flashcards.** A great way to refresh your memory is to review with flashcards. Put the Spanish word on one side and either an English word or a drawing on the other. Then pair up with a classmate to quiz one another on the words.
- **Look for meaning within the context of a sentence.** If you can't remember a word or phrase, try reading or listening to the entire sentence, and see if you can figure out its meaning based on what else is being said.

Go Online
PHSchool.com
For: More Tips for Studying Spanish
Web Code: jbe-0003

Study Tips

Here are some easy tips to help you learn Spanish.

- **You don't need to understand everything.** When reading a text or listening to someone speak Spanish, don't worry about knowing the meaning of every word. Focus on what you *do* know, and look for context cues to help you with the rest. You'll be surprised at how much you understand!
- **Look for opportunities to practice your Spanish.** If you wait until you think your Spanish is perfect, you will have missed many opportunities to use it. Take risks! You will learn from your mistakes. Concentrate on *what* you are saying, and *how* you say it will soon come naturally.
- **Look for Strategy and ¿Recuerdas? boxes.** Throughout **Realidades,** you'll see boxes that will help you learn something new or remind you of something you've already learned.
- **Go beyond the book.** Look for ways to practice your Spanish outside of class. Practice with a friend, look for Spanish words on products you use every day, talk with Spanish speakers, or use the Internet. You can also visit the Web pages for **Realidades** at **PHSchool.com.** Throughout the book you'll find **Go Online** icons with **Web Codes** that give you direct access to additional practice or information on the Internet.
- **Have fun!** The goal of studying Spanish is to communicate! In **Realidades** Level B, you'll find lots of activities that allow you to work with other students, play games, act out skits, explore the Internet, create projects, and use technology. Try out all of these activities and you'll have fun while your Spanish gets better and better.

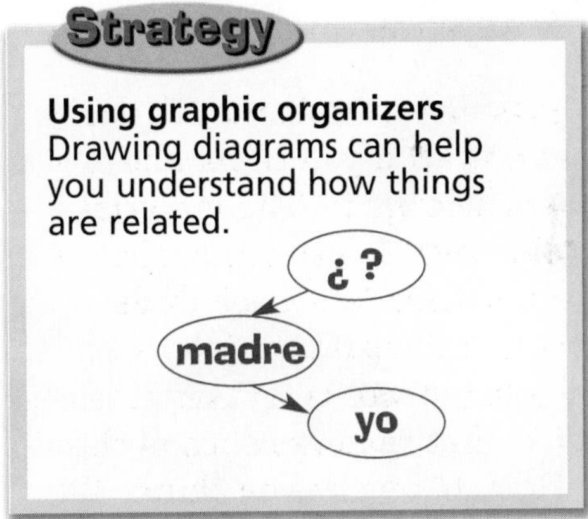

¿Recuerdas?

Use *señor, señora,* and *señorita* when talking **to** adults. Use *el* in front of *señor* and *la* in front of *señora* or *señorita* when talking **about** adults.

Montando en monopatín en el sur de California

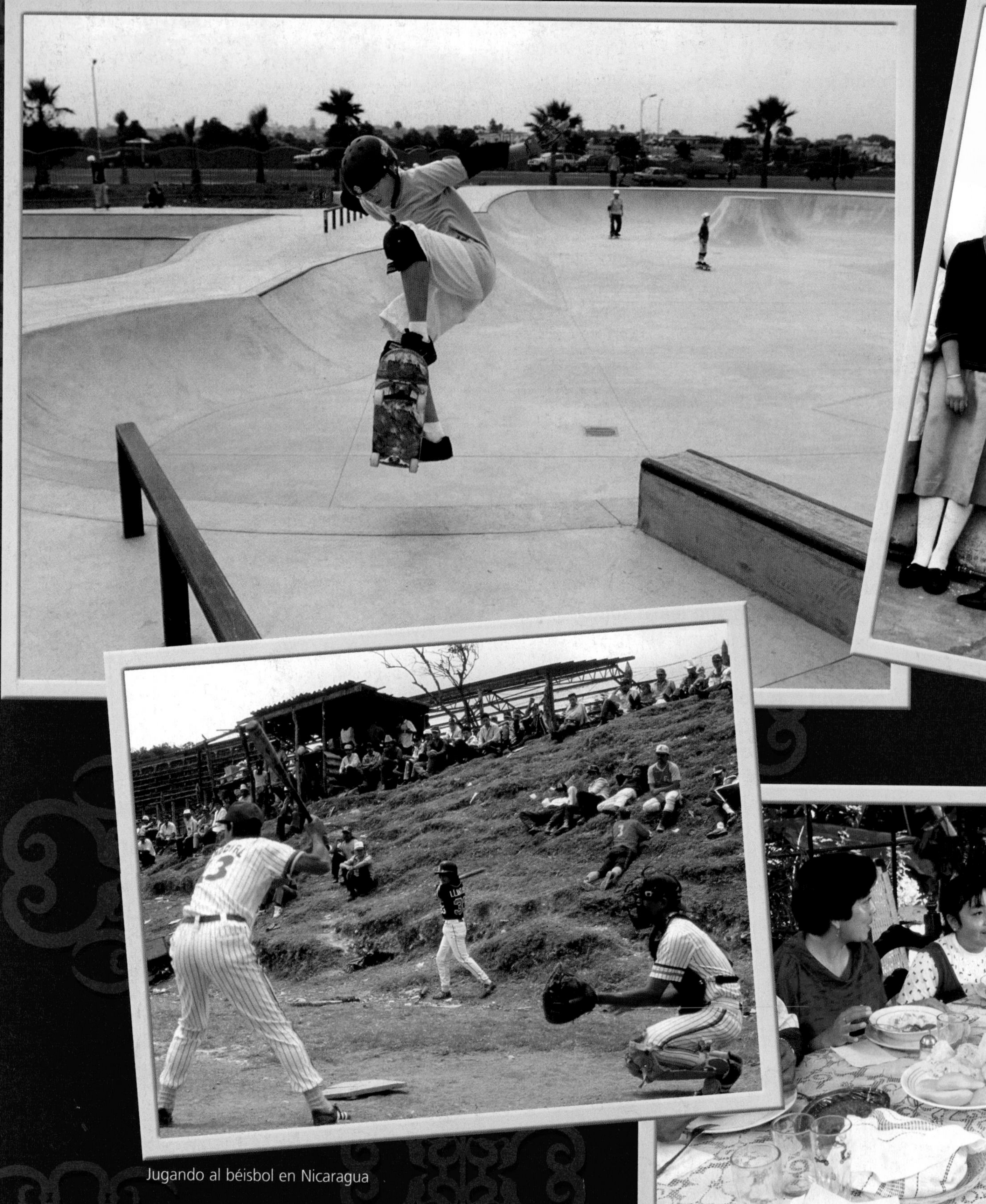

Jugando al béisbol en Nicaragua

antes en Valle de Bravo, México

Un almuerzo en familia

Para empezar

Objectives

1 Mis amigos y yo

- Talk about what you like and don't like to do
- Describe yourself and other people

2 La escuela

- Talk about the classes you have
- Describe your classroom
- Ask and tell who is doing an action

3 La comida

- Talk about foods and beverages for breakfast, lunch, and dinner
- Discuss food, health, and exercise

4 Los pasatiempos

- Talk about locations in your community
- Talk about leisure activities
- Tell where you go
- Ask questions

1 Mis amigos y yo

Objectives

- Talk about what you like and don't like to do
- Describe yourself and other people

bailar

escuchar música

nadar

escribir cuentos

montar en monopatín

correr

esquiar

dibujar

cantar

pasar tiempo con amigos

ver la tele

usar la computadora

hablar por teléfono

tocar la guitarra

leer revistas

¿Qué te gusta hacer?

to tell what you like to do

(A mí) me gusta ___.
(A mí) me gusta más ___.
(A mí) me gusta mucho ___.
A mí también
ir a la escuela
jugar videojuegos
montar en bicicleta
patinar
practicar deportes
trabajar

to say what you don't like to do

(A mí) no me gusta ___.
(A mí) no me gusta nada ___.
A mí tampoco.

to ask others what they like to do

¿Qué te gusta hacer?
¿Qué te gusta más?
¿Te gusta ___?
¿Y a ti?

other useful words and expressions

ni . . . ni	sí
o	también
pues	y

For: Vocabulary Practice
Web Code: jbd-0001

artístico, -a

desordenado, -a

impaciente

trabajador, -a

perezoso, -a

atrevido, -a

talentoso, -a

gracioso, -a

reservado, -a

estudioso, -a

sociable

deportista

Y tú, ¿cómo eres?

to talk about what you and others are like

bueno, -a
inteligente
ordenado, -a
paciente
serio, -a
simpático, -a

to tell people what someone likes or doesn't like

le gusta . . .
no le gusta . . .

to describe someone

soy
no soy
es

other useful words and expressions

a veces
muy
pero
según
según mi familia

to tell whom you are talking about

el chico
la chica
yo
él
ella

¡Hola!

Me llamo Jaime Ordóñez Soriano. Soy de Santiago de los Caballeros en la República Dominicana. Yo soy deportista y un poco reservado. Me gusta leer libros de historia y montar en bicicleta. Mi amiga Clara es de Camagüey, Cuba. No es ni deportista ni reservada. Ella es muy talentosa, pero yo no. No me gusta ni tocar la guitarra ni dibujar. Tampoco me gusta bailar. Y tú, ¿cómo eres? ¿Qué te gusta hacer?

Leer/Escribir

Hola, soy Jaime

Read the letter from your new pen pal, Jaime. Number your paper from 1–6 and for each of Jaime's statements, write *cierto* if it is true, or *falso* if it is false. Correct the false statements.

1. Yo soy de Camagüey.
2. Mi amiga Clara no es reservada.
3. Yo soy muy talentoso.
4. Me gusta leer revistas.
5. No me gusta ni bailar ni dibujar.
6. Me gusta montar en bicicleta.

¿Recuerdas?

In Spanish, you might use one or more negatives after answering "no".

—¿Te gusta cantar?

—**No, no** me gusta **nada.**

If you want to say that you do not like either of two choices, use *ni… ni:*

- **No** me gusta **ni** nadar **ni** dibujar.

Gramática • Repaso

Infinitives

Verbs are words that are most often used to name actions. The most basic form of a verb is called the **infinitive.** In English, you can spot infinitives because they usually have the word "to" in front of them. Spanish infinitives are only one word, and always end in *-ar, -er,* or *-ir:*

nadar, leer, escribir

The verb *gustar*

It's easy to talk about the things you like to do once you know the infinitive. Just add the infinitive to *te gusta* or *me gusta.*

¿Te gusta **practicar deportes?**

Sí, me gusta **correr.**

Dibujar/Hablar

¿Te gusta dibujar?

1. On a sheet of paper, make simple sketches of three activities that you like to do, and three that you do not like to do.
2. Work with a partner. Exchange your sketches and take turns asking each other whether or not you like doing each activity shown.

Modelo

A —*¿Te gusta bailar?*
B —*No, no me gusta bailar. ¿Y a ti?*
A —*Sí, me gusta mucho bailar con mis amigos.*
o:—*A mí tampoco. Me gusta más cantar.*

Escribir/Hablar

Y tú, ¿qué dices?

1. ¿Qué te gusta hacer en invierno? ¿Qué te gusta hacer en verano?
2. ¿Qué te gusta hacer más después de las clases?
3. ¿Qué no te gusta hacer los fines de semana?
4. ¿Qué revistas te gusta leer? ¿Qué libros?
5. ¿Con quién te gusta hablar por teléfono?

Gramática • Repaso

Adjectives

Words that describe people and things are called adjectives *(adjetivos)*.

In Spanish, most adjectives have both masculine and feminine forms. The masculine form usually ends in the letter *-o* and the feminine form usually ends in the letter *-a*.

Masculine adjectives are used to describe masculine nouns and feminine adjectives are used to describe feminine nouns.

Paco es ordenad**o** y simpátic**o**.

Marta es ordenad**a** y simpátic**a**.

Adjectives that end in *-e* describe both masculine and feminine nouns.

Anita es inteligent**e** y Pedro es inteligent**e** también.

When the masculine form of an adjective ends in *-or*, its feminine form ends in *-ora*.

Juan Carlos es trabajad**or** y Marilú es trabajad**ora** también.

Some adjectives that end in *-a*, such as *deportista*, describe both masculine and feminine nouns. You will need to learn which adjectives follow this pattern.

Tomás es deportist**a** y Raquel es deportist**a** también.

Actividad 4

jbd-0099

Escuchar

Los amigos de Jorge

Listen to Jorge describe his friends. Write the numbers 1–5 on a sheet of paper. For each of his statements, write the name of the activity you think his friends would prefer.

1. ver la tele o estudiar
2. correr o dibujar
3. leer o jugar videojuegos
4. montar en monopatín o escribir cuentos
5. hablar por teléfono o usar la computadora

Actividad 5

Escribir

¿Cómo son los estudiantes?

Number your paper from 1–6. Use the words in the box below to write a sentence describing each of the following people.

Paloma

Modelo

Paloma es trabajadora.

atrevido	gracioso
talentoso	perezoso
sociable	trabajador
desordenado	

1. 
Gloria

2. 
Lola

3. 
Felipe

4. 
Marisol

5. 
Juan

6. 
Carolina

Leer/Escribir

En la clase de español de Jaime

Unscramble the following descriptions from your pen pal Jaime's letter in which he talks about people in his Spanish class. Write your paragraph on a sheet of paper.

Me gusta mucho mi clase de español.

1. estudioso soy chico un yo.
2. Cruz una es profesora la paciente Sra. muy.
3. seria chica una es Ana.
4. no un Rafael chico es serio.
5. él un gracioso chico es.

Me gusta ir a la escuela y pasar tiempo con amigos.

¿Recuerdas?

In Spanish, adjectives usually come after the noun they describe. Notice how *artística* follows *chica* in this sentence:

- Margarita es **una chica artística.**

Hablar

¿Cómo eres y qué te gusta hacer?

Working with a partner, find out what each other is like. Ask questions using the following adjectives and answer following the model.

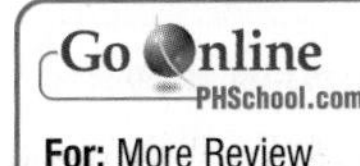

Modelo

A —*¿Eres talentoso(a)?*
B —*Sí, soy un(a) chico(a) talentoso(a). Me gusta mucho escribir cuentos.*
o: *Pues, no soy un(a) chico(a) muy talentoso(a). Me gusta más ver la tele.*

Estudiante A

artístico, -a
deportista
estudioso, -a
perezoso, -a
reservado, -a
talentoso, -a

¡Respuesta personal!

Estudiante B

¡Respuesta personal!

2 La escuela

Objectives

- Talk about the classes you have
- Describe your classroom
- Ask and tell who is doing an action

to talk about your school day
la clase
en la . . . hora
la tarea

to describe school activities
enseñar
estudiar
hablar

to describe your classes
aburrido, -a
difícil
divertido, -a
fácil
favorito, -a
interesante
práctico, -a
más . . . que

El horario de clases

primera hora	tecnología
segunda hora	arte
tercera hora	ciencias sociales
cuarta hora	ciencias naturales
quinta hora	el almuerzo
sexta hora	español
séptima hora	matemáticas
octava hora	inglés
novena hora	educación física

to talk about things you need for school
la calculadora
la carpeta de argollas
el diccionario
necesito
necesitas

other useful words and expressions
a ver . . .
para . . .
¿Quién?
mucho, -a

Tu día en la escuela

Tu sala de clases

to identify gender and quantity of nouns

los, las

unos, unas

to indicate possession

de

mi

tu

to identify (description, quantity)

Es un(a)

Hay

¿Qué es esto?

to talk about classroom items

el disquete

la mochila

la pantalla

el ratón

el teclado

to indicate location

al lado de la/del

allí

aquí

debajo de la/del

delante de la/del

detrás de la/del

¿Dónde?

en

encima de la/del

Go Online PHSchool.com
For: Vocab. Practice
Web Code: jbd-0003

Horario

Estudiante: Gabriela del Mar Romero

1ª hora:	inglés
2ª hora:	matemáticas
3ª hora:	tecnología
4ª hora:	arte
5ª hora:	educación física
6ª hora:	almuerzo
7ª hora:	ciencias naturales
8ª hora:	español
9ª hora:	ciencias sociales

jbd-0099

Escuchar

¿Para qué clase?

Look at the schedule above as you listen to Gabriela get ready for school. Write the numbers 1–5 on a sheet of paper. For each statement that you hear, write the class period that Gabriela is gathering items for.

Escribir/Hablar

¿Cómo es tu horario?

1. Using Gabriela's schedule as a model, write your own schedule on a sheet of paper.

2. With a partner, use your schedules to talk about your classes.

Modelo

A —*Para ti, ¿qué clase es más fácil?*
B —*Para mí, la clase de arte es más fácil. Me gusta mucho dibujar.*
A —*¿En qué hora es la clase?*
B —*Es en la segunda hora.*

Estudiante A

fácil
aburrida
difícil
interesante
práctica
divertida

Estudiante B

¡Respuesta personal!

Gramática • Repaso

Subject pronouns

The subject of a sentence tells who is doing the action. You can also use subject pronouns, which replace people's names.

Eduardo toca muy bien la guitarra.
Él toca muy bien la guitarra.

Laura y yo practicamos muchos deportes.
Nosotros practicamos muchos deportes.

Here are the subject pronouns in Spanish:

yo	I	**nosotros** **nosotras**	we *(masc., masc./fem.)* we *(fem.)*
tú	you *(familiar)*	**vosotros** **vosotras**	you *(masc., masc./fem.)* you *(fem.)*
usted (Ud.)	you *(formal)*	**ustedes (Uds.)**	you *(formal)*
él **ella**	he she	**ellos** **ellas**	they *(masc., masc./fem.)* they *(fem.)*

Present tense of *-ar* verbs

You will want to use verbs in ways other than in the infinitive form. To create the present-tense form of most *-ar* verbs, you first drop the *-ar* ending, leaving the stem. Then you add new endings to the stem. These verb endings tell you who is doing the action.

Here are the present-tense forms of the verb *hablar:*

(yo)	**hablo**	(nosotros) (nosotras)	**hablamos**
(tú)	**hablas**	(vosotros) (vosotras)	**habláis**
Ud. (él) (ella)	**habla**	Uds. (ellos) (ellas)	**hablan**

Actividad 10 **Escribir**

Las actividades de mis amigos

Use the words in the box below to write complete sentences about what you and your friends do.

estudiar	montar en monopatín
usar la computadora	escuchar música
patinar	trabajar
nadar	bailar

¡Respuesta personal!

Modelo

Mi amigo(a) *(nombre)*
Mi amiga Laura nada todos los días.

1. yo
2. mi mejor *(best)* amigo(a)
3. mi profesor(a)
4. los estudiantes en mi clase de español
5. mis amigos y yo

Hablar

¿Qué hacen los fines de semana?

With a partner, take turns asking about what you and your friends do on the weekends.

Modelo

A —*¿Estudias tú los sábados?*
B —*Sí, yo estudio los sábados.*
A —*¿Y tus amigos?*
B —*Sí, mis amigos y yo estudiamos mucho.*
o: *No, ellos no estudian, pero usan la computadora.*

Estudiante A

¡Respuesta personal!

Estudiante B

¡Respuesta personal!

Escribir

¿Generalmente dónde están?

Number your paper from 1–5. For each of the times below, write a sentence to tell where you and the people you know generally are.

Modelo

el domingo a las ocho de la mañana: *(nombre)* y *(nombre)*
El domingo a las ocho de la mañana, Joaquín y Sarita están en la iglesia.

1. el lunes a las diez de la mañana: tu mejor amigo(a) *(nombre)*
2. el miércoles al mediodía: la profesora *(nombre)*
3. el sábado a las ocho de la noche: tú
4. el viernes a la una de la tarde: los profesores *(nombre)* y *(nombre)*
5. el domingo a las once de la mañana: tu amigo(a) *(nombre)* y tú

¿Recuerdas?

Estar is irregular because the *yo* form doesn't follow a regular pattern, and because *estás, está,* and *están* require accent marks. *Estar* is used to tell how someone feels or where something is located.

- **Estoy** en en la escuela.

Hablar

¿Qué hay y dónde está?

With a partner, take turns asking if various items are in the following picture, and where each item is located.

Modelo

A —*¿Hay una computadora?*
B —*Sí, hay una computadora.*
A —*Pues, ¿dónde está?*
B —*Está encima de la mesa.*

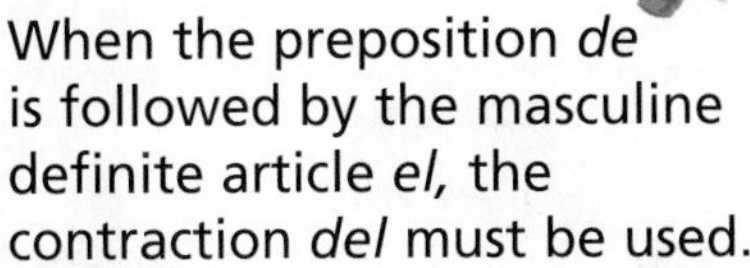

¿Recuerdas?

When the preposition *de* is followed by the masculine definite article *el,* the contraction *del* must be used.

- La computadora está encima **del** escritorio.

Escribir/Hablar

Juego

Make a list of five items you can see in your classroom for which you know the names in Spanish. With a partner, describe where each item is, and your partner will guess which item you are talking about.

Modelo

A —*Está al lado de la puerta, debajo del sacapuntas.*
B —*¿Es la papelera?*
A —*¡Claro que sí!*
o:—*No, está cerca de la papelera, pero no es la papelera.*

For: More Review
Web Code: jbd-0004

3 La comida

Objectives

- Talk about foods and beverages for breakfast, lunch, and dinner
- Discuss food, health, and exercise

en el desayuno

el pan tostado

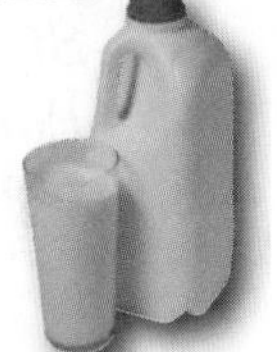

la leche

el café

el cereal

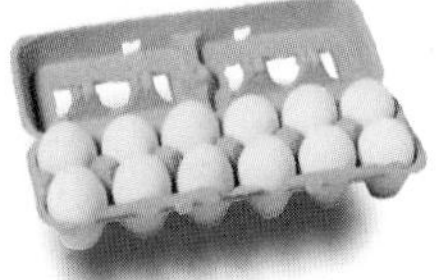

los huevos

el jugo de manzana

en el almuerzo

el sándwich de jamón y queso

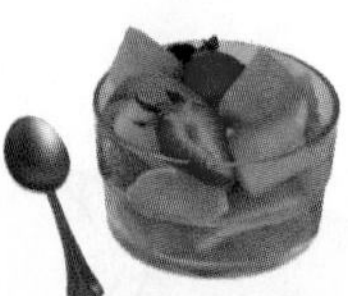

la ensalada de fruta

las papas fritas

la limonada

el té helado

la sopa de verduras

¿Desayuno o almuerzo?

to talk about breakfast

el desayuno
el jugo de naranja
el pan
el plátano
la salchicha
el té
el tocino
el yogur

to show surprise

por supuesto
¡Qué asco!
¿Verdad?

to indicate how often

nunca
siempre
todos los días

to talk about lunch

el agua
la ensalada
las fresas
la galleta
la hamburguesa
la manzana
el perrito caliente
el refresco
la pizza

to talk about eating and drinking

beber
comer
la comida
compartir

to say that you like / love something

Me/te encanta(n) ____.
Me/te gusta(n) ____.

other useful words and expressions

comprender
con
¿Cuál?
más o menos
sin

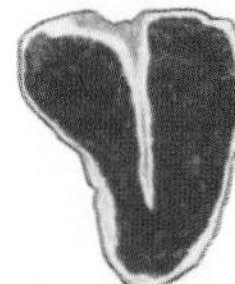
el bistec

la cebolla

las judías verdes

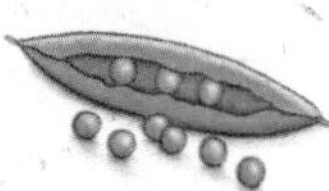
los guisantes

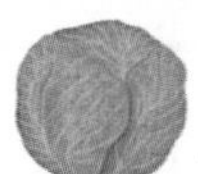
la lechuga

las uvas

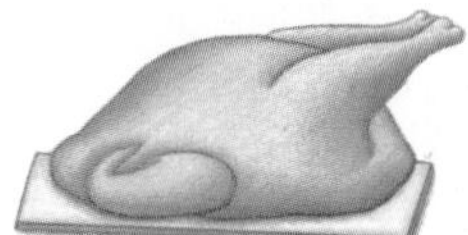
el pollo

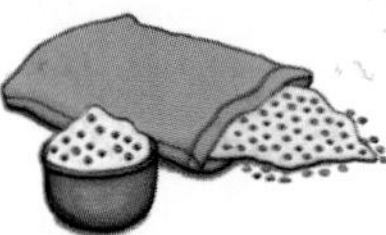
el arroz

los espaguetis

los tomates

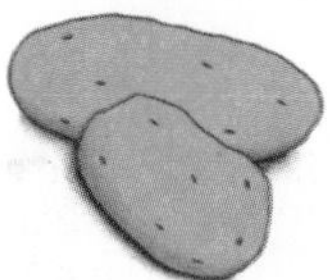
las papas

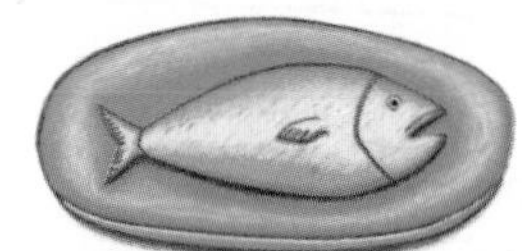
el pescado

la carne

la mantequilla

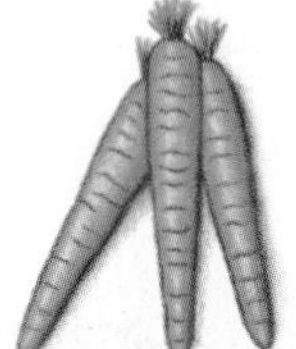
las zanahorias

Para mantener la salud

to talk about being hungry and thirsty
Tengo hambre.
Tengo sed.

to talk about dessert
el helado
los pasteles

to describe something
horrible
malo, -a
sabroso, -a

to indicate agreement and disagreement
Creo que . . .
Creo que sí/no.
(No) estoy de acuerdo.

to discuss health
caminar
hacer ejercicio
(yo) hago
(tú) haces
levantar pesas
para la salud
para mantener la salud

other useful words and expressions
algo
cada día
muchos, -as
¿Por qué?
porque
todos, -as
(yo) prefiero
(tú) prefieres

Café Miami

Menú del día

El desayuno

cereal con plátanos	$2.75
huevos con tocino y pan tostado	$3.50
huevos con salchichas y pan tostado	$3.50
ensalada de frutas	$3.25
con yogur	$4.00

El almuerzo

sándwiches con papas fritas	
de jamón	$3.25
de jamón y queso	$3.75
perrito caliente con papas fritas	$3.75
hamburguesa con papas fritas	$4.25
pizza	$2.50
ensalada	$2.75
sopa de verduras con ensalada y pan	$4.25

La cena

bistec con papas y judías verdes	$8.25
pollo con arroz y zanahorias	$7.25
pescado con arroz y guisantes	$8.00
espaguetis con salsa de tomate y queso	$6.50

ensalada de lechuga y tomate incluida con todas las cenas

El postre

pasteles del día	$2.75
helado	$2.00

Bebidas

refrescos	$0.95
té helado	$0.75
limonada	$0.95
jugo de naranja	$1.05
jugo de manzana	$1.05
té o café	$0.75
leche	$0.85

Hablar

¿Qué te gusta comer?

With a partner, look at the menu above to talk about what you like to eat and drink for breakfast, lunch, and dinner.

Modelo

A —*¿Qué te gusta comer en el desayuno?*
B —*Me gusta el tocino y me encantan los huevos.*
A —*¿Y para beber?*
B —*Pues, me gusta mucho el jugo de naranja.*

¿Recuerdas?

Use *me gusta* and *me encanta* to talk about a singular noun.

- Me encant**a** el café, pero no me gust**a** la leche.

Use *me gustan* and *me encantan* to talk about a plural noun.

- Me gust**an** los plátanos, y me encant**an** las uvas.

Gramática • Repaso

Present tense of *-er* and *-ir* verbs

To create the present-tense forms of *-er* and *-ir* verbs, drop the endings from the infinitives, and add the appropriate verb endings to the stem.

Here are the present-tense forms of regular *-er* verbs:

como	comemos
comes	coméis
come	comen

Here are the present-tense forms of regular *-ir* verbs:

comparto	compartimos
compartes	compartís
comparte	comparten

Escribir

¿Qué hacen para mantener la salud?

Write sentences to say what the following people do or don't do to stay healthy, based on what you see in the drawings.

Modelo

tú

Tú bebes leche.

1. 
Juan/correr

2. 
Laura y Ana/comer

3. 
Pedro y yo/beber

4. 
Manuela y Rosa/compartir

5. 
Roberto/comer

6. **¡Respuesta personal!**
yo

Hablar

¿Qúe bebes y qué comes?

With a partner, talk about what you eat and drink for breakfast, lunch, and dinner.

Modelo

A —*¿Comes salchichas en el desayuno?*
B —*Sí, me encantan. Como salchichas en el desayuno los domingos.*
o:—*No, no me gustan nada. Nunca como salchichas.*

Estudiante A

las papas fritas
el cereal
la ensalada
los pasteles
el pollo
el pescado
el café
los refrescos
la leche

¡Respuesta personal!

Estudiante B

me gusta(n)
me encanta(n)
no me gusta(n) nada
¡Qué asco!

¡Respuesta personal!

Gramática • Repaso

The plurals of adjectives

Just as adjectives agree with nouns depending on whether they are masculine or feminine, they also agree according to whether the nouns are singular or plural. To make adjectives plural, just add *-s* after the vowel at the end of the adjective. If the adjective ends in a consonant, add *-es.*

La manzana es buena para la salud. **Las** manzana**s** son buena**s** para la salud.

El pastel aquí es popular. **Los** pastel**es** del Café Nuñoz son popular**es.**

When an adjective describes a group including both masculine and feminine nouns, use the masculine plural form.

Las zanahorias y **los** tomates son buen**os** para la salud.

Escribir

¿Cómo son los estudiantes?

Using the words from the list below, write sentences to describe Alejo and his friends. Write your sentences on a sheet of paper.

> **¿Recuerdas?**
>
> *Ser,* which means "to be," is an irregular verb. Use *ser* to describe what a person or thing is like. Here are the present-tense forms:
>
> | soy | somos |
> |---|---|
> | eres | sois |
> | es | son |

deportista	atrevido
talentoso	trabajador
perezoso	estudioso
generoso	

¡Respuesta personal!

Clara y Paula

Modelo

Clara y Paula son estudiosas. Estudian mucho.

1. 

Juanita y yo

2. 

Ana y María

3. 

Joaquín y Luis

4. 

Claudia y Marisa

5. 

los estudiantes en mi clase de arte

6. 

Natalia y Angelito

Pensar/Escribir/Hablar

¿Qué comemos para mantener la salud?

1. On a separate sheet of paper, copy this food pyramid and fill in at least two items for each category.

2. Work with a partner. For each category on the food pyramid, take turns asking and answering questions about what you prefer to eat or drink and why you like those items.

Modelo

A —*¿Qué frutas prefieres comer?*
B —*Me gustan mucho las fresas y las manzanas.*
A —*Y, ¿por qué?*
B —*Porque son muy sabrosas y son buenas para la salud. Yo soy deportista y necesito mantener la salud.*

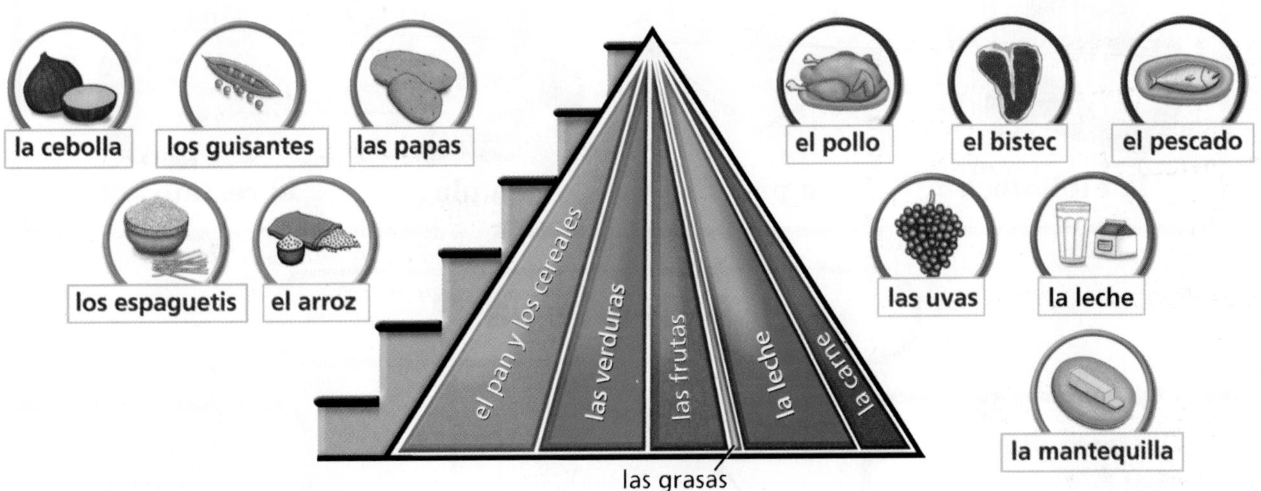

Escribir/Hablar

Y tú, ¿qué dices?

1. ¿Qué prefieres comer en el desayuno? ¿En el almuerzo?
2. ¿Qué frutas son buenas para la salud? ¿Qué verduras?
3. ¿Qué comida que es buena para la salud te gusta comer?
4. ¿Qué comida que es mala para la salud te gusta comer?
5. ¿Qué actividades te gusta hacer para mantener la salud?

For: More Review
Web Code: jbd-0006

4 Los pasatiempos

Objectives

- Talk about locations in your community
- Talk about leisure activities
- Tell where you go
- Ask questions

las montañas

el parque

el centro comercial

ir de compras

el trabajo

la lección de piano

el cine

ver una película

el campo

la biblioteca

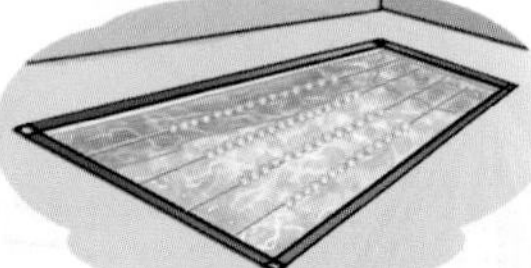
la piscina

la playa

el restaurante

¿Adónde vas?

to tell where you go and with whom

a
a la, al *(a + el)*
¿Adónde?
a casa
¿Con quién?
con mis / tus amigos
solo, -a

other useful words and expressions

¿De dónde eres?
de
generalmente
¡No me digas!
para + *infinitive*

to talk about places

Me quedo en casa.
la casa
en casa
el gimnasio
la iglesia
la mezquita
la sinagoga
el templo

to talk about when things are done

¿Cuándo?
después
después (de)
los fines de semana
los lunes, los martes . . .
el tiempo libre

el baile

el concierto

la fiesta

el partido

ir de pesca

jugar al básquetbol

jugar al fútbol americano

jugar al vóleibol

jugar al tenis

jugar al golf

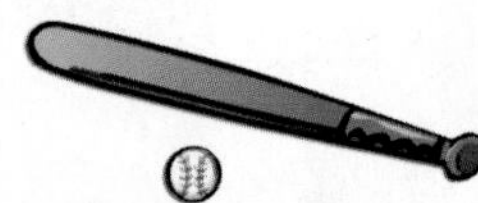
jugar al béisbol

jugar al fútbol

¿Quieres ir conmigo?

to tell what time something happens

¿A qué hora?
a la una
a las ocho
de la mañana
de la noche
de la tarde
este fin de semana
esta noche
esta tarde

to describe how someone feels

cansado, -a
contento, -a
enfermo, -a
mal
ocupado, -a
triste

to extend, accept, or decline invitations

conmigo
contigo
(yo) puedo
(tú) puedes
¡Ay! ¡Qué pena!
¡Genial!
lo siento
¡Oye!
¡Qué buena idea!
(yo) quiero
(tú) quieres
¿Te gustaría?
Me gustaría
Tengo que ___.

other useful words and expressions

demasiado
entonces
un poco (de)
ir + a + *infinitive*
(yo) sé
(tú) sabes

Go Online PHSchool.com
For: Vocabulary Practice
Web Code: jbd-0007

¿Adónde va Carmen?

Listen to Carmen describe her plans for the week. As you hear each statement she makes, point to the place on the map where she is going.

¿Recuerdas?

To say where someone is going, use the verb *ir*. Here are the present-tense forms:

voy	vamos
vas	vais
va	van

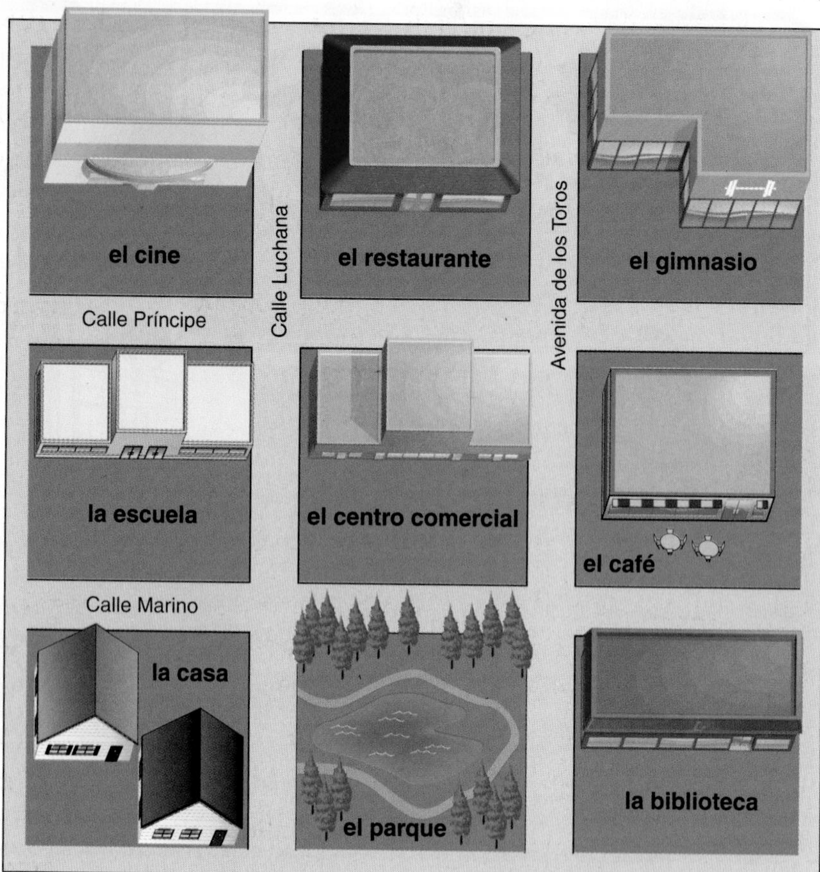

Actividad 22 Leer/Escribir

Los fines de semana de Arturo

Read Arturo's description of his weekends. Number your paper from 1–5, and write the appropriate form of the verb *ir*.

Me encantan los fines de semana. A veces me quedo en casa, pero generalmente __1.__ al parque para correr. Los sábados por la noche, mis amigos y yo __2.__ al cine. Me gustan mucho las películas. Mi mejor amigo, Jonatán, siempre __3.__ conmigo. Muchos de mis amigos son estudiosos y __4.__ a la biblioteca los sábados. ¿Y tú? ¿Adónde __5.__ este fin de semana?

Gramática • Repaso

Asking questions

In Spanish, when you ask a question with an interrogative word (*who, what, where,* etc.), you put the verb before the subject.

¿Qué **bebe María** en el café?

¿Por qué **estudian Juan y Flor** en la biblioteca?

Here are some interrogative words you know:

¿Qué?	**¿Adónde?**
¿Cómo?	**¿De dónde?**
¿Quién(es)?	**¿Cuál?**
¿Con quién(es)?	**¿Por qué?**
¿Dónde?	**¿Cuándo?**
¿Cuántos(as)?	

Leer/Escribir

¡Qué chica curiosa!

Isabel is a very curious person. She can't stop asking questions. Number your paper from 1–5 and for each of her questions, write the letter of the answer that corresponds to what she asks.

1. ¿Qué hay en tu mochila?
2. ¿Con quién vas al cine?
3. ¿Por qué van Julio y Rosibel a la biblioteca?
4. ¿Dónde está el cine?
5. ¿Quién va al parque?

a. Clara, Lucía y yo vamos al parque.
b. El cine está al lado del restaurante.
c. Hay una carpeta y dos libros porque yo voy a la escuela.
d. Porque ellos necesitan estudiar.
e. Voy al cine con mis amigos.

Escribir/Hablar

¿Adónde vas los fines de semana?

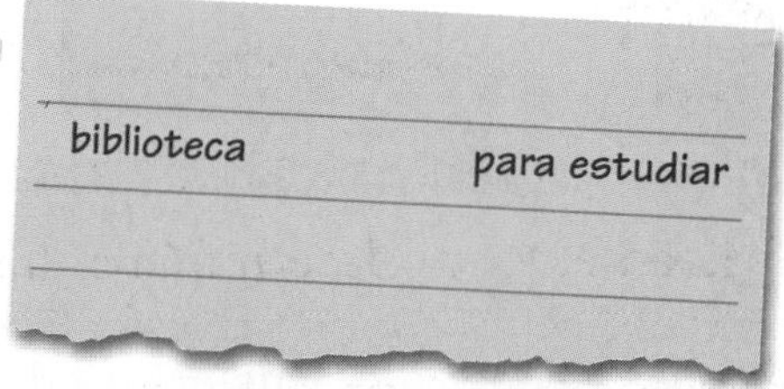

1. Use the map in Actividad 21 to make a list of three places you go to and the reasons why you go there.
2. Exchange your list with a partner, and write two questions about each activity that you see on the list.

Modelo

¿Cuándo vas a la biblioteca para estudiar?

3. With your partner, use your questions to talk about where you go.

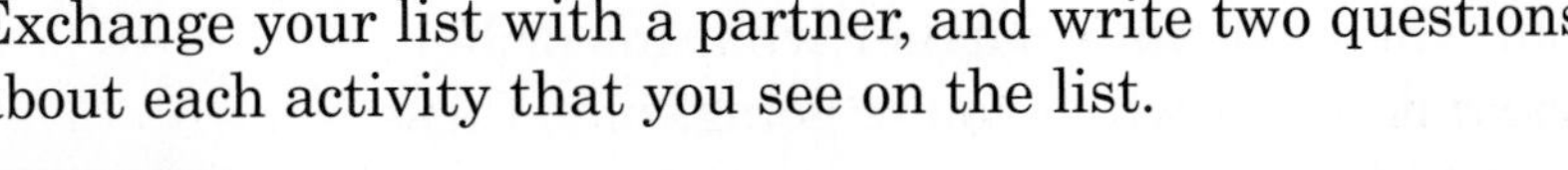

Modelo

A —*¿Cuándo vas a la biblioteca para estudiar?*
B —*Voy a la biblioteca los lunes después de las clases.*
A —*¿Y con quién vas?*
B —*Generalmente yo voy con mis amigos.*

Gramática • Repaso

Ir + a + infinitive

Just as you use "to be going" + an infinitive in English to say what you are going to do, in Spanish you use a form of the verb *ir* + *a* + an infinitive to express the same thing.

Voy a correr hoy.

¿Tú **vas a jugar** al golf esta tarde?

Escribir

¿Qué van a hacer tú y tus amigos?

On a sheet of paper, write sentences that tell what the following people are going to do at different times.

Modelo

mi amigo(a) *(nombre)* / sábado por la mañana
Mi amiga Eliana va a ver la tele el sábado por la mañana.

1. yo / lunes por la tarde
2. mi amigo(a) *(nombre)* / mañana por la noche
3. mi profesor(a) de español / después de las clases
4. mis amigos y yo / sábado por la noche
5. los estudiantes en la clase de español / mañana en la clase

Escribir/Hablar

¿Qué vas a hacer?

Make a chart like this one to describe five things you're going to do, when you are going to do them, and with whom. Then ask your partner what his or her plans are. Use the following words to talk about when you're going to do these things: *esta tarde, esta noche, mañana, el lunes . . . , el fin de semana.*

¿Qué?	¿Cuándo?	¿Con quién?
tocar la guitarra	esta tarde	mis amigos

Modelo

A —*¿Qué vas a hacer esta tarde?*
B —*Esta tarde mis amigos y yo vamos a tocar la guitarra.*

Gramática • Repaso

The verb *jugar*

Use the verb *jugar* to talk about playing a sport or a game. Even though *jugar* uses the same endings as the other *-ar* verbs, it has a different stem in some forms. For those forms, the *-u-* becomes *-ue-*. This kind of verb is called a "stem-changing verb."

Here are the present-tense forms of *jugar:*

juego	jugamos
juegas	jugáis
juega	juegan

Escribir/Hablar

En el club deportivo

1. Write a list of four activities from Club Deporte al Máximo and choose a time for each activity.

2. Get together with three other students and talk about the activities that you have chosen. Keep track of your group's answers to use the information in step 3.

Modelo

A —*Mario, ¿juegas al tenis?*
B —*Sí, juego al tenis.*
A —*¿A qué hora juegas al tenis?*
B —*A las dos.*

3. Write six sentences about the sports and games the students in your group play at the club.

Modelo

Mario juega al tenis y Ana y Geraldo juegan al fútbol. Todos jugamos al golf.

Club Deporte al Máximo
Actividades de verano

básquetbol
10:00 A.M., 12:00 P.M., 2:00 P.M., 4:00 P.M

béisbol
11:00 A.M., 1:00 P.M., 3:00 P.M., 5:00 P.M.

fútbol americano
10:00 A.M., 12:00 P.M., 2:00 P.M., 4:00 P.M

fútbol
9:00 A.M., 11:00 A.M., 1:00 P.M., 3:00 P.M.

golf
11:00 A.M., 1:00 P.M., 3:00 P.M., 5:00 P.M.

tenis
10:00 A.M., 12:00 P.M., 2:00 P.M., 4:00 P.M

vóleibol
11:00 A.M., 1:00 P.M., 3:00 P.M., 5:00 P.M.

¡También tenemos videojuegos! 10:00 A.M. – 4:00 P.M.

Escribir/Hablar

Y tú, ¿qué dices?

1. ¿Adónde vas después de las clases? ¿Qué te gusta hacer allí?
2. ¿Dónde estudias? ¿Estudias solo(a) o con un amigo(a)?
3. ¿Cuándo pasas tiempo con tus amigos? ¿Adónde van ustedes?
4. ¿Qué vas a hacer este sábado? ¿Y el domingo?
5. ¿Adónde vas este verano? ¿Qué vas a hacer allí?

For: More Review
Web Code: jbd-0008

A ver si puedes . . .

Now that you've completed *Para empezar,* you should be able to complete these practice tasks . . .

Chapter Review

Before you move on, check to see if you . . .

- **can perform the tasks on pp. 28–29**

Escuchar

jbd-0099

1. Listen to an interview with a professional tennis player. a) What is she like?; b) What are two things she likes doing?; c) What is one thing she dislikes doing?; d) What does she do to stay healthy?

2. Listen as two students describe what they typically eat and drink for breakfast. Which one is most like the kind of breakfast you eat? Which foods mentioned do you not like?

Hablar

1. You are trying to find out the name of someone in your class. You ask the students sitting next to you, but they don't understand whom you are talking about. Describe what the person you are trying to identify is like and tell where he or she is in the classroom. Give at least three statements to describe his or her location in relation to various classroom objects.

2. Your best friend calls to find out where you are going and what you are going to do this weekend. Mention at least three places you plan to go and three things you plan to do. For example, you might say *Voy a hacer ejercicio en el gimnasio a las 4:30.*

Go Online PHSchool.com
For: More Practice
Web Code: jbd-0009

Leer

1. You are checking your e-mail and receive several responses to invitations that you sent out last week for a party at your house. Read them to see why some people declined the invitation.

   a) Me gustaría, pero no puedo. Tengo que trabajar el sábado.

   b) ¡Genial! ¡Una fiesta! Ay, pero no puedo, voy de pesca.

   c) ¿A las seis? No puedo. Juego un partido de fútbol a las siete.

Escribir

1. A school in Uruguay wants to exchange e-mails with your school. Tell your e-pal your name and describe your class schedule. Include a description of your favorite class.

2. Your family is going to host an exchange student from Madrid, Spain. His name is Alejandro and he is going to spend the summer with you. Write him a note to find out more about him and to tell him about you. Ask him with whom he spends time on weekends and where he goes. Tell him about the places you and your friends go in your community and how you spend your free time.

Tema 5 • Fiesta en familia

Fondo cultural

Carmen Lomas Garza (1948–) is best known for her paintings that show Mexican American family life in her native South Texas in the 1950s.

- What do you see in the painting that would make this family celebration similar to or different from family parties that you're familiar with?

"Barbacoa para cumpleaños / Birthday Party Barbecue" (1993), Carmen Lomas Garza

Alkyds on canvas, 36 x 48 inches. ©1993 Carmen Lomas Garza (reg. 1994). Photo credit: M. Lee Fatherree. Collection of Federal Reserve Bank of Dallas.

Una fiesta de cumpleaños

Chapter Objectives

- Describe families
- Talk about celebrations and parties
- Ask and tell ages
- Express possession
- Understand cultural perspectives on family and celebrations

Video Highlights

A primera vista: *¡Feliz cumpleaños!*

GramActiva Videos: the verb *tener;* possessive adjectives

Videomisterio: *¿Eres tú, María?*, Episodio 1

Country Connection

As you learn about family celebrations and parties, you will make connections to these countries and places:

Más práctica

- *Real.* para hispanohablantes, pp. 170–171

For: Online Atlas
Web Code: jbe-0002

Una comida al aire libre con toda la familia

A primera vista

Vocabulario y gramática en contexto

jbd-0587

Objectives

Read, listen to, and understand information about
- families
- parties and celebrations

Más vocabulario

el padrastro	stepfather
la madrastra	stepmother
el hermanastro	stepbrother
la hermanastra	stepsister

mis abuelos

Ricardo
mi **abuelo,** 68

Ana María
mi **abuela,** 61

mis padres

mis tíos

María
mi **madre,** 39

José Antonio
mi **padre,** 42

Josefina
mi **tía,** 38

Andrés
mi **tío,** 42

Capitán
mi **perro**

Michi
mi **gato**

mis hermanos

mis primos

Angélica
mi **hermana,** 16

Cristina
yo, 13

Esteban
mi **hermano,** 15

Carolina
mi **prima,** 15

Gabriel
mi **primo,** 11

“¡Hola! Me llamo Cristina. Hoy es mi **cumpleaños.** Toda mi familia va a **preparar** una fiesta para **celebrar.** ¡Va a ser muy divertido!”.

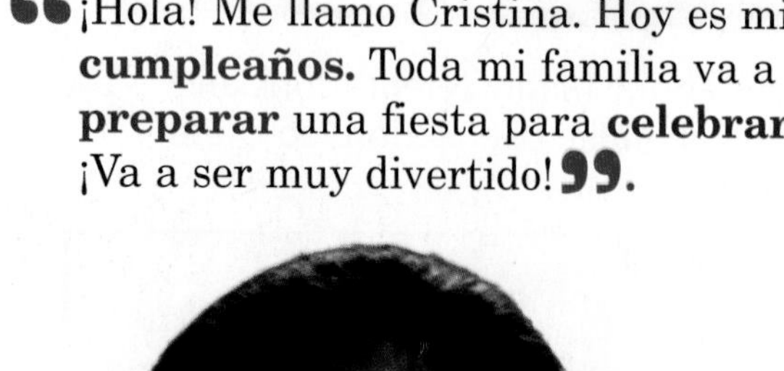

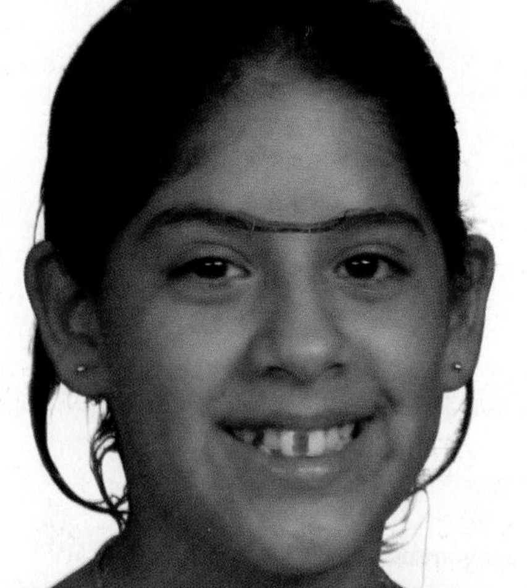

“Aquí está mi familia. Tengo dos hermanos: mi hermana **mayor,** Angélica, **que tiene 16 años,** y mi hermano, Esteban, que tiene 15 años. Y aquí están mis primos: Carolina tiene 15 años. **Su** hermano **menor** Gabriel, tiene **sólo** 11 años”.

“Mira a **las personas** de **las fotos.** Es la familia de mi tía Josefina. Mi tío Andrés es **el esposo** de Josefina. Ellos tienen dos **hijos: su hijo** Gabriel y su **hija** Carolina”.

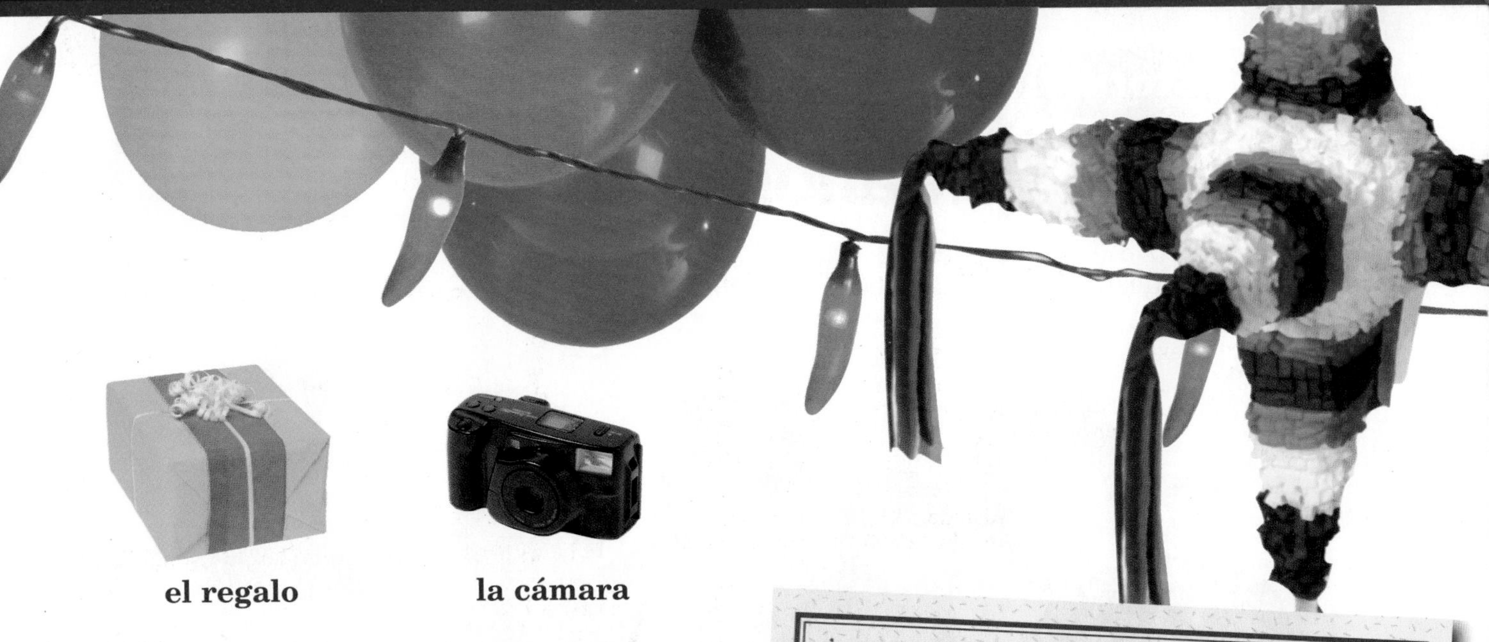

el regalo **la cámara**

“Hoy es el cumpleaños de Cristina. Tengo un regalo para ella. Es una cámara. A Cristina **le encanta sacar fotos**”.

jbd-0587

Escuchar

La familia de Cristina

Listen as Cristina describes her family. If her statement is true, give a “thumbs-up” sign. If it is false, give a “thumbs-down” sign.

jbd-0587

Escuchar

Preparamos la fiesta

Now listen as Cristina and her mother prepare for a birthday party. Look at the items in the party shop ad on this page and touch each item they mention.

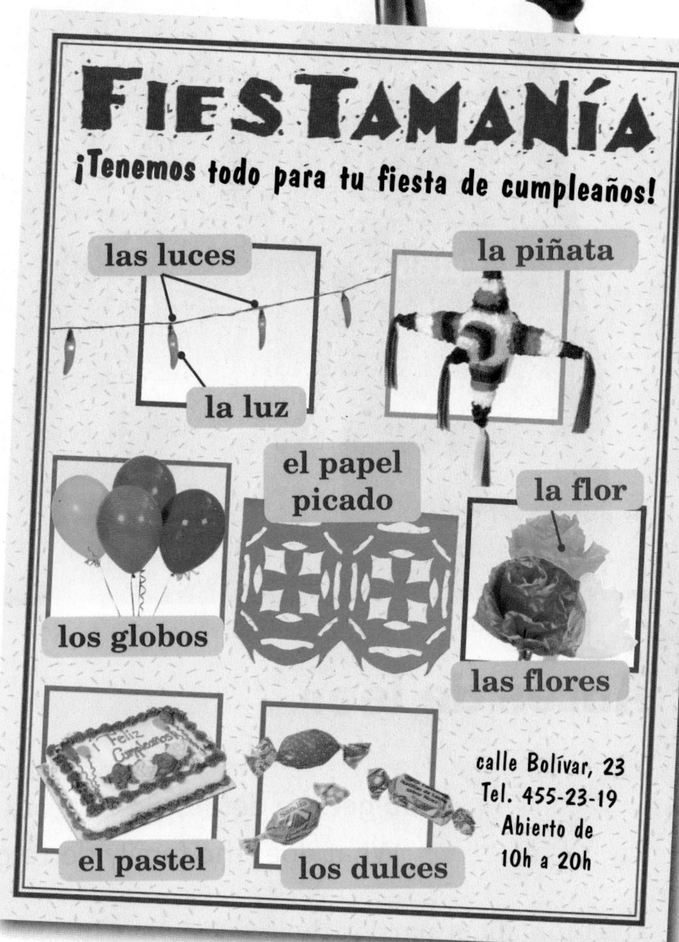

Más práctica

- Practice Workbook, pp. 1–2: 5A-1, 5A-2
- WAV Wbk.: Writing, p. 8
- Guided Practice: Vocab. Flash Cards, pp. 149–154
- *Real.* para hispanohablantes, p. 172

jbd-0587 

¡Feliz cumpleaños!

¿Qué pasa en la fiesta de Cristina? Lee la historia.

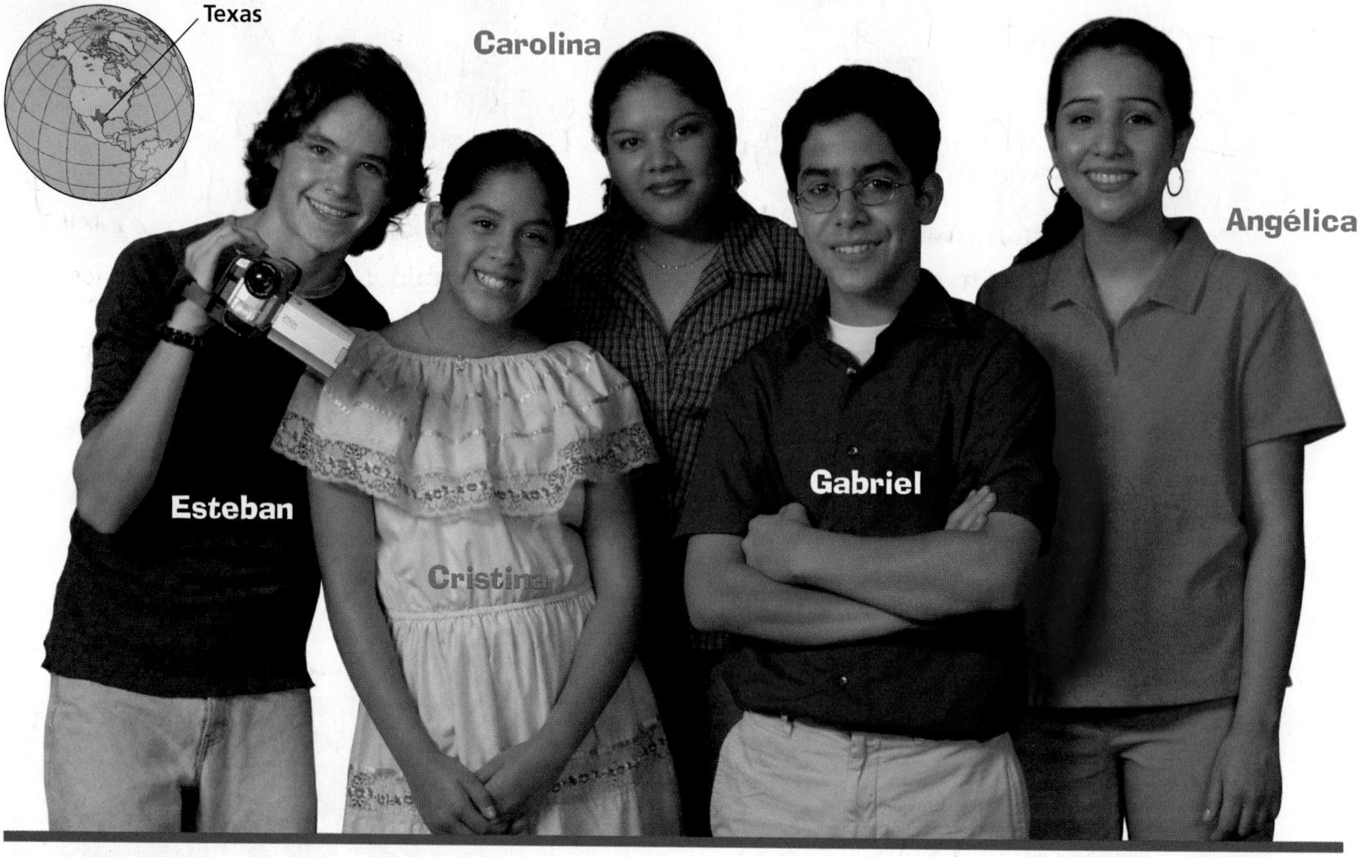

Texas

Carolina

Angélica

Esteban

Gabriel

Cristina

Antes de leer

Using visuals Look at the pictures as you read to help you get the details of the story.

- What does the family do to get ready for the party?

1. Think about parties that you or your friends have had. Who was invited? What were you celebrating?
2. What do you or your friends do to prepare for parties that you give?
3. What activities are common at birthday parties that you go to? What are some similarities and differences between what you are used to and what you see in the *Videohistoria* photos?

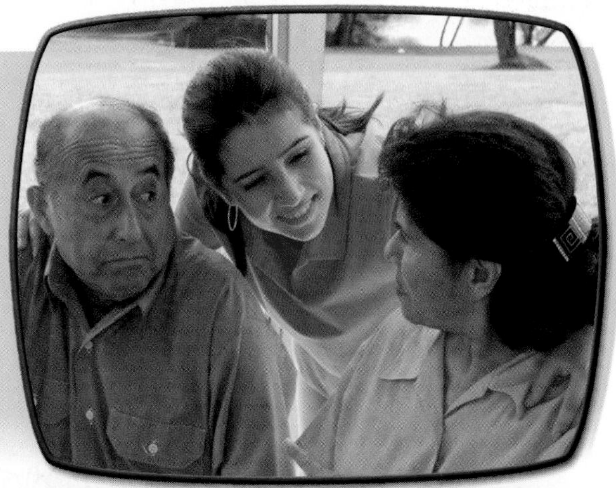

1 **Esteban:** Vamos a **hacer un video.** Uno . . . dos . . . tres . . . ¡Acción!

Angélica: Hola, me llamo Angélica. Hoy es el cumpleaños de **nuestra** hermana, Cristina. Todos están aquí para celebrar.

2 **Angélica:** Aquí están mis abuelos. **¿Y cuántos años tienen Uds.?**

Abuelo: Pues, yo tengo sesenta y ocho años y tu abuela . . .

Abuela: Por favor, Ricardo. Angélica, ¡qué pregunta!

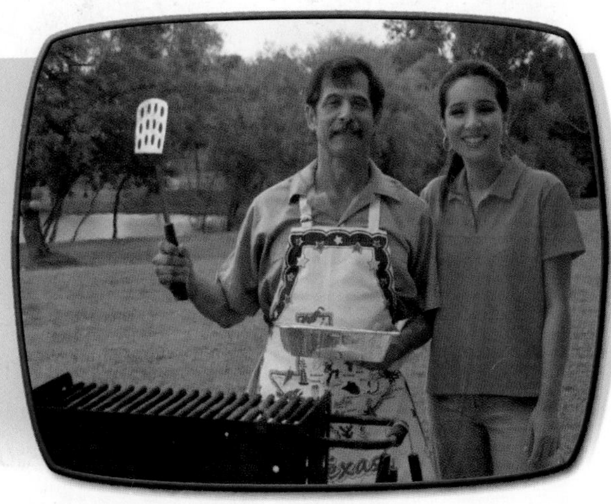

3 **Angélica:** Aquí está Gabriel, mi primo menor. Le gusta mucho el fútbol. Y aquí está mi prima. ¿Cómo te llamas?

Carolina: Pero, Angélica, tú sabes mi nombre.

Angélica: Sí, pero es para el video. Por favor . . .

4 **Angélica:** Él es **nuestro** padre. ¿Qué haces, **papá?**

Padre: Voy a preparar unas hamburguesas y después voy a sacar fotos de la fiesta.

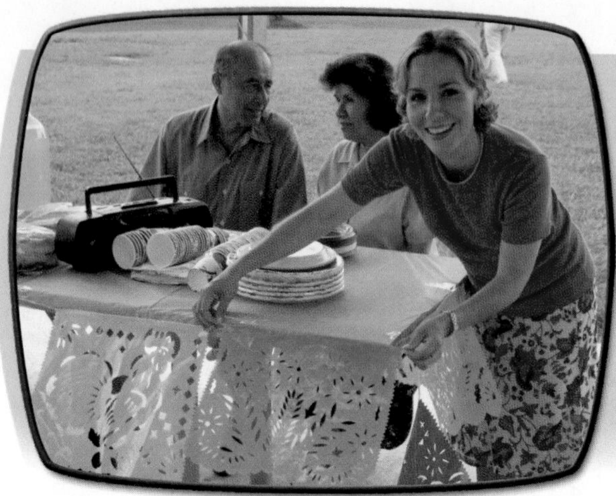

5 **Angélica:** Aquí está mi madre. A **mamá** le gustan **las decoraciones.**

Madre: Sí. A mí **me encanta decorar** con papel picado.

6 **Angélica:** Y aquí está Cristina. Hoy es su cumpleaños. **¡Feliz cumpleaños!**

Cristina: ¿Cuándo puedo **abrir** mis regalos?

Angélica: Ahora no. Primero, la piñata.

7 **Padre:** ¡Vamos, Gabriel! ¿Puedes **romper** la piñata?

Gabriel: ¡Por supuesto!

Todos: *Dale, dale, dale, no pierdas el tino, porque si lo pierdes, pierdes el camino.*

¡Crac! *Gabriel rompe la piñata y...*

8 **Madre:** ¡Gabriel! ¡La piñata! ¡El pastel! ¡Ay, no!

Leer/Escribir

Asociaciones

Number your paper from 1–5. Write the name of the *Videohistoria* character who would be associated with each of the following.

1.

2. 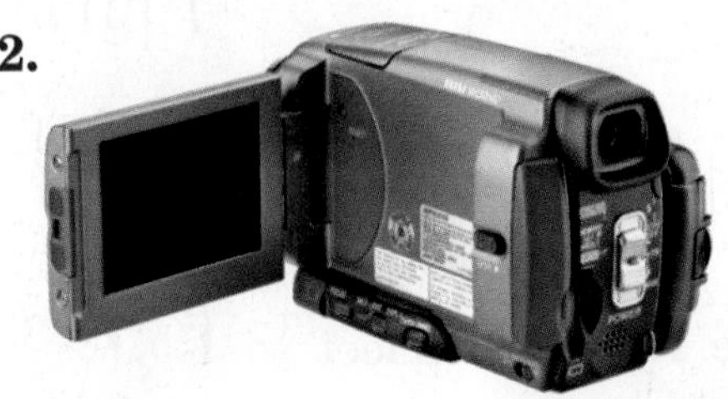

3. 

4. 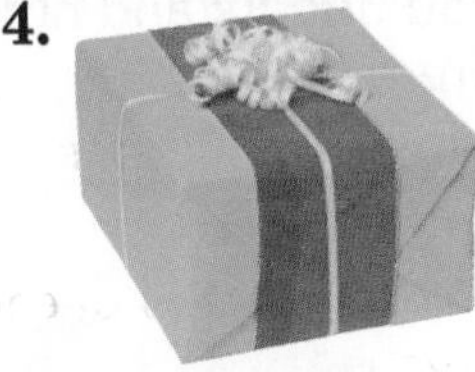 

5. 

Escribir/Hablar

¿Comprendes?

1. ¿Quién va a hacer el video, Gabriel o Esteban?
2. ¿Quién tiene sesenta y ocho años, el abuelo o la abuela?
3. ¿A quién le gusta jugar al fútbol, a Esteban o a Gabriel?
4. ¿Qué va a hacer el padre, decorar o preparar hamburguesas?
5. ¿Con qué decora la madre, con globos o con papel picado?
6. ¿Quién rompe la piñata, Cristina o Gabriel?

Leer/Escribir

Primero . . . y después . . .

Esteban is trying to edit his video. Help him out by putting the following people in the order that they are interviewed in the *Videohistoria*. Number your paper from 1–8 and write the names on your paper.

Gabriel	Padre
Abuela	Angélica
Madre	Cristina
Abuelo	Carolina

Más práctica

- Practice Workbook, pp. 3–4: 5A-3, 5A-4
- WAV Wbk.: Video, pp. 1–3
- Guided Practice: Vocab. Check, pp. 155–158
- *Real.* para hispanohablantes, p. 173

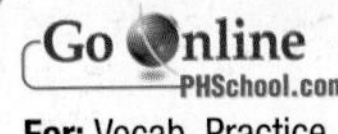

For: Vocab. Practice
Web Code: jbd-0502

Manos a la obra

Vocabulario y gramática en uso

Objectives

- Communicate about families and parties
- Ask and tell what people have
- Ask and tell people's ages
- Tell to whom something belongs
- Learn to use the verb *tener* and possessive adjectives

Pensar/Escribir

Un árbol genealógico

José is explaining his family tree. Number a sheet of paper from 1–8, then write the correct words to complete the sentences based on what you see in the family tree.

Strategy

Using graphic organizers
Drawing diagrams can help you understand how things are related.

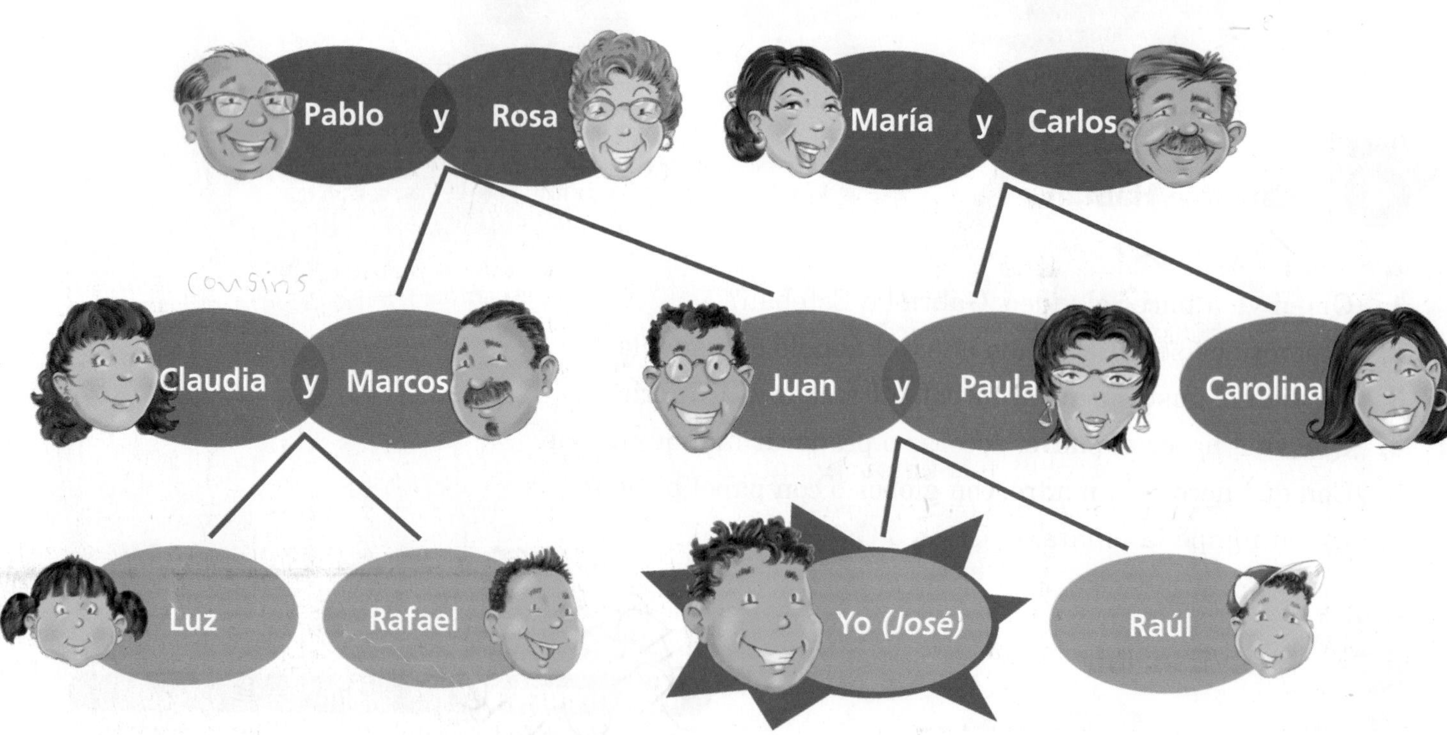

1. Juan es mi *(tío / padre)*.
2. Marcos es mi *(abuelo / tío)*.
3. Rafael es mi *(hermano / primo)*.
4. Rosa es mi *(madre / abuela)*.
5. Carolina es mi *(tía / prima)*.
6. Paula es mi *(madre / tía)*.
7. Raúl es mi *(primo / hermano)*.
8. Luz es mi *(abuela / prima)*.

Leer/Escribir

¿Quién es?

Find out how each member of Ana Sofía's family is related to her by completing her sentences. Number your paper from 1–8 and write the appropriate word.

Modelo

La madre de mi madre es mi abuela.

1. La esposa de mi tío es mi ___.
2. El padre de mi padre es mi ___.
3. El hijo de mi madrastra es mi ___.
4. Paco y Ana son mis tíos. Sus hijos son mis ___.
5. El hermano de mi madre es mi ___.
6. Los padres de mi madre son mis ___.
7. La hija de mi padrastro es mi ___.
8. El hermano de mi prima es mi ___.

Leer/Escribir

En la fiesta de cumpleaños

Complete the description of Cristina's birthday by choosing the correct word in parentheses. Write your answers on a separate sheet of paper.

Hoy __1.__ *(celebramos / sacamos)* la fiesta de cumpleaños de mi hermana menor, Cristina. ¿Cuántos años __2.__ *(es / tiene)* ella? Trece.

A nuestra madre __3.__ *(le / me)* encantan las fiestas. Mi mamá y mi hermana __4.__ *(decoran / rompen)* el patio con __5.__ *(luces / pasteles)* y __6.__ *(fiestas / flores)*. A __7.__ *(nuestro / tu)* hermano le gusta hacer un __8.__ *(regalo / video)* o __9.__ *(abrir / sacar)* fotos de la fiesta. Siempre hay una piñata que nosotros __10.__ *(preparamos / rompemos)*. En la piñata hay __11.__ *(dulces / flores)* sabrosos. Ahora Cristina va a __12.__ *(romper / abrir)* sus regalos.

El papel picado Mexican families frequently decorate for celebrations by using *papel picado*. It is made by folding and cutting layers of paper to create designs or scenes that are then hung as decorations.

- What crafts do you know that use similar techniques?

"Haciendo papel picado / Making papel picado" (1999), Carmen Lomas Garza

Black paper cutout, 22" x 30". ©1998 Carment Lomas Garza. Photo Credit: Northern Lights, Collection of Carmen Lomas Garza.

Escribir/Hablar

Preparaciones para la fiesta

You are preparing a party for someone in your family.

1. On a sheet of paper, make a chart like the one you see here. In the first column, write a list of six items you think you will need for the party. The items can be decorations, food, beverages, gifts, etc. In the second column, list six family members who are going to the party. Be sure to tell how they are related to you.

2. Compare your list with that of a partner.

Necesito	La familia
unas flores	mi prima Marta

Modelo

A —*¿Qué necesitas para la fiesta?*
B —*Necesito flores.*
A —*Yo también necesito flores.*
o:—*No necesito flores; necesito globos.*
A —*¿Quién va a la fiesta?*
B —*Mi prima Marta va a la fiesta.*

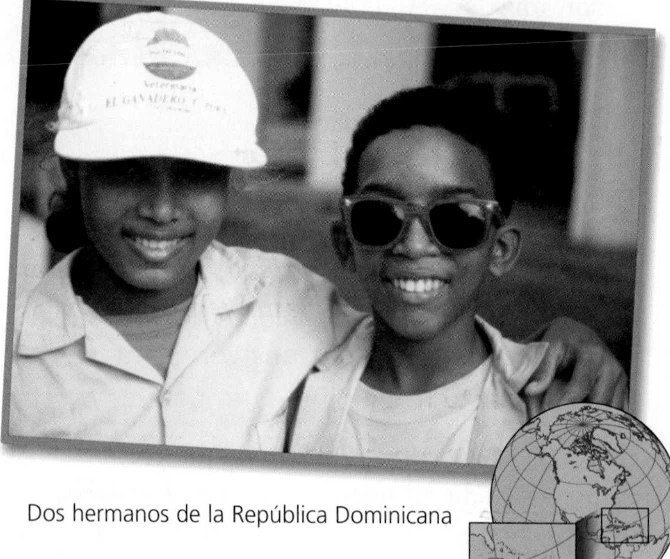

Dos hermanos de la República Dominicana

Hablar

Mi familia

You're at a friend's birthday party. You've just made a new friend, and you want to know more about one another. Work with a partner to ask and tell about your families.

Modelo

hermanos
A —*¿Tienes hermanos?*
B —*Sí, tengo un hermano y una hermana.*
o:—*No, no tengo hermanos.*
A —*¿Cómo se llaman?*
B —*Mi hermano se llama David y mi hermana se llama Abby.*

Estudiante A

1. tíos
2. primos
3. un abuelo
4. una hermana mayor
5. hermanos menores
6. una tía favorita
7. una abuela
8. un gato o un perro

Estudiante B

¡Respuesta personal!

Para decir más . . .
el (la) hijo(a) único(a) only child

Escribir

El cumpleaños de Carlitos

Tío Jorge is throwing Carlitos a birthday party. Look at the picture below and then tell what the various people are doing.

Modelo

Tío David
Tío David habla con Tío Jorge.

1. Tío Jorge
2. Tía Ana y Tía Rosita
3. Benjamín
4. Carlitos
5. Eliana y Glenda

Hablar

A mi familia le gusta . . .

With a partner, talk about the activities that your family, or another family, likes to do.

Modelo

primo
A —*¿Qué le gusta hacer a tu primo?*
B —*Le gusta sacar fotos.*

Estudiante A

1. padre
2. madre
3. abuelo
4. hermana
5. prima
6. tío favorito
7. perro o gato

Estudiante B

Escribir/Hablar

Y tú, ¿qué dices?

1. Describe a una persona de tu familia o de otra familia. ¿Cómo se llama? ¿Cuántos años tiene? ¿Cómo es? ¿Qué le gusta hacer?
2. ¿Tienes un perro o un gato? ¿Cómo se llama? ¿Cuántos años tiene?
3. ¿Qué te gusta hacer durante *(during)* una fiesta de cumpleaños?

Gramática

The verb *tener*

The verb *tener* is used to show relationship or possession.

Tengo un hermano mayor. — ***I have** an older brother.*
Tenemos un regalo para Tere. — ***We have** a gift for Tere.*

Some expressions in Spanish use *tener* where in English we use "to be."

Mi primo **tiene** dieciséis años. — *My cousin **is** sixteen years old.*
Tengo hambre y sed. — ***I am** hungry and thirsty.*

Here are all the present-tense forms of *tener:*

(yo)	**tengo**	(nosotros) (nosotras)	**tenemos**
(tú)	**tienes**	(vosotros) (vosotras)	**tenéis**
Ud. (él) (ella)	**tiene**	Uds. (ellos) (ellas)	**tienen**

¿Recuerdas?

You have been using the verb *tener* for several chapters.

- **¿Tienes** sed?
- **Tengo** que hacer ejercicio.

GramActiva VIDEO

Want more help with the verb *tener?* Watch the **GramActiva** video.

Escribir

Las familias que tenemos

El Sr. Torre and his class are describing their families. Match the people in the first column with their family members in the second column. Write your sentences on a sheet of paper.

1. Eduardo
2. Yo
3. Carolina y Sabrina
4. Esteban y yo
5. Y tú, Juan, ¿ . . . ?

a. tengo un padrastro
b. tiene una esposa
c. tienes dos hermanastras
d. tenemos cinco tíos
e. tienen muchos primos

¡Rompecabezas!

Number your paper from 1–4. Complete the following sentences by writing the appropriate form of the verb *tener.* Then try to solve the math puzzle.

El total de las edades *(ages)* de los hijos en nuestra familia es 100. Marta __1.__ 19 años. Paco y yo __2.__ dos años menos que Marta. Laura y Eva __3.__ cinco años menos que Paco y yo. ¿Cuántos años __4.__ nuestro hermano mayor, Enrique?

Actividad 16 — Hablar

¿Cúantos años tienen?

Look at the photos of Guillermo and his family and friends. Describe them by saying how old everyone is. Then interview three of your classmates to find out how old they are.

mi padre / 52

Modelo

El padre de Guillermo tiene cincuenta y dos años.

1.

mi madre / 43

2.

mis primos / 20

3.

yo / 13

4.

mis amigos y yo / 13

5.

mi abuela / 72

6.

Y tú, / ¿cuántos . . . ?

Actividad 17 — Hablar

¿Qué hay para la fiesta?

You are organizing a birthday party. With a partner, ask and answer questions about what people have for the party.

Ana

Modelo

A —*¿Qué tiene Ana?*
B —*Ana tiene la piñata.*

1. David

2. Yolanda

3. tu abuela

4. tú

5. Uds.

6. Juan y Marcos

Hablar/Escribir

Entrevista

Interview a partner. Find out the answers to the following questions. Your partner may answer based on his or her own family or on a TV family. Write your partner's answers so that you can report your interview to the class.

1. ¿Cómo te llamas y cuántos años tienes? ¿Qué te gusta hacer?
2. ¿Cuántos hermanos mayores o menores tienes?
3. ¿Cómo se llaman tus hermanos(as) y cuántos años tienen?
4. ¿Cómo son tus hermanos(as)?
5. ¿Qué le gusta hacer a uno(a) de tus hermanos(as)?
6. ¿Tienes perros o gatos? ¿Cómo se llama(n)?

Nota

To say that a person likes or loves something, use *le gusta(n)* or *le encanta(n).* When you include the name of the person or the pronoun, be sure to add *a:*

- **A Pedro le gustan** los dulces.
- **A ella le encanta** sacar fotos.

Escribir/Hablar

¡Reportaje!

Based on your notes from Actividad 18, write a report of your interview. Your teacher may ask you to read your report to the class.

Modelo

Anita tiene 13 años y le encanta escuchar música. Anita tiene tres hermanos: un hermano mayor y dos hermanos menores. Son simpáticos y deportistas. Su hermano mayor, Pedro, tiene 16 años. Sus hermanos menores se llaman Lisa y José. Ellos tienen sólo once y ocho años. A José le gusta jugar al básquetbol. Anita no tiene ni perros ni gatos.

"La molendera" (1924), Diego Rivera

Oil on canvas, 35 7/16 x 46 1/16 in. Museo Nacional de Arte Moderno, Instituto Nacional de Bellas Artes, Mexico City, D.F., Mexico. © Banco de Mexico Diego Rivera & Frida Kahlo Museums Trust. Av. Cinco de Mayo n.º 2. Col. Centro, Del. Cuauhtemoc 06059, México, D.F. Reproduction authorized by the *Instituto Nacional de Bellas Artes y Literatura.* Courtesy of Art Resource, NY.

Diego Rivera (1886–1957) This painting by Mexican muralist Diego Rivera shows a woman grinding maize on a *metate,* a utensil used for grinding grain. This is one of many paintings in which Rivera portrays the daily life of the indigenous peoples of Mexico.

- Through paintings, an artist conveys feelings to the viewer. What do you think Rivera wants you to feel about this woman and her task?

Pronunciación

jbd-0588

The letters *p, t,* and *q* 

In English, the consonants *p, t, q,* and the hard *c* sound are pronounced with a little puff of air.

Hold a tissue loosely in front of your mouth as you say these English words. You will notice that the tissue moves.

pan	papa	too	tea
comb	case	park	take

Now say these Spanish words with the tissue in front of your mouth. Try to say the consonants so that there is no puff of air and the tissue does not move.

pan	papá	tú	tía
cómo	queso	parque	taco

Try it out! Listen to this nursery rhyme. Listen particularly for the *p, t,* and *q* sounds. Then repeat the rhyme.

Tortillitas para mamá
Tortillitas para papá
Las quemaditas,[1] para mamá
Las bonitas,[2] para papá

[1]the burned ones [2]the pretty ones

Actividad 20 **Escribir/Hablar**

Preparaciones para una fiesta de cumpleaños

Contesta las preguntas.

Cuando una familia celebra un cumpleaños, ¿quién tiene que...

1. ...decorar la casa? ¿Con qué?
2. ...preparar la comida y las bebidas?
3. ...comprar los regalos?
4. ...hacer el pastel?
5. ...hacer el video o sacar fotos?

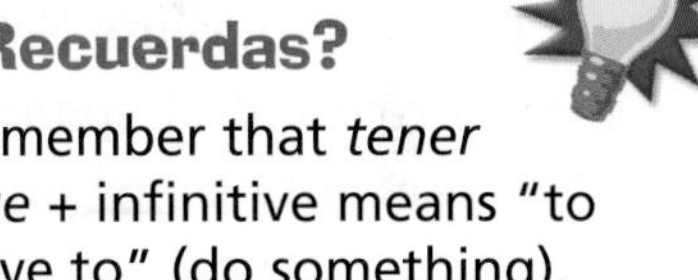

¿Recuerdas?

Remember that *tener que* + infinitive means "to have to" (do something).

- Sofía **tiene que decorar** el pastel.

Celebrando un cumpleaños con una piñata

Leer/Escribir

La familia de Pablo

Look carefully at the photograph of Pablo's family, the royal family of Spain, as they celebrate his special day. As Pablo describes this family photo, complete the story with the appropriate forms of the verb *tener*.

Me llamo Pablo Nicolás Urdangarín y de Borbón. Mi cumpleaños es el 6 de diciembre. Nosotros __1.__ muchas fiestas en mi familia. En la foto celebramos un día muy especial para mí. Es el día de mi bautizo. (Yo) __2.__ un hermano mayor que se llama Juan Valentín. También (yo) __3.__ dos primos: Felipe, que __4.__ dos años, y una prima, Victoria. Victoria __5.__ sólo tres meses más que yo. Felipe y Victoria son los hijos de mis tíos, la infanta[1] Elena y su esposo, Jaime. Están a la derecha en la foto. A la izquierda están mi tío—el príncipe Felipe— y mis padres. Mi hermano está en los brazos de mi padre, Iñaki. Yo estoy en los brazos de mi mamá, la infanta Cristina. Mis abuelos, el rey Juan Carlos y la reina Sofía, __6.__ 62 años. Ellos son los reyes[2] de España. ¿ __7.__ tú tíos y primos? Me encanta tener una familia grande.

[1]In the Spanish royal family, *una infanta* is a princess *(una princesa)* who is not heir to the throne.
[2]Note that *el rey + la reina = los reyes.*

La familia de Juan Carlos I, rey de España

Fondo cultural

La familia real *(royal)* de España Juan Carlos I and Sofía have been king and queen of Spain since 1975.

- What other countries can you name that are ruled by a monarchy?

Más práctica

- Practice Workbook, p. 5: 5A-5
- WAV Wbk.: Writing, p. 9
- Guided Practice: Grammar Acts., pp. 159–160
- *Real.* para hispanohablantes, pp. 174–177

Go Online PHSchool.com
For: *Tener*
Web Code: jbd-0504

Leer/Hablar/Pensar

¿Quiénes son los miembros de la familia real?

Work with a partner to identify the members of the royal family. Use the photograph and answers from Actividad 21 to help.

Modelo

A —*Creo que el número uno es el tío de Pablo. Se llama Felipe.*
B —*Estoy de acuerdo.*
o: —*No estoy de acuerdo.*

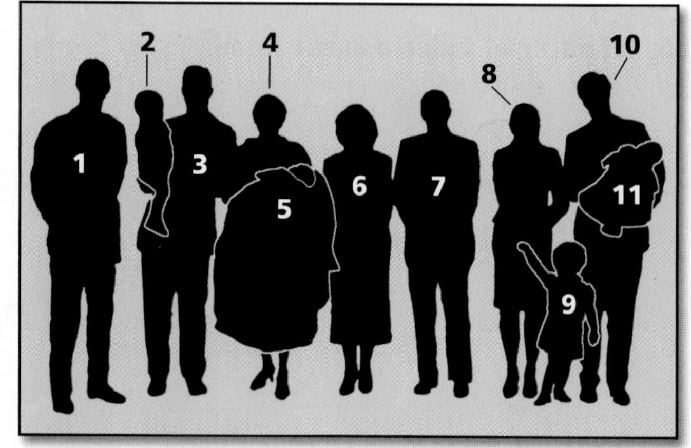

Leer/Pensar

La familia de Carlos IV

Before the age of photography, painted portraits were used to capture the images of people. Look carefully at the painting *La familia de Carlos IV* by Francisco de Goya and then read about the family.

Pensar/Hablar

Carlos IV y su familia

Work with a partner. Point to different people in Goya's painting of the royal family and ask your partner who he or she thinks they are.

Modelo

A —*¿Quién es?*
B —*Creo que es el hijo menor.*

"Autorretrato" (ca. 1815)
Oil on canvas. Academia de San Fernando, Madrid, Spain. Courtesy of The Bridgeman Art Library International Ltd.

Francisco de Goya (1746–1828) was one of the greatest Spanish painters and is considered by many to be the "Father of Modern Art." He was known for a wide range of art themes, including portraits of the royal family and other members of the nobility.

Conexiones — El arte

La familia real tiene mucha importancia en la historia de España. Es el año 1800: Carlos IV (cuarto) no es un rey popular y muchas personas creen que es demasiado indeciso[1]. En este cuadro[2] del pintor Francisco de Goya, puedes ver a la familia del rey Carlos IV. Carlos IV reinó[3] de 1788 a 1808.

- El pintor también está en el cuadro. ¿Puedes ver a Goya? ¿Dónde está?

[1]indecisive [2]painting [3]reigned

"La familia de Carlos IV" (1800), Francisco de Goya

Oil on canvas. 110 1/4" x 132 1/4 " (280 x 336 cm). Museo Nacional del Prado, Madrid. Photo credit: Scala / Art Resource, NY.

Fondo cultural

Dos familias reales The family photo of the Spanish royal family on p. 46 was taken in the year 2000, 200 years after Goya painted the portrait of Juan Carlos I's ancestor and his family. Study the two pictures as you answer these questions.

- In what ways are the two pictures similar? How are they different? How would you compare them to your own family portraits?

Gramática

Possessive adjectives

You use possessive adjectives to tell what belongs to someone or to show relationships. In English, the possessive adjectives are *my, your, his, her, its, our,* and *their.*

Here are the possessive adjectives in Spanish:

mi(s)	nuestro(s) nuestra(s)
tu(s)	vuestro(s) vuestra(s)
su(s)	su(s)

Javier y yo, con **nuestra** abuela

Mis padres, con **su** regalo

¿Recuerdas?

You know that *de* shows possession or relationship and is the equivalent of *-'s* and *-s'*:

- el regalo **de** Ana
- los primos **de** mis amigos

Like other adjectives, possessive adjectives agree in number with the nouns that follow them. Only *nuestro* and *vuestro* have different masculine and feminine endings.

mi cámara	mis cámaras
nuestro abuelo	nuestros abuelos
nuestra hija	nuestras hijas

Su and *sus* can have many different meanings: *his, her, its, your,* or *their.* To be more specific, you can use *de* + noun or pronoun.

sus flores = las flores **de ella**

sus regalos = los regalos **de Javier y Carlos**

GramActiva VIDEO

Want to learn more about possessive adjectives? Watch the **GramActiva** video.

Escribir

Muchos primos

Felipe's class is talking about their cousins. Number your paper from 1–6. Find out the names of everyone's cousins by matching the sentences in the first column with the sentences in the second column.

1. Yo tengo un primo.
2. Karin y yo tenemos dos primos.
3. Nosotros tenemos una prima.
4. También tengo tres primas.
5. Javier y Clara tienen un primo.
6. Ud. tiene dos primas.

a. Sus primas se llaman María y Ana.
b. Mi primo se llama Roberto.
c. Nuestra prima se llama Nelia.
d. Su primo se llama Gilberto.
e. Mis primas se llaman Micaela, Sara y Cristina.
f. Nuestros primos se llaman Luisa y Carlos.

Leer/Escribir

La Cenicienta y su familia

Complete the following story about *La Cenicienta* with the appropriate word or possessive adjective. Write your answers on a sheet of paper. *La Cenicienta* is a character from a well-known story. Who is she?

Cenicienta tiene una madrastra y dos hermanastras muy perezosas. **1.** *(Sus / Tus)* hermanastras se llaman Griselda y Anastasia. **2.** *(Nuestra / Su)* madrastra y **3.** *(su / sus)* hermanastras siempre dicen: "¡Cenicienta! Tenemos hambre. ¿Dónde está **4.** *(mi / nuestra)* comida?". Cada mañana Griselda le dice: "Quiero **5.** *(mi / su)* desayuno. ¿Dónde está?". Una noche Cenicienta va al baile del príncipe. Él le pregunta a Cenicienta: "¿Cómo te llamas? ¿Quiénes son **6.** *(tu / tus)* padres?". Las hermanastras **7.** *(de / su)* Cenicienta ven al príncipe cuando baila con Cenicienta. Ellas dicen: "¡ **8.** *(Nuestra / Su)* hermanastra baila con el príncipe! ¡Qué ridículo!".

Hablar

¿Dónde están las decoraciones?

You and your friend are looking for some things for a school party. Ask and answer questions about where you can find the decorations and other items you need.

Modelo

A —*¿Dónde están las luces de Renaldo?*
B —*Sus luces están en la oficina.*

Estudiante A

1. tus flores
2. los regalos de Uds.
3. mi piñata
4. el papel picado de Lupe
5. los globos de Marta y Tere
6. mis luces

Estudiante B

en la sala de clases
debajo de la mesa
allí
en la oficina
al lado de la silla
detrás de la puerta
en el escritorio

¡Respuesta personal!

Actividad 28 Leer/Escribir/Hablar

¿Quién es tu héroe?

Read this ad and answer the questions that follow.

1. In this ad, who is the hero? Whose hero is he?
2. Work with a partner to find out about his or her hero. Ask and answer following the model.

Modelo

A —*¿Quién es tu héroe o heroína? ¿Cómo es?*
B —*Mi heroína es mi madre. Es muy inteligente.*

Actividad 29 Escribir/Hablar/GramActiva

Juego

1 Working with a partner, make a set of two cubes using the template your teacher will give you.

- **Cube 1** Write a different subject pronoun on each side.
- **Cube 2** Write a different classroom object on each side. Make three of them singular and three of them plural.
- **Both cubes** Write a different point value from 1 to 6 on each side.

Modelo

Uds. tienen su calculadora.

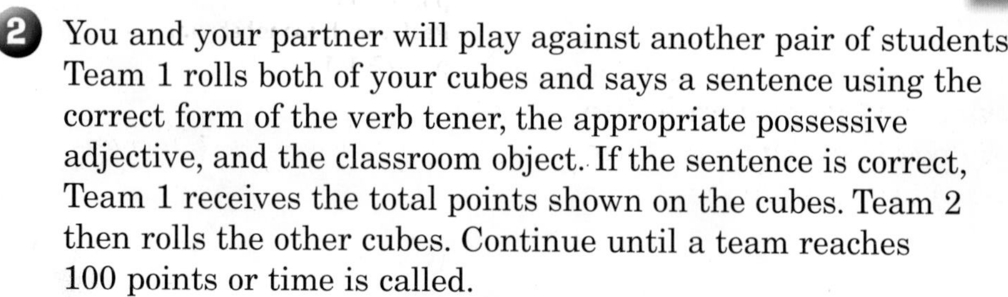

2 You and your partner will play against another pair of students. Team 1 rolls both of your cubes and says a sentence using the correct form of the verb tener, the appropriate possessive adjective, and the classroom object. If the sentence is correct, Team 1 receives the total points shown on the cubes. Team 2 then rolls the other cubes. Continue until a team reaches 100 points or time is called.

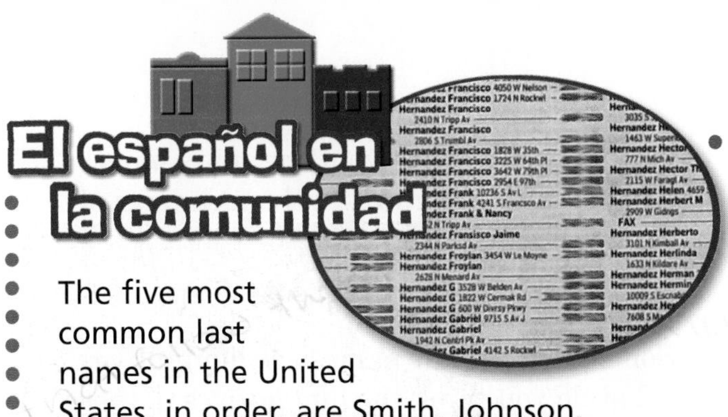

El español en la comunidad

The five most common last names in the United States, in order, are Smith, Johnson, Williams, Jones, and Brown. The five most common last names in the United States for people of Spanish-speaking heritage, in order, are García, Martínez, Rodríguez, Hernández, and López.

- Look up these names in your local phone book. Count the number of entries for each. Do the numbers in your community match the statement made above? Can you identify two other Hispanic last names that are common in your community or that you are familiar with?

Escribir/Hablar

¿Qué tienen que comprar para sus profesores?

You and your classmates are celebrating *el Día de los profesores.* What gifts do each of you need to buy, and for whom?

1. Write the names of five teachers and the classes that they teach. Beside each name, write one item that you think is a good gift for that teacher.

2. Interview a partner to find out what gifts they have to buy and for whom.

Modelo

A —*¿Qué tienes que comprar para tus profesores?*
B —*Tengo que comprar una calculadora para la Sra. Cantos, mi profesora de matemáticas, y un diccionario para el Sr. Aldea, mi profesor de español.*

3. Write a paragraph to describe what gifts your partner has to buy and for whom.

Modelo

Ana tiene que comprar una calculadora para la Sra. Cantos, su profesora de matemáticas. También tiene que comprar un diccionario para el Sr. Aldea, su profesor de español.

Para decir más . . .

comprar to buy

¿Recuerdas?

You have already been using vocabulary for classroom supplies.

Más práctica

- Practice Workbook, pp. 6–7: 5A-6, 5A-7
- WAV Wbk.: Writing, p. 10
- Guided Practice: Grammar Acts., pp. 161–162
- *Real.* para hispanohablantes, pp. 178–181

For: Possessive Adjs.
Web Code: jbd-0505

Exploración del lenguaje

Diminutives

In Spanish you can add the suffix *-ito(a)* to a word to give it the meaning of "small" or "little." It can also be used to show affection. Words with this suffix are called diminutives *(diminutivos)*.

abuelo → abuel**ito**

perros → perr**itos**

hermana → herman**ita**

Now that you know what the suffix *-ito(a)* means, can you figure out the meanings of these words?

abuelita gatito Miguelito hijita

Some very popular names are diminutives. What do you think the diminutives of these names are?

Ana Juana Eva Lola

Leer/Pensar

¡Feliz cumpleaños!

Read the birthday card. Who is it for? Find the diminutives. What words in the poem do you understand? How many objects can you name in Spanish in the picture?

jbd-0588

Leer/Escuchar

La fiesta de cumpleaños

On a sheet of paper, write the numbers from 1–6. Read the birthday card and listen to the statements. If a statement is true *(cierto)* write *C;* if it is false *(falso)* write *F.*

Hay luces, y flores,
y lindos globitos, un pastelito sabroso,
y muchos regalitos,

y una piñata,
y seis perritos que cantan y bailan,
muy contentitos,

porque hoy cumples...
¡6 añitos!

Felipe

Hablar/Escribir

Un cumpleaños divertido

1. Find out from your classmates what they consider to be a great birthday. Make a chart like the one below on a sheet of paper and complete the first row about yourself.

2. Then survey four classmates to find out what their preferences are and record the information in the chart.

Modelo

¿En qué mes es tu cumpleaños?
¿Cuál es tu actividad y lugar (place) *favorito?*
¿Cuáles son tus comidas favoritas?

	Mes del cumpleaños	Actividad y lugar favorito	Comidas favoritas
yo	julio	comer / un restaurante	pastel y helado
Miguel	enero	abrir regalos / en casa	pizza y ensalada
Anita	julio	bailar / un baile	hamburguesas y helado

3. Write a paragraph describing the person you interviewed whose idea of a great birthday celebration is most like your own. Describe the similarities, but also mention differences.

Modelo

Nuestro cumpleaños es en julio. Nuestra comida favorita es el helado. A ella le gustan las hamburguesas pero a mí me gusta el pastel. Mi lugar favorito para mi cumpleaños es un restaurante porque me gusta comer. Su lugar favorito es un baile porque le gusta bailar.

Escuchar/Hablar

¿Quién es esta persona?

Use your completed chart from Actividad 33 and describe a classmate to the class. Do not give that person's name. The class will try to guess whom you are describing.

Modelo

Su cumpleaños es en enero. Para su cumpleaños le gusta abrir regalos en casa. Sus comidas favoritas en su cumpleaños son pizza y ensalada. ¿Quién es?

Un chico chileno con su mejor amigo

¡Adelante!

Objectives

- Read about a *miniteca*
- Learn to make *papel picado*
- Describe pictures of your family
- Watch *¿Eres tú, María?*, Episodio 1

Lectura

¡Te invitamos a nuestra miniteca!

Muchos jóvenes hispanos celebran una ocasión especial con una miniteca. Sus padres y uno o varios amigos organizan la miniteca en una casa o en un lugar especial. Decoran el sitio al estilo de una discoteca pequeña. Las luces, la decoración y la música hacen un ambiente[1] divertido para los jóvenes. En las minitecas los jóvenes tienen la oportunidad de escuchar música, bailar, comer y pasar tiempo con los amigos y sus padres. Las minitecas son una costumbre de los jóvenes en países hispanos, especialmente Colombia y Venezuela.

Aquí está la invitación a la miniteca de María y Andrea para celebrar el fin de año del octavo grado.

[1]atmosphere

Strategy

Scanning
What information would you expect to find on an invitation? Read quickly through this invitation and find the names of the two people who are inviting you to the *miniteca*, where it is taking place, and when.

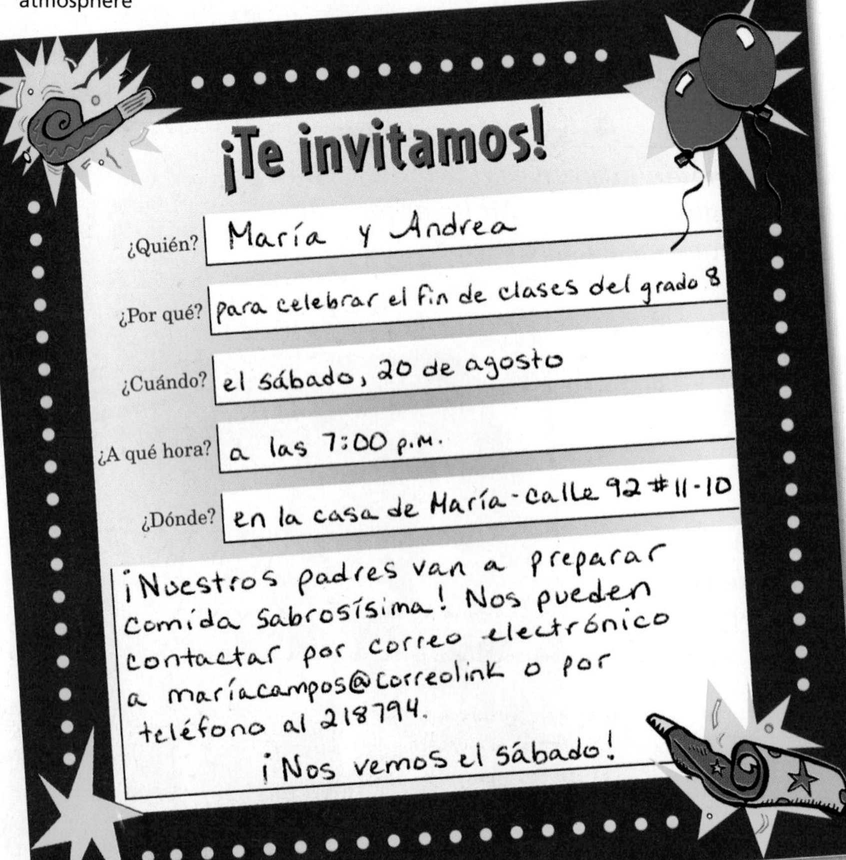

¡Te invitamos!

¿Quién? María y Andrea

¿Por qué? para celebrar el fin de clases del grado 8

¿Cuándo? el sábado, 20 de agosto

¿A qué hora? a las 7:00 p.m.

¿Dónde? en la casa de María - Calle 92 #11-10

¡Nuestros padres van a preparar comida sabrosísima! Nos pueden contactar por correo electrónico a mariacampos@correolink o por teléfono al 218794.

¡Nos vemos el sábado!

"El sábado va a ser un día muy divertido. Vamos a bailar, comer y celebrar el fin del octavo grado con todos nuestros amigos. Tenemos que sacar fotos y hacer un video para nunca olvidar[2] el momento."

[2]forget

“Aquí estamos María y yo. Es un día muy especial y todos nuestros amigos están en la casa para celebrar. Todo está perfecto para la miniteca: la comida, las decoraciones y la música. ¡Estamos felices!”.

¿Comprendes?

1. ¿Cuál es la fecha de la miniteca de María y Andrea?
2. Necesitas veinte minutos para ir de tu casa a la casa de María. ¿A qué hora tienes que salir *(leave)* de tu casa?
3. ¿Qué ocasión van a celebrar María, Andrea y sus amigos? ¿Quién va a ayudar a María y Andrea a organizar la miniteca?
4. ¿Qué actividad de la miniteca te gusta más?

Fondo cultural

La quinceañera is a special celebration of a girl's fifteenth birthday also called *los quince,* or *los quince años.* It celebrates the girl becoming a more responsible and involved part of society. During this special occasion friends and family attend mass and then an elaborate party. It is customary for the girl celebrating her *quinceañera* to dance the first dance, a waltz, with her father. This tradition is especially important in Mexico, Central America, Hispanic American countries in the Caribbean, as well as among the Spanish-speaking population in the United States.

- Think about an event in the lives of your friends that has the importance of a *quinceañera* celebration. How are the events similar or different?

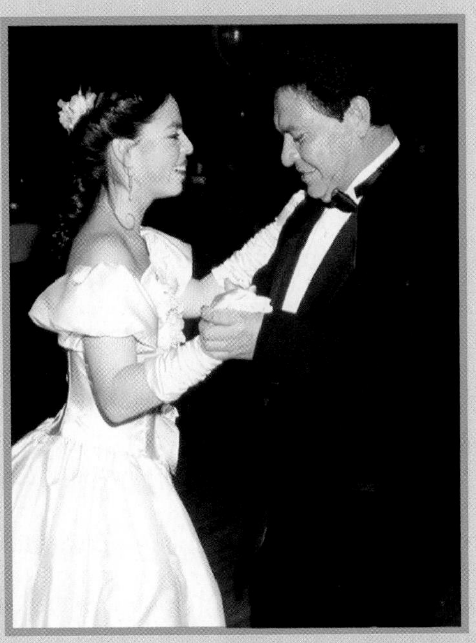

Más práctica

- **WAV Wbk.: Writing, p. 11**
- **Guided Practice: *Lectura*, p. 163**
- ***Real.* para hispanohablantes, pp. 182–183**

La cultura en vivo

El papel picado

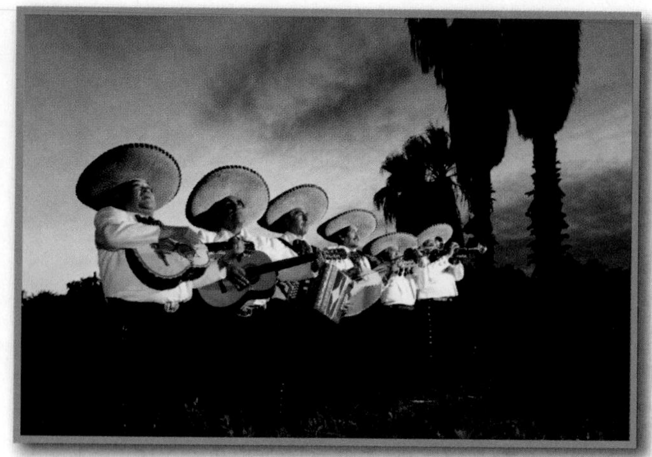

Una fiesta con música de mariachi

As you've seen in this chapter, *el papel picado* (cut-paper decorations) is a well-known Mexican craft. Tissue paper is cut into small patterns similar to making paper snowflakes. The cut paper is then hung on string to make a banner to use as decoration at many different celebrations. Here's how to make *papel picado* to decorate your classroom.

Materials

- colored tissue paper cut into 12" x 18" sheets
- scissors
- stapler
- string

1 2 3

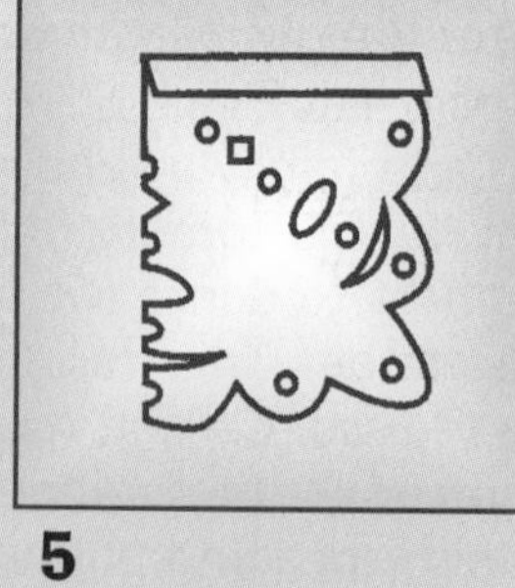

4 5 6

Directions

1 Spread the tissue paper flat. Fold down 1" on the 18" side for making a hanging flap.

2 Fold the paper in half on the 12" side and crease on the fold to make a sharp line.

3 Fold the paper twice diagonally.

4 Cut out designs along the folded edge. Experiment with snowflake or other geometric designs.

5 Cut a scalloped design on the outside edge.

6 Open the cutout and staple to a string to hang across a room to decorate for a *fiesta*.

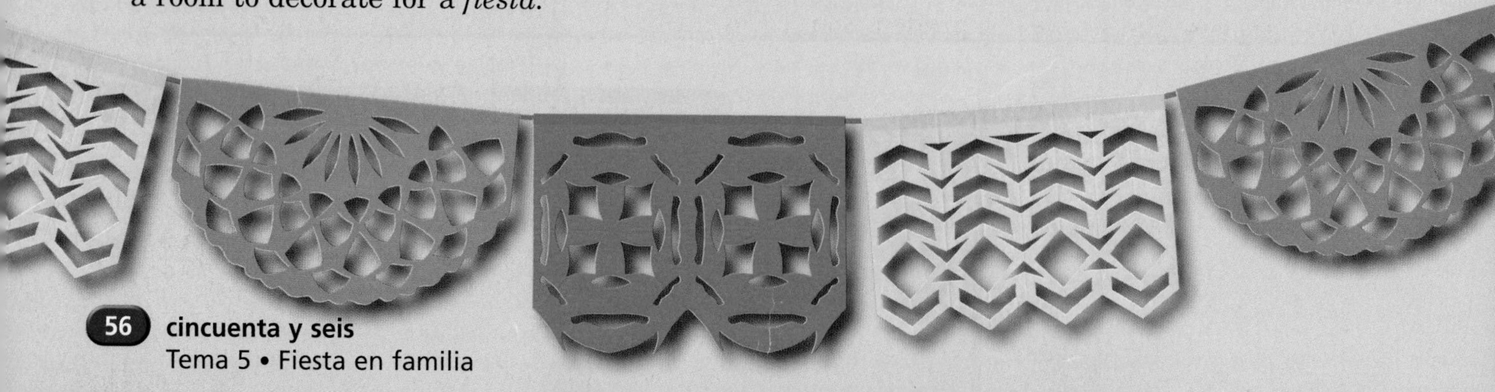

Presentación oral

Mi familia

Task

You are on an exchange program in Chile and your host family wants to know about your family back home. Show them photographs of three family members and talk about the people shown.

1 Prepare Bring in three family photos or "create" a family using pictures from a magazine. Use a chart like this one to think through what you want to say about each person.

Nombre	Es mi . . .	Edad	Actividad favorita
Isabel	hermana menor	9 años	le gusta cantar

2 Practice Go through your presentation several times. You can use your notes in practice, but not when you present. Try to:

- provide all the information on each family member
- use complete sentences
- speak clearly

Strategy

Using graphic organizers
Simple charts can help you organize your thoughts for presentation.

Modelo

Se llama Isabel. Ella es mi hermana menor y tiene 9 años. A Isabel le gusta cantar. Es muy artística.

3 Present Show your pictures and give the information about each person.

4 Evaluation Your teacher may give you a rubric for how the presentation will be graded. You will probably be graded on:

- how complete your preparation is
- how much information you communicate
- how easy it is to understand you

Videomisterio

¿Eres tú, María?

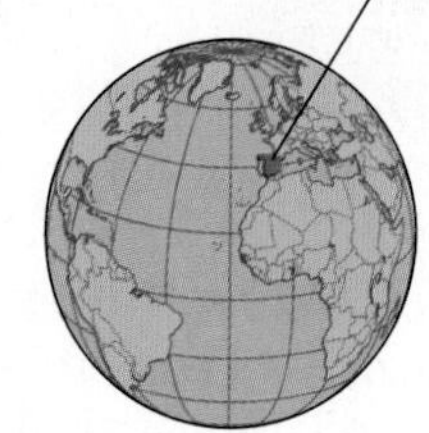

Episodio 1

Antes de ver el video

Personajes importantes

Nota cultural In many apartment buildings in Spain, you will find a *portero* or *portera*. In exchange for a small salary and free apartment (in Spain, an apartment is called *un piso),* this person watches over the building and its residents, doing small chores such as taking messages and receiving packages. Because the *portero* or *portera* knows everyone in the building, he or she is often a good source of information about the residents.

Resumen del episodio

Estamos en el piso de Lola Lago, una detective que trabaja en Madrid, la capital de España. Es la una de la mañana. Desde[1] su balcón, ella ve a dos personas hablando enfrente de un edificio.[2] ¿Qué pasa? Más tarde, Lola encuentra[3] algo muy importante en la calle.[4] Al día siguiente,[5] doña Lupe, la portera del edificio, entra en el piso de doña Gracia y . . .

[1]From [2]building [3]finds [4]street [5]The next day

Palabras para comprender

investigar	to investigate
las llaves	keys
el periódico	newspaper
el piso	apartment; floor *(of a building)*

"¿Qué es esto?
Mañana voy a investigar".

"A ver. Unas llaves . . ."

"¡Ay de mí! Necesito una ambulancia. Plaza del Alamillo. Número 8. Tercer piso. ¡Rápido!".

Después de ver el video

¿Comprendes?

Lee las frases y decide si son ciertas o falsas. Si una frase es falsa, escríbela con la información correcta.

1. Es la una de la tarde cuando Lola entra en su piso.
2. Ella está sola en su piso.
3. Lola ve a dos hombres hablando en la calle.
4. Las dos personas están muy contentas.
5. Lola encuentra un llavero con las iniciales "J.R.D.".
6. Lola compra *(buys)* una revista en la mañana.
7. Doña Lupe entra en el piso de Lola con el periódico.

Go Online PHSchool.com **For:** More on *¿Eres tú, María?* **Web Code:** jbd-0507

Chapter Review

Repaso del capítulo

To prepare for the test, check to see if you . . .

- know the new vocabulary and grammar
- can perform the tasks on p. 61

Vocabulario y gramática

jbd-0589 

to talk about family members

los abuelos	grandparents
el abuelo	grandfather
la abuela	grandmother
el esposo, la esposa	husband, wife
los hermanos	brothers; brother(s) and sister(s)
el hermano	brother
la hermana	sister
el hermanastro	stepbrother
la hermanastra	stepsister
los hijos	children; sons
el hijo	son
la hija	daughter
los padres (papás)	parents
el padre (papá)	father
la madre (mamá)	mother
el padrastro	stepfather
la madrastra	stepmother
los primos	cousins
el primo	(male) cousin
la prima	(female) cousin
los tíos	uncles; aunt(s) and uncle(s)
el tío	uncle
la tía	aunt

to discuss and compare ages

¿Cuántos años tiene(n) ___?	How old is / are ___?
Tiene(n) ___ años.	He / She is / They are ___ (years old).
mayor, *pl.* **mayores**	older
menor, *pl.* **menores**	younger

to talk about people

la persona	person

to name animals

el gato	cat
el perro	dog

to discuss what someone likes

(a + *person*) **le gusta(n) / le encanta(n)**	he / she likes / loves

For *Vocabulario adicional,* see pp. 336–337.

to describe activities at parties

abrir	to open
celebrar	to celebrate
decorar	to decorate
las decoraciones	decorations
hacer un video	to videotape
el video	video
preparar	to prepare
romper	to break
sacar fotos	to take photos
la foto	photo
la cámara	camera

to discuss celebrations

el cumpleaños	birthday
¡Feliz cumpleaños!	Happy birthday!
los dulces	candy
la flor, *pl.* **las flores**	flower
el globo	balloon
la luz, *pl.* **las luces**	light
el papel picado	cut-paper decorations
el pastel	cake
la piñata	piñata
el regalo	gift, present

other useful words

que	who, that
sólo	only

to indicate possession or relationship

tener *to have*

tengo	**tenemos**
tienes	**tenéis**
tiene	**tienen**

possessive adjectives

mi(s) my	**nuestro(s), -a(s)** our
tu(s) your	**vuestro(s), -a(s)** your
su(s) your *(formal),* his, her, its	**su(s)** your *(pl.),* their

Más práctica

- Practice Workbook: Puzzle, p. 8
- Practice Workbook: Organizer, p. 9

For: Test Preparation
Web Code: jbd-0508

Preparación para el examen

On the exam you will be asked to . . .	Here are practice tasks similar to those you will find on the exam . . .	If you need review . . .
jbd-0589  **1 Escuchar** Listen to and understand someone's description of a family member	At a friend's party, a woman is telling you stories about her brother, Jorge. a) How old is her brother? b) Who is older, the woman or her brother? c) What does her brother like to do?	**pp. 32–37** *A primera vista* **p. 39** Actividad 7 **p. 41** Actividades 12–13 **p. 44** Actividad 18
 **2 Hablar** Describe some members of your family and what they like to do	At your first Spanish Club meeting, your teacher requests that all of you try to talk to each other in Spanish. Since you just learned how to talk about your family, you feel confident that you can talk about some of your family members. Tell about: a) how they are related to you; b) their ages; c) what they like to do; d) their personalities.	**pp. 32–37** *A primera vista* **p. 39** Actividad 7 **p. 41** Actividad 12 **p. 44** Actividad 19 **p. 48** *Gramática: Possessive adjectives* **p. 53** Actividades 33–34
 **3 Leer** Read and understand someone's description of a problem he or she is having with a family member	Read this letter to an advice columnist. Can you describe in English what Ana's problem is? Querida Dolores: Yo soy la hija menor de una familia de seis personas. Uno de mis hermanos mayores, Nacho, siempre habla de mí con mis padres. A él le encanta hablar de mis amigos y de mis actividades. Tenemos una familia muy simpática, pero ¡Nacho me vuelve loca! —Ana	**pp. 32–37** *A primera vista* **p. 39** Actividades 7–8 **p. 46** Actividad 21 **p. 49** Actividad 26
4 Escribir Write a brief note telling at least two facts about a friend or family member	The party planner at a local restaurant is helping you plan a birthday party for your cousin. Write a brief note telling her your cousin's name, age, two things he or she likes to do at a party, the kinds of decorations he or she likes, and one thing he or she loves to eat.	**p. 39** Actividad 8 **p. 41** Actividad 13 **p. 44** Actividad 19 **p. 53** Actividad 34
 **5 Pensar** Demonstrate an understanding of some ways that Spanish-speaking families celebrate special occasions	Think about what you would consider your most important birthday. Based on what you know about important family traditions, describe why a fifteenth birthday is important for a young Spanish-speaking girl and what you would expect to see at her celebration.	**pp. 32–37** *A primera vista* **p. 39** *Fondo cultural* **pp. 54–55** *Lectura* **p. 56** *La cultura en vivo*

Tema 5 • Fiesta en familia

Fondo cultural

Extended families tend to be close-knit in Spanish-speaking cultures. Parents, children, grandparents, aunts, uncles, and cousins get together often for meals or just to spend time together, and not just on special occasions. In fact, it is not uncommon for three generations to live under one roof or in the same neighborhood.

- How does the idea of extended families in Spanish-speaking cultures compare with what happens with you and your friends?

"Orgullo de familia" (1997), Simón Silva

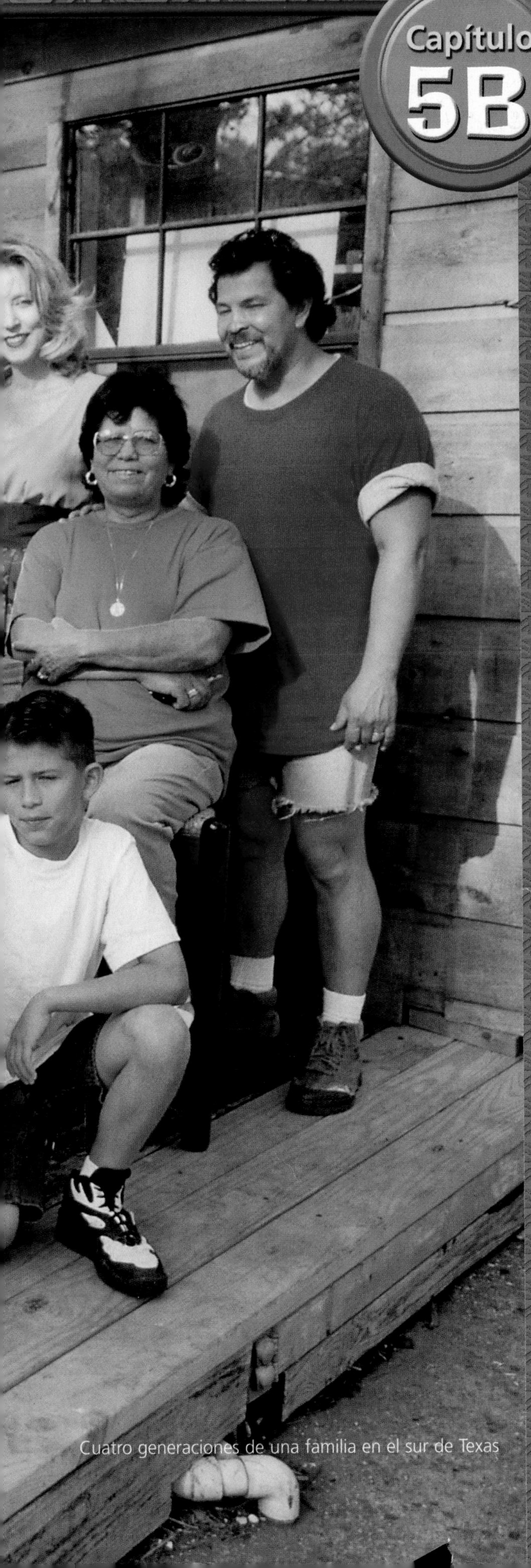

Cuatro generaciones de una familia en el sur de Texas

Capítulo 5B

¡Vamos a un restaurante!

Chapter Objectives

- **Talk about family celebrations**
- **Describe family members and friends**
- **Ask politely to have something brought to you**
- **Order a meal in a restaurant**
- **Understand cultural perspectives on family celebrations**

Video Highlights

A primera vista: ***En el restaurante Casa Río***
GramActiva Videos: **the verb *venir;* the verbs *ser* and *estar***
Videomisterio: ***¿Eres tú, María?,*** **Episodio 2**

Country Connection

As you learn about family celebrations, describing family members, and restaurants, you will make connections to these countries and places:

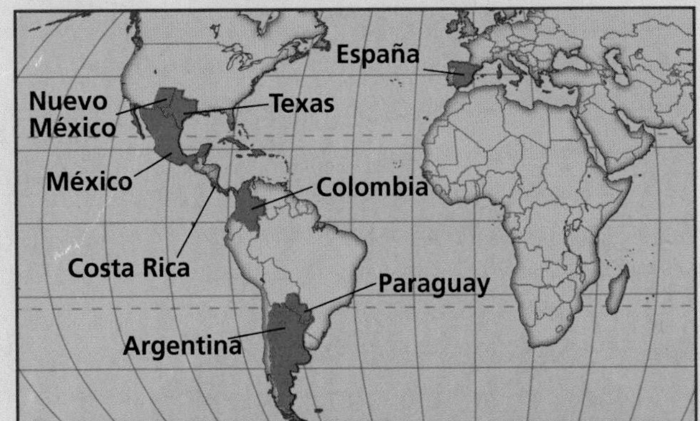

Más práctica

- ***Real.*** **para hispanohablantes, pp. 190–191**

Go Online PHSchool.com **For:** Online Atlas **Web Code:** jbe-0002

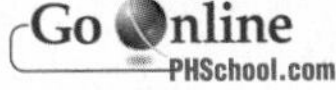

A primera vista

Vocabulario y gramática en contexto

Objectives

Read, listen to, and understand information about
- descriptions of family members
- restaurant vocabulary
- table settings

jbd-0597

—Abuelito, ¿quiénes son las personas en la foto?

—La mujer es tu abuela y el hombre, soy yo. Y aquí está tu papá. Tiene sólo seis años.

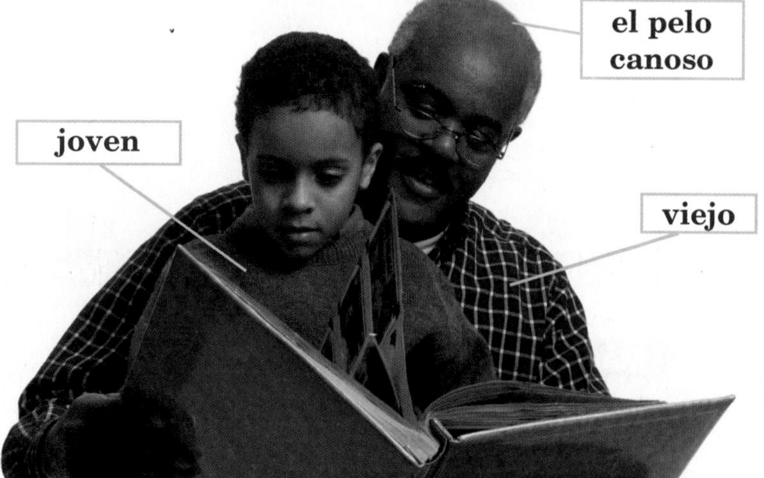

—¿Quién es **el joven** alto y **guapo?**

—Es tu primo Rafael.

—¿Y **la joven** baja al lado de primo Rafael?

—Es su amiga, Sara. Y estas **otras** personas son amigos también.

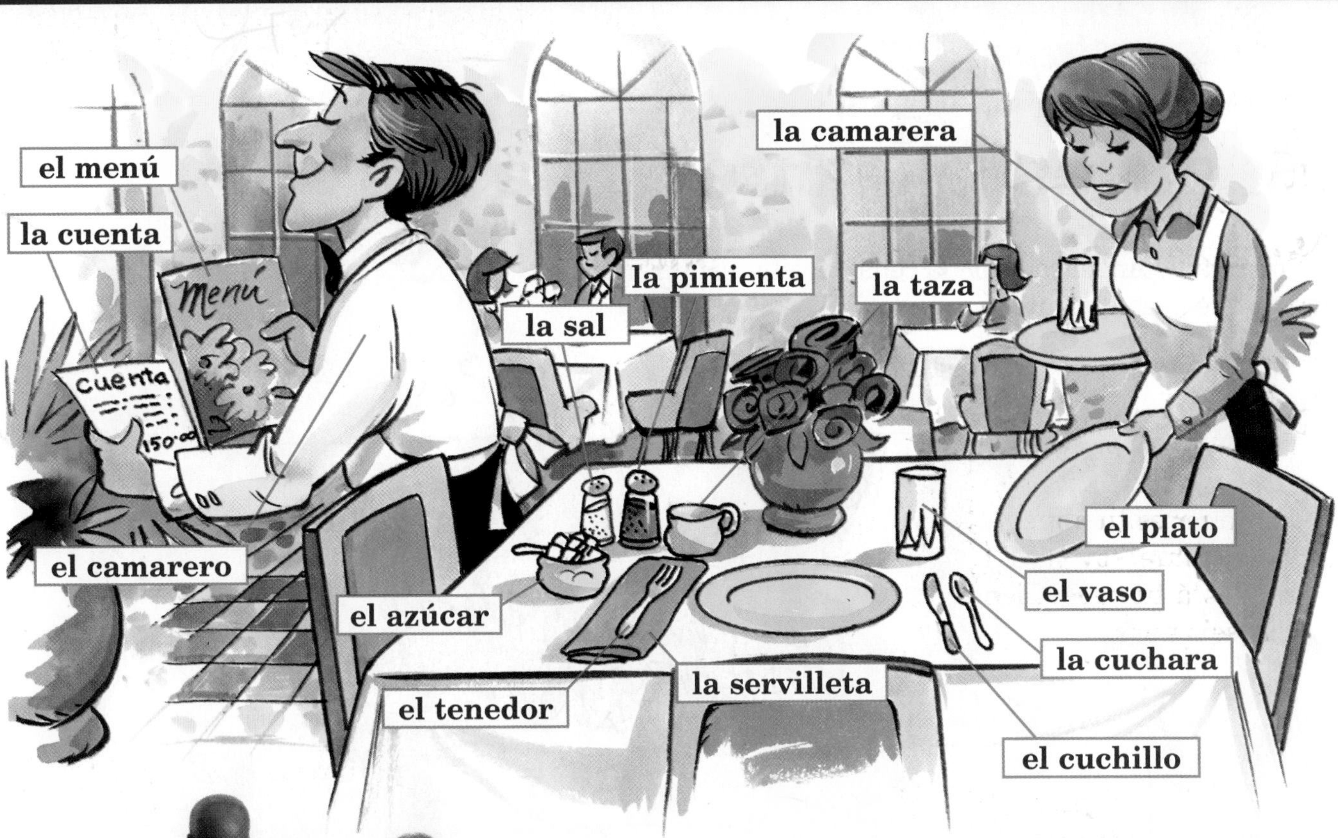
el menú
la cuenta
Menú
Cuenta
150.00
la pimienta
la sal
la camarera
la taza
el plato
el camarero
el azúcar
el vaso
la cuchara
la servilleta
el tenedor
el cuchillo

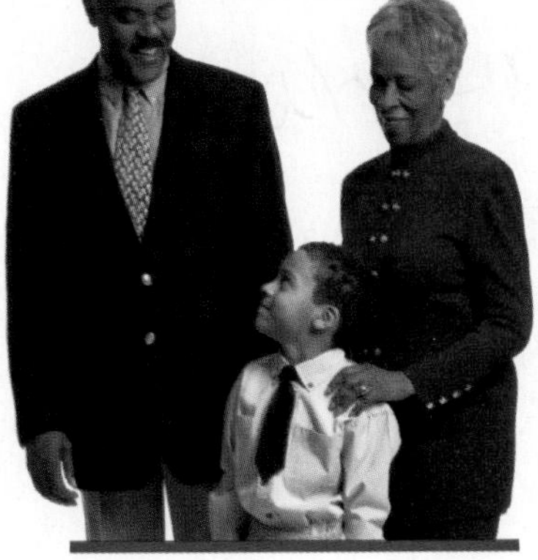

—Abuela, ¿qué celebramos esta noche?
—Es el cumpleaños de tu abuelo.
—¿Quiénes **vienen** a la fiesta?
—Toda la familia **viene.**

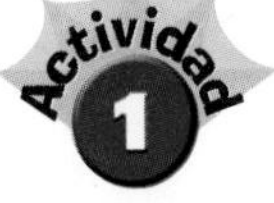

Actividad 1

jbd-0597

Escuchar

¿Quiénes vienen?

Paquito is showing the family album to a friend. Point to the different pictures as he describes the people in the photographs.

Actividad 2

jbd-0597

Escuchar

¿Qué necesitas para . . . ?

You will hear seven statements about the table setting. If a statement is correct, indicate *cierto* by raising one hand. If a statement is incorrect, indicate *falso* by raising two hands.

Más práctica

- **Practice Workbook, pp. 10–11: 5B-1, 5B-2**
- **WAV Wbk.: Writing, p. 18**
- **Guided Practice: Vocab. Flash Cards, pp. 165–170**
- ***Real.* para hispanohablantes, p. 192**

Go Online
PHSchool.com
For: Vocab. Practice
Web Code: jbd-0511

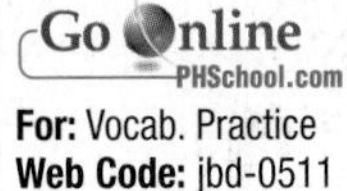

jbd-0597

En el restaurante Casa Río

La familia de Angélica come la cena en este restaurante. Lee lo que pasa durante la comida.

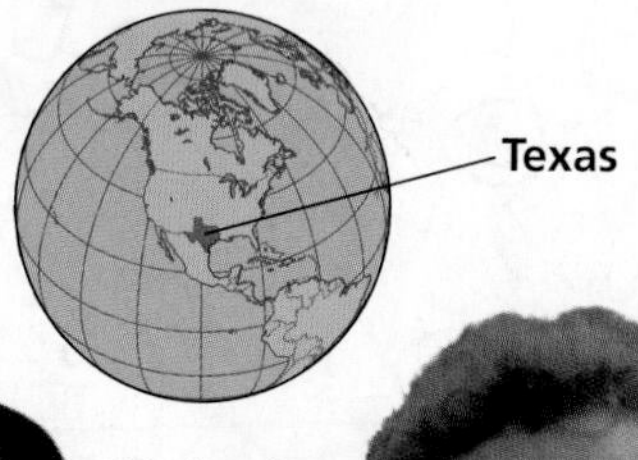

Texas

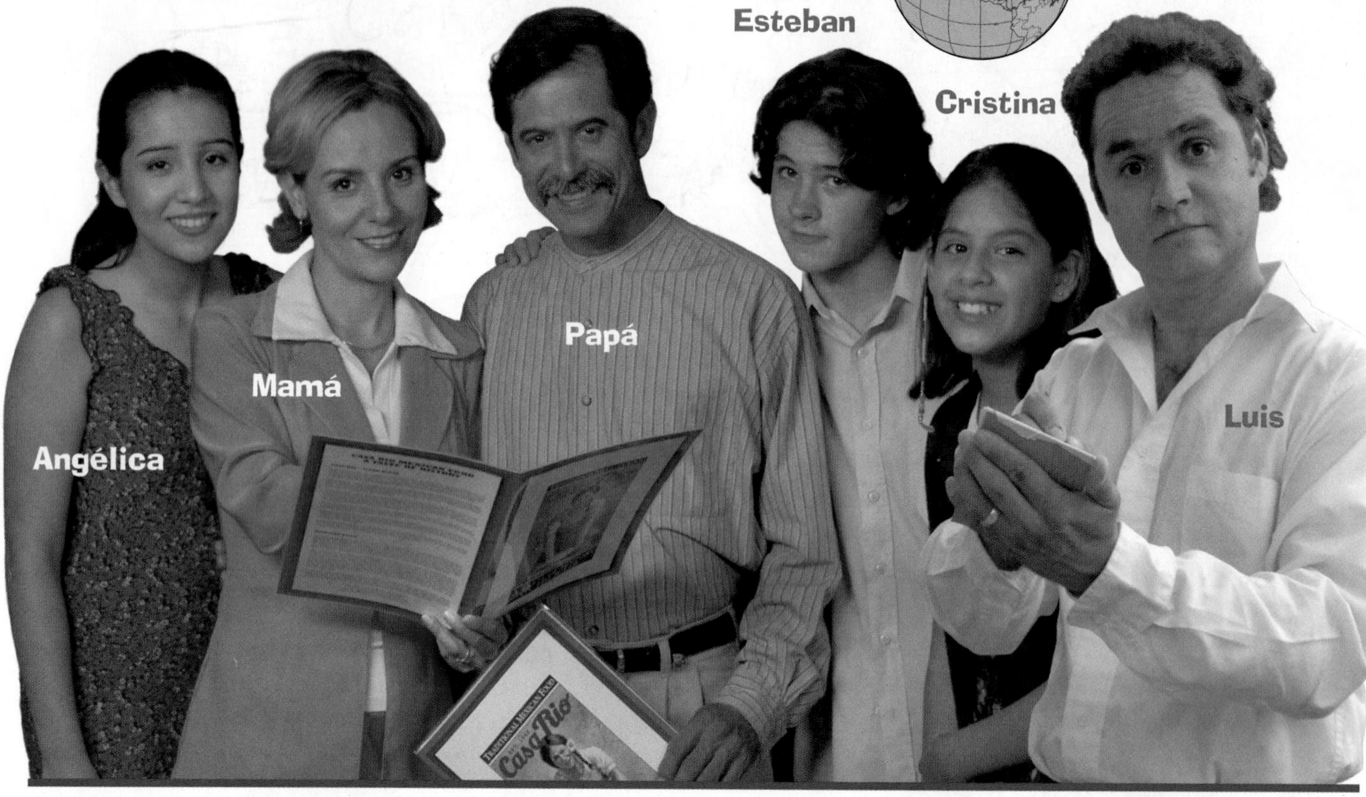

Esteban

Cristina

Papá

Mamá

Angélica

Luis

Antes de leer

Scanning You can use scanning to help you get an idea of what you might find in a reading. Think about what a waiter might say to you when you order in a restaurant.

- Look quickly through the dialogue and find three expressions that the waiter uses.

Before you read the *Videohistoria,* use the photos to help you answer the following questions.

1. How do you think the waiter is feeling when he first comes to the table?
2. What are some different foods available at this restaurant?
3. Are the members of the family enjoying their food? Why or why not?

1 **Luis:** Bienvenidos al restaurante Casa Río. Soy Luis, su mesero. Hoy es mi primer día de trabajo. Estoy un poco nervioso. El menú está en la mesa.

También se dice . . .

el / la camarero, -a = el / la mesero, -a *(México, Puerto Rico)*; el / la mozo, -a *(Argentina, Puerto Rico, Bolivia)*

2 **Luis:** ¿Qué va a **pedir** Ud. de bebida?

Papá: ¡Uy! **Tengo calor.** Para mí, un té helado.

Mamá: Y yo **tengo frío.** Para mí, café.

3 **Luis:** Y ahora . . . , **¿qué desean** Uds. **de plato principal?**

Angélica: **Quisiera** el arroz con pollo.

Esteban: Para mí, una hamburguesa con papas fritas.

4 **Luis:** ¿Y qué desea Ud.?

Cristina: **¿Me trae** las fajitas de pollo, por favor?

Luis: ¡Muy bien!

5 **Esteban:** Señor, **me faltan** un cuchillo y un tenedor.

Luis: ¡Ah, sí! En un momento **le traigo** un cuchillo y un tenedor.

6 **Luis:** ¿Y para quién son las enchiladas?

Angélica: Creo que son para el señor de pelo castaño.

Luis: ¡Oh! ¡Gracias!

Angélica: De nada.

7 **Luis:** ¿Necesitan **algo más?** ¿Y cómo está la comida?

Mamá: La comida aquí es **deliciosa. ¡Qué rica!**

8 **Luis:** Ahora, ¿desean **postre?**

Mamá: Y **otro** café, por favor.

Papá: Para mí, nada. Pero quisiera un café, yo también. Ahora **tengo sueño.**

Leer/Escribir

¿Mesero o cliente?

Read each of the following sentences from the *Videohistoria.* Number your paper from 1–6. If the sentence is something the waiter says, write *mesero* and if it is something one of the customers says, write *cliente.*

1. Bienvenidos al restaurante Casa Río.
2. ¿Me trae las fajitas de pollo, por favor?
3. ¿Necesitan algo más?
4. ¿Qué desean Uds. de plato principal?
5. Señor, me faltan un cuchillo y un tenedor.
6. ¿Y para quién son las enchiladas?

Leer/Escribir

¿Qué piden?

Help Luis by making a list of the food and drinks that Angélica's family orders. Copy this bill on your own paper and complete it based on the *Videohistoria.*

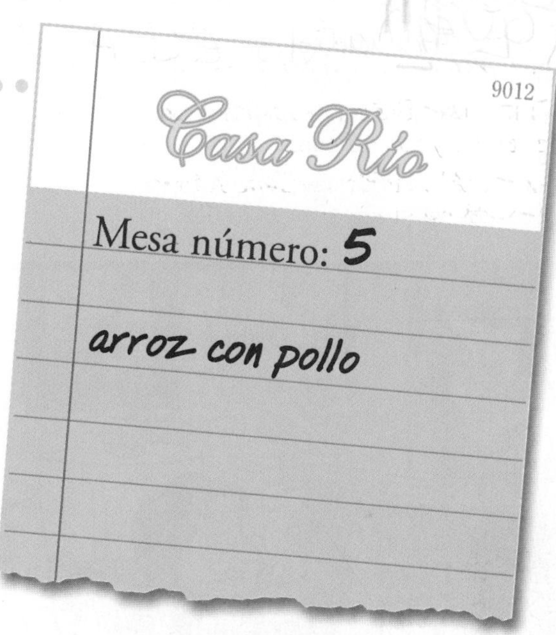

Escribir/Hablar

¿Comprendes?

1. ¿Cómo se llama el restaurante?
2. ¿Cómo se llama el camarero?
3. ¿Por qué está nervioso el camarero?
4. ¿Quiénes quieren café?
5. ¿Quién tiene sueño?
6. Según la mamá, ¿cómo es la comida?

Más práctica

- Practice Workbook, pp. 12–13: 5B-3, 5B-4
- WAV Wbk.: Video, pp. 12–14
- Guided Practice: Vocab. Check, pp. 171–174
- *Real.* para hispanohablantes, p. 193

For: Vocab. Practice
Web Code: jbd-0512

Manos a la obra

Vocabulario y gramática en uso

Objectives

- Describe people and foods
- Order a meal in a restaurant
- Learn to use the verb *venir*
- Know some uses of the verbs *ser* and *estar*

Escribir

Las personas en el restaurante

Look at the scene of the restaurant below. Number your paper from 1–6 and write a sentence to describe the following people.

Modelo

Daniela
Daniela es joven y tiene pelo negro.

1. el Sr. Ortega
2. la Sra. Ortega
3. Milagros
4. Luz
5. Eduardo
6. el Sr. Ramos

jbd-0598

Escuchar

¿Quiénes son?

You will hear descriptions of the people in the drawings below. Number your paper from 1–5, and write the name of the person who is being described.

También se dice . . .

pelirrojo, -a = colorado, -a *(Argentina);* colorín, colorina *(Chile)*

el pelo = el cabello *(muchos países)*

rubio, -a = güero, -a *(México)*

Eduardo, 15

Rosalía, 14

Lucía, 18

Alejandro, 20

María Elena, 60

Jorge, 65

Escribir

Descripciones

Choose four people from the drawings above and write three sentences to describe each person.

Modelo

El joven muy alto es Eduardo. Tiene 15 años. Tiene el pelo castaño. Le gusta jugar al tenis.

¿Recuerdas?

Adjectives agree in number and gender with the nouns they modify.

Leer/Escribir

Las asociaciones

Number your paper from 1–7. Complete the following paragraph with the appropriate word from the list.

postre	sal
taza	camarero
corto	joven
baja	azúcar

Yo soy un __1.__ y trabajo en el restaurante todos los viernes. Tengo el pelo __2.__ y soy bajo. Los viernes Carlitos y el Sr. Mendoza vienen a comer en el restaurante. El chico es __3.__ pero su abuelo es viejo. Al Sr. Mendoza le gusta pedir un plato de bistec con papas fritas y una __4.__ de café. Siempre necesita __5.__ para las papas y __6.__ para el café. A Carlitos le gusta pedir arroz con pollo de plato principal, y helado con fresas de __7.__.

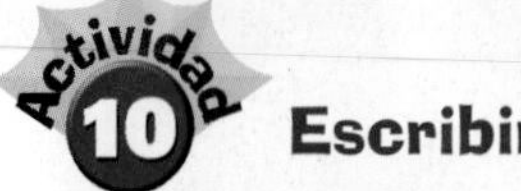

Escribir

¿Me trae . . . ?

You ordered the following items in a restaurant, but your waiter has not brought you all the utensils you need for eating them. Ask him for the missing items.

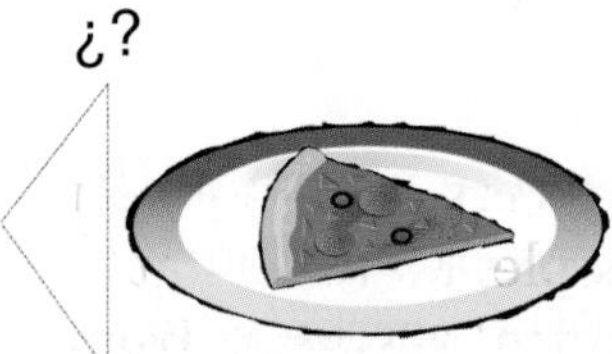

Modelo

¿Me trae una servilleta?

1. 

2.  

3. 

4. 

5. 

6. 

Fondo cultural

En el restaurante Getting a server's attention at a restaurant in a Spanish-speaking country sometimes differs from how it is done in other cultures. For example, in Costa Rica people often make a *pfft* sound to get a server's attention, while in Colombia people may raise or clap their hands. Be careful in using this sort of attention-getting device—it may seem rude when done by someone from outside the culture!

- How do you get a server's attention in a restaurant? Compare this to what is acceptable in some Spanish-speaking countries.

Leer/Hablar

En el restaurante

With a partner, read the conversation between a waiter and two young people. Match what the waiter says with the logical response from the customers to recreate the conversation.

Un restaurante en la Argentina

El camarero

1. Buenas noches. ¿Qué desean de bebida?
2. ¿Qué desea pedir de plato principal?
3. ¡Ay, señor! Le falta el cuchillo, ¿no?
4. ¿Le gusta la sopa?
5. Señorita, ¿qué desea Ud. de postre?
6. Señor, ¿le traigo otra bebida?
7. ¿Desean Uds. algo más?
8. Gracias por venir a nuestro restaurante.

Los jóvenes

a. Sí, está deliciosa. Umm. ¡Qué rica!
b. No, sólo la cuenta, por favor.
c. Quisiera el arroz con pollo, por favor.
d. De nada. Hasta luego.
e. Un helado, por favor.
f. Sí. ¿Me trae uno, por favor?
g. Para mí, un refresco y, para la señorita, un té helado.
h. Sí, por favor. Tengo mucha sed.

Escribir/Hablar

¿Qué te gusta pedir?

Write a sentence telling what you like to order in each of the following situations.

Modelo

Cuando tengo hambre, me gusta pedir pizza en un restaurante.

1.

2.

3.

4.

5.

Hablar

Juego

1. Work in groups of three or four. Your teacher will give you copies of pictures of various table items. Cut or tear the pictures apart to make cards.

2. Arrange the pictures in a table setting on a desk. While the other players have their backs turned, hide one or more of the cards. Then ask: *¿Qué me falta?* The first player to say correctly *Te falta(n)*... and name the missing item(s) receives a point.

3. Put the hidden items back on the desk and continue playing until all players have had a chance to hide items. The player with the most points is the winner.

Nota

When one item is missing, use *me/te falta.* When more than one item is missing, use *me/te faltan.*

Exploración del lenguaje

Adjectives ending in *-ísimo*

Muy + an adjective can be expressed in another way by adding the correct form of *-ísimo* to the adjective. The *-ísimo* ending conveys the idea of "extremely."

un chico muy guapo = un chico guap**ísimo**
una clase muy difícil = una clase dificil**ísima**

Adjectives that end in *-co* or *-ca* have a spelling change to *-qu-*. The *-o* or *-a* is dropped.

unos pasteles muy ri**cos**
= unos pasteles ri**quísimos**

Try it out! Rework the following phrases using the correct *-ísimo* form.

un perro muy perezoso = ¿ ?
dos libros muy interesantes = ¿ ?
una clase muy aburrida = ¿ ?
unas chicas muy simpáticas = ¿ ?

Leer/Pensar/Escribir

Café Buen Libro

Read the review of the *Café Buen Libro*. Then, based on what the people listed below are looking for, decide whether or not you would recommend that they go to this café. Number your paper from 1–6 and write *sí* if you recommend the café to that person, or *no* if you do not.

Café Buen Libro
Nuevo León, 28

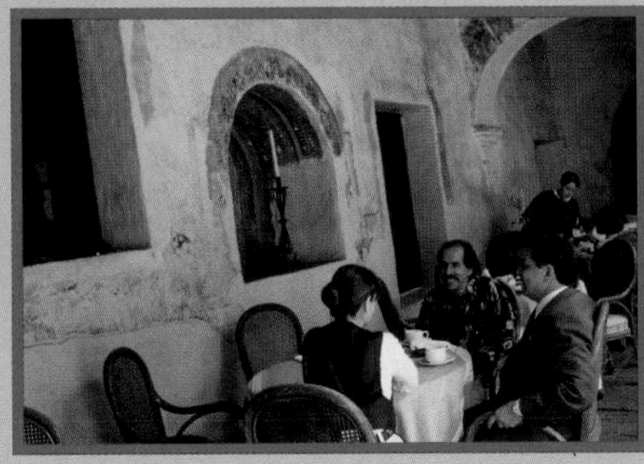

✓✓ ++ $ ☺☺

Es un café tranquilo con un ambiente* intelectual donde puedes pasar el tiempo en la compañía de un buen amigo o un buen libro. Los precios son muy razonables. Puedes comer un sándwich, una ensalada, un postre riquísimo o simplemente beber un café. También tienen lo último en libros, videos y música. Un "plus" es la presentación de grupos musicales los fines de semana.

Ambiente
aburrido ✓
tranquilo ✓✓
fantástico ✓✓✓
Comida y bebida
regular +
buena ++
excelente +++
Precios
barato $
medio $$
caro $$$
Servicio
regular ☺
bueno ☺☺
superior ☺☺☺

*atmosphere

1. **Carmen:** "Quisiera comer un bistec sabroso".
2. **Marta:** "Me encanta escuchar música".
3. **Diego:** "Tengo muchísima hambre y poco tiempo".
4. **Lupe:** "Me gusta pasar tiempo con otras personas interesantes y graciosas".
5. **Ana:** "No tengo mucho dinero *(money)* ahora".
6. Y a ti, ¿te gustaría ir al Café Buen Libro? ¿Por qué?

Escribir/Hablar

¿Quién viene a la fiesta?

1 Imagine you are planning a party and can invite any three people you want. They can be famous people who live today, people who lived long ago, or people you know personally. On a sheet of paper, write their names and why you want to invite each one.

Modelo

Albert Einstein viene a la fiesta porque es inteligente y talentoso.

2 Now, work with a partner to talk about who is coming to the party. Take turns asking and answering each other's questions.

Modelo

A —*¿Quién viene a la fiesta?*
B —*Albert Einstein viene.*
A —*¿Por qué?*
B —*Porque él es inteligente y talentoso.*

Gramática

The verb *venir*

You use *venir* to say that someone is coming to a place or an event.

¿A qué hora **vienes** a mi casa?
*When **are you coming** to my house?*

Siempre **vengo** a esta playa.
*I **always come** to this beach.*

Here are all the present-tense forms:

(yo) **vengo**	(nosotros) (nosotras) **venimos**
(tú) **vienes**	(vosotros) (vosotras) **venís**
Ud. (él) (ella) **viene**	Uds. (ellos) (ellas) **vienen**

GramActiva VIDEO

Want more help with *venir?* Watch the **GramActiva** video.

Leer/Escribir

¿Cómo vienen?

Your friend Antonio has invited you and some friends to his family's house for a party this weekend. Number your paper from 1–6 and complete his note with the appropriate forms of the verb *venir* to explain how and when everyone is coming.

> ¡Hola a todos!
>
> La cena es este fin de semana. Yo __1.__ en bicicleta con mi amiga Marta. Nosotros __2.__ a las dos porque ella trabaja hasta la una. Mi abuela __3.__ en tren[1] con mis tíos. Ellos __4.__ a las once para ayudar[2] con la cena. Mis hermanitos también __5.__ en tren con mis tíos. Mi hermana mayor Cecilia __6.__ en autobús más tarde.
>
> ¡Nos vemos el sábado!

[1]train [2]to help

jbd-0598

Escuchar/Escribir/Dibujar

Escucha, escribe y dibuja

Roberto, a friend of Antonio, is also going to Antonio's party with his family. You will hear a description of Roberto's family. On a sheet of paper, write the four descriptions you hear and then draw a picture of the family. Compare your drawing with a partner's.

Una fiesta en familia

Escribir

¿A qué hora vienen?

There is a party at your school on Saturday night. On a separate sheet of paper, write sentences telling when the following people will come to the party.

Tomás

Modelo

Tomás viene a la fiesta a las siete y media.

1. Mariana y Carmen

2. yo

3. Verónica

4. tú

5. José

6. los chicos

Hablar

¿Qué traen a tu casa?

You are at a friend's house. Talk about what different people bring when they come over to visit.

Modelo

A —*Cuando tus tíos vienen a tu casa, ¿traen algo?*
B —*Sí, generalmente traen el postre.*
o:—*No, generalmente no traen nada.*

Nota

Traer, "to bring," follows the pattern of *-er* verbs except for the irregular *yo* form: *traigo.*

- Mañana **traigo** pasteles para todos.
- Y tú, **¿traes** bebidas?

Estudiante A

1. tu(s) abuelo(s)
2. tu mejor amigo(a)
3. tus amigos
4. tus tíos
5. tus primos
6. los amigos de tus padres

Estudiante B

el plato principal
el postre
un regalo
flores
nada

¡Respuesta personal!

Escribir/Hablar

¿Quiénes vienen?

You are talking with friends at a school party. Answer the following questions.

1. ¿Quiénes vienen a la fiesta? ¿A qué hora vienen?
2. ¿Vienen todos los profesores a la fiesta? ¿Qué traen ellos?
3. ¿Traen los estudiantes pizza o sándwiches? ¿Frutas o pasteles?
4. ¿Quién trae las decoraciones? ¿Qué traes tú?

Más práctica

- Practice Workbook, p. 14: 5B-5
- WAV Wbk.: Writing, p. 19
- Guided Practice: Grammar Acts., pp. 175–176
- *Real.* para hispanohablantes, pp. 194–197

For: *Venir*
Web Code: jbd-0513

Gramática

The verbs *ser* and *estar*

You know that both *ser* and *estar* mean "to be." Their uses, however, are different.

(yo)	soy	(nosotros) (nosotras)	somos
(tú)	eres	(vosotros) (vosotras)	sois
Ud. (él) (ella)	es	Uds. (ellos) (ellas)	son

(yo)	estoy	(nosotros) (nosotras)	estamos
(tú)	estás	(vosotros) (vosotras)	estáis
Ud. (él) (ella)	está	Uds. (ellos) (ellas)	están

Use *ser* to talk about characteristics that generally do not change. *Ser* is used for descriptions that are not about conditions or location. For example:

- who a person is or what a person is like
- what something is or what something is like
- where a person or thing is from

Teresa **es** mi prima. **Es** muy graciosa.

Los tacos **son** mi comida favorita. **Son** riquísimos.

Mis tíos **son** de México. **Son** muy simpáticos.

Use *estar* to talk about conditions that tend to change. For example:

- how a person feels
- where a person or thing is

¿Dónde **está** Mariana? No **está** aquí.

No puede venir hoy porque **está** muy enferma.

GramActiva VIDEO

Want more help with *ser* and *estar*? Watch the **GramActiva** video.

Actividad 21 **Escribir**

Mi amigo(a) y yo

1. Copy this chart on a sheet of paper. Fill in the chart correctly by choosing words from the box at right that best describe what one of your friends is like and how he or she is feeling.

Mi amigo(a) está	Mi amigo(a) es
cansado(a)	trabajador(a)

2. Choose words from the list that describe you and write sentences to tell how you are feeling and what you are like.

alto, -a	ocupado, -a
bajo, -a	ordenado, -a
contento, -a	pelirrojo, -a
cansado, -a	popular
desordenado, -a	reservado, -a
enfermo, -a	rubio, -a
guapo, -a	trabajador, -a
nervioso, -a	

¡Respuesta personal!

Modelo

Yo soy trabajador. Estoy muy cansado.

Leer/Escribir

En el restaurante mexicano

Read the following descriptions of people in a restaurant in San Antonio, Texas. Based on the picture below, write sentences telling where the people are in the restaurant.

Modelo

El Sr. Ramos no es joven. Es muy gracioso. Está contento hoy porque está en el restaurante con su familia.

El Sr. Ramos está al lado de la mujer con pelo castaño y delante de los dos chicos jóvenes.

1. Miguelito es joven. Tiene cinco años. Su hermana está enferma pero él está de buena salud. Sus padres son muy graciosos.
2. Ana, Diana y Sabrina son hermanas. Son jóvenes y muy deportistas. Están tristes y aburridas hoy porque llueve y no pueden jugar al fútbol.
3. El Sr. Soriano es serio y muy inteligente. Quisiera comer con su familia pero su esposa y sus dos hijos están en Nueva York y él está en San Antonio para el trabajo.
4. Esteban es muy trabajador. Es alto y rubio. Tiene treinta años. No es serio pero ahora está muy ocupado.
5. Elena es joven y muy talentosa. Tiene pelo largo. Está nerviosa hoy porque tiene un concierto muy importante.

Leer/Escribir

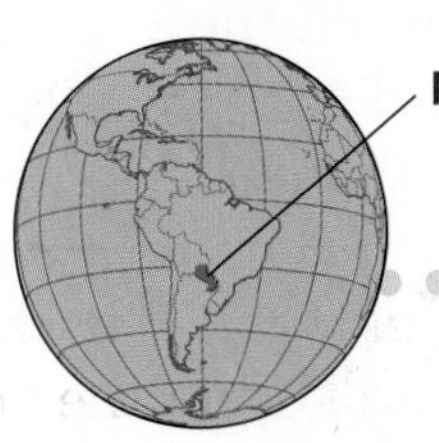

Entrevista con una chef

Number your paper 1–10. Complete the following interview with Chef Ortiz with the appropriate form of the verb *ser* or *estar.*

— Bienvenida, Chef Ortiz. ¿Cómo __1.__ Ud. hoy?
— __2.__ muy bien, gracias.
— Ud. trabaja aquí en Asunción ahora pero, ¿de dónde __3.__ Ud. originalmente?
— Mi familia y yo __4.__ del campo.
— Y ¿cuál __5.__ su trabajo aquí?
— Yo __6.__ directora de los chefs en el famoso restaurante La Capital.
— La Capital __7.__ un restaurante muy popular aquí. ¿Dónde __8.__ el restaurante?
— Al lado de la catedral.
— Los platos en su restaurante __9.__ muy típicos de Paraguay, ¿no?
— Sí, y según los clientes, la comida en nuestro restaurante __10.__ deliciosa.

¡Qué rico!

Hablar

¿Y las otras personas?

You were supposed to meet your friend and his or her family at a café, but only your friend is there. Ask your partner questions to find out what the members of his or her family are like and why they are not at the café.

Modelo

A —*¿Por qué no está tú primo?*
B —*Porque está en la escuela.*
A —*¿Cómo es?*
B —*Mi primo es inteligente y trabajador.*

Estudiante A

abuelo, -a
padre
madre
tío, -a
primo, -a
hermano, -a
amigo, -a

¡Respuesta personal!

Estudiante B

la escuela
casa
el trabajo
la lección
la biblioteca
ocupado, -a
artístico, -a
estudioso, -a
inteligente
perezoso, -a
trabajador, -a

¡Respuesta personal!

Strategy

Using rhymes
To remember the uses of *estar*, memorize this rhyme:

For how you feel
And where you are,
Always use the verb *estar*.

Pronunciación

jbd-0598

The letters *b* and *v*

In Spanish, *b* and *v* are pronounced the same. At the beginning of a word or phrase, *b* and *v* sound like the *b* in *boy*. Listen to and say these words:

voy	vienen	viejo
bolígrafo	bien	video

In most other positions *b* and *v* have a softer "b" sound. The lips barely touch as the *b* or *v* sound is pronounced. Listen to and say these words:

abuelo	joven	globo
divertido	huevos	Alberto

Try it out! Listen to and say this *trabalenguas:*

Cabral clava un clavo.
¿Qué clavo clava Cabral?

Leer/Pensar

Un postre delicioso

Your grandmother has given you her recipe for *arroz con leche* and you want to try it out. But the ingredients are given in *gramos* and *litros* and you don't know what the customary measure equivalents are. Study the conversion chart, convert the measurements given in the recipe, and answer the questions.

Conexiones
Las matemáticas

ARROZ CON LECHE

Para 8

300 gramos de arroz
3 litros de leche
400 gramos de azúcar
un poco de vainilla
canela[1]

Pon el arroz en remojo[2] con la leche una hora y media. Luego cocina a fuego lento[3] una hora más o menos. Añade[4] el azúcar y la vainilla y cocina unos cinco minutos más.

Pon el arroz en el refrigerador y esparce[5] un poco de canela encima.

Multiplica los kilos, gramos o litros por su medida[6] correspondiente en el sistema que usas.

1 kilo (kg) = 2.2 libras *(pounds)*
1 gramo (g) = 0.035 onzas *(ounces)*
1 litro (l) = 1.057 cuartos *(quarts)*

Calcula las onzas o los cuartos que hay en 300 gramos de arroz, tres litros de leche y 400 gramos de azúcar.

- ¿Cuántas libras hay en dos kilos de pollo?

[1]cinnamon [2]soak [3]cook slowly [4]Add [5]sprinkle [6]measurement

El español en el mundo del trabajo

How can you combine an interest in nutrition and health with skills in Spanish? Here's one example. The U.S. Department of Agriculture provides the public with a wide range of nutritional information through print materials and Web sites. Much of this information is available in Spanish. There is a need for federal employees who are knowledgeable to translate and work with the Spanish-speaking community on issues related to nutrition.

- What other jobs can you think of that would combine communication skills with a knowledge of nutrition?

USDA Building in Washington, D.C.

Actividad 26 — **Escribir/Hablar**

Conversación en el restaurante

1. Write a list of five food items and three drinks that you might order in a restaurant.

2. Exchange lists with your partner. Take turns playing the waiter and the customer. Use your lists as a menu and ask what the various items are like. The server will answer using words from the list.

bueno (para la salud)	sabroso
malo (para la salud)	delicioso
rico	horrible
riquísimo	¡Qué asco!

Modelo

A —*¿Cómo está el pollo?*
B —*El pollo está riquísimo y es bueno para la salud.*

3. Now that the items have been served, ask and answer about how they taste.

Modelo

A —*¿Cómo está el pollo?*
B —*¡Qué asco! Está horrible.*

Nota

To describe what a food item is like in general, use *ser*. To describe how a food item tastes at a particular time, use *estar*.

Fondo cultural

El menú del día In many Spanish-speaking countries, restaurants and cafés often offer *un menú del día* or, as they are called in some parts of Mexico, *una comida corrida.* These menus usually offer one to three choices for each course at a reasonable fixed price.

- Do any restaurants that you know offer something similar to *el menú del día?* What would be the advantages and disadvantages of ordering from *un menú del día?*

Escribir

El menú del día

Use the *menú del día* from the Restaurante Hidalgo to write five questions that a waiter or waitress might ask and five questions that a customer might ask. Don't forget to use the formal *Ud.* in your questions.

Modelo

el (la) camarero(a)	el (la) cliente
¿Qué desea pedir de plato principal?	¿Cómo está el bistec?

Restaurante Hidalgo

Menú del día

$20,00

Sopas y Ensaladas
Ensalada de tomate y cebolla
Sopa de verduras
Sopa Hidalgo

Verduras
Papas fritas
Papas al horno
Guisantes con jamón

Platos principales
Bistec
Pescado
Arroz con pollo

Postres
Pastel de chocolate
Helado de mango o papaya
Frutas frescas

Hablar

En el restaurante

Get together with a partner and use the questions that you wrote in Actividad 27 to play the roles of a server and customer at the Restaurante Hidalgo. Don't forget to use the formal *Ud.* in your conversation.

Modelo

A —*¿Qué desea pedir de plato principal?*
B —*No sé. ¿Cómo está el bistec?*
A —*Está muy sabroso.*
B —*¡Genial! Quisiera el bistec, por favor.*

También se dice . . .

el menú = la carta *(México, España)*

Escribir/Hablar

Y tú, ¿qué dices?

1. ¿Cuál es tu restaurante favorito?
2. ¿Dónde está el restaurante?
3. ¿Cómo son los camareros allí?
4. ¿Cuál es el plato principal que te gusta comer allí? ¿Cómo es?
5. ¿Te gusta pedir postre cuando comes allí? ¿Cómo es?

Más práctica

- Practice Workbook, pp. 15–16: 5B-6, 5B-7
- WAV Wbk.: Writing, p. 20
- Guided Practice: Grammar Acts., pp. 177–178
- *Real.* para hispanohablantes, pp. 198–201

For: *Ser* vs. *estar*
Web Code: jbd-0514

¡Adelante!

Objectives

- **Read a letter about a visit to Santa Fe, New Mexico**
- **Learn about *la sobremesa***
- **Write a review of a restaurant**
- **Watch *¿Eres tú, María?*, Episodio 2**

Lectura

Una visita a Santa Fe

Lee esta carta que escriben Alicia y Pedro. Ellos hablan de una visita que hacen sus primos a Santa Fe. ¿Qué cosas interesantes van a hacer? ¿Qué van a visitar?

Strategy

Skimming
Before you read this letter, make a list of three pieces of information you might expect to find. Quickly skim the letter. What information did you find that was on your list?

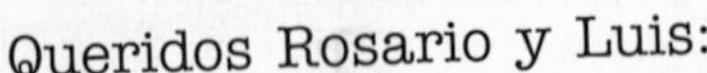

Queridos Rosario y Luis:

¡Esperamos[1] su visita en agosto! Aquí en Santa Fe vamos a hacer muchas cosas. ¿Saben que es una ciudad[2] con más de 400 años de historia y cultura? Vamos a visitar museos, tiendas y vamos a comer comida típica. ¡Los cinco días van a pasar rápidamente![3]

Tenemos planes para pasar una noche muy especial en honor de su visita. Vamos a comer en un "restaurante" histórico que se llama Rancho de las Golondrinas.[4] Está a diez millas de nuestra casa, al sur de Santa Fe. El Rancho, en realidad, no es un restaurante; es una casa española.

Durante los días de su visita, el Rancho va a celebrar "un fandango," un baile histórico y típico, con una cena tradicional. Toda la comida es riquísima, pero nuestro plato favorito es el chile con carne y queso. Después de comer, vamos a bailar. ¡No sabemos bailar pero va a ser muy divertido! Mandamos[5] el menú con la carta.

¡Nos vemos en agosto!

Sus primos de Nuevo México,

Alicia y Pedro

Un paraje[6] en El Camino Real[7] desde la Ciudad de México hasta Santa Fe, es del año 1710. Ahora es un museo.

[1]We're looking forward to [2]city [3]quickly [4]Swallows
[5]We're sending [6]a stopping place [7]the Royal Highway

Menú del Fandango

Sopas
Sopa de arroz
Garbanzos con chile

Plato principal
Pollo relleno[8]
Chile con carne y queso

Postre
Bizcochitos[9]
Pudín del arroz con leche

Bebidas
Chocolate mexicano
Ponche
Café

[8]Stuffed chicken [9]Cookies

La Capilla de San Miguel, la iglesia más vieja de Santa Fe, del año 1610

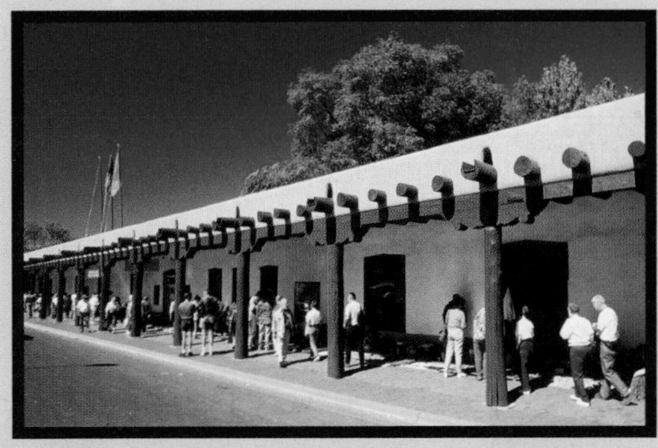

El Palacio de los Gobernadores, construído en 1610, es el edificio *(building)* público más viejo de los Estados Unidos que todavía se usa. Ahora es un museo de historia.

¿Comprendes?

1. ¿Cuáles son cuatro actividades que van a hacer durante la visita? ¿Cuál te gustaría hacer en Santa Fe?
2. ¿Por qué es importante Santa Fe?
3. ¿Por qué quieren ir Alicia y Pedro al Rancho de las Golondrinas?
4. Si no te gusta nada la comida picante *(spicy)*, ¿qué debes pedir del menú?
5. ¿Por qué es importante La Capilla de San Miguel?

¡A pensar! Santa Fe was established thirteen years before the Plymouth Colony was settled by the *Mayflower* Pilgrims. It has been a seat of government for Spain, Mexico, the Confederacy, and the United States.

- Find out when the oldest building in your community was built. How does it differ in age from the *Palacio de los Gobernadores* in Santa Fe?

Más práctica

- WAV Wbk.: Writing, p. 21
- Guided Practice: *Lectura*, p. 179
- *Real.* para hispanohablantes, pp. 202–203

For: Internet Activity
Web Code: jbd-0515

Perspectivas del mundo hispano

A la hora de comer

Una familia en Escazú, Costa Rica

Imagine that you had two hours for lunch every day. Or imagine that every time you ate a meal, you sat down at a table with a friend or family member and had a lengthy conversation. Now imagine that you didn't jump up from dinner as soon as you finished eating. What do these situations have in common?

In many Spanish-speaking cultures, even ordinary mealtimes are considered social events, a time to spend enjoying food and company. People often take time after a meal to relax, to sit around the table and enjoy a good conversation or just to have a laugh. This custom, called the *sobremesa,* is more important in many cultures than getting to the next appointment or saving time and money by buying a quick meal.

A los jóvenes de muchos países hispanos les gusta pasar el tiempo de la sobremesa con amigos o con la familia.

Not surprisingly, most Spanish-speaking countries have very few drive-through restaurants. Since people rarely take food "to go," they might be surprised if you suggested grabbing a sandwich to eat in the car. In fact, many cars don't have cup holders.

Check it out! Figure out how much time you and your family spend at breakfast, lunch, and dinner on days when you're not in school or at work. Compare your results with those of your classmates. Then complete the following statements about practices among families in your community.

Modelo

En mi comunidad, es común *(common)* comer el desayuno en quince minutos.

1. En mi comunidad, es común comer el desayuno en ___ minutos.
2. En mi comunidad, es común comer el almuerzo en ___ minutos.
3. En mi comunidad, es común comer la cena en ___ minutos.

Think about it! What does your research say about the importance of relaxing and enjoying a leisurely meal with friends and family? How does it compare with what happens during meals in Spanish-speaking countries? Consider the two different attitudes towards mealtime. What benefits might each one have?

Presentación escrita

Un restaurante muy bueno

Task

Your school is developing a community guide for Spanish-speaking residents. Your class is in charge of writing about restaurants. Write a review of your favorite restaurant.

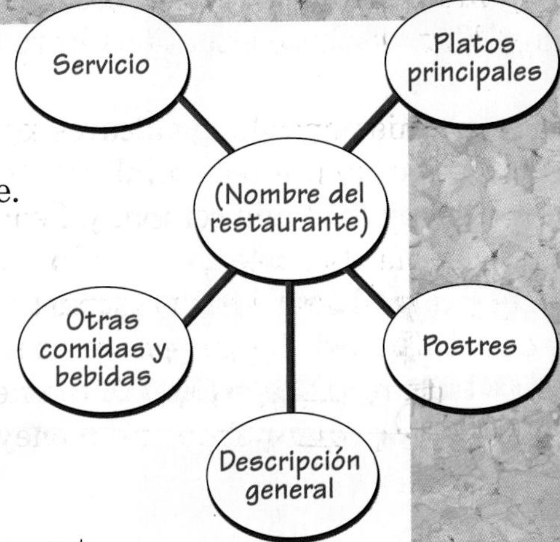

1. **Prewrite** Think about the restaurant you and your family like best. Copy the word web. Write the name of the restaurant you are reviewing in the middle circle. Write words and expressions associated with each category inside the appropriate circles.

2. **Draft** Write your review of the restaurant using information from the word web. Try to include any information that might persuade others to try the restaurant.

3. **Revise** Read through your review and check for agreement, verb forms, and spelling. Share your review with a partner. Your partner should check the following:
   - Did you provide information about all categories?
   - Did you use the correct forms of the verbs?
   - Do you have any errors in spelling or agreement?
   - Is the review persuasive?

Strategy

Persuasion
Give specific information and concrete examples to persuade your readers to try a restaurant.

4. **Publish** Write a final copy of your review and make any necessary changes or additions. You may want to add illustrations and include your review in a booklet with your classmates' reviews or in your portfolio.

5. **Evaluation** Your teacher may give you a rubric for grading the review. You may be evaluated on:
   - how complete the task was
   - how you used new and previously learned vocabulary
   - how accurate the agreement, verb forms, and spelling are
   - correct use of verbs

Videomisterio

¿Eres tú, María?

Episodio 2

Antes de ver el video

Personajes importantes

Resumen del episodio

En este episodio, la ambulancia llega[1] y lleva[2] a doña Gracia Requena al hospital. También llegan dos inspectores de policía. Le hablan a doña Lupe, la portera, sobre el incidente en el piso de doña Gracia. Lola se presenta[3] a los dos hombres y les dice[4] lo que sabe del incidente.

[1] arrives [2] takes away [3] introduces herself [4] tells them

Nota cultural In the cities and towns of Spain and many Spanish-speaking countries, you will find *plazas,* open squares that are surrounded by buildings. The *plazas* are the social center of the community or neighborhood. They may contain benches, trees and flowers, statues, and fountains. In the evening, neighbors will spend time in the *plaza* sharing details about families, daily events, politics, and many other topics.

Palabras para comprender

vive *(vivir)*	she lives *(to live)*
la sobrina	niece
esperar	to wait
anoche	last night
vi *(ver)*	I saw *(to see)*
una barba	beard
¿Quién era?	Who was she?
ayudar	to help
saber	to know

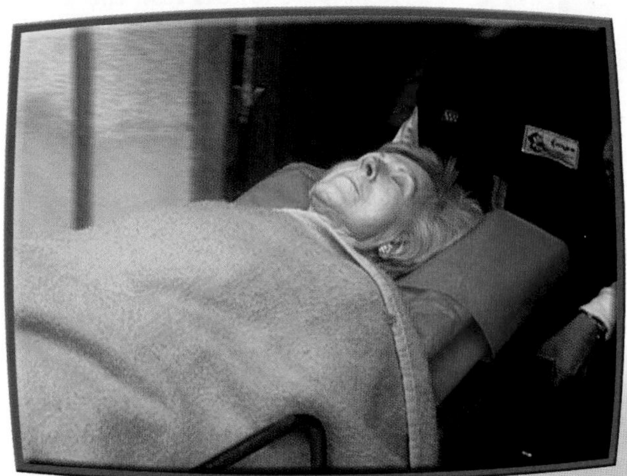

"Es doña Gracia Requena. Vive en el tercer piso con su sobrina, María".

"Anoche a la una de la mañana, vi a un hombre y a una mujer".

—¿Ud. es detective pero no tiene una descripción exacta ni del hombre ni de la mujer?

—A la una de la mañana es imposible ver mucho, ¿no?

Después de ver el video

¿Comprendes?

A. ¿Quién . . . ?

1. ¿Quién es la víctima?
2. ¿Quiénes viven en el tercer piso?
3. ¿Quién es la sobrina?
4. ¿Quién es doña Lupe?
5. ¿Quiénes llegan para investigar el crimen?
6. ¿Quién espera en la plaza?
7. ¿Quién dice que es imposible ver mucho a la una de la mañana?
8. ¿Quién quiere ayudar a los inspectores?

B. Escoge una de las fotos de esta página y escribe tres frases para describir la foto.

Go Online PHSchool.com **For:** More on *¿Eres tú, María?* **Web Code:** jbd-0507

Chapter Review

Repaso del capítulo

To prepare for the test, check to see if you...

- know the new vocabulary and grammar
- can perform the tasks on p. 91

Vocabulario y gramática

jbd-0599 

to talk about people

el hombre	man
la mujer	woman
el joven	young man
la joven	young woman

to describe people and things

alto, -a	tall
bajo, -a	short *(stature)*
corto, -a	short *(length)*
guapo, -a	good-looking
joven	young
largo, -a	long
viejo, -a	old
el pelo	hair
canoso	gray
castaño	brown (chestnut)
negro	black
rubio	blond
pelirrojo, -a	red-haired

to describe how someone is feeling

tener calor	to be warm
tener frío	to be cold
tener sueño	to be sleepy

to talk about food

delicioso, -a	delicious
desear	to want
pedir *(e → i)*	to order
el plato principal	main dish
de plato principal	as a main dish
el postre	dessert
de postre	for dessert
rico, -a	rich, tasty

For *Vocabulario adicional,* see pp. 336–337.

to describe table settings

el azúcar	sugar
la cuchara	spoon
el cuchillo	knife
la pimienta	pepper
el plato	plate, dish
la sal	salt
la servilleta	napkin
la taza	cup
el tenedor	fork
el vaso	glass

to talk about eating out

el camarero, la camarera	waiter, waitress
la cuenta	bill
el menú	menu

to express needs

Me falta(n)...	I need...
Quisiera	I would like
traer	to bring
Le traigo...	I will bring you...
¿Me trae...?	Will you bring me...?
yo traigo	I bring

other useful words and expressions

ahora	now
¿Algo más?	Anything else?
De nada	You're welcome
otro, -a	other, another
¡Qué + *adjective!*	How...!

venir *to come*

vengo	venimos
vienes	venís
viene	vienen

Más práctica

- Practice Workbook: Puzzle, p. 17
- Practice Workbook: Organizer, p. 18

For: Test Preparation
Web Code: jbd-0516

Preparación para el examen

On the exam you will be asked to . . .	Here are practice tasks similar to those you will find on the exam . . .	If you need review . . .
jbd-0599  **1 Escuchar** Listen and understand as people complain to room service that something is missing from their order	As you listen to complaints about room service, see if you can tell if there is a) missing silverware; b) missing food; c) missing condiments; d) all of the above.	**pp. 64–69** *A primera vista* **p. 65** Actividad 2 **p. 73** Actividad 11 **p. 74** Actividad 13 **p. 82** Actividad 26 **p. 83** Actividad 27
 **2 Hablar** Describe physical characteristics of family members to another person	Your aunt and uncle are going to celebrate their anniversary with you in a restaurant, but they're late. You describe them to the waiter so that he can recognize them when they arrive. Mention at least two physical characteristics about each person, such as hair color, height, or age.	**pp. 64–69** *A primera vista* **p. 70** Actividad 6 **p. 71** Actividad 7 **p. 76** Actividad 17
3 Leer Read and understand a letter about an upcoming visit with a relative	As you read part of a letter about an upcoming trip to Santa Fe, can you determine what the writers are most looking forward to in the trip? What questions do they have about it? Queridos Alicia y Pedro: Nosotros también esperamos impacientemente nuestra visita a Santa Fe en el verano. Me encanta la idea de visitar una ciudad con mucha historia. Nuestra ciudad también es muy histórica. ¿Qué es una comida típica del Rancho de las Golondrinas?	**p. 75** Actividad 14 **pp. 84–85** *Lectura*
 **4 Escribir** Write a short report telling whether people are coming to an event and what they are bringing with them	You and your classmates decide to bring either a main dish, dessert, eating utensils, glassware, plates, or condiments for the Spanish Club party. Write a note to the club president indicating who is coming and what they are bringing. For example: *Ryan viene y trae las servilletas.*	**p. 76** Actividad 16 **p. 77** Actividades 19–20 **p. 87** *Presentación escrita*
 **5 Pensar** Demonstrate an understanding of cultural perspectives regarding meals	Think about how you spend lunch or dinner time during the school week. What would be at least three things that would be different at mealtime if you were an exchange student in a Spanish-speaking country? What is a *sobremesa?*	**p. 72** *Fondo cultural* **p. 82** *Fondo cultural* **p. 86** *Perspectivas del mundo hispano*

Fondo cultural

Salvador Dalí (1904–1989) was a painter born in Figueras, Spain. This is one of his most famous paintings, made when he was only 20. Here he has painted his sister, who appears only from the back.

- Why do you think that Dalí painted her looking out the window rather than facing the viewer?

"Muchacha en la ventana" (1924), Salvador Dalí

Calle Caminito, en Buenos Aires, Argentina

En mi dormitorio

Chapter Objectives

- Talk about your bedroom
- Describe bedroom items and electronic equipment
- Make comparisons
- Understand cultural perspectives on homes

Video Highlights

A primera vista: ***El cuarto de Ignacio***

GramActiva Videos: making comparisons; the superlative; stem-changing verbs: *poder* and *dormir*

Videomisterio: *¿Eres tú, María?*, Episodio 3

Country Connection

As you learn how to describe your bedroom, you will make connections to these countries and places:

Más práctica

- *Real.* para hispanohablantes, pp. 210–211

For: Online Atlas
Web Code: jbe-0002

A primera vista

Vocabulario y gramática en contexto

jbd-0687

Objectives

Read, listen to, and understand information about
- bedroom items
- electronic equipment
- colors

“Tengo **un dormitorio pequeño.** Las paredes son azules. Tengo carteles de mis grupos musicales favoritos en las paredes. Generalmente, mi dormitorio está muy desordenado, pero hoy está ordenado. No comparto el dormitorio con otra persona—es mi **propio** dormitorio.

En mi dormitorio tengo todas mis **posesiones más importantes:** mi guitarra, mis discos compactos, mis fotos, mi computadora. ¿Por qué me gusta mucho mi dormitorio? ¡Está encima del garaje! ¡Es **el mejor** dormitorio para tocar y escuchar música!”.

los colores

amarillo, -a

anaranjado, -a

azul

blanco, -a

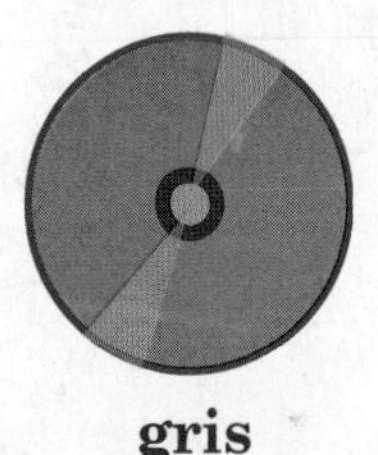
gris

marrón

—¿Te gusta el disco compacto de Mano Negra?

—¡Por supuesto! Me encanta su música. Pero es **menos** interesante **que** la música de Mecano.

—A mis padres les encanta escuchar música. Me gustaría tener mi propio equipo de sonido.

**El televisor* refers to the actual appliance. *La televisión (tele)* is the programming that is watched.

negro, -a

verde

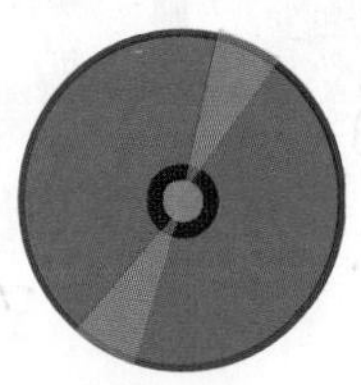
rojo, -a

morado, -a

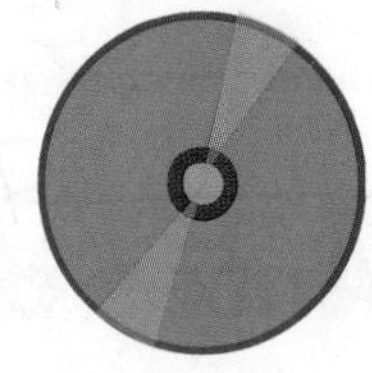
rosado, -a

jbd-0687

Escuchar

Las posesiones

Listen as Marcos describes his bedroom. Look at the picture and touch each item as he mentions it.

jbd-0687

Escuchar

Los colores

As you hear a color named, point to an item on these pages that is that color.

Más práctica

- Practice Workbook, pp. 19–20; 6A-1, 6A-2
- WAV Wbk.: Writing, p. 29
- Guided Practice: Vocab. Flash Cards, pp. 181–186
- *Real.* para hispanohablantes, p. 212

Go Online
PHSchool.com
For: Vocab. Practice
Web Code: jbd-0601

Videohistoria

jbd-0687

El cuarto de Ignacio

También se dice . . .

el dormitorio = el cuarto *(España)*

¡El cuarto de Ignacio está muy desordenado!

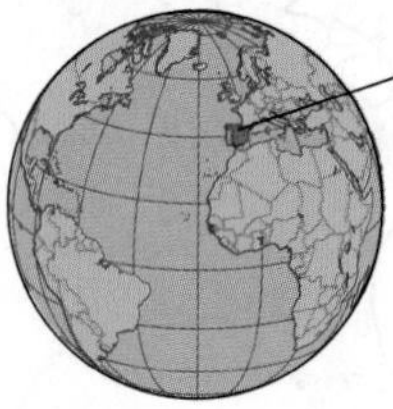

Antes de leer

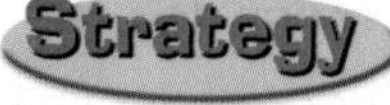

Using prior experience Have you ever had someone go in and change things around in your room? How did you feel?

- Look at the photos and guess how Ignacio feels about his mother moving things around in his room.

1. Scan the reading for words that are familiar to you. What things has Mamá moved around, based on the words you have picked out?
2. Look at photo 8 and make a prediction about how Ignacio and his mother feel at the end of the story.

1 **Mamá:** Mira este cuarto . . . ¡qué **feo!** ¡Está muy desordenado! Ignacio, ¿cómo puedes hacer esto?

2 **Mamá:** **¿De qué color** es esta camiseta? ¿Gris? ¿Blanca? Y esta camiseta de muchos colores, ¿qué es? ¡Ay, tengo que trabajar mucho en este cuarto!

3 **Mamá:** ¿Qué **podemos** hacer con este cuarto? El cuadro va en la pared y la lámpara va en la mesita. ¡Ay, ay, ay!

4 **Ignacio:** ¡Mamá! ¡Mi cuarto! ¡Mis **cosas!** ¿Dónde están?

5 **Mamá:** Tu cuarto está mucho más **bonito.** Los libros **grandes** están aquí, y **a la izquierda** están las revistas. Y los discos compactos están **a la derecha de** los libros. Es mejor, ¿no crees?

6 **Ignacio:** Mamá, no es el **mismo** cuarto. **Para ti,** está **mejor que** antes, pero **para mí,** está **peor.** Tengo todas mis posesiones más importantes aquí y ahora no sé dónde están.

7 **Mamá:** Pero Ignacio, ¿cómo puedes **dormir** con todas las cosas encima de la cama?

Ignacio: Mamá, siempre **duermo** bien.

Mamá: ¡Ay! Está bien. Nunca más voy a organizar tu cuarto.

8 **Ignacio:** ¡Eres la mejor mamá! Muchas gracias.

Mamá: De nada, Ignacio.

Leer/Escribir

Según mamá

Escribe los números del 1 al 5 en una hoja de papel. Escribe frases para describir dónde debe estar cada uno de estos objetos, según Mamá.

1. 
2. 3. 

4. 
5. 

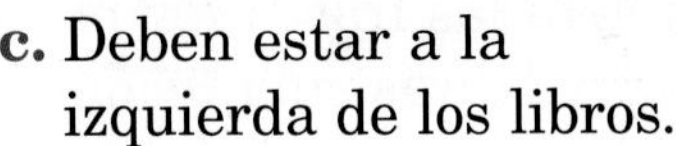

a. Debe estar en la pared.
b. Deben estar a la derecha de los libros.
c. Deben estar a la izquierda de los libros.
d. Debe estar en la mesa.
e. Deben estar al lado de las revistas.

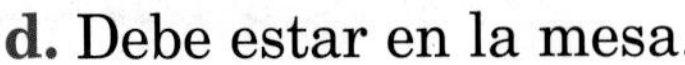

Leer

¿Mamá o Ignacio?

Read the following sentences and decide if Mamá or Ignacio would say each one. Write the name of the person on your paper.

1. Creo que el cuarto es muy feo cuando está desordenado.
2. Tengo una camiseta blanca y otra camiseta de muchos colores.
3. Voy a organizar el cuarto.
4. No estoy contento cuando veo el cuarto ordenado.
5. Para mí, el cuarto es peor cuando está desordenado.
6. Ahora que el cuarto está más ordenado, no sé dónde están mis cosas.
7. Nunca más voy a organizar el cuarto de mi hijo.
8. Puedo dormir con todas las cosas encima de la cama.

Nota

Use reading strategies such as looking for cognates and understanding words from context when you read direction lines in Spanish. Here are some typical words you will see:

completa *complete*
contesta *answer*
dibuja *draw*
escoge *choose*
escribe *write*
escucha *listen*
lee *read*
habla *speak*
mira *look*
pregunta *ask*
trabaja *work*
una frase *a sentence*
una hoja de papel *a piece of paper*
una palabra *a word*
una respuesta *an answer*

Más práctica

- Practice Workbook, pp. 21–22: 6A-3, 6A-4
- WAV Wbk.: Video, pp. 22–24
- Guided Practice: Vocab. Check, pp. 187–190
- *Real.* para hispanohablantes, p. 213

Manos a la obra

Vocabulario y gramática en uso

Objectives

- Name items found in a bedroom
- Talk about electronic equipment
- Use colors to describe things
- Use comparatives and superlatives
- Learn to use the verbs *poder* and *dormir*

Escribir

Palabras opuestas

Completa las frases con el opuesto *(opposite)* de las palabras subrayadas *(underlined)*.

1. El cuadro no es bonito, es feo.
2. Mi dormitorio no está ordenado, está ___.
3. La mesita no está a la derecha de la cama, está a la ___.
4. Mi despertador no es negro, es ___.
5. Mi dormitorio no es grande, es ___.
6. Para mí, estudiar es peor que ver la tele, no es ___.

Making word associations
Learning vocabulary as opposites helps you make quick associations to other words.

jbd-0688

 **Escuchar/Dibujar/Escribir**

Escucha, dibuja y escribe

Copy this drawing on a sheet of paper. You will hear Celia describing her room. As she mentions objects, draw them in the correct places in the room. Then label each object in Spanish.

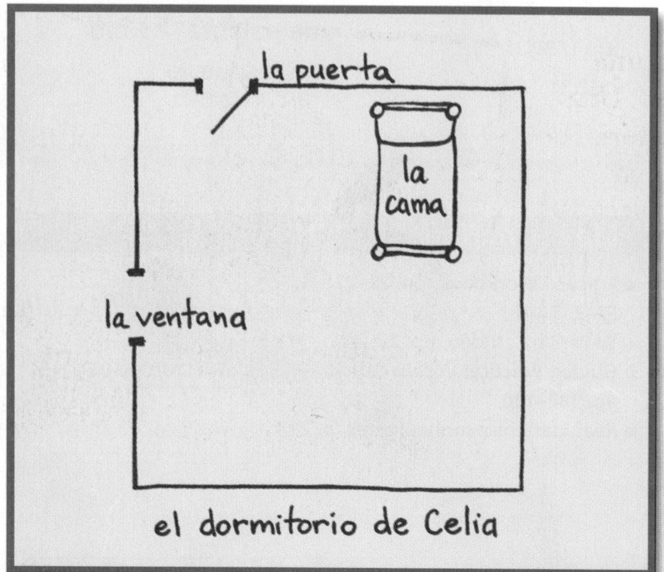

También se dice . . .

el dormitorio = la habitación, la alcoba (España); la pieza (Argentina, Chile); la recámara (México)

bonito = lindo (México); mono (España)

marrón = de color café, castaño, de color chocolate (México, América del Sur)

la cómoda = el gavetero, el buró (México, otros países)

el armario = el guardarropa, el ropero (México, otros países)

pequeño = chico (México, otros países)

Dibujar/Escribir

Mi dormitorio

1. Dibuja tu propio dormitorio o tu dormitorio ideal. Escribe los nombres de ocho cosas en el dibujo.

2. Escribe siete frases para describir o *(either)* tu dormitorio o el dormitorio de Celia de la Actividad 6.

Modelo

El espejo está al lado de la cama.
Las cortinas en el dormitorio son largas.

¿Recuerdas?

Use *estar* to tell the location of items.

Use *ser* to tell what items are like.

Hablar

¿Qué dormitorio es?

Trabaja con otro(a) estudiante. Muestra *(Show)* los dibujos de tu dormitorio y del dormitorio de Celia a tu compañero(a). Lee una de las frases que escribiste *(that you wrote)* en la Actividad 7. Tu compañero(a) tiene que identificar qué dormitorio describes.

Modelo

A —*El espejo está al lado de la cama.*
B —*Es tu propio dormitorio.*
o: —*Es el dormitorio de Celia.*

Strategy

Labeling
Put Spanish labels on the items in your bedroom so that you will see them every day. This will help you learn new words quickly.

Escuchar/Hablar

Juego

Trabajen con un grupo de tres personas. Necesitan una moneda *(coin)* y uno de los dibujos de la Actividad 7. Una persona describe dónde está la moneda en el dormitorio. Los otros dos tratan de colocar *(try to place)* la moneda en el cuarto correctamente. La primera persona que coloca la moneda correctamente recibe un punto.

Modelo

La moneda está debajo de la cama.

  **Leer/Pensar/Hablar**

¿Quién soy yo?

Aquí tienes una adivinanza *(riddle)* popular en las escuelas primarias en México. Trabaja con otro(a) estudiante para resolver la adivinanza.

> **Cine no soy,**
> **Radio tampoco.**
> **Tengo pantalla**
> **Y me creen poco.**
>
> **¿Quién soy yo?**

    **Hablar/Escribir**

Tus propias cosas

1 Habla con otro(a) estudiante sobre las cosas que tienes en tu dormitorio. Pregunta y contesta según el modelo. Escribe las respuestas en una hoja de papel.

Modelo

A —*¿Tienes tu propia videocasetera?*
B —*Sí, tengo mi propia videocasetera. ¿Y tú?*
A —*No, pero puedo usar la videocasetera de mi familia.*

Estudiante A

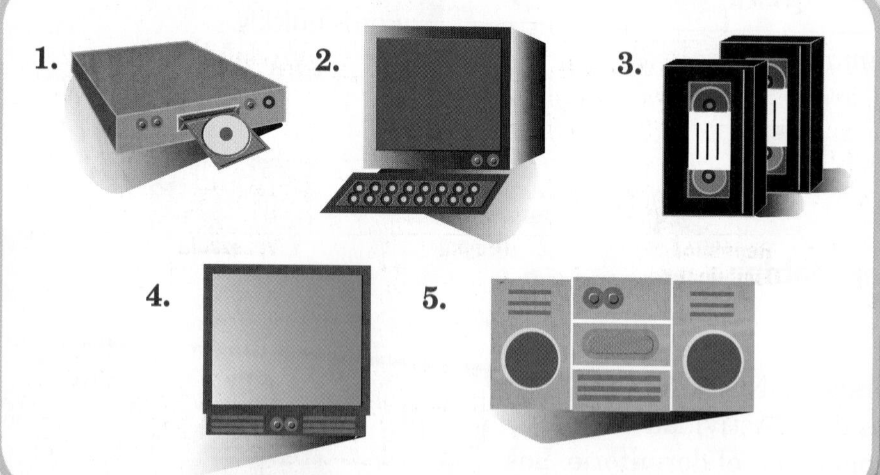

Estudiante B

Sí, tengo mi propio(a) . . .
No, pero comparto . . . con . . .
No, pero puedo usar . . . de mi familia.
No, no tengo . . .
(No) me gustaría . . .

¡Respuesta personal!

2 Trabajen con otra pareja. Sumen *(Add together)* los resultados del paso *(step)* 1. Escriban frases para presentar los resultados a la clase. Compartan los resultados del grupo de ustedes con los otros grupos y sumen los resultados de toda la clase.

Modelo

Once estudiantes tienen computadoras en sus casas.

Actividad 12

Hablar

Las banderas

Working with a partner, describe the colors of the following flags from different Spanish-speaking countries. Your partner will name all countries whose flag it could be.

Mi familia es de Puerto Rico.

Modelo

A —*La bandera tiene los colores rojo, amarillo y verde.*

B —*¿Es la bandera de Bolivia?*

A —*Sí.*

Argentina

Bolivia

Chile

Colombia

Costa Rica

Cuba

Ecuador

El Salvador

España

Guatemala

Guinea Ecuatorial

Honduras

Nicaragua

Panamá

Paraguay

Perú

Puerto Rico

República Dominicana

Uruguay

Venezuela

Fondo cultural

La bandera mexicana has a fascinating history. According to tradition, the Aztecs were to build their capital city, Tenochtitlán, where they found an eagle perched on a cactus and devouring a serpent. This image is what you see on the Mexican flag today.

- What flags can you identify in the United States that also contain a symbol with historical significance?

La bandera de México

Hablar

¿De qué color es . . . ?

Trabaja con otro(a) estudiante y habla de tu dormitorio. Describe el color de cada palabra en la lista.

Modelo

A —*¿De qué color es la alfombra en tu dormitorio?*
B —*La alfombra es amarilla.*
o: *No tengo alfombra en mi dormitorio.*

cama	equipo de sonido
paredes	cortinas
lámparas	alfombra
cómoda	

¡Respuesta personal!

¿Recuerdas?

Remember, when colors describe an object, they are adjectives. Adjectives agree with the noun they describe in both number and gender. If a color ends in a consonant, add *-es* regardless of gender.

- Las cortin**as** son roj**as**.
- Las cortin**as** son azul**es**.

Pensar/Escribir

¿De qué color es tu día?

¿Cuáles son los colores que asocias con estas palabras? Escribe los colores.

Modelo

regular *gris*

1. contento
2. triste
3. calor
4. frío
5. artístico
6. sociable
7. horrible
8. gracioso
9. reservado
10. aburrido

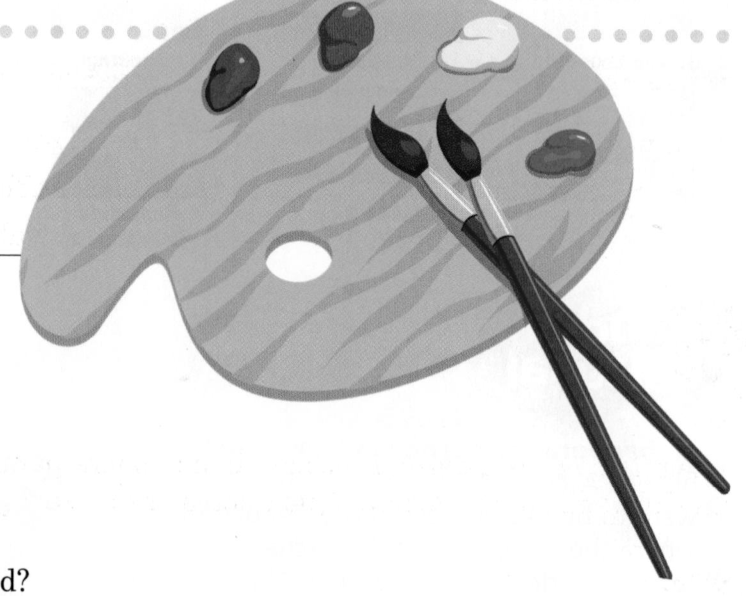

Y para ti, ¿cuál es el color de tu personalidad?

  **Leer/Pensar/Escribir**

¿Qué significan los colores?

En la psicología, hay un estudio de los significados *(meanings)* de diferentes colores en diferentes culturas. Lee las descripciones aquí para contestar las preguntas.

Conexiones
Las ciencias sociales

En muchas culturas, el verde significa buena salud, la primavera, las plantas y tranquilidad. Es un color de la paz[1].

El blanco, en las culturas de las Américas, significa generalmente inocencia y paz. En ciertas culturas asiáticas, el blanco significa la muerte[2].

El color que expresa energía, pasión y acción en muchas culturas diferentes es el rojo.

En muchas culturas, el amarillo significa atención, precaución, el sol y energía. Es muy fácil ver el amarillo y se usa mucho para los taxis.

Un color que expresa protección, autoridad, confianza[3] y armonía es el azul. Vemos este color mucho en los uniformes de la policía y los militares.

[1]peace [2]death [3]confidence

Find words or expressions in the reading to explain the following uses of color:

- yellow traffic light
- green recycling symbol
- blue police uniform
- red roses for Valentine's day

 **Escribir/Hablar**

Una bandera para ti

Imagina que vas a diseñar *(design)* una bandera para una organización, un club o un equipo *(team)*. ¿Qué colores vas a usar? ¿Por qué?

 **Escribir/Hablar**

Y tú, ¿qué dices?

1. ¿Cuáles son tus colores favoritos? ¿Qué posesiones tienes en tu dormitorio de estos colores?
2. Escribe una lista de cinco cosas que están en tu dormitorio y el color de cada cosa. Por ejemplo: *Tengo una lámpara anaranjada.*

Gramática

Making comparisons

Just as you can use *más . . . que* to compare two things, you can also use **menos . . . que** *(less . . . than).*

El disco compacto de Los Toros es **menos** popular **que** el disco compacto de Los Lobos.

*The CD by Los Toros is **less** popular **than** the CD by Los Lobos.*

The adjectives *bueno(a), malo(a), viejo(a),* and *joven* and the adverbs *bien* and *mal* have their own comparative forms. *Más* and *menos* are not used with these comparative adjectives and adverbs.

Adjective	Adverb	Comparative	
bueno, -a	bien	mejor (que)	*better than*
malo, -a	mal	peor (que)	*worse than*
viejo, -a		mayor (que)	*older than*
joven		menor (que)	*younger than*

Mejor, peor, mayor, and *menor* have plural forms that end in *-es.*

Los discos compactos son **mejores que** los casetes.

¿Recuerdas?

You have learned to use *más . . . que* to compare two things.

- La clase de inglés es **más** interesante **que** la clase de matemáticas.

GramActiva VIDEO

Want more help with comparisons? Watch the **GramActiva** video.

Escribir/Hablar

Las personas en mis fotos

Your friend wants to know about the people in the photos that you have in your room. On a separate sheet of paper, write sentences about people you know by completing the sentences with the names of friends or family members.

1. ___ es más alto(a) que ___.
2. ___ es menos deportista que ___.
3. ___ es mayor que ___.
4. ___ es menor que ___.
5. ___ es más deportista que ___.
6. ___ es menos serio(a) que ___.
7. ___ es más artístico(a) que ___.
8. ___ es menos atrevido(a) que ___.

jbd-0688

Escuchar/Escribir

Dos dormitorios

En una hoja de papel, escribe los números del 1 al 6. Escucha las seis comparaciones de los dormitorios de Paco y Kiko. Escribe *C* (cierto) o *F* (falso).

El dormitorio de Paco

El dormitorio de Kiko

Leer/Escribir

Quiero decorar mi propio dormitorio

Lee el correo electrónico de Alicia sobre su idea del dormitorio perfecto. En una hoja de papel, escribe los números del 1 al 6. ¿Cuál es tu opinión? Indica para cada frase si estás de acuerdo con ella o no. Si no estás de acuerdo, ¿por qué no?

¡Hola!

¿Quieres un dormitorio bonito? Tengo mi propio dormitorio y es perfecto. ¡Es fácil de hacer! Necesitas pensar en:

1. **las paredes:** Las paredes moradas son menos feas que las paredes blancas.
2. **las cortinas:** Las cortinas anaranjadas son mejores que las cortinas azules.
3. **la alfombra:** Una alfombra roja es menos seria que una alfombra gris.
4. **la comóda:** Una cómoda bonita es más importante que un estante bonito.
5. **los carteles:** Los carteles de actores son más interesantes que los carteles de deportes.
6. **el televisor:** Un televisor con videocasetera es más popular que un televisor con lector DVD. Tengo buenas ideas, ¿no estás de acuerdo?

Hasta luego,
Alicia

Modelo

el equipo de sonido: Los equipos de sonido grandes son mejores que los equipos de sonido pequeños.

Sí, estoy de acuerdo. Para mí, los equipos de sonido grandes son mejores que los equipos de sonido pequeños.

o: *—No estoy de acuerdo. Para mí, los equipos de sonido pequeños son mejores que los equipos de sonido grandes.*

o: *—No estoy de acuerdo. Para mí, los equipos de sonido grandes son peores que los equipos de sonido pequeños.*

   Escribir/Hablar

¡Viva la música!

1. Escribe cinco frases con comparaciones de los varios tipos de música que ves aquí. Usa estos *(these)* adjetivos en la forma correcta con *más . . . que* o *menos . . . que.*

aburrido, -a	interesante
bonito, -a	serio, -a
divertido, -a	triste
feo, -a	popular
importante	

Para decir más . . .

el blues	el jazz
la música clásica	la música rap
la música folklórica	la salsa
la música hip-hop	la música reggae
la música rock	

Modelo

Para mí, la salsa es más divertida que la música rap.

2. Lee tus comparaciones a otro(a) estudiante para ver si Uds. están de acuerdo.

Modelo

A —*Para mí, la salsa es más divertida que la música rap.*
B —*Sí, estoy de acuerdo, pero la salsa es menos popular que la música rap.*

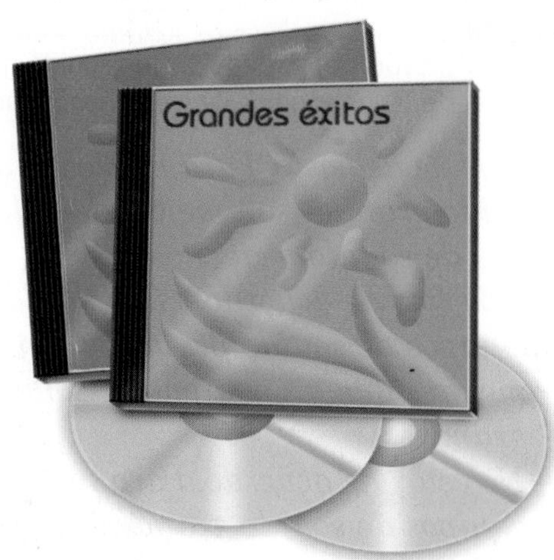

Fondo cultural

El Grammy latino Since 2000, the Latin Grammy awards have recognized the talent of many Spanish and Portuguese-speaking artists every year. In 2005, Juanes won three Grammys for best rock song, music video, and rock solo artist.

- Who are some Latin recording artists you enjoy and what is their music like?

El cantante Juanes, de Colombia

Pronunciación

jbd-0688

The letters *r* and *rr* 

Except at the beginning of a word or after *l* or *n*, the sound of the letter *r* is similar to the *dd* in the English word *ladder*. Listen to and say these words:

derecha	quiero	amarillo	bandera
pero	puerta	alfombra	morado

The sound of the letter *rr* is similar to saying "batter, batter, batter" over and over again very quickly. Listen to and say these words:

perro	correr	guitarra	marrón
aburrido	arroz	pelirrojo	horrible

When *r* is the first letter of a word or comes after *l* or *n*, it is pronounced like the *rr*.

Roberto	Rita	Ricardo	rojo	regalo
rubio	radio	reloj	romper	Enrique

Try it out! Listen to and say this *trabalenguas:*

Erre con erre cigarro,
erre con erre barril.
Rápido corren los carros
cargados de azúcar del ferrocarril.

Actividad 22 **Escribir/Hablar**

¿Cómo se comparan los dos?

With a partner, choose two people or things for each category below. On your own sheet of paper compare the two. Your partner will do the same. Then take turns reading your comparisons and giving your opinions.

1. actividades
2. deportes
3. clases
4. comidas
5. libros o revistas
6. personas famosas

Modelo

A —*Para mí, ir al cine es mejor que ver un video.*
B —*Estoy de acuerdo. Ir al cine es mejor que ver un video.*
o: —*No estoy de acuerdo. Ver un video es más divertido que ir al cine.*

Actividad 23 **Escribir/Hablar**

Y tú, ¿qué dices?

1. ¿Cómo es tu dormitorio? ¿Está más o menos ordenado que los dormitorios de tus amigos?
2. Describe a tu mejor amigo(a). ¿Es más serio(a) que tú? ¿Quién es más deportista?
3. ¿Cómo son tus clases? ¿Son menos aburridas que las clases de tus amigos? Explica.
4. ¿Cómo es la comida en la escuela? ¿Es mejor que la comida en un restaurante?
5. Compara tus dos grupos musicales favoritos.

Más práctica

- Practice Workbook, p. 23: 6A-5
- WAV Wbk.: Writing, p. 30
- Guided Practice: Grammar Acts., p. 191
- *Real.* para hispanohablantes, pp. 214–217

For: Comparisons
Web Code: jbd-0603

Gramática

The superlative

To say that someone or something is the "most" or "least," use:

definite article **(el, la, los, las)** + noun + **más / menos** + adjective

La foto de mi familia es **la posesión más importante** para mí.

To say that someone or something is the "best" or the "worst," use:

definite article + **mejor(es) / peor(es)** + noun

Rojo y azul son **los mejores colores** para mi dormitorio.

GramActiva VIDEO

Want more help with the superlative? Watch the **GramActiva** video.

Escribir

Espejo, espejo de la pared . . .

Imagine you have a magic mirror on the wall in your room. How would it complete these sentences? Write the sentences on a separate sheet of paper.

1. La persona más inteligente es ___.
2. El peor actor es ___.
3. Las clases más interesantes son ___.
4. El videojuego menos divertido es ___.
5. Los mejores discos compactos son ___.
6. El color menos bonito es ___.

Hablar

Las casas de los ricos y famosos

Una persona del programa de televisión "Las casas de los ricos y famosos" está en tu casa. Habla con él/ella sobre las cosas especiales en tu casa. Pregunta y contesta según el modelo.

Modelo

cuadro / bonito

A —*Para ti, ¿cuál es el cuadro más bonito?*

B —*Para mí, el cuadro más bonito es el cuadro de las flores rojas y amarillas.*

1. posesión / importante
2. disco compacto / mejor
3. video / interesante
4. foto / bonita
5. videojuego / divertido

Escribir

No me gustan mucho

Do you like some things better than others in your room? Describe the things that you like the least in your room. For each object below use one of the adjectives in the word box.

bonito, -a	feo, -a
interesante	aburrido, -a
importante	mejor
divertido, -a	peor

Modelo

El cartel menos bonito en mi dormitorio es el cartel de los gatos.

o: *El cartel más feo en mi dormitorio es el cartel de los gatos.*

1. los discos compactos
2. los cuadros
3. el libro
4. el video
5. la foto
6. la posesión

Hablar

¡No seas tan negativo(a)!

Using the information from Actividad 26, tell your partner about the worst things in your room. Your partner will try to get you to be more positive by asking you about the best things in your room.

Modelo

A —*El cartel menos bonito en mi dormitorio es el cartel de los gatos.*

B —*¿Cuál es el cartel más bonito en tu dormitorio?*

A —*El cartel más bonito es el cartel de los perros.*

Escribir/Hablar

Y tú, ¿qué dices?

1. ¿Cuál es la película más graciosa? ¿Y cuál es la película más seria?
2. Según tus amigos y tú, ¿cuál es el grupo musical más popular? ¿Y cuál es el grupo musical menos popular?
3. ¿Quién es tu amigo(a) menos reservado(a)? ¿Y quién es tu amigo(a) menos atrevido(a)?
4. ¿Para ti, cuál es el mejor mes del año? ¿Y cuál es el peor mes del año? ¿Por qué?

Más práctica

- Practice Workbook, p. 24: 6A-6
- WAV Wbk.: Writing, p. 31
- Guided Practice: Grammar Acts., p. 192
- *Real.* para hispanohablantes, p. 217

For: Superlatives
Web Code: jbd-0604

Gramática

Stem-changing verbs: *poder* and *dormir*

Like *jugar*, *poder* and *dormir* are stem-changing verbs. They have a change from *o→ue* in all forms except *nosotros* and *vosotros*. Here are the present-tense forms:

(yo)	**puedo**	(nosotros) (nosotras)	**podemos**
(tú)	**puedes**	(vosotros) (vosotras)	**podéis**
Ud. (él) (ella)	**puede**	Uds. (ellos) (ellas)	**pueden**

(yo)	**duermo**	(nosotros) (nosotras)	**dormimos**
(tú)	**duermes**	(vosotros) (vosotras)	**dormís**
Ud. (él) (ella)	**duerme**	Uds. (ellos) (ellas)	**duermen**

¿Recuerdas?

You use *puedo* and *puedes* to say what you can or cannot do.

- ¿**Puedes** ir a la fiesta conmigo? No, no **puedo**.

GramActiva VIDEO

Want more help with these stem-changing verbs? Watch the **GramActiva** video.

Actividad 29 Leer/Escribir/Pensar

Rompecabezas

¿Cuántas horas duermen las personas en esta familia? Escribe la forma apropiada del verbo *dormir* para cada frase. Después contesta la pregunta.

¡Mis hermanos y yo __1.__ 50 horas al día! Es mucho, ¿no? Tomás, mi hermano mayor, __2.__ menos, seis horas al día. Catalina __3.__ más horas que todos—cuatro horas más que Tomás. Guillermo y yo __4.__ el mismo número de horas. Juntos *(Together)* nosotros __5.__ el mismo número de horas que Tomás y Catalina. Paco y Laura __6.__ el mismo número de horas.

¿Cuántas horas duerme cada persona (Tomás, Catalina, Guillermo, Paco, Laura y yo)?

Fondo cultural

La siesta, an afternoon nap after the large midday meal, is a custom that has been observed in Spain and other Spanish-speaking countries for many centuries. However, with modern-day pressures and in larger cities, many people no longer take off work for *la siesta*.

- What do you think would be some advantages and disadvantages of a *siesta* in your daily life?

En España, muchas tiendas se cierran entre las 14:00 y las 16:30 horas.

jbd-0688

Escuchar/Escribir/Hablar

El Campamento Nadadivertido

It's the first day at your summer camp, el Campamento Nadadivertido. Your friend never listens to anything. Listen to the camp rules and answer your friend's questions.

1. ¿Podemos usar el equipo de sonido en la tarde?
2. ¿Quiénes no pueden ir a los dormitorios de los chicos?
3. ¿Podemos ver la televisión o videos en los dormitorios?
4. ¿Cuándo podemos escuchar discos compactos?
5. ¿Podemos beber refrescos en la cama?
6. ¿Podemos dormir hasta *(until)* las nueve?

Nota

When the forms of *poder* are followed by another verb, the second verb is in the infinitive form.

- No **puedo dormir** bien cuando tengo calor.

Escribir/Hablar

Las reglas

You are baby-sitting two children and you don't know the rules of the house. First, write five questions to ask the children. Then, working in groups of three, use the verbs in the box below to ask and answer questions according to the model.

comer	ir
beber	jugar
ver	escuchar

Modelo

A —*¿Uds. pueden comer helado después de las siete?*

B —*No, nunca podemos comer helado después de las siete.*

o:—*¡Claro! Siempre podemos comer helado después de las siete.*

Hablar

¡Podemos hacer muchas cosas!

Trabaja con otro(a) estudiante para decir qué pueden hacer diferentes personas con las posesiones que tienen.

Modelo

Marcos / sacar fotos

A —*¿Marcos puede sacar fotos?*

B —*¡Claro que sí! Tiene una cámara muy buena.*

o: —*No. No tiene una cámara.*

Estudiante A

1. Uds. / ver películas en casa
2. Raquel / hacer la tarea de álgebra
3. tu papá (o tu mamá) / usar el Internet
4. tú / escuchar discos compactos
5. Guillo y Patricio / jugar videojuegos

Estudiante B

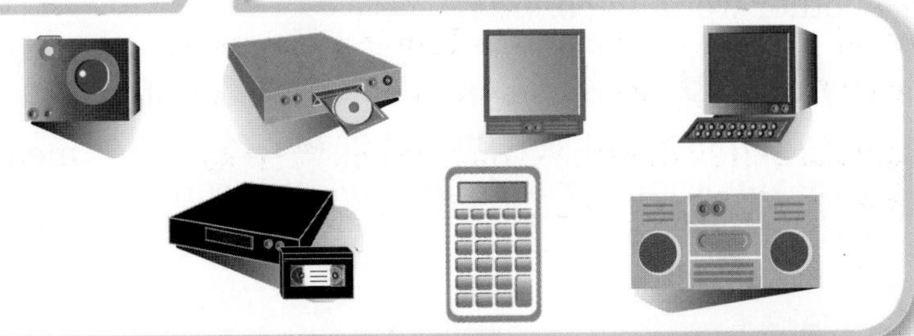

Leer/Escribir/Hablar

¿Duermes bien?

Lee este artículo de una revista y contesta las preguntas.

1. Según el artículo, ¿cuál es el problema?
2. ¿Qué porcentaje de las personas duerme menos de ocho horas diarias durante la semana?
3. ¿El artículo presenta estas ideas? Contesta *sí* o *no*.

   Las personas que duermen poco . . .
   . . . generalmente están más cansadas.
   . . . trabajan mejor.
   . . . juegan mucho y hacen ejercicio.
   . . . son menos sociables.
4. Y tú, durante los fines de semana, ¿cuántas horas duermes en la noche?

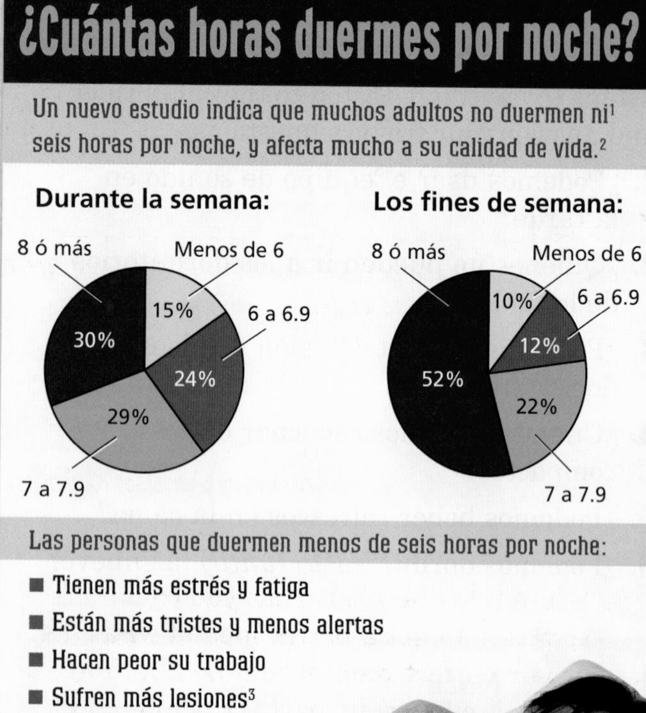

¿Cuántas horas duermes por noche?

Un nuevo estudio indica que muchos adultos no duermen ni[1] seis horas por noche, y afecta mucho a su calidad de vida.[2]

Las personas que duermen menos de seis horas por noche:

- Tienen más estrés y fatiga
- Están más tristes y menos alertas
- Hacen peor su trabajo
- Sufren más lesiones[3]
- Tienen más problemas de relaciones interpersonales
- Comen más de lo usual
- Tienen menos energía

[1]not even [2]quality of life [3]injuries

Exploración del lenguaje

Using root words

You can build your vocabulary, both in Spanish and in English, if you recognize the root of a word and know its meaning.

For example, because you know the root of one word, ***comer***, you can more easily learn another word, *la* ***comida***.

Try it out! Because you know the root of ***beber***, you can easily remember *la* __?__. And since you know *ver la* ***televisión***, you can easily recognize *el* __?__.

Once you learn another language, your mastery of your own language can increase. In part, this is because you begin to use the words from your second language to help you understand words in English that are new to you.

Try it out! Since you know *verde*, *azul*, and *gris*, what do you think these words mean?

verdant fields *azure* sky a *grizzled* old man

Actividad 34 — Escribir/Hablar

Juego

Work with a partner to write a description of three items. Then get together with another group and read your descriptions. The other group will try to guess which items you are describing. The group to guess the items in the least amount of time wins.

Modelo

A —*Es una cosa que toca música. Puede ser grande o pequeño. Está en muchas casas. ¿Qué es?*
B —*Es un equipo de sonido.*

Strategy

Circumlocution
When you don't know or can't remember the word for something, you can describe it. You can tell what it is used for, what size it is, what color it is, where it is often found, and so on.

Actividad 35 — Escribir/Hablar/Dibujar

Y tú, ¿qué preguntas?

1. Write five questions that you could ask someone to get a better idea of what his or her perfect room would be like. You can ask what your partner is like and what his or her favorite activities, colors, and interests are.
2. Ask your questions and write your partner's responses.
3. Draw the perfect room for your partner based on the responses to your questions. Show your drawing to your partner and explain why you think the room is perfect.

Modelo

El dormitorio es especial para ti porque tus colores favoritos son azul y rojo. Hay una foto de Lleyton Hewitt en la cómoda porque te gusta mucho el tenis. Hay muchas fotos en las paredes porque sacas fotos de tus amigos también. Tú eres muy gracioso y desordenado. Hay muchos videos y revistas en la cama. Te gusta escuchar la música hip-hop. Aquí, en el estante, están tus discos compactos.

El español en la comunidad

In many U.S. communities, you can see the influence of Spanish-style architecture. Spanish-style buildings often have tile roofs, stucco exteriors, and interior courtyards or patios.

- Identify houses, buildings, or neighborhoods in your community that feature this style. Draw or take a picture of one example.

Más práctica

- Practice Workbook, p. 25: 6A-7
- Guided Practice: Grammar Acts., pp. 193–194
- *Real.* para hispanohablantes, p. 218

For: *o* → *ue* Verbs
Web Code: jbd-0605

¡Adelante!

Objectives

- Read a letter and response in an advice column
- Learn about *las luminarias*
- Talk about how a person's bedroom reflects his or her personality
- Watch *¿Eres tú, María?*, Episodio 3

Lectura

El desastre en mi dormitorio

Lee esta carta *(letter)* a Querida Magdalena. Ella da soluciones para los problemas de los jóvenes en una revista.

Strategy

Using cognates
As you read the letter and response, look for cognates to help you better understand Rosario's problem. Try to guess the meaning of some of the cognates: *el desorden, la situación, recomendar, considerar.*

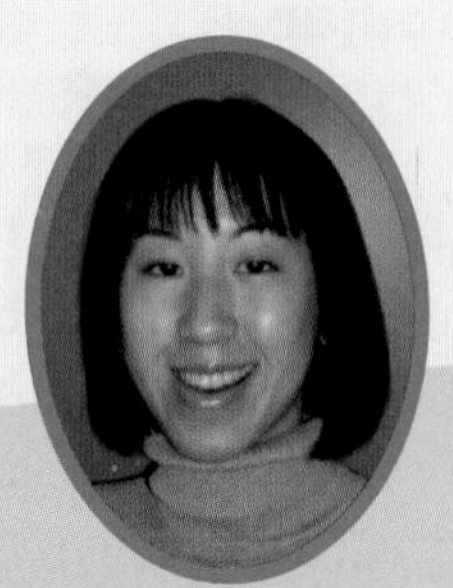

Con tu amiga Magdalena

Querida Magdalena:

Mi problema tiene un nombre; es mi hermana, Marta. Compartimos el mismo dormitorio y estoy desesperada. Todo en mi lado del dormitorio está en orden. Pero su lado es un desastre. Ella es la reina del desorden. Le encanta comer en el dormitorio. Hay pizza debajo de la cama. Hay botellas de agua en la mesita. Hay postre en el escritorio. Es horrible. Siempre deja[1] ropa,[2] videos y todas sus posesiones en el suelo,[3] en la mesita y en la cama. ¡No hay ni un libro en el estante!

Y ella no escucha sus propios discos compactos—¡no! Escucha mis discos compactos y sin pedir[4] permiso. Y escucha música a toda hora (y a un volumen muy alto) y ¡yo no puedo dormir!

Las paredes en su lado del dormitorio son negras. Es el peor color y es feísimo. Mi color favorito es amarillo, claro. Es más bonito que negro, ¿no?

Estoy cansada de compartir el dormitorio con ella y su desorden.
¿Qué debo hacer?

Rosario Molino
Montevideo, Uruguay

[1]leaves [2]clothing [3]floor [4]asking for

Mi problema tiene un nombre; es mi hermana, Marta.

¡Es difícil compartir un dormitorio con otra persona!

Querida Rosario:

¡Qué problema! Es difícil compartir un dormitorio con otra persona, especialmente si la persona es tu hermana. Uds. son muy diferentes, ¿no? Tú eres más ordenada que ella. Ella cree que el color negro es el más bonito.

Necesitas hablar con tu hermana delante de tus padres. Tienes que explicar[5] la situación y recomendar unas soluciones. Es necesario encontrar[6] un punto intermedio.[7] Si la situación no es mejor después de unas semanas, tienes que considerar la posibilidad de separar el dormitorio con una cortina. ¡Pero no debe ser una cortina ni negra ni amarilla!

Tu amiga,
Magdalena

[5]explain [6]to find [7]middle ground

¿Comprendes?

Lee las frases y decide quién dice *(says)* la frase. ¿Es Rosario, Marta o su madre?

1. "Pero me gusta comer en la cama y escuchar música".
2. "Soy una persona muy simpática y el color amarillo representa mi personalidad".
3. "Estoy muy ocupada y no tengo tiempo para 'un dormitorio perfecto".
4. "Uds. tienen que respetar las posesiones de la otra".
5. "Mi color favorito es el negro. No me gustan los colores amarillo, anaranjado o azul".
6. "Ella debe pedir permiso para escuchar mis discos compactos".
7. "Tu hermana no es ordenada como tú. Tienes que ser más paciente".

Y tú, ¿qué dices?

¿Eres desordenado(a) como *(like)* Marta o eres ordenado(a) como Rosario? ¿En qué? Incluye dos ejemplos en tu respuesta.

Los aparatos electrónicos Throughout the Spanish-speaking world you will find the latest electronic devices: DVD players, stereo sound systems, cell phones, computers, etc. No matter the country, there is a demand for movies, music, and instant communication.

- What are some advantages and disadvantages of the new global community brought about by these technological innovations?

Más práctica

- WAV Wbk.: Writing, p. 32
- Guided Practice: *Lectura*, p. 195
- *Real.* para hispanohablantes, pp. 222–223

For: Internet Activity
Web Code: jbd-0606

La cultura en vivo

Las luminarias

En Santa Fe, Nuevo México

To celebrate Christmas in Mexico and the southwest United States, countless bags, tons of sand, and candles are transformed into flickering outdoor lanterns called *luminarias.* They are lined up along window ledges, walkways, and roofs and are lit to welcome visitors.

This tradition dates back more than 300 years, when villagers along the Río Grande built bonfires to light and warm their way to church on Christmas Eve. The *luminarias* used today go back to the 1820s, when traders introduced brown paper into the region and candles were set in sand in the bottom of the paper bags.

Try it out! Here's how you can make your own *luminarias.*

Materials

- 12" paper lunch bags
- sand
- small flashlights
- scissors

Figure 1

Figure 2

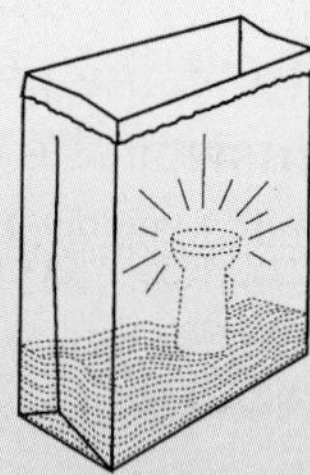

Figure 3

Directions

1 Trace a pattern on the side of the bag, leaving at least 4 inches at the top and 3 inches at the bottom. You may want to use the pattern in Fig. 1 or create your own.

2 Cut out the design, cutting through both sides of the bag. *(Fig. 1)*

3 Open the bag and fold down a 2" cuff around the top. *(Fig. 2)*

4 Fill the bag $\frac{1}{4}$ full of sand.

5 Place a flashlight in the sand. *(Fig. 3)*

6 Place the completed *luminarias* along your walkway, turn on the small flashlights, and enjoy these symbols of hope and joy for any special occasion.

Variations

1 Use white or brightly colored bags.

2 Paste white or pastel tissue paper behind the cut-out design.

3 Cut a scalloped edge along the top of the bag instead of folding down the cuff.

4 Instead of sand, use soil, cat litter, or gravel to hold the flashlight in place.

Think about it! What kind of decorations do you use for special events? How is light used in different cultures to celebrate events?

Presentación oral

La personalidad de un dormitorio

Task

You are doing a study on how a bedroom can reflect the personality of its owner(s). Use a photograph or drawing of a bedroom and talk about what its contents and colors tell about the personality of the owner.

Using graphic organizers
A word web can help you organize your thoughts for a presentation.

1. **Prepare** Bring in a picture of a bedroom. It can be a photo you took, one cut out from a magazine, or a picture that you draw. Use this word web to think through what you want to say about the room and the personality of the person who decorated it. Then answer the questions.
   - En tu opinion, ¿cómo es la persona que vive *(lives)* en el dormitorio? ¿Qué le gusta hacer?

2. **Practice** Go through your presentation several times. You can use your notes in practice, but not when you present. Try to:
   - support your statements with examples
   - use complete sentences
   - speak clearly
3. **Present** Show your picture and give the information about the bedroom and the personality behind it. Don't forget to stand up straight and project your voice!
4. **Evaluation** Your teacher may give you a rubric for how the presentation will be graded. You probably will be graded on:
   - how complete your preparation is
   - how much information you communicate
   - how easy it is to understand you

Videomisterio

¿Eres tú, María? Episodio 3

Antes de ver el video

Personajes importantes

Paco, quien trabaja en la oficina de Lola y la ayuda con las investigaciones

Margarita, la secretaria de la oficina

Nota cultural *El País* is probably Spain's most widely read and influential newspaper. You can consult an electronic version of *El País* on the Internet.

Resumen del episodio

Este episodio es muy importante. Lola le explica a Paco lo que pasó[1] en el incidente del domingo pasado.[2] En otra escena, Lola habla con doña Lupe quien le describe el incidente en el piso de doña Gracia. También doña Lupe le explica a Lola la historia de la familia de doña Gracia. ¿Por qué cree que María va a recibir toda la fortuna de doña Gracia?

[1] what happened [2] last Sunday

Palabras para comprender

dinero	money
periodista	newspaper reporter
¿Qué pasó . . . ?	What happened . . . ?
No ve casi nada.	She can hardly see anything.
abro	I open
muerta	dead
busco	I'm looking for
¿Robaron . . . ?	Did they steal . . . ?
las joyas	jewels
accidente de coche	car accident
Pasó antes de venir a vivir con doña Gracia.	It happened before she came to live with doña Gracia.
Pasó tres meses . . .	She spent three months . . .
el nieto	grandson
No viene aquí nunca.	He never comes here.
No conoce a su abuela.	He doesn't know his grandmother.

La familia Requena

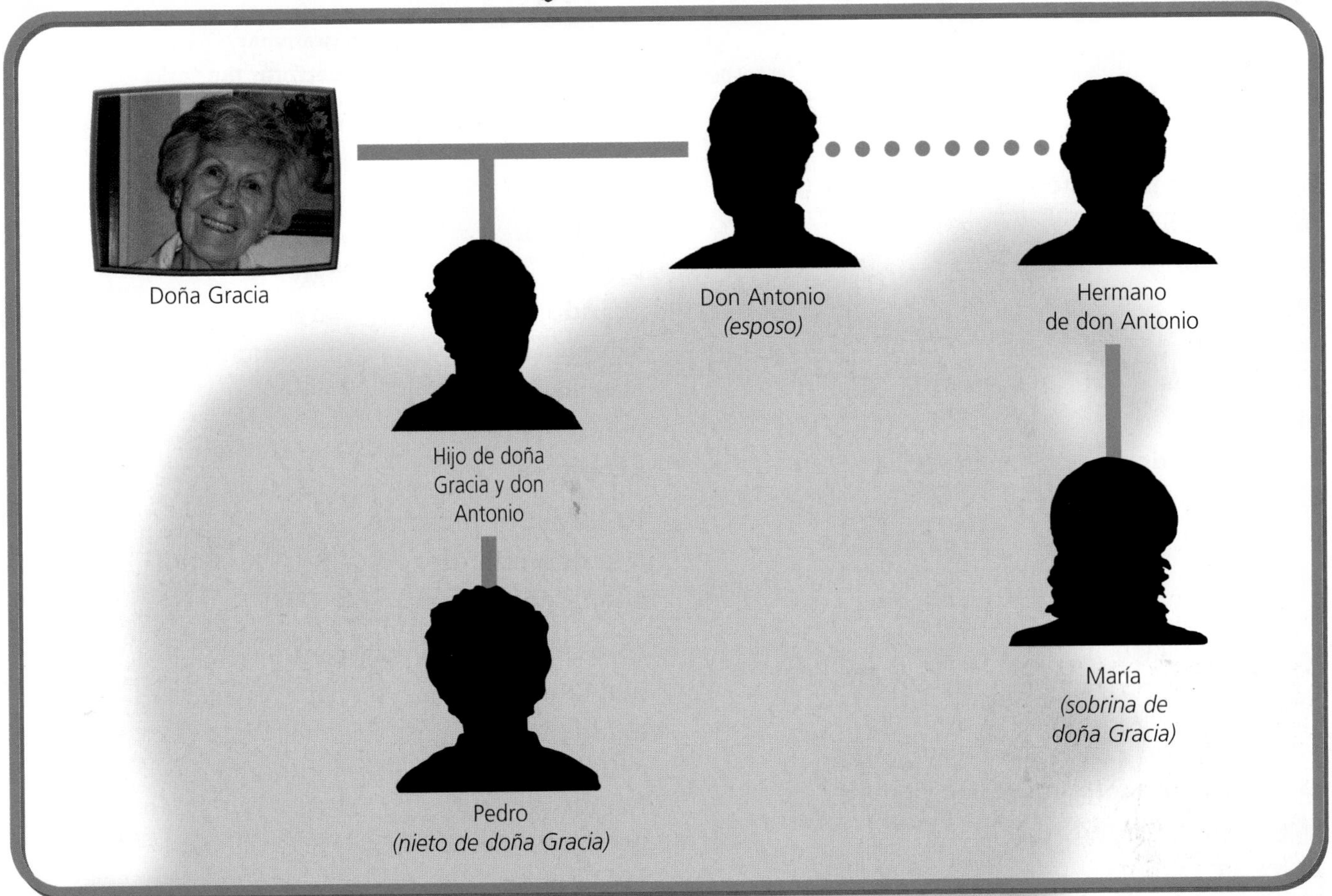

Doña Gracia

Don Antonio
(esposo)

Hermano
de don Antonio

Hijo de doña
Gracia y don
Antonio

María
*(sobrina de
doña Gracia)*

Pedro
(nieto de doña Gracia)

Después de ver el video

¿Comprendes?

Completa cada frase con la palabra apropiada del recuadro.

periodista	**joyas**
hija	**conoce**
fortuna	**dinero**
accidente de coche	**sobrina**

1. Según Paco, si no hay cliente, si no hay ___, entonces no hay nada.
2. Lola dice que trabaja para *El País,* un periódico importante en España, y es ___.
3. María es la ___ de Lorenzo Requena y la ___ de doña Gracia.
4. Doña Gracia es muy rica. Tiene una fortuna en dinero, ___ y arte.
5. Antes de venir a vivir con doña Gracia, a María le pasó un grave ___.
6. Pedro, el nieto de doña Gracia, vive en Italia y su abuela no lo ___.
7. Según doña Lupe, María va a recibir la ___ de doña Gracia.

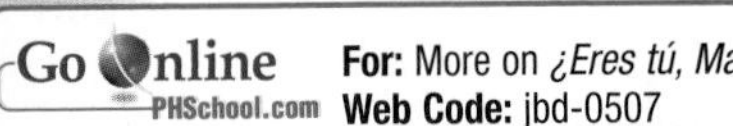

For: More on *¿Eres tú, María?*
Web Code: jbd-0507

Repaso del capítulo

Chapter Review

To prepare for the test, check to see if you . . .

- know the new vocabulary and grammar
- can perform the tasks on p. 123

Vocabulario y gramática

jcd-0689

to talk about things in a bedroom

la alfombra	rug
el armario	closet
la cama	bed
la cómoda	dresser
las cortinas	curtains
el cuadro	painting
el despertador	alarm clock
el dormitorio	bedroom
el espejo	mirror
el estante	shelf, bookshelf
la lámpara	lamp
la mesita	night table
la pared	wall

to talk about electronic equipment

el disco compacto	compact disc
el equipo de sonido	sound (stereo) system
el lector DVD	DVD player
el televisor	television set
el video	videocassette
la videocasetera	VCR

to talk about colors

¿De qué color . . . ?	What color . . . ?
los colores	colors
amarillo, -a	yellow
anaranjado, -a	orange
azul	blue
blanco, -a	white
gris	gray
marrón	brown
morado, -a	purple
negro, -a	black
rojo, -a	red
rosado, -a	pink
verde	green

to describe something

bonito, -a	pretty
feo, -a	ugly
grande	large
importante	important
mismo, -a	same
pequeño, -a	small
propio, -a	own

to indicate location

a la derecha (de)	to the right (of)
a la izquierda (de)	to the left (of)

to compare and contrast

mejor(es) que	better than
el / la mejor; los / las mejores	the best
menos . . . que	less, fewer . . . than
peor(es) que	worse than
el / la peor; los / las peores	the worst

other useful words and expressions

la cosa	thing
para mí	in my opinion, for me
para ti	in your opinion, for you
la posesión	possession

stem-changing verbs: *dormir* and *poder*

duermo	**dormimos**
duermes	**dormís**
duerme	**duermen**

puedo	**podemos**
puedes	**podéis**
puede	**pueden**

For *Vocabulario adicional,* see pp. 336–337.

Más práctica

- Practice Workbook: Puzzle, p. 26
- Practice Workbook: Organizer, p. 27

Go Online PHSchool.com
For: Test Preparation
Web Code: jbd-0607

Preparación para el examen

On the exam you will be asked to . . .	Here are practice tasks similar to those you will find on the exam . . .	If you need review . . .
jbd-0689  **1 Escuchar** Listen to and understand descriptions of bedrooms	You will be spending a month in a Spanish immersion camp. You go to the camp Web site and click on the audio descriptions of the student rooms. Which items are provided? Which items do you have to bring?	**pp. 94–99** *A primera vista* **p. 100** Actividad 6 **p. 101** Actividad 8 **p. 102** Actividad 11
 **2 Hablar** Ask and answer questions about your bedroom and that of a classmate	You are asked to survey several classmates about their bedrooms in order to describe the "typical" teenage room. Ask a partner at least three questions including: a) information about the color of his or her room; b) whether or not there is a TV or sound system in the room; c) whether he or she is able to study well in the room; d) what is on the walls.	**pp. 94–99** *A primera vista* **p. 101** Actividad 8 **p. 102** Actividad 11
 **3 Leer** Read and understand descriptions of bedroom colors that are associated with particular personality types	Decorators say that the colors of a room's walls should match the personality of the person living in it. Based on the descriptions of a "yellow personality" and a "blue personality," what kind of room best suits you? Why or why not? A las personas más sociables les gustan los dormitorios amarillos. Es el color más popular para los jóvenes a quienes les gusta hablar y hablar por teléfono. ¡Ellos son los mejores amigos! Al contrario, a las personas más serias les gustan los dormitorios azules. Ellos son los mejores estudiantes y los peores cómicos.	**p. 104** Actividad 14 **p. 105** Actividad 15 **pp. 116–117** *Lectura*
4 Escribir Write a short paragraph comparing your bedroom to a friend's bedroom	After surveying classmates, you are asked to write a comparison of your room to that of one of the people you surveyed. Use the information from Task 2 to practice. You might compare: a) the colors; b) the sizes; c) the types of furniture in the rooms; d) the number of different things on the walls.	**p. 101** Actividad 7 **p. 107** Actividad 19 **p. 119** *Presentación oral*
 **5 Pensar** Demonstrate an understanding of cultural perspectives regarding a celebration	Explain the historical significance of *las luminarias*. What is the history of other decorations used in the celebrations of different cultures?	**p. 118** *La cultura en vivo*

hello

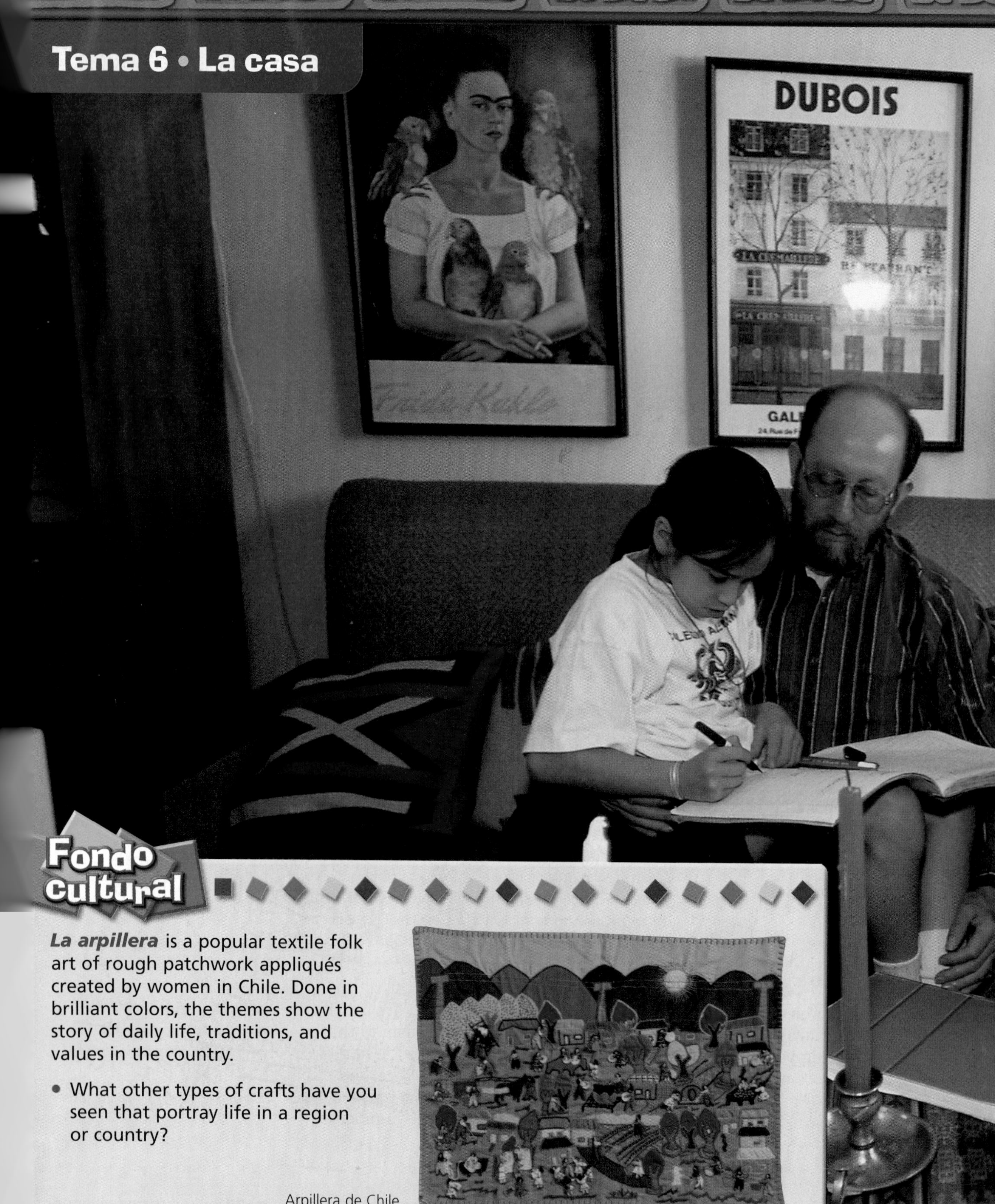

Fondo cultural

La arpillera is a popular textile folk art of rough patchwork appliqués created by women in Chile. Done in brilliant colors, the themes show the story of daily life, traditions, and values in the country.

- What other types of crafts have you seen that portray life in a region or country?

Arpillera de Chile

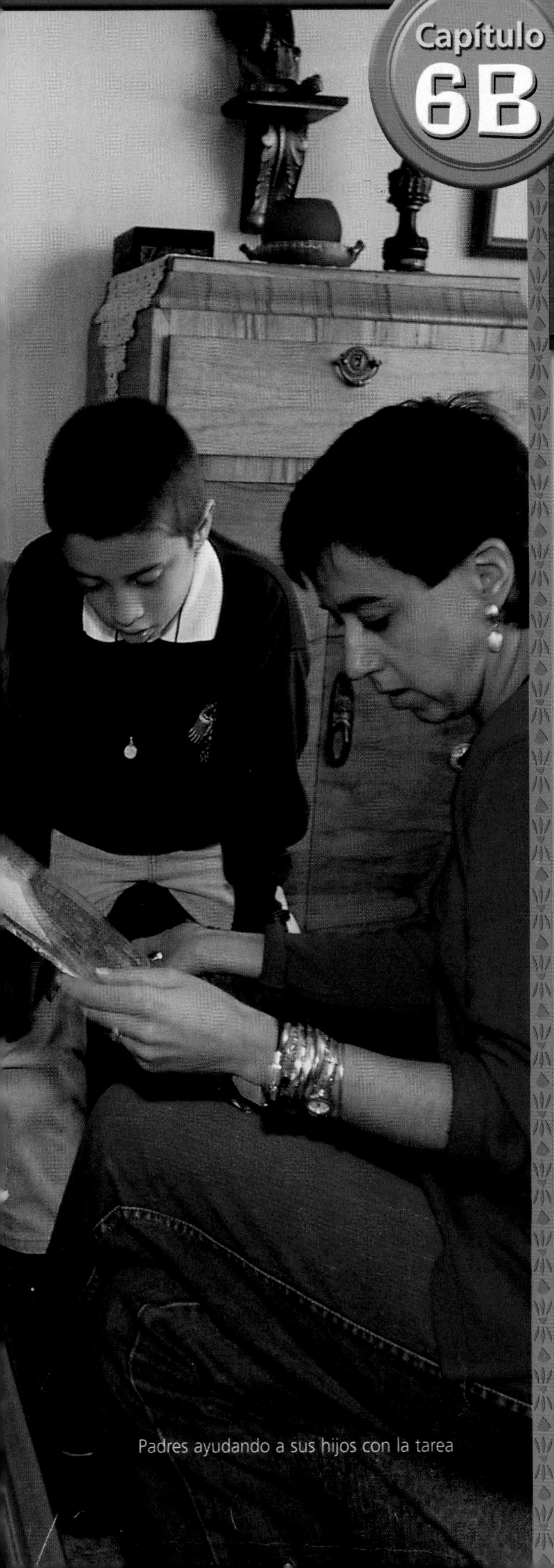

Padres ayudando a sus hijos con la tarea

Capítulo 6B

¿Cómo es tu casa?

Chapter Objectives

- Identify rooms in a house
- Name household chores
- Tell where you live
- Understand cultural perspectives on different types of housing

Video Highlights

A primera vista: ***Los quehaceres de Elena***
GramActiva Videos: **affirmative** ***tú*** **commands; the present progressive tense**
Videomisterio: ***¿Eres tú, María?*****, Episodio 4**

Country Connection

As you learn about rooms in a house and household chores, you will make connections to these countries and places:

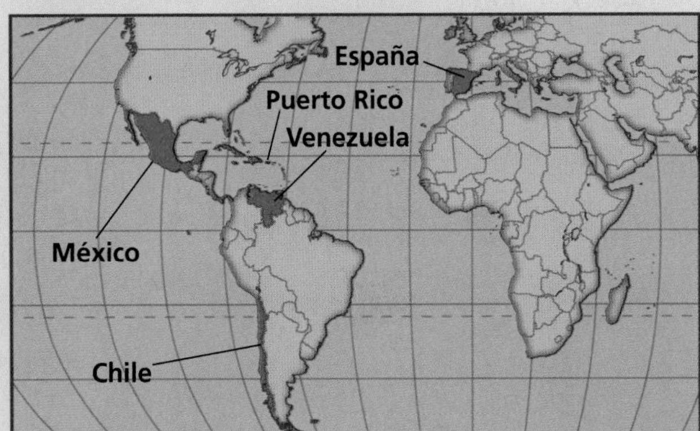

Más práctica

- ***Real.*** **para hispanohablantes, pp. 230–231**

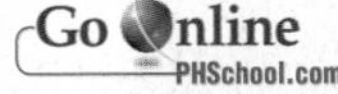

Go Online PHSchool.com — **For:** Online Atlas **Web Code:** jbe-0002

A primera vista

Vocabulario y gramática en contexto

jbd-0697

Objectives

Read, listen to, and understand information about
- **rooms in a house**
- **household chores**
- **how to tell someone to do something**

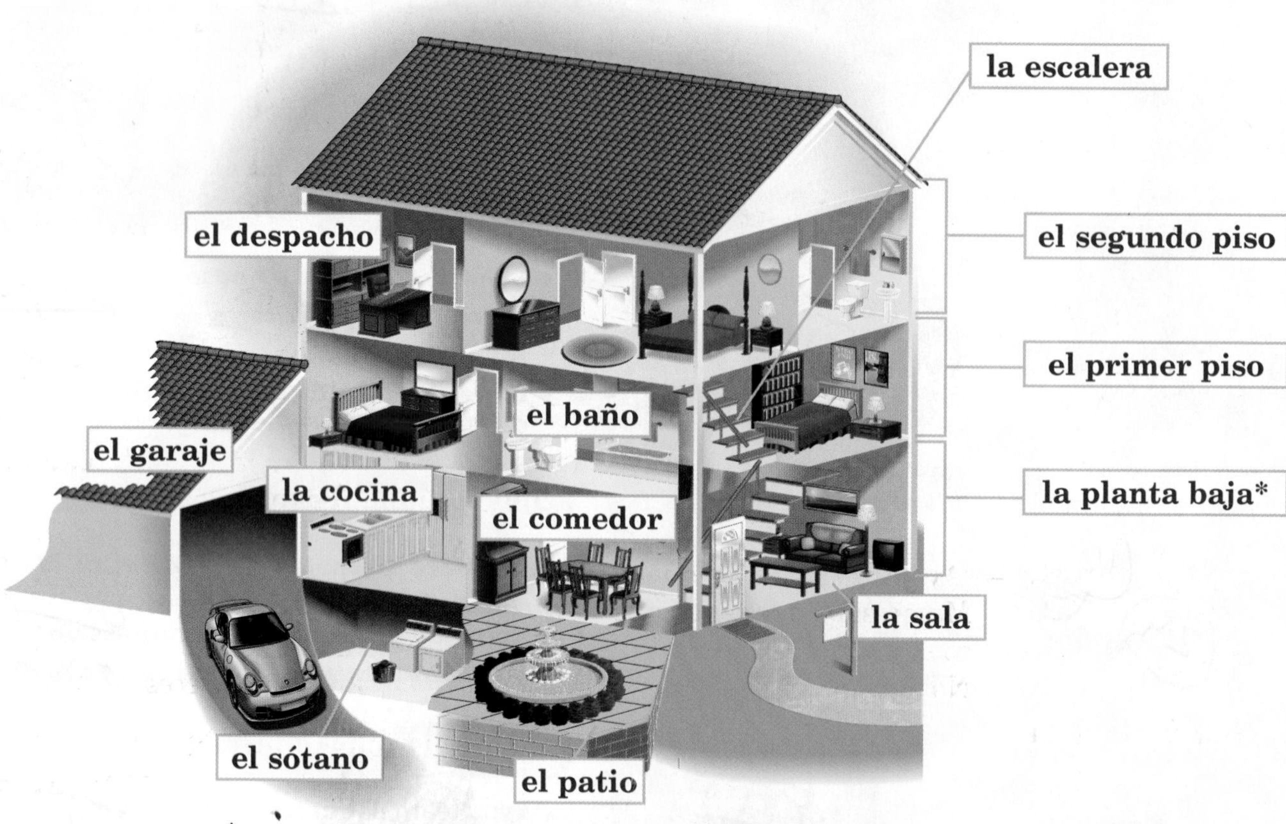

*In most countries, Spanish speakers call the ground floor in a multistory building *la planta baja*, the second floor *el primer piso*, the third floor *el segundo piso*, the fourth floor *el tercer piso*, and so on.

—Me gustaría ver esta casa. Es grande y bonita.
—Sí, tiene tres dormitorios y un despacho. Y también tiene una cocina moderna, **si** te gusta cocinar.

Se vende

Casa particular de tres pisos y sótano. Sala grande, cocina moderna, comedor, despacho, 2 baños, 3 dormitorios, garaje. Llama al 555-37-89.

Más vocabulario

el apartamento apartment
cerca (de) close (to), near
lejos (de) far (from)
bastante enough, rather

lavar los platos sucios

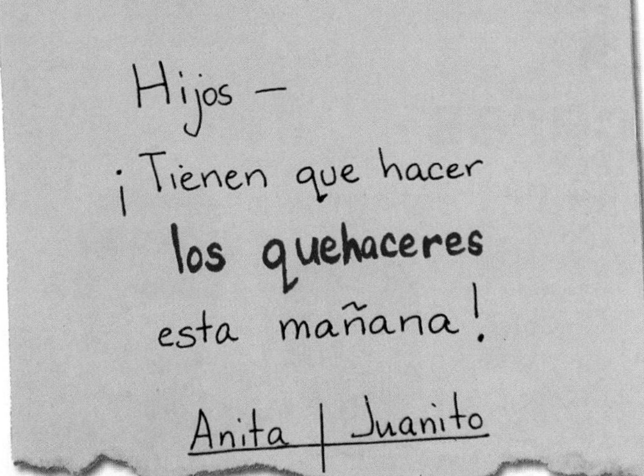

cortar el césped

poner la mesa

lavar el coche

pasar la aspiradora

dar de comer al perro

lavar la ropa

sacar la basura

cocinar

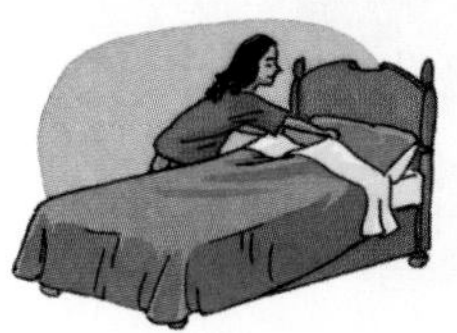

hacer la cama

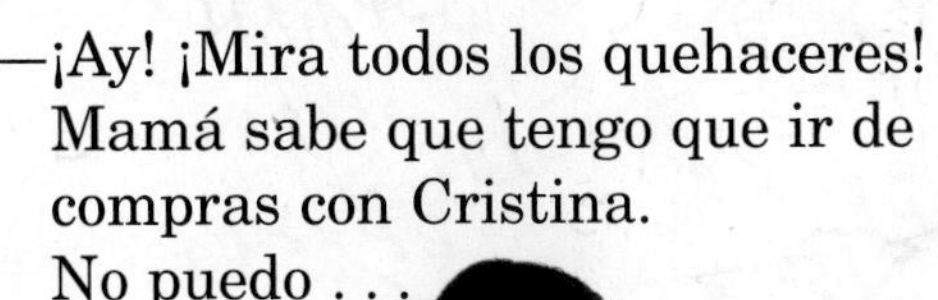

—¡Ay! ¡Mira todos los quehaceres! Mamá sabe que tengo que ir de compras con Cristina. No puedo . . .

—Yo voy a jugar al fútbol a la una. Y tengo más quehaceres que tú.

quitar el polvo

arreglar el cuarto

limpiar el baño

Actividad 1

jbd-0697

Escuchar

La casa de Elena

Escucha a Elena describir su casa. Señala cada cuarto que describe.

Actividad 2

jbd-0697

Escuchar

¿Es lógico o no?

Escucha cada frase. Si es lógica, haz el gesto del pulgar hacia arriba *("thumbs-up" sign)*. Si no es lógica, haz el gesto del pulgar hacia abajo *("thumbs-down" sign)*.

Más práctica

- **Practice Workbook, pp. 28–29: 6B-1, 6B-2**
- **WAV Wbk.: Writing, p. 39**
- **Guided Practice: Vocab. Flash Cards, pp. 197–202**
- ***Real.* para hispanohablantes, p. 232**

For: Vocab. Practice
Web Code: jbd-0611

Videohistoria

jbd-0697

Los quehaceres de Elena

Elena no quiere hacer sus quehaceres. ¿Qué hace ella?

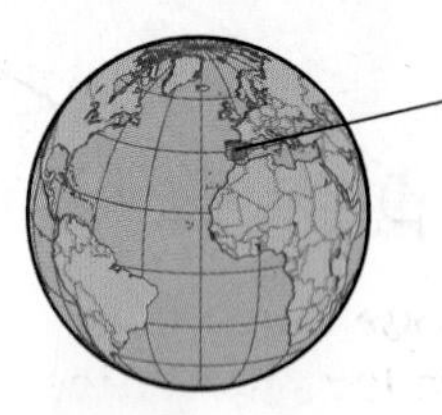

Antes de leer

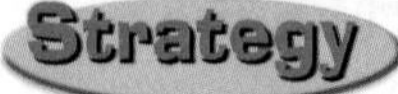
Strategy

Using language knowledge Using what you already know about a language can help you understand better when you read.

- You have just learned the infinitives for various household chores. Can you list the four activities that Elena tells Jorgito to do in photo 5?

Before reading the *Videohistoria*, use the photos to consider the following:

1. What does Elena have to do? How does she feel about this?
2. What do you think Jorgito expects in return for doing Elena's chores?
3. How do their parents react to the condition of the house when they arrive home? Who do they think has done all the work? Why?

1 **Elena:** ¡Hola! Bienvenidos a mi casa. **Vivo** en el número 12 de la calle Apodaca. Vamos a entrar. Mi casa es su casa.

2 **Elena:** ¡Ay, no! Veo que tengo más quehaceres. Siempre lavo los platos sucios y **pongo** la mesa para la cena. ¡Y ahora necesito hacer más trabajo!

3 **Elena:** ¿Me **ayudas** con los quehaceres?

Jorgito: Quiero **dinero.**

Elena: No te **doy** dinero, pero puedes escuchar discos compactos en mi dormitorio.

4 **Jorgito:** A ver. Si hago unos de los quehaceres, me **das** los discos y escucho música por una hora.

Elena: Media hora.

Jorgito: Cuarenta y cinco minutos.

Elena: Está bien.

5 **Jorgito:** **¿Cuáles** son los quehaceres que necesito hacer?

Elena: **Pon** la mesa, lava los platos sucios en la cocina, **haz** la cama en mi dormitorio y da de comer al perro.

6 **Mamá:** Elena, ¡qué trabajadora eres!

Papá: ¡Cómo ayudas en casa! Das de comer al perro, lavas los platos, **pones** la mesa . . .

Elena: Ah, . . . **¿Recibo** mi dinero?

Mamá: **Un momento.** ¿Tu dormitorio está **limpio?**

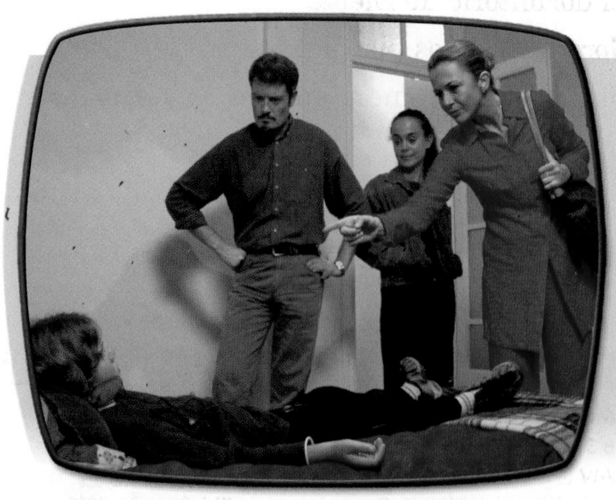

7 **Mamá:** ¡Jorgito! ¡Qué perezoso eres! **¿Qué estás haciendo?**

Jorgito: Pero, . . . pero, . . .

Papá: Ni pero ni nada. ¡Jorgito, a tu dormitorio! Vamos a ver . . .

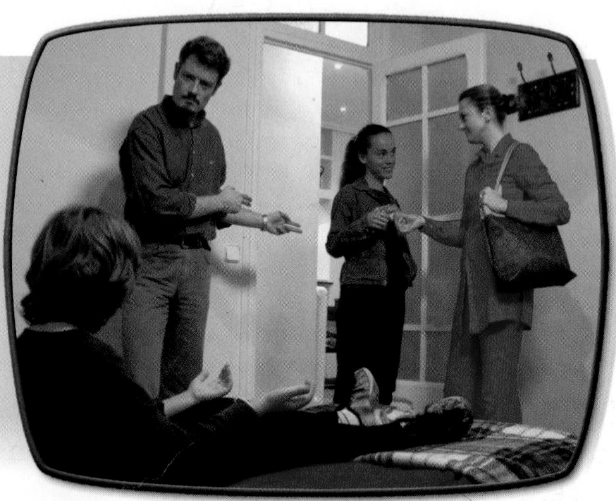

8 **Mamá:** Elena, tu dinero.

Elena: Gracias, mamá.

Papá: Jorgito, ¿cómo puedes vivir así? Tienes que arreglar tu cuarto, hijo: haz la cama, quita el polvo, pasa la aspiradora . . .

Jorgito: Pero, Elena . . .

Elena: ¡Adiós! ¡Voy al cine!

Leer/Escribir

La lista de quehaceres

Lee esta lista de quehaceres y escoge los que necesitan hacer Elena y Jorgito. En una hoja de papel, escribe la lista de todos los quehaceres que tienen que hacer.

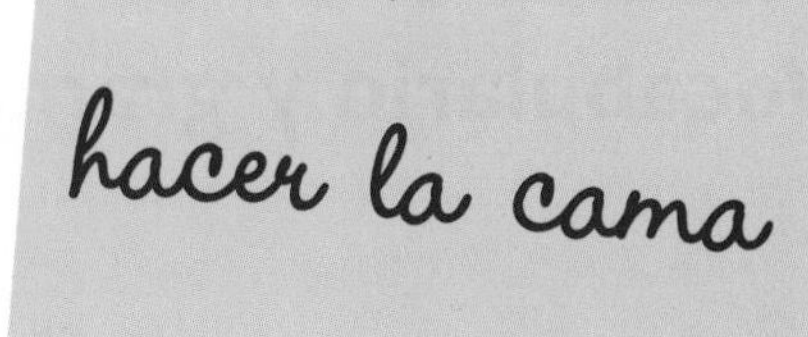

cortar el césped	quitar el polvo
dar de comer al perro	pasar la aspiradora
lavar los platos	poner la mesa
limpiar el baño	sacar la basura

Leer/Escribir

¿Para quién trabaja?

Jorgito hace unos quehaceres para Elena y unos para arreglar su propio dormitorio. Lee estas frases y escribe *C* (cierto) o *F* (falso) según lo que hace en la *Videohistoria*.

1. Jorgito tiene que hacer la cama de Elena y también su propia cama.
2. Elena tiene que quitar el polvo.
3. Jorgito da de comer al perro para Elena.
4. Jorgito tiene que pasar la aspiradora en el dormitorio de Elena.
5. Jorgito lava los platos para Elena.
6. Jorgito pone la mesa en su dormitorio.

Leer/Escribir

¿Comprendes?

Todas estas frases son falsas. Para cada una, escribe una frase nueva con la información correcta según la *Videohistoria*.

1. Elena nunca pone la mesa en su casa.
2. A Jorgito no le gusta escuchar los discos compactos.
3. Si hace uno de los quehaceres, Jorgito puede escuchar una hora de música.
4. Según los padres, Elena es muy perezosa.
5. Según los padres, Jorgito es trabajador.
6. Ahora Jorgito va al cine.

Más práctica

- **Practice Workbook, pp. 30–31: 6B-3, 6B-4**
- **WAV Wbk.: Video, pp. 33–35**
- **Guided Practice: Vocab. Check, pp. 203–206**
- ***Real.* para hispanohablantes, p. 233**

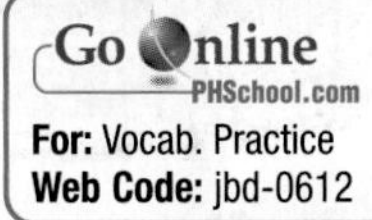

For: Vocab. Practice
Web Code: jbd-0612

Manos a la obra

Vocabulario y gramática en uso

Objectives

- Know the rooms of a house
- Talk about chores around the house
- Learn to use familiar *tú* commands and the present progressive tense

Leer/Escribir

¿Dónde estás?

Lee las frases para decidir en qué cuarto estás. Escribe los números del 1 al 7 en una hoja de papel y completa las frases con la palabra apropiada de la lista.

1. Hay una cama y dos mesitas en ___.
2. El coche siempre está en ___.
3. Hay un sofá y dos sillas en ___.
4. Los tenedores y los cuchillos están en ___.
5. Hay un espejo muy grande en ___.
6. La computadora y el escritorio están en ___.
7. Hay una mesa y cuatro sillas en ___.

el comedor	el garaje
el baño	el dormitorio
la sala	el despacho
la cocina	

Escribir

¿En qué piso viven?

You are in front of the apartment building from where the Ramírez family will be moving. Look at the buzzer panel to identify on what floor their neighbors live. Write your answers on a separate sheet of paper.

Modelo

El Sr. Álvarez
El Sr. Álvarez vive en el segundo piso.

1. Javier y Ana Ríos
2. Luis Méndez
3. Jorge y Carmen Benítez
4. Marta Herrera
5. La Sra. Lopera
6. Paco y Juana Ramos

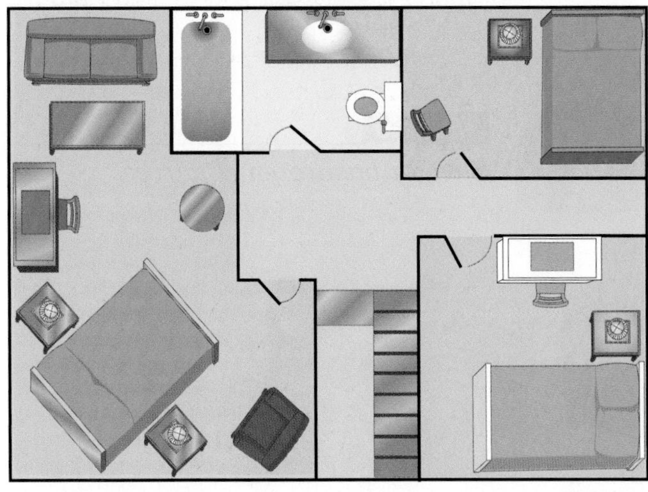

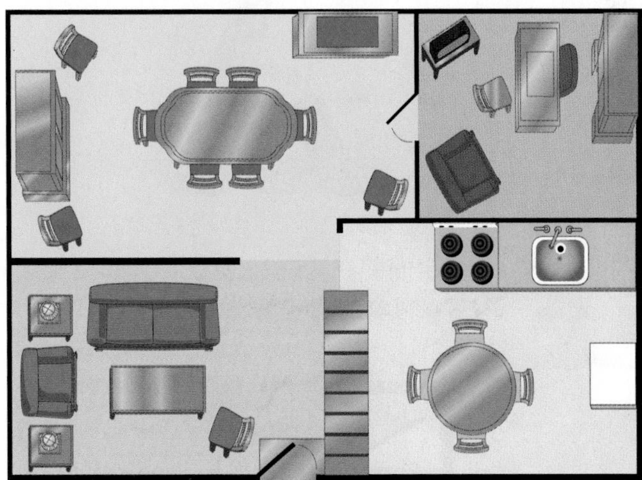

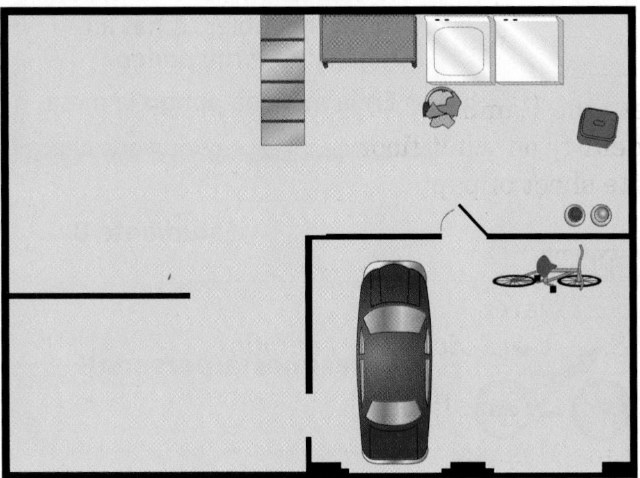

Actividad 8

jbd-0698

Escuchar/Escribir

La casa de los Ramírez

Los Ramírez van a comprar la casa que ves aquí. En una hoja de papel escribe los números del 1 al 8 y escribe el nombre de cada cuarto que describen.

Nota

Primero(a) and *tercero(a)* become *primer* and *tercer* before a masculine singular noun.

- Mi dormitorio está en el **primer** piso.
- Su apartamento está en el **tercer** piso.

Actividad 9

Escribir/Escuchar/Hablar

¿Cierto o falso?

Escribe cinco frases para indicar dónde están los cuartos en la casa de los Ramírez. Las frases pueden ser ciertas o falsas. Lee tus frases a otro(a) estudiante, quien va a indicar si las frases son ciertas o falsas. Si son falsas, tiene que dar la información correcta.

Modelo

A —*La sala está en el primer piso.*
B —*Falso. La sala está en la planta baja.*

También se dice . . .

la sala = el salón *(muchos países);* el living *(España)*

el despacho = la oficina *(muchos países)*

el piso = la planta *(muchos países)*

el apartamento = el piso *(España);* el departamento *(muchos países)*

Escribir

¿En qué cuarto?

Siempre ayudas a tu familia con los quehaceres. Escribe una frase para decir dónde haces estos *(these)* quehaceres.

Modelo

Saco la basura en el garaje.

1. 
2. 
3. 
4. 
5. 
6. 

Hablar

¿Dónde pongo la silla?

Ayudas a tu amigo(a) a mudarse *(move)* a su nueva casa pero no sabes dónde poner sus posesiones. Con otro(a) estudiante, pregunta y contesta según el modelo.

Modelo

A —*¿Dónde pongo la silla?*
B —*Vamos a poner la silla en el comedor.*

Nota

Poner, "to put," is also used in the expression *poner la mesa,* "to set the table." It has an irregular *yo* form: *pongo.*

- En la mañana **pongo** la mesa.

Estudiante A

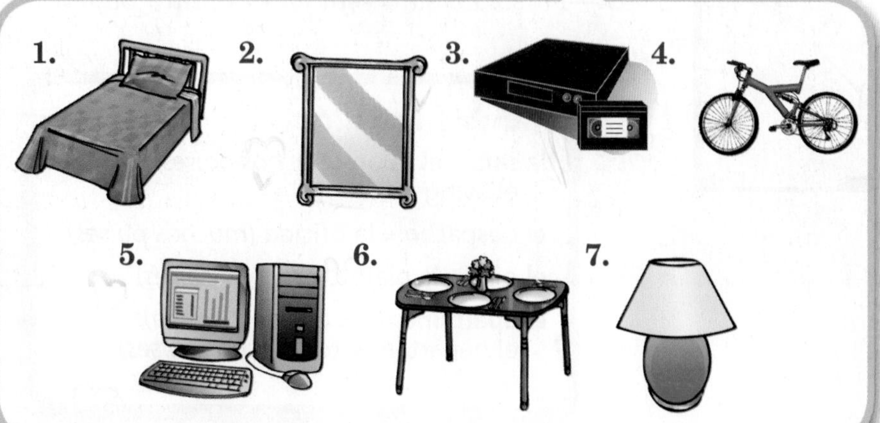

Estudiante B

¡Respuesta personal!

  Escribir

En mi casa hay . . .

Haz una lista de los cuartos en tu casa o apartamento. Al lado de cada cuarto, escribe por lo menos *(at least)* dos cosas que hay en el cuarto.

Los cuartos	Las cosas
mi dormitorio	una cama

  Hablar

¿Qué hay en nuestras casas?

Con otro(a) estudiante, usa tu lista de la Actividad 12 para hablar de los cuartos en su casa o apartamento, y de las cosas que hay en cada uno.

Modelo

A —*¿Hay un comedor en tu casa?*
B —*Sí, hay un comedor.*
A —*¿Qué hay en tu comedor?*
B —*Hay una mesa y unas sillas.*

Fondo cultural

El patio in an apartment building in a large Spanish city is usually just an open area in the center of the building. In southern Spain, however, houses are often built around *patios*, which may have gardens as well as a fountain. The Moors brought this architectural style to Spain, and the Spaniards then carried it over to the Americas.

- How does the Spanish patio differ from what a patio is in your community? How is it similar?

Un patio típico en Córdoba, España

Actividad 14 **Hablar**

¿Cómo ayudas en casa?

¿Ayudas mucho en casa? Habla de tus quehaceres con otro(a) estudiante.

Modelo

A —*¿Tienes que lavar el coche?*
B —*Sí, lavo el coche todos los sábados.*

Estudiante A

1. 2. 3.

4. 5. 6.

Estudiante B

a veces
mucho
todos los días
todos los (sábados)
en el (verano)
los fines de semana
nunca

Nota

Dar means "to give" and is used in the expression *dar de comer,* "to feed." It has an irregular *yo* form: *doy.*

- En mi casa **doy** de comer al perro.

Exploración del lenguaje

Nouns that end in *-dor* and *-dora*

Every day you use appliances and gadgets to help with different tasks: a calculator, a computer, a stapler, a copier, a dryer, etc. Many of these words in English add the ending *-er* or *-or* to the verb that tells what the device is for. Spanish follows a similar pattern. Look at these words you already know and identify the pattern: *despertador, computadora, calculadora, aspiradora.* Can you guess what the corresponding verbs are and what they mean?

Try it out! Read each statement on the left and decide which appliance is needed.

1. Tengo calor.
2. ¿Dónde está el pan tostado?
3. Mi ropa está sucia.
4. Necesito leche para el cereal.

a. Está en la tostadora.
b. Ponla en la lavadora.
c. Está en el refrigerador.
d. Necesitas el ventilador.

Leer/Escribir/Hablar

¿Quién hace los quehaceres?

Un artículo de la revista española *Muy* explica quién hace la mayoría de *(most of)* los quehaceres de la casa. Estudia las gráficas a la derecha y haz comparaciones entre *(between)* las mujeres y los hombres españoles. Después, explica si las mujeres hacen los siguientes quehaceres mucho más, un poco más, o menos que los hombres.

Modelo

lavar los platos
Según el artículo, las mujeres lavan los platos mucho más que los hombres.

1. comprar cosas para la familia cada día
2. preparar la comida y la cena
3. cuidar *(to take care of)* el coche
4. cuidar a las personas enfermas de la familia
5. lavar y planchar *(iron)* la ropa
6. ir al banco
7. limpiar la casa

*Together

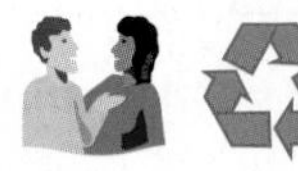

Escribir/Hablar

¿Dónde vives?

Escribe una lista de cinco lugares *(places)* en tu comunidad, como la escuela, el centro comercial, la biblioteca, etc. Pregunta a otro(a) estudiante si vive cerca o lejos de estos lugares.

Modelo

El cine Rex
A —*¿Vives cerca del cine Rex?*
B —*Sí, vivo bastante cerca del cine.*
o:—*No, vivo muy lejos.*

Gramática

Affirmative *tú* commands

When you tell friends, family members, or young people to do something, you use an affirmative *tú* command. To give these commands, use the same present-tense forms that you use for *Ud., él, ella.*

Infinitive	Ud./él/ella	Affirmative *tú* commands
hablar	habla	¡Habla!
leer	lee	¡Lee!
escribir	escribe	¡Escribe!

- Certain verbs, like *poner* and *hacer*, have irregular command forms.

  Jorgito, ¡**pon** la mesa!

  Jorgito, ¡**haz** tu cama!

¿Recuerdas?

In the direction lines of many activities, you have already seen many affirmative commands.

- **Habla** con otra persona.
- **Lee** las frases.
- **Escribe** la palabra apropiada.

GramActiva VIDEO

Want more help with the affirmative *tú* commands? Watch the **GramActiva** video.

Actividad 17 Escuchar/GramActiva

"Simón dice . . ."

Escucha y sigue *(follow)* las instrucciones de tu profesor(a) o de otro(a) estudiante. Si no dicen *"Simón dice,"* no debes hacer la acción.

Actividad 18 Escribir

¿Me ayudas?

Vienen unos amigos a tu casa para almorzar y tu madre necesita ayuda con los quehaceres. Completa la nota con la forma correcta del verbo apropiado para saber que tienes que hacer. Escribe las frases completas en una hoja de papel.

Modelo

Saca la basura.

Viene la familia Sánchez a casa para almorzar. Voy al trabajo esta mañana. ¿Me ayudas con los quehaceres?

Por favor:

1. ____ el polvo del despacho.
2. ____ el baño.
3. ____ tu dormitorio.
4. ____ la cama en mi dormitorio.
5. ____ la aspiradora en la sala.
6. ____ la mesa para el almuerzo.

¡Muchísimas gracias!

Mamá

  **Pensar/Escribir**

¿Responsable o irresponsable?

You need to make a decision: be responsible and do the household chores that need to be done, or be irresponsible and do things that are more fun. On a separate sheet of paper, make two lists: one titled *Responsable* and the other titled *Irresponsable*. For each list, write five sentences using the words in the box.

cocinar	limpiar
cortar	leer
escuchar	poner
hacer la tarea	ver
lavar	

¡Respuesta personal!

También se dice . . .

cocinar = guisar *(España)*

cortar el césped = cortar la hierba, cortar el pasto *(muchos países);* cortar el zacate *(México)*

lavar los platos = fregar los platos *(España)*

quitar el polvo = sacudir los muebles *(México);* *desempolvar (Bolivia)*

   **Hablar**

Un(a) niño(a) difícil

Estás cuidando a un(a) niño(a) difícil que quiere hacer muchas cosas. Tienes que indicar dónde él debe hacer estas actividades. Con otro(a) estudiante, explica dónde debe hacer varias actividades.

Modelo

A —*Yo quiero comer el almuerzo.*
B —*Está bien, pero por favor, come el almuerzo en la cocina.*

Estudiante A

1. hablar por teléfono
2. tocar la guitarra
3. limpiar los zapatos sucios
4. escuchar la radio
5. ver una película en el lector DVD
6. jugar videojuegos

Estudiante B

el baño
la cocina
el comedor
el cuarto
el despacho
el garaje
la sala
el sótano

¡Respuesta personal!

  **Leer/Escribir**

Menos quehaceres, más tiempo libre

Tu amiga Carmen tiene un problema y te escribe una carta *(letter)*. Lee su carta y escribe tus recomendaciones en otra carta, usando los verbos de la lista.

Modelo

Mi querida Carmen, aquí están mis recomendaciones: Corre en el parque, . . .

correr	jugar
dormir	levantar pesas
estudiar	ver
hacer ejercicio	

¡Respuesta personal!

¡Hola!

Tengo un problema grande. Nunca paso tiempo con mis amigos y no estoy en buena forma. ¡No tengo tiempo libre! Durante la semana tengo clases y en los fines de semana arreglo mi cuarto, limpio el baño, quito el polvo de toda la casa . . . ¡Hago quehaceres todo el día! Quisiera hacer cosas más divertidas. Siempre tengo mucho sueño y poca energía. Nunca hago ejercicio. No estoy muy enferma pero quisiera estar mejor de salud. ¿Qué debo hacer?

Tu amiga desesperada,

Carmen

  **Hablar/Escribir**

Muchos quehaceres

Tienes muchos quehaceres en casa, pero no los quieres hacer. ¡A ver si tu hermanito(a) puede hacer todo! Primero di *(say)* lo que está sucio (o lo que no está limpio). Luego di lo que tiene que hacer.

¿Recuerdas?

Adjectives agree in number and gender with the nouns they modify.

- **La** casa está suci**a**.
- **Los** plato**s** están limpi**os**.

Modelo

Los platos están sucios.
o: *Los platos no están limpios.*
Lava los platos, por favor.

1. 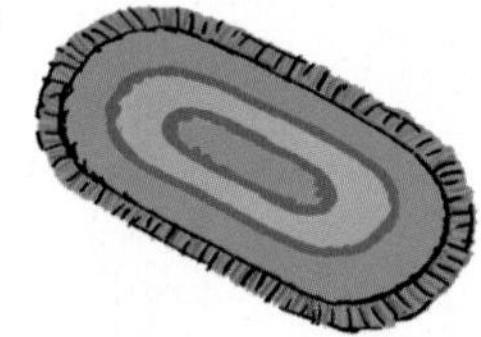
2. 
3. 
4.   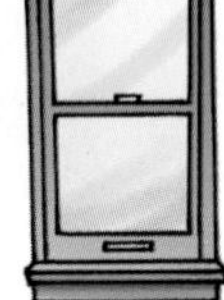 
5. 
6. 

  **Hablar**

Compartir el trabajo

Tú y tus amigos van a tener una fiesta en tu casa. Tus padres están de acuerdo, pero Uds. tienen que arreglar la casa antes de la fiesta. Lee la lista de todos los quehaceres que necesitas hacer. Trabaja con otro(a) estudiante para decidir cómo compartir el trabajo.

Modelo

A —*Limpia el baño.*
B —*No me gusta nada limpiar el baño. ¿Por qué no limpias tú el baño? Yo paso la aspiradora.*
A —*Está bien. Pasa la aspiradora y yo puedo limpiar el baño.*
o:—*Bueno, pasa la aspiradora pero yo quiero hacer las camas.*

Antes de la fiesta necesitan:

- cortar el césped
- hacer todas las camas
- arreglar los dos dormitorios
- limpiar el baño
- pasar la aspiradora en el despacho
- sacar la basura de la cocina
- quitar el polvo de la sala
- poner las bicicletas en el garaje

Más práctica

- Practice Workbook, p. 32: 6B-5
- WAV Wbk.: Writing, p. 40
- Guided Practice: Grammar Acts., pp. 207–208
- *Real.* para hispanohablantes, pp. 234–237

For: Affirmative *Tú* Commands
Web Code: jbd-0613

Pronunciación

jbd-0698

The letters *n* and *ñ* 

In Spanish, the letter *n* sounds like the *n* in *no*. Listen to and say these words:

anaranjado	nieva	nadar	joven	desayuno
necesito	encantado	número	nombre	donde

However, the sound changes when there is a tilde (~) over the *n*. The *ñ* then sounds like the *-ny-* of the word *canyon*. Listen to and say these words:

señor	otoño	español	enseñar	año
montañas	niña	mañana	piñata	cumpleaños

Try it out! Listen to this *trabalenguas* and then try to say it.

El Sr. Yáñez come ñames[1] en las mañanas con el niño.

[1]yams

Gramática

The present progressive tense

When you want to emphasize that an action is happening *right now,* you use the present progressive tense.

Paco **está lavando** los platos. — *Paco **is washing** dishes **(now).***
Estoy haciendo la cama. — ***I'm making** the bed **(now).***

To form the present progressive tense, use the present-tense forms of *estar* + the present participle. The present participle is formed by dropping the ending of the infinitive and adding *-ando* for *-ar* verbs or *-iendo* for *-er* and *-ir* verbs.

(yo)	**estoy**	**lavando** **comiendo** **escribiendo**	(nosotros) (nosotras)	**estamos**	**lavando** **comiendo** **escribiendo**
(tú)	**estás**	**lavando** **comiendo** **escribiendo**	(vosotros) (vosotras)	**estáis**	**lavando** **comiendo** **escribiendo**
Ud. (él) (ella)	**está**	**lavando** **comiendo** **escribiendo**	Uds. (ellos) (ellas)	**están**	**lavando** **comiendo** **escribiendo**

- *Leer* has an irregular spelling in the present participle: *leyendo.*

¿Recuerdas?

You use the present tense to talk about an action that regularly takes place, or that is happening now.

- Paco **lava** los platos.
  *Paco **washes** the dishes.*
  OR
  *Paco **is washing** the dishes.*

GramActiva VIDEO

Want more help with the present progressive tense? Watch the **GramActiva** video.

Escribir

¿Qué están haciendo ahora?

Mira este dibujo y en una hoja de papel, escribe seis frases para decir cuáles quehaceres están haciendo estas personas.

Modelo
Roberto está quitando el polvo.

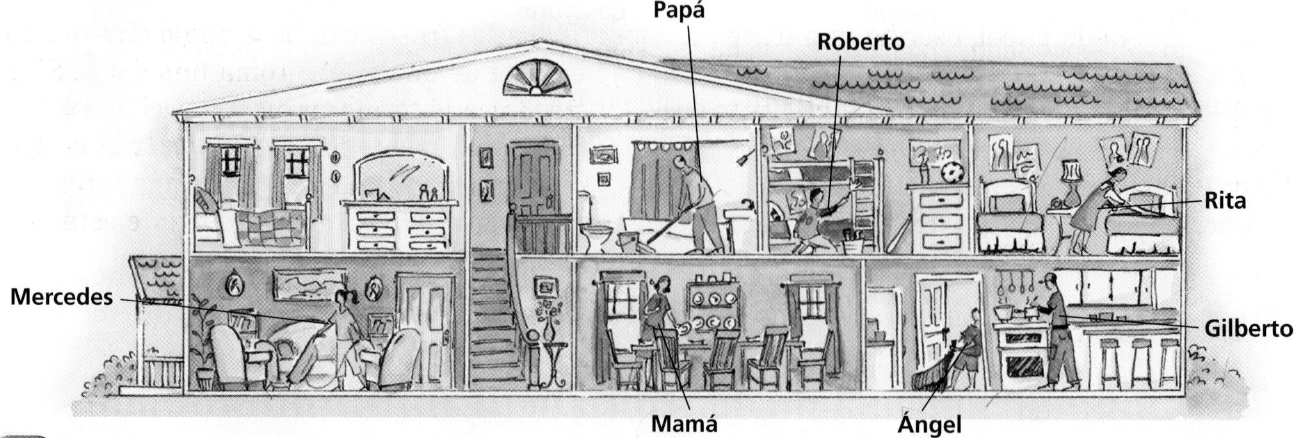

jcd-0698

Escuchar/Escribir 

Escucha y escribe

Estos hermanos tienen muchos quehaceres. Escucha y escribe la pregunta de la madre y las excusas de los hijos.

Hablar

Un momento, por favor

A veces no podemos hacer los quehaceres porque estamos haciendo otras cosas. Trabaja con otro(a) estudiante para dar un mandato y una excusa.

Modelo

A —*Por favor, da de comer al perro.*
B —*No puedo. Estoy estudiando para un examen.*

Estudiante A

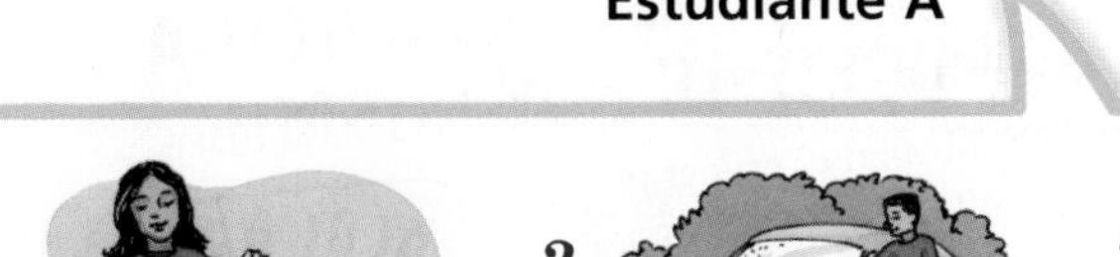

1. 
2. 
3. 
4. 
5. 
6. 

Estudiante B

Un momento . . .	estudiar
No puedo . . .	hacer
Lo siento . . .	jugar
Me gustaría pero . . .	escuchar
	tocar
	escribir
	comer
	beber
	hablar

¡Respuesta personal!

Escribir/Hablar/GramActiva

Juego

1. En una hoja de papel, escribe una frase para explicar lo que está haciendo una persona (usa la forma tú). En otra hojita, escribe una frase para explicar lo que están haciendo dos personas (usa la forma Uds.).

Modelo

Estás levantando pesas.
Uds. están esquiando.

2. Todas las frases van boca abajo *(facedown)* encima de una mesa. Toma una frase. Si la frase usa la forma tú, haz la acción solo(a). Si la frase usa la forma Uds., haz la acción con otro(a) estudiante. Los compañeros tienen que adivinar *(guess)* lo que estás (están) haciendo.

Actividad 28 Leer/Pensar

¿Qué casa están buscando?

En Santiago, Chile, tres personas están buscando *(looking for)* una nueva casa y leen el anuncio a la derecha. ¿Quién crees que va a comprar *(buy)* la casa?

José Guzmán: "Quiero vivir bastante cerca de mi trabajo. Para mi esposa es importante tener una cocina equipada. Prefiero una casa con sólo un piso porque mis padres van a vivir con nosotros y las escaleras son muy difíciles para ellos".

Alejandro Lara: "Mis padres y yo vivimos en un apartamento ahora. Quiero una casa con tres dormitorios porque mis primos vienen a nuestra casa a veces. No quiero una casa muy grande porque no me gusta ni pasar la aspiradora ni limpiar los baños".

Dora Peña: "Mi familia y yo estamos buscando una casa nueva. Tenemos dos hijas y mi mamá vive con nosotros. Quiero una casa con un dormitorio un poco separado para mi mamá. Prefiero tener alfombra en los dormitorios porque nuestras hijas juegan mucho allí".

Chile

LAS MEJORES CASAS EN LA AVENIDA LA FLORIDA

CASA VENEZIA: 310 m² 3 PISOS
DESDE CHP[1] 40.000.000

FERNANDO MILLÁN
AVENIDA MARTÍNEZ
ROJAS MAGALLANES
ENRIQUE OLIVARES
oficina
AVENIDA LA FLORIDA

Planta baja: Amplia sala • Comedor separado • Cocina y baño de visitas
Primer piso: Dormitorio principal, más 2 dormitorios y otro baño
Segundo piso: Amplio dormitorio con baño completo y una gran sala de estar

«VISITE NUESTRA OFICINA Y COMPRE HOY MISMO»

- Cerámica en el primer piso
- Alfombra en dormitorios
- Cocina equipada
- Papel vinílico en paredes
- Armarios terminados
- Ventanas de aluminio
- Amplio jardín

CASAS ROJAS
MAGALLANES 3400

¡Llame hoy! 232 9980

[1] Pesos chilenos

El español en el mundo del trabajo

Across the country, "For Sale" signs in Spanish are appearing on lawns, in front of apartment buildings, and in office complexes.

- Look for ads in Spanish in the real estate section of your local newspaper.

Leer/Pensar

¿Dónde viven?

En Caracas, la capital de Venezuela, analizaron *(they analyzed)* dónde viven unos 2.7 millones de habitantes. Según los estudios, ¿viven más personas en casas o en apartamentos? ¿Viven en casas y apartamentos grandes o pequeños? Estudia las gráficas y contesta las preguntas.

Nota

Do you see the pattern in the following numbers?

100,000 = cien mil
200,000 = doscientos mil
300,000 = trescientos mil

But watch out for 500,000:

542,656 = quinientos cuarenta y dos mil, seiscientos cincuenta y seis

1,000,000 = un millón

Conexiones
Las matemáticas

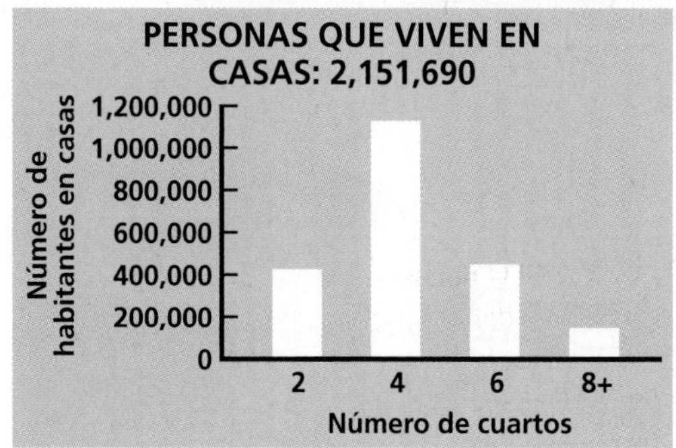

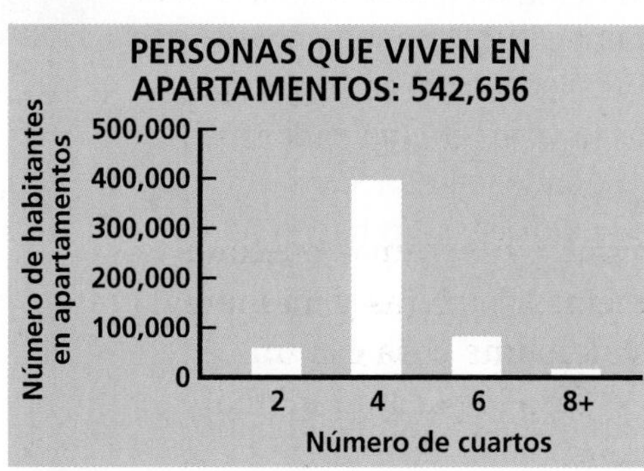

1. ¿Cuántas personas viven en una casa con dos cuartos? ¿Cuántas viven en un apartamento con dos cuartos?
2. ¿Cuántas personas viven en una casa con ocho o más cuartos? ¿Cuántas viven en un apartamento con ocho o más cuartos?
3. Calcula el porcentaje de personas que viven en una casa con cuatro cuartos. Calcula el porcentaje de personas que viven en un apartamento con cuatro cuartos.

Dibujar/Escribir/Hablar

¿Qué están haciendo todos?

Haz un dibujo de tres personas que están haciendo diferentes actividades. En otra hoja de papel, escribe dos preguntas sobre lo que está haciendo cada persona. Trabaja en un grupo de tres. Da tu dibujo a los otros estudiantes y lee tus preguntas. Tus compañeros tienen que contestar.

Modelo

A —*¿Qué está haciendo la chica?*
B/C —*Está lavando los platos sucios.*

Más práctica

- Practice Workbook, pp. 33–34: 6B-6, 6B-7
- WAV Wbk.: Writing, p. 41
- Guided Practice: Grammar Acts., pp. 209–210
- *Real.* para hispanohablantes, pp. 238–239

For: Present Progressive
Web Code: jbd-0614

¡Adelante!

Objectives

- **Read a version of *Cinderella***
- **Learn about houses in the Spanish-speaking world**
- **Create a flyer to sell a house or apartment**
- **Watch *¿Eres tú, María?*, Episodio 4**

Lectura

Lee esta historia sobre una joven que se llama Cantaclara.

Skimming
This reading is based on the story of Cinderella. Quickly skim the story and find characters and dialogue that remind you of *Cinderella.*

Cantaclara

Hay una muchacha que se llama Cantaclara. Ella vive con su madrastra y sus dos hermanastras, Griselda y Hortencia. Las cuatro viven en una casa grande y Cantaclara hace todos los quehaceres. Sus dos hermanastras y su madrastra no hacen nada.

—Cantaclara, saca la basura. Y después, pon la mesa —dice la madrastra.

—Cantaclara, haz mi cama y limpia el baño —dice Griselda.

—Haz mi cama también —dice Hortencia.

—Un momento. Estoy lavando los platos ahora mismo —dice Cantaclara.

¡Pobre[1] Cantaclara! Hace todos los quehaceres y cuando trabaja, ella canta. Tiene una voz[2] muy clara y le encanta cantar.

Un día, Cantaclara entra en el dormitorio de Griselda para hacer la cama. Ve en la televisión un anuncio[3] para un programa muy popular que se llama *La estrella*[4] *del futuro*. En la televisión hay un señor que dice: "¡Hola, amigos! ¿Tienen talento? ¿Cantan bien? ¿Por qué no cantan para nosotros? ¡Pueden tener un futuro fantástico y recibir muchísimo dinero!".

Cantaclara está muy contenta. Ella puede cantar. Ella quiere un futuro fantástico. En este momento, ella decide cantar para el programa *La estrella del futuro*.

[1]Poor [2]voice [3]ad [4]star

Es la noche del programa. Después de hacer todos los quehaceres, Cantaclara está saliendo[5] de casa cuando su madrastra le habla.

—Cantaclara, ¿adónde vas?

—Quiero salir por unas horas, madrastra. ¿Está bien?

—Ahora no. Tienes que limpiar la cocina —contesta la madrastra. —Está muy sucia.

—Pero, madrastra, tengo que . . .

—¡No importa, Cantaclara! ¡Limpia la cocina!

Cantaclara mira su reloj. Sólo tiene una hora. Va a la cocina y limpia todo. Trabaja muy rápidamente. Después de cuarenta y cinco minutos, termina el trabajo.

Cantaclara llega[6] al programa y canta su canción favorita. ¡Por supuesto ella canta mejor que todos![7] Ella va a tener un futuro fantástico y va a recibir muchísimo dinero.

Son las ocho de la noche. La madrastra y las dos hermanastras están en la sala y ven su programa favorito. Pero, ¿qué es esto? ¡Ven a Cantaclara en la pantalla!

—Mira, mamá. ¡Es Cantaclara! —dice Hortencia.

—¡Oh, no! Si Cantaclara es la nueva estrella del futuro, ¿quién va a hacer los quehaceres? —pregunta Griselda.

[5]is leaving [6]arrives [7]anyone else

¿Comprendes?

Pon las frases en orden según la historia.

1. Ella decide cantar en el programa *La estrella del futuro.*
2. Cantaclara es la persona que canta mejor en el programa.
3. Ella está lavando los platos.
4. Ella tiene que limpiar la cocina.
5. Ella ve el anuncio para *La estrella del futuro.*
6. Griselda no sabe quién va a hacer los quehaceres.
7. Cantaclara vive en una casa grande con su madrastra y dos hermanastras.
8. Son las ocho de la noche y la madrastra y las hermanastras están viendo la tele.

Fondo cultural

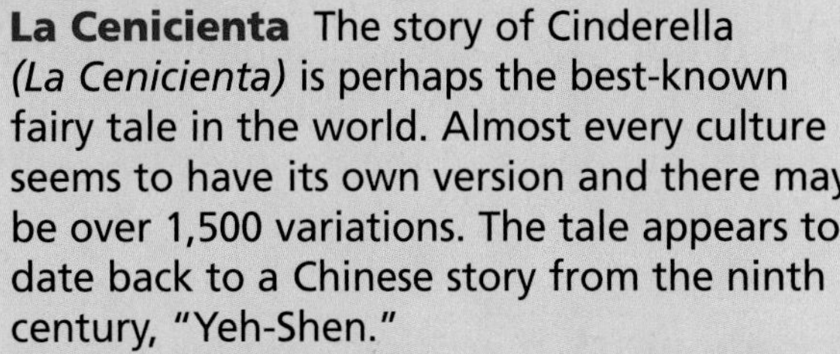

La Cenicienta The story of Cinderella *(La Cenicienta)* is perhaps the best-known fairy tale in the world. Almost every culture seems to have its own version and there may be over 1,500 variations. The tale appears to date back to a Chinese story from the ninth century, "Yeh-Shen."

- What aspects of the story might change from culture to culture?

Más práctica

- **WAV Wbk.: Writing, p. 42**
- **Guided Practice: *Lectura*, p. 211**
- ***Real.* para hispanohablantes, pp. 242–243**

For: Internet Activity
Web Code: jbd-0615

Perspectivas del mundo hispano

¿Cómo son las casas en el mundo hispano?

In many Spanish-speaking countries the architectural features of houses are very different from those in the United States. Houses tend to be separated from the outside by a barrier such as a tall wall or fence. The owner would open a gate to enter the property where there may be a carport or small outside area. In many communities, the outside wall of the house is located directly on the sidewalk and the front windows may contain bars or *rejas.* The doors may be large wooden or metal doors. A plain walled exterior gives no hints about what may be a beautiful, comfortable interior.

Inside, a home will often have an open space in the middle called the *patio.* Many rooms of the house open onto the *patio,* and it is a place for the family to meet, eat meals, talk, and spend time together. Privacy is valued, and the home and family activities are shielded from view from the outside.

Homes in Spanish-speaking countries are used for the family and to entertain very close relatives and friends. It is unusual to invite non-family members such as coworkers or casual friends into the home. Parties often take place in restaurants or small reception halls.

Check it out! Look around your neighborhood. How does the architecture of houses compare with the design of houses in the Spanish-speaking world?

Think about it! If architectural features of houses in Spanish-speaking countries imply a desire for privacy, what do the architectural features of houses in the United States imply? How does the concept of a *patio* compare in these cultures?

El patio de una casa en Córdoba, España

Una calle en una zona residencial en San Juan, Puerto Rico

Una casa en Caracas, Venezuela

Presentación escrita

Se vende casa o apartamento

Task
You have been asked to create a flyer in Spanish to promote the sale of your family's house or apartment. Create an attractive and inviting flyer that will make your home, or your dream house if you prefer, appealing to a potential buyer.

1 **Prewrite** Think about the information you want to include in your flyer. Read these questions and jot down what you'd like to say about the house or apartment.

- En general, ¿cómo es la casa o el apartamento?
- ¿Cuántos cuartos hay? ¿Qué son? ¿Cómo son? ¿Cuáles son los colores?
- ¿Hay algo especial en la casa (piscina, cuarto especial)?
- Incluye *(Include)* otra información importante como la dirección *(address)* y el precio *(price).*

Strategy

Using key questions
Answering key questions can help you think of ideas for writing.

2 **Draft** Look at the ad on p. 144 to help you design your flyer. Use the answers to the Prewrite questions. Include an illustration and other features to make it attractive. Begin with the phrase *Se vende casa* or *Se vende apartamento.*

3 **Revise** Read through your ad to see that you have included all the information that a potential buyer might want. Make sure the words are spelled correctly. Share your flyer with a partner, who will check the following:

- Is the flyer neat and attractive and does it include a visual?
- Is the key information provided?
- Does it make you want to look at the property?

4 **Publish** Write a final copy of your flyer, making any necessary changes. You may want to include it with your classmates' flyers in a collection called *Se venden casas y apartamentos,* or in your portfolio.

5 **Evaluation** Your teacher may give you a rubric for grading the flyer. You probably will be graded on:

- neatness and attractiveness
- use of vocabulary
- amount of information provided

Videomisterio

¿Eres tú, María? Episodio 4

Antes de ver el video

Personajes importantes

Carmela, una buena amiga de Lola

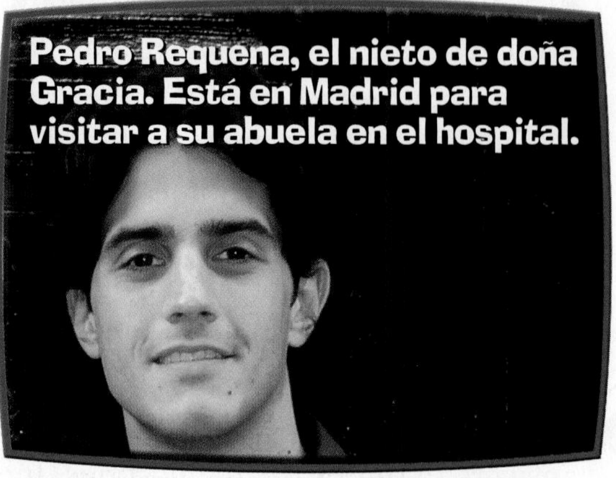

Pedro Requena, el nieto de doña Gracia. Está en Madrid para visitar a su abuela en el hospital.

Nota cultural *Tapas* are popular appetizers in Spain. *Tapas* come in small servings called *raciones,* and can be almost anything: olives, seafood, meat, cheese, vegetables, shellfish, or any dish the chef cares to prepare. Eating *tapas* is a social event. Friends eat, drink, and relax as they talk. When you are done, you are charged according to how many platefuls of *tapas* you ate.

Resumen del episodio

Doña Gracia está mucho mejor y puede ir a casa en unos días. Pero no recuerda mucho del incidente. Lola llama por teléfono a su buena amiga, Carmela. Las dos van a un café para hablar y Carmela le dice a Lola que una de sus amigas, Rosalinda, trabaja en el hospital San Carlos. Es el hospital donde está doña Gracia. Deciden ir al hospital para hablar con Rosalinda y ver a doña Gracia. A la mañana siguiente,[1] Lola habla con Pedro Requena.

[1] next

Palabras para comprender

fui a visitarla	I went to visit her
¿Habló del incidente?	Did she talk about the incident?
¿Sabe . . .	Does she know . . . ?
Lo único que recuerda . . .	The only thing she remembers . . .
un golpe	hit, blow
ahora mismo	right away
preguntar por	to ask about
los churros	fried dough pastries
No estoy pensando en . . .	I'm not planning to . . .
Voy a pensarlo.	I'll think about it.

“Lo único que recuerda es un golpe aquí, en la cabeza. ¿La verdad? No sabe nada”.

“Soy Pedro Requena. Exacto, el nieto de la Sra. Gracia Requena. Voy ahora mismo para el hospital”.

—Si necesita más información, aquí tiene mi número de teléfono.

—Gracias, señorita. Voy a pensarlo.

Después de ver el video

¿Comprendes?

A. Lee las frases y ponlas *(put them)* en el orden cronológico.

1. Pedro no sabe si quiere contratar a una detective.
2. Lola y Carmela van al café a comer unas tapas.
3. Lola habla con Pedro y le da su número de teléfono.
4. Paco y Lola hablan en la oficina.
5. Pedro Requena habla por teléfono con el Dr. Sánchez Mata.
6. Doña Lupe dice que fue al hospital y habló con doña Gracia.
7. Carmela dice que su amiga, Rosalinda, trabaja en el hospital San Carlos.

B. Lee las frases y escribe el nombre de la persona que dice cada frase: Pedro, Carmela, Lola, doña Lupe o Paco.

1. No podemos trabajar si no hay cliente y no hay dinero.
2. Buenas noticias. Doña Gracia está mejor.
3. ¿Quieres tomar un café conmigo?
4. Mi amiga trabaja allí. Puedes hablar con doña Gracia.
5. No estoy pensando en contratar a un detective.

For: More on *¿Eres tú, María?*
Web Code: jbd-0507

Repaso del capítulo

Chapter Review

To prepare for the test, check to see if you . . .

- know the new vocabulary and grammar
- can perform the tasks on p. 153

Vocabulario y gramática

jcd-0699

to talk about where someone lives

cerca (de)	close (to), near
lejos (de)	far (from)
vivir	to live

to talk about houses or apartments

el apartamento	apartment
el baño	bathroom
la cocina	kitchen
el comedor	dining room
el cuarto	room
el despacho	home office
la escalera	stairs, stairway
el garaje	garage
el piso	story, floor
la planta baja	ground floor
el primer piso	second floor
la sala	living room
el segundo piso	third floor
el sótano	basement

to name household chores

arreglar el cuarto	to straighten up the room
ayudar	to help
cocinar	to cook
cortar el césped	to cut the lawn
dar (yo doy, tú das)	to give
dar de comer al perro	to feed the dog
hacer la cama	to make the bed
lavar (el coche, los platos, la ropa)	to wash (the car, the dishes, the clothes)
limpiar el baño	to clean the bathroom
pasar la aspiradora	to vacuum
poner (yo pongo, tú pones)	to put, place
poner la mesa	to set the table
los quehaceres	chores
quitar el polvo	to dust
sacar la basura	to take out the trash

to describe household items

limpio, -a	clean
sucio, -a	dirty

other useful words and expressions

bastante	enough; rather
¿Cuáles?	Which (ones)?
el dinero	money
un momento	a moment
¿Qué estás haciendo?	What are you doing?
recibir	to receive
si	if, whether

affirmative *tú* commands

For regular verbs, use the *Ud.*/*él*/*ella* form:

-ar:	**habla**
-er:	**lee**
-ir:	**escribe**

For *hacer* and *poner:*

hacer	**haz**
poner	**pon**

present progressive tense

Use the present-tense forms of *estar* + the present participle to say that you are doing something right now.

present participles:

-ar:	stem + **-ando** → lav**ando**
-er:	stem + **-iendo** → com**iendo**
-ir:	stem + **-iendo** → escrib**iendo**

For *Vocabulario adicional,* see pp. 336–337.

Más práctica

- Practice Workbook: Puzzle, p. 35
- Practice Workbook: Organizer, p. 36

Go Online PHSchool.com
For: Test Preparation
Web Code: jbd-0616

Preparación para el examen

On the exam you will be asked to . . .	Here are practice tasks similar to those you will find on the exam . . .	If you need review . . .
jbd-0699  **1 Escuchar** Listen to and understand teenagers' excuses for not doing a particular chore at the moment they are asked to do it	As you listen to a teenager explain to his mother why he can't do a particular chore at the moment, identify: a) what the mother wants the teenager to do; b) what the teenager says he is busy doing.	**pp. 126–131** *A primera vista* **p. 134** Actividad 10 **p. 136** Actividad 14 **p. 143** Actividades 25–26
2 Hablar Give advice to others about how to be successful in school	Your school counselors have asked you to participate in an orientation for new Spanish-speaking students. Offer each student in the group a piece of advice. For example, you might say *Escucha bien en clase* or *Haz la tarea.*	**p. 140** Actividad 21
 **3 Leer** Read and understand ads for apartments that you might find in the classified section of a Spanish-language newspaper	A friend is moving to Spain and asks you to help find an apartment. He wants a two-bedroom, two-bath apartment with a small kitchen. He wants to live near a gym and a library. Read this ad and answer the following: a) Is this a good apartment for him?; b) How many of his requested features does it have?; c) What other features that are mentioned might he like? Este maravilloso apartamento tiene todo. Está cerca de un parque y un gimnasio moderno. Tiene una cocina pequeña, pero totalmente equipada. Tiene dos dormitorios con estantes y un baño muy grande. También tiene televisión por satélite y un garaje privado. No se permiten animales.	**pp. 126–131** *A primera vista* **p. 133** Actividades 8–9 **p. 144** Actividad 28 **p. 149** *Presentación escrita*
 **4 Escribir** Write a list of household chores that you are willing to do	You and your classmates are offering to do chores to earn money for your Spanish club. Make a list of at least eight chores that you would be willing to do.	**pp. 126–131** *A primera vista* **p. 134** Actividades 10–11 **p. 136** Actividad 14 **p. 137** Actividad 15 **p. 140** Actividad 22
 **5 Pensar** Demonstrate an understanding of cultural perspectives regarding houses	Explain how the architechtural features of many houses in the Spanish speaking world reflect the importance the owners place on privacy. How do these features compare to those in homes in the United States?	**p. 135** *Fondo cultural* **p. 148** *Perspectivas del mundo hispano*

Tema 7 • De compras

Mercado en Otavalo, Ecuador

Fondo cultural

Joan Miró (1893–1983) was born near Barcelona. He painted this self-portrait in 1919, when he was 26 years old. Here he portrays himself wearing a *garibaldina*, or cardigan, a collarless sweater or jacket that buttons in the front. *Garibaldinas* were popular at the time, and they were usually red, a color that makes this portrait even more intense.

- How do fashions change across time, or from culture to culture? Give three examples.

"El joven de la garibaldina roja" (autorretrato) (1919), Joan Miró

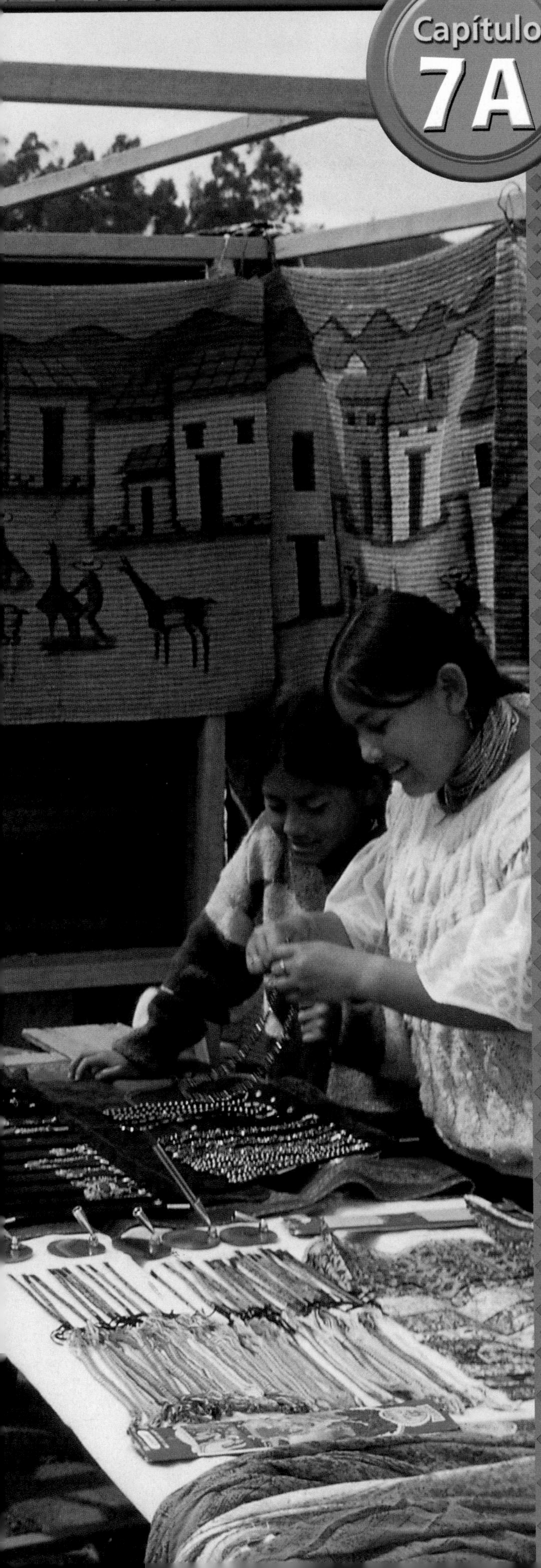

Capítulo 7A

¿Cuánto cuesta?

Chapter Objectives

- Talk about clothes, shopping, and prices
- Describe your plans
- Talk about what you want and what you prefer
- Point out specific items
- Understand cultural perspectives on shopping

Video Highlights

A primera vista: ***Una noche especial***

GramActiva Videos: **stem-changing verbs:** ***pensar, querer,*** **and** ***preferir;*** **demonstrative adjectives**

Videomisterio: ***¿Eres tú, María?,*** **Episodio 5**

Country Connection

As you learn about clothing and shopping, you will make connections to these countries and places:

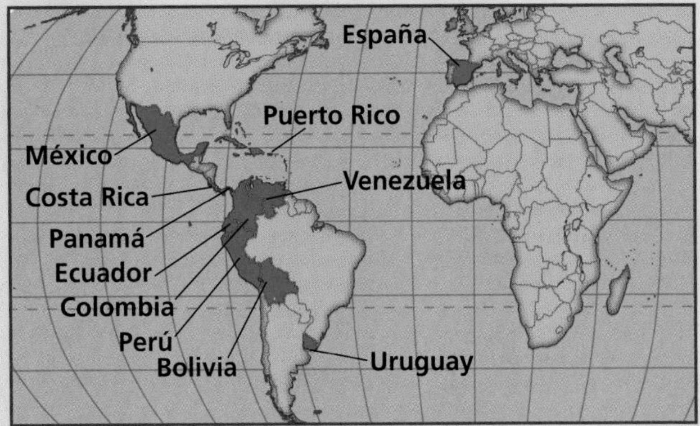

Más práctica

- *Real.* para hispanohablantes, pp. 250–251

Go Online PHSchool.com **For:** Online Atlas **Web Code:** jbe-0002

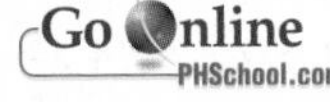

A primera vista

Vocabulario y gramática en contexto

Objectives

Read, listen to, and understand information about
- **shopping for clothes**
- **plans, desires, and preferences**

jbd-0787

Tienda de ropa La Preferida

ROPA ELEGANTE

el traje
el vestido
la camisa
los pantalones
los calcetines
las botas
los zapatos

ROPA DEPORTIVA

la camiseta
la gorra
el traje de baño
los pantalones cortos

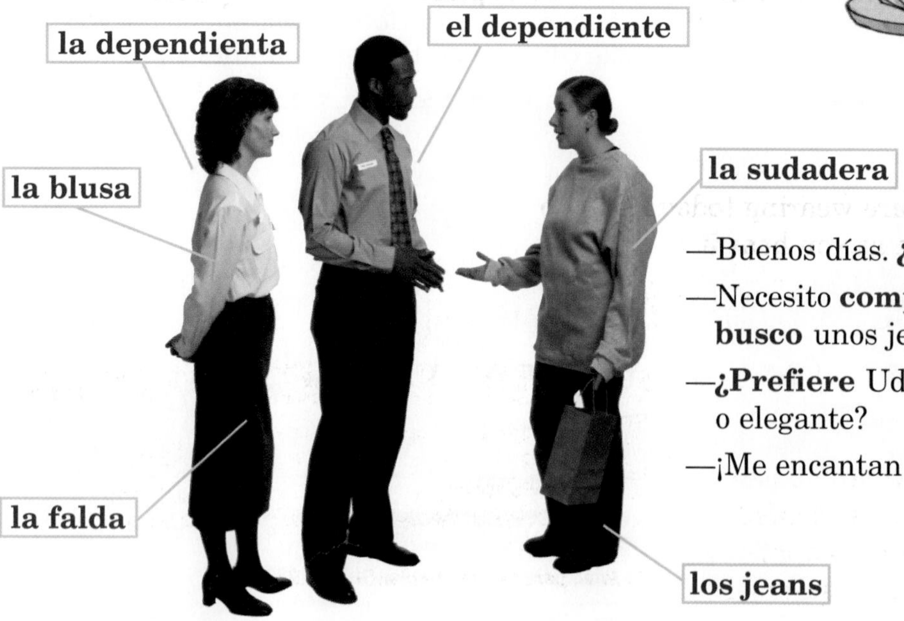

la dependienta
el dependiente
la blusa
la sudadera
la falda
los jeans

—Buenos días. **¿En qué puedo servirle?**

—Necesito **comprar** una blusa. Y también **busco** unos jeans **nuevos.**

—**¿Prefiere** Ud. **llevar** una blusa deportiva o elegante?

—¡Me encantan las blusas deportivas!

—¿Qué **piensas** comprar hoy?

—Necesito comprar un abrigo. Me gusta **ese** abrigo. **¿Entramos** en **la tienda?**

—¡Uf! **Me queda mal.**

—**Tienes razón.** Es demasiado grande.

—**¿Cómo me queda este** abrigo?

—**Te queda bien.** Me gusta. ¿Qué piensas?

—Me gusta también. **¿Cúanto cuesta?**

—A ver... Cuesta ochocientos pesos. Es un buen **precio,** ¿no?

doscientos pesos

300

trescientos pesos

cuatrocientos pesos

quinientos pesos

seiscientos pesos

setecientos pesos

ochocientos pesos

novecientos pesos

mil pesos

jbd-0787

Escuchar

¿Qué ropa llevan?

Listen to what different people are wearing today. Point to the picture of each clothing item as you hear it.

jbd-0787

Escuchar

¿Verano o invierno?

On a sheet of paper, draw a snowman on one side and the sun on the other. If a statement you hear is most logical for winter, hold up the snowman. If it is most logical for summer, hold up the sun.

Más práctica

- Practice Workbook, pp. 37–38: 7A-1, 7A-2
- WAV Wbk.: Writing, p. 49
- Guided Practice: Vocab. Flash Cards, pp. 213–218
- *Real.* para hispanohablantes, p. 252

Videohistoria

jbd-0787 

Una noche especial

¿Por qué necesita ir de compras Teresa? Lee la historia.

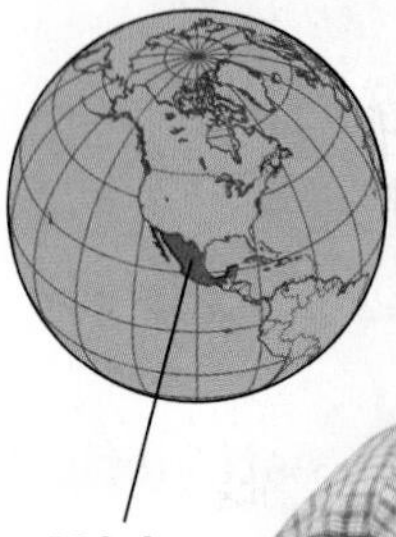

Antes de leer

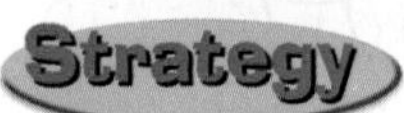

Using questions as a guide for reading Before you read the *Videohistoria,* read the questions in Actividad 5 to help you focus on the information that is most important.

- What are three specific things that you should be thinking about as you read the *Videohistoria?*

1. Think about the last time you went clothes shopping. What were you looking for? Did you buy something? If so, was it expensive? If not, why didn't you buy anything? What do you expect Teresa and Claudia to talk about when Teresa tries to buy something to wear to the party?
2. Compare how Ramón is dressed in photo 6 and how he is dressed in photo 8. What are the differences? What are the similarities?

1 **Teresa: Esta** falda no me queda bien y este vestido no me gusta. No sé qué llevar para la fiesta.

Claudia: Pues, puedes comprar ropa nueva. Hay una tienda **de ropa** aquí cerca y tienen ropa muy bonita.

Teresa: Sí, **quizás** una falda nueva . . . **¡Vamos!**

2 **Claudia:** ¡Mira esta tienda!

Teresa: Mmmm . . . No sé. No tengo mucho dinero y **esa** ropa es muy cara.

Claudia: ¡Vamos! **¡Queremos** ver qué tienen!

3 **Teresa: Perdón,** ¿señora?

Dependienta: ¿Sí? ¿En qué puedo servirle, señorita?

Teresa: Busco ropa para llevar a una fiesta. Me gustaría comprar esta falda y esta blusa.

Claudia: A ver . . . ¿Cuánto **cuestan?**

Teresa: ¡Seiscientos pesos! Pero, ¡es mucho dinero!

4 **Dependienta:** Bueno, aquí hay ropa que no cuesta **tanto.**

Claudia: Mira, Teresa. Esta falda cuesta trescientos pesos. ¿Qué piensas?

Teresa: ¡Genial! Y este suéter cuesta doscientos pesos. **Los dos** no cuestan tanto.

5 **Manolo:** Ramón, son las ocho. La fiesta es a las nueve, ¿recuerdas?

Ramón: Sí, sí, tienes razón. Vamos.

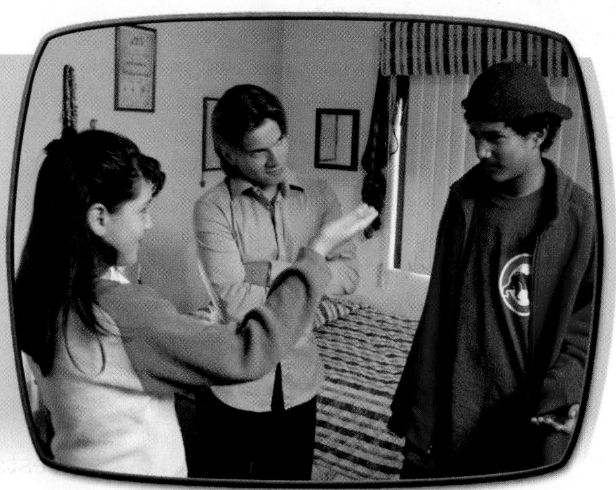

6 **Berta:** Ramón, ¿tú piensas llevar esa ropa a la fiesta de Teresa? ¡**Esos** jeans y esa camiseta y . . . esa gorra! No, no puedes.

Ramón: ¿Y por qué no?

Berta: Uhm . . . Pues, aquí en México no llevamos esa ropa a las fiestas.

7 **Ramón:** ¡Yo quiero llevar mi gorra favorita, y me gustan **estos** jeans!

Manolo y Berta: Te ayudamos.

8 **Teresa:** ¡Hola! Buenas noches. Pero, ¿dónde está la gorra?

Actividad 3 Leer/Escribir

¿Sí puedes o no puedes?

Lee estas frases de Ramón. En una hoja de papel, escribe *sí puedes* si según Berta y Manolo es algo que Ramón puede llevar a la fiesta o *no puedes* si según ellos es algo que no puede llevar a la fiesta.

1. Quiero llevar mis jeans a la fiesta.
2. Pienso llevar unos pantalones negros a la fiesta.
3. Pienso llevar mi gorra favorita a la fiesta.
4. Voy a llevar una camisa blanca a la fiesta.
5. Quiero llevar una camiseta a la fiesta.

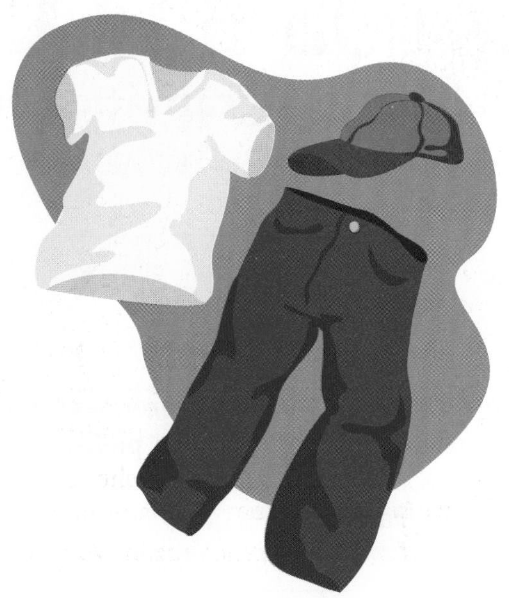

Actividad 4 Leer/Pensar

¿Cierto o falso?

Lee las frases y escribe *C* (cierto) o *F* (falso), según la *Videohistoria*.

1. Claudia y Teresa buscan ropa para una fiesta.
2. Teresa tiene un vestido que le gusta mucho y no quiere ropa nueva.
3. A Ramón le encanta llevar su gorra.
4. La tienda no tiene ropa que cuesta menos que seiscientos pesos.
5. Teresa puede comprar un suéter con doscientos pesos.
6. Para Berta y Manolo, no es importante la ropa que lleva Ramón a la fiesta.

Actividad 5 Hablar/Escribir

¿Comprendes?

1. ¿Por qué no está contenta Teresa? ¿Adónde va ella?
2. Según Claudia, ¿qué puede hacer Teresa?
3. ¿Adónde van las dos?
4. ¿Tiene Teresa mucho o poco dinero?
5. ¿Por qué no compra Teresa la primera falda y blusa?
6. ¿Cuánto cuestan la segunda falda y blusa?
7. ¿Qué quiere llevar Ramón a la fiesta?
8. Cuando Ramón entra en la casa de Teresa, ¿qué lleva?

Más práctica

- Practice Workbook, pp. 39–40: 7A-3, 7A-4
- WAV Wbk.: Video, pp. 43–45
- Guided Practice: Vocab. Check, pp. 219–222
- *Real.* para hispanohablantes, p. 253

Manos a la obra

Vocabulario y gramática en uso

Objectives

- Talk about shopping for clothes
- Discuss how clothes fit and how much they cost
- Ask and tell what you or others plan to do
- Ask and tell what you or others want and prefer
- Point things out using demonstrative adjectives

Escribir

¿Qué piensas llevar?

¡Es importante llevar ropa diferente en diferentes ocasiones! ¿Qué ropa piensas llevar a estos lugares *(places)* o actividades? Escribe las frases.

Modelo

la casa de un amigo
Pienso llevar unos jeans y una camiseta.

1. la playa
2. un baile formal
3. un concierto
4. las montañas
5. un partido de béisbol

Escribir

¿Qué ropa llevan en el cuadro?

Escribe cuatro o más frases que describen la ropa que lleva la familia en este cuadro de Fernando Botero.

Modelo

La madre lleva . . .

Fernando Botero (1932–) is a very famous artist from Medellín, Colombia. His paintings and sculptures feature people and objects that are puffed up to an exaggerated size. The figures celebrate life while making fun of what they represent.

- What statement might an artist like Botero be making when his artwork presents humorous portrayals of politicians and prominent people?

"En familia" (1983), Fernando Botero
Courtesy of the Marlborough Gallery, New York.

jbd-0788

Escuchar/Escribir

Escucha y escribe

Trabajas en una tienda de ropa y escuchas los comentarios de diferentes personas que buscan ropa. Escribe los números del 1 al 6 en una hoja de papel y escribe las frases que escuchas. Después indica con (+) o (–) si piensas que las personas van a comprar la ropa.

También se dice . . .

la camiseta = la playera (México); la polera (Chile); la remera (Argentina)

la chaqueta = la chamarra (México, Bolivia); la campera (Argentina, Chile, Paraguay, Uruguay)

los jeans = los mahones (el Caribe); las mezclillas (México); los vaqueros (Argentina, España); el pantalón vaquero (España)

el suéter = el jersey (España); la chompa (Bolivia, Ecuador, Paraguay, Perú, Uruguay)

Escribir/Hablar

En el almacén Buenprecio

Haz una lista de seis artículos de ropa que te gustaría comprar. Después, con otro(a) estudiante, mira el directorio del almacén Buenprecio y decide dónde puedes encontrar *(find)* la ropa en tu lista.

Modelo

A —*¿Dónde están las botas?*
B —*Están en la planta baja.*

Bienvenidos al almacén Buenprecio	
3	**Ropa para mujer. Vestidos. Faldas y blusas. Abrigos. Futura mamá.**
2	**Ropa para hombre. Pantalones. Camisas. Trajes. Chaquetas.**
1	**Ropa deportiva. Camisetas. Gorras. Sudaderas. Zapatos de tenis.**
PB	**Zapatos. Botas. Calcetines.**
S	**Café. Discos. Libros. Videos.**

Hablar

¿En qué puedo servirle?

Tú vas de compras y hablas con un(a) dependiente(a). Con otro(a) estudiante, pregunta y contesta según el modelo. Escoge *(choose)* cinco artículos de ropa.

Modelo

A —*¿En qué puedo servirle, señor (señorita)?*
B —*Me gustaría comprar una camisa nueva.*
A —*¿De qué color?*
B —*Estoy buscando una camisa blanca.*

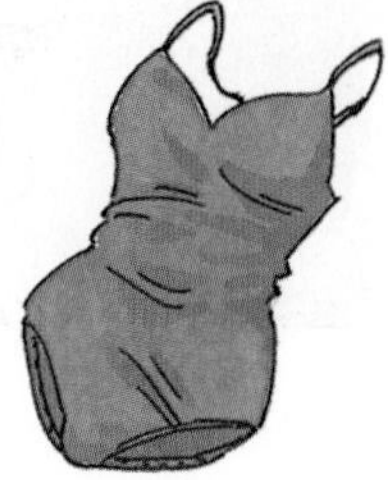

Escribir/Hablar

Juego

1. Escribe una descripción de la ropa de una persona en tu clase. Incluye dos o más cosas que lleva y los colores de la ropa.

2. Juega con otro(a) estudiante. Lee tu descripción. Tu compañero(a) tiene que identificar a la persona que describes. Antes de decir *(Before saying)* su nombre, él o ella tiene que hacer tres preguntas para saber más cosas. Por ejemplo: *¿Lleva una sudadera azul? ¿Tiene zapatos negros? ¿Sus calcetines son blancos? ¿Es Mateo?*

Fondo cultural

El dinero The currencies of Bolivia, Peru, and Costa Rica are all different. Just as the United States has the dollar, Spanish-speaking countries have their own national currencies.* In Bolivia, the official currency is the *boliviano*; in Peru it's the *nuevo sol*, and in Costa Rica, people use the *colón*. The images on the printed money honor each country's history and culture.

- How do the images that appear on bills and coins in Spanish-speaking countries compare to those in the United States?

*Puerto Rico and Ecuador use the United States dollar.

jbd-0788

Escuchar/Escribir

¿Cuánto cuesta en Montevideo?

Estás comprando ropa en Montevideo, Uruguay. Escucha los precios en pesos uruguayos. Escribe en tu hoja de papel el precio que escuchas.

1. la camiseta
2. el suéter
3. la blusa
4. el vestido
5. el traje de baño
6. la chaqueta

Modelo

los zapatos
Escuchas: *Los zapatos cuestan mil ochocientos veinte pesos.*
Escribes: *1.820 pesos*

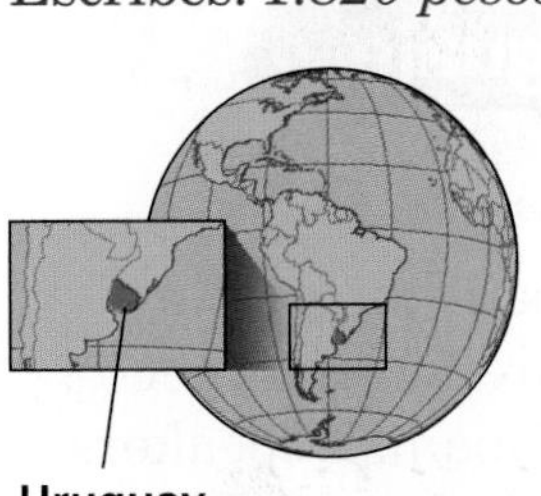

Hablar

¿Cuánto cuesta esa ropa?

Tú y tu amigo(a) van de compras. Con otro(a) estudiante, pregunta y contesta cuánto cuesta esta ropa. Los precios están en nuevos pesos uruguayos (UYU).

195 pesos

Modelo

A —*¿Cuánto cuestan los calcetines?*
B —*Cuestan cuatrocientos pesos.*

1.  800 pesos

2.  775 pesos

3.  950 pesos

4.  2100 pesos

5.  700 pesos

6.  625 pesos

Pensar/Leer/Hablar

En la tienda

Con otro(a) estudiante lee la conversación entre un(a) dependiente(a) y un(a) joven. Empareja *(Match)* lo que dice el(la) dependiente(a) con lo que contesta el(la) joven.

el(la) dependiente(a)

1. Buenas tardes. ¿En qué puedo servirle?
2. ¿Qué color prefiere Ud.?
3. Pues, estos pantalones son muy populares.
4. Sólo 50 dólares.
5. Pues, hay otros pantalones que no cuestan tanto.
6. Creo que te quedan muy bien.

el(la) joven

a. Perdón... ese precio es demasiado para mí.
b. Entonces voy a comprar estos pantalones.
c. Quiero comprar unos pantalones nuevos.
d. Son bonitos. A ver si me quedan bien.
e. No sé—quizás negro.
f. Me gustan. ¿Cuánto cuestan?

Exploración del lenguaje

Nonverbal language

You've already learned about the gesture *¡Ojo!*, which means "be careful." Another common gesture used by Spanish speakers conveys the meaning "a lot of money." This gesture is made by holding the hand palm-up and rubbing the fingertips together. It is often accompanied by expressions such as *¡Cuesta muchísimo!* or *Es mucho dinero.* It can even be used when you're describing someone who is rich.

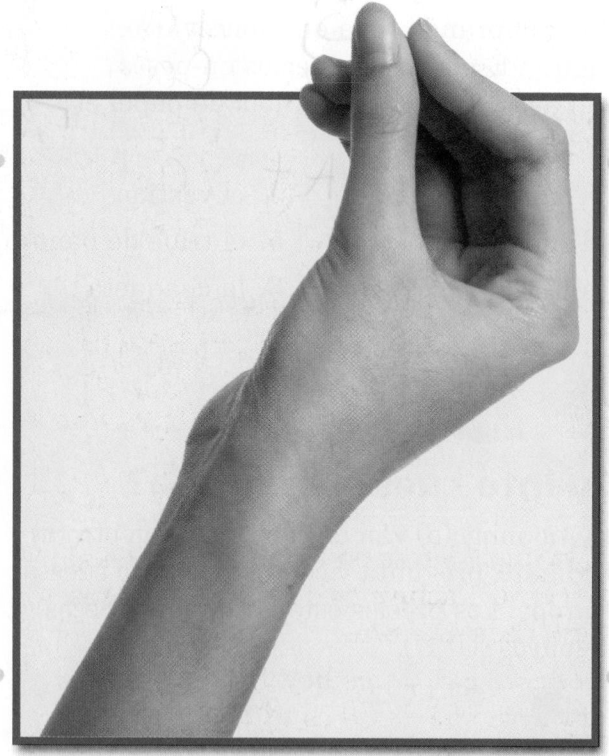

Hablar

¿Cómo me queda?

Estás en una tienda de ropa. Te pruebas *(You're trying on)* la ropa y necesitas la opinión honesta de tu amigo(a). Tu amigo(a) siempre te hace *(gives you)* comentarios. Escoge dos artículos de ropa.

Nota

Me/te queda(n) follows the same pattern as *me/te gusta(n).*

- La camisa **me** queda bien pero los jeans **me** qued**an** mal.

Modelo

A —*¿Me queda bien el traje? ¿Qué piensas?*
B —*Te queda bien. ¡Qué guapo estás!*

Estudiante A

Estudiante B

Te queda(n) bien/mal.
Es/son muy/bastante/ demasiado...
¡Qué guapo/bonita estás!
(No) me gusta(n) mucho.

Escribir/Hablar

Y tú, ¿qué dices?

1. ¿Qué ropa llevas en el verano? ¿Y en el invierno? Incluye tres artículos de ropa para cada estación.
2. Describe qué llevas hoy. ¿Cuál de los artículos que llevas es tu favorito?
3. Describe qué llevas cuando estás en casa. ¿Cómo es diferente de la ropa que llevas a clases?
4. ¿Quién compra ropa, tú o tus padres? ¿Dónde te gusta ir de compras?
5. ¿Cuáles son tres artículos de ropa que te gustaría comprar? ¿Cuánto cuesta cada uno? ¿Cuál es el total?
6. Describe alguna ropa nueva que tienes.

Gramática

Stem-changing verbs: *pensar, querer, preferir*

Verbs like *pensar* ("to think," "to plan"), *querer* ("to want"), and *preferir* ("to prefer") are *e→ie* stem-changing verbs. The *-e-* of the stem changes to *-ie-* in all forms except *nosotros* and *vosotros*. Here are the forms:

(yo)	**pienso** **quiero** **prefiero**	(nosotros) (nosotras)	**pensamos** **queremos** **preferimos**
(tú)	**piensas** **quieres** **prefieres**	(vosotros) (vosotras)	**pensáis** **queréis** **preferís**
Ud. (él) (ella)	**piensa** **quiere** **prefiere**	Uds. (ellos) (ellas)	**piensan** **quieren** **prefieren**

- Use the infinitive for any verb that follows pensar, querer, or preferir.

¿Piensas comprar esa blusa?
Do you plan to buy *that blouse?*

¿Recuerdas?

You have used *quiero/quieres* and *prefiero/prefieres* to say what you want or prefer.

GramActiva VIDEO

Want more help with stem-changing verbs? Watch the **GramActiva** video.

Escribir

Ropa para el fin de semana

Tú y tus amigos piensan comprar ropa para las cosas que quieren hacer este fin de semana. En una hoja de papel, escribe frases para decir qué quieren hacer y qué ropa piensan comprar.

Modelo

Mi amigo Manuel quiere ir a una fiesta y piensa comprar una camisa y unos pantalones.

1. Yo
2. Mi amigo
3. Mi amiga
4. Mis amigos
5. Mis amigos y yo

querer ir a

- un partido de béisbol
- la playa
- las montañas
- un restaurante elegante
- un baile en la escuela
- la biblioteca
- **¡Respuesta personal!**

pensar + comprar

- un traje
- unos pantalones
- una camisa
- una falda
- una camiseta
- un traje de baño
- unas botas
- una sudadera
- un vestido
- un suéter
- **¡Respuesta personal!**

jbd-0788

Escuchar/Escribir

¿Qué piensan llevar?

1. En una hoja de papel, escribe los números del 1 al 6. Escucha lo que quieren o piensan hacer diferentes personas y escribe las frases.

2. Escribe otra frase para decir qué piensan llevar las personas para sus actividades.

Modelo

Mis primas quieren ir a un baile el viernes. Piensan llevar una falda y una blusa.

Escribir

¿Qué prefieren comprar?

Después de dos semanas de trabajo, todos los jóvenes tienen dinero y quieren ir de compras. Escribe frases para decir qué prefieren comprar y cuándo piensan ir de compras.

Catalina/el sábado

Modelo

Catalina quiere ir de compras. Prefiere comprar unos pantalones cortos. Piensa ir a la tienda de ropa el sábado.

1. Isidoro y Lorenzo/esta tarde

2. Julia y yo/mañana

3. Javier/este fin de semana

4. yo/¿ ?

Hablar

¿Qué piensas hacer?

Habla con otro(a) estudiante sobre qué piensas hacer tú y qué piensan hacer otras personas.

Modelo

tu amigo(a)/después de las clases

A —*¿Qué piensa hacer tu amigo después de las clases?*

B —*Mi amigo David piensa montar en monopatín.*

Estudiante A

1. tus amigos(as)/mañana
2. tu familia/este fin de semana
3. tus amigos y tú/esta tarde
4. tú / el domingo
5. tu amigo(a)/esta noche

Estudiante B

¡Respuesta personal!

Escribir/Hablar

¿Adónde quieren ir?

1 Copia la gráfica en una hoja de papel y escribe los nombres de tres personas con quienes vas a salir. ¿Adónde quieren ir Uds. y qué piensan hacer?

¿Con quién?	¿Adónde?	¿Qué?
Pepe	al gimnasio	levantar pesas

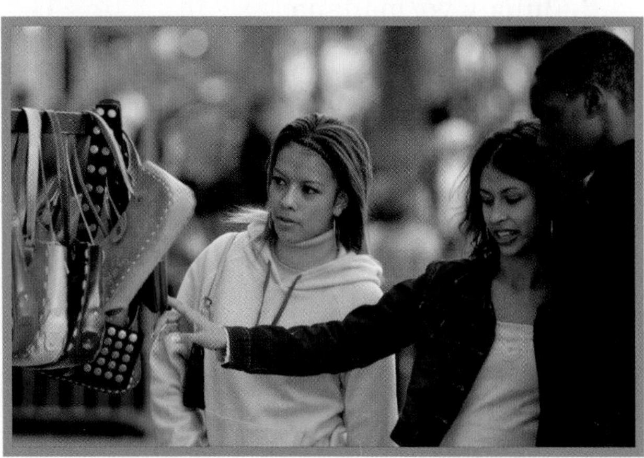

Pensamos comprar algo en el mercado.

2 Dile *(Tell)* a otro(a) estudiante adónde quieren ir tú y la otra persona. Tu compañero(a) va a adivinar *(guess)* qué piensan hacer Uds. Puede continuar adivinando hasta *(until)* decir la actividad correcta.

Modelo

A —*Pepe y yo queremos ir al gimnasio.*

B —*¿Uds. piensan jugar al básquetbol?*

A —*No, no pensamos jugar al básquetbol.*

B —*¿Uds. piensan levantar pesas?*

A —*Sí, tienes razón. Pensamos levantar pesas.*

Hablar

¿Qué prefieres llevar cuando . . . ?

Invita a un(a) compañero(a) a hacer estas actividades, y habla de la ropa que prefieren llevar.

1. la piscina
2. el parque
3. el gimnasio
4. un partido de fútbol
5. una fiesta
6. un concierto de rock

Modelo

A —*¿Quieres ir al cine conmigo?*
B —*Sí, quiero ir. ¿Qué piensas llevar?*
A —*Generalmente cuando voy al cine prefiero llevar unos jeans y una camiseta.*
B —*Bueno, yo pienso llevar una camiseta también, pero pienso llevar pantalones negros.*

Pronunciación

The letter *z*

jbd-0788 

In most Spanish-speaking countries, the letter *z* sounds like the *s* in *see*. Listen to and say these words:

zapato	arroz	almuerzo	cabeza
izquierda	haz	razón	nariz
	azul	quizás	

In many parts of Spain, however, the letter *z* is pronounced something like the *th* in *think*. Listen again to the words as a Spaniard says them. Then practice saying the words as if you were in Spain.

Try it out! Listen to *"En la puerta del cielo"* ("At Heaven's Gate"), a traditional poem from Puerto Rico. Then say the poem aloud.

En la puerta del cielo,
venden zapatos
para los angelitos
que andan descalzos.

Escribir/Hablar

Y tú, ¿qué dices?

1. ¿Qué piensas hacer después de clases hoy? ¿Qué ropa piensas llevar?
2. ¿Qué ropa piensas llevar a clase mañana?
3. ¿Dónde prefieres comprar ropa elegante? ¿Ropa deportiva?
4. ¿Con quién prefieres ir de compras? ¿Por qué?
5. ¿Quieres comprar ropa nueva? ¿Por qué sí o por qué no? ¿Cuándo piensas ir de compras?

Más práctica

- Practice Workbook, p. 41: 7A-5
- WAV Wbk.: Writing, p. 50
- Guided Practice: Grammar Acts., pp. 223–224
- *Real.* para hispanohablantes, pp. 254–257

For: *e* → *ie* Verbs
Web Code: jbd-0704

Gramática

Demonstrative adjectives

You use demonstrative adjectives to point out nouns: ***this*** *cap,* ***these*** *socks,* ***that*** *shirt,* ***those*** *shoes.* Notice that "this" and "these" refer to things that are close to you, while "that" and "those" refer to things that are at some distance from you.

Here are the corresponding demonstrative adjectives in Spanish. Like other adjectives, demonstrative adjectives agree in gender and number with the nouns that follow them.

	"this," "these"	*"that," "those"*
SINGULAR	**este** suéter **esta** falda	**ese** vestido **esa** chaqueta
PLURAL	**estos** suéteres **estas** faldas	**esos** vestidos **esas** chaquetas

Strategy

Using rhymes to remember meaning
To remember the difference between these demonstrative adjectives that are spelled very similarly, memorize this rhyme:

"This" and "these" both have *t's*,
"That" and "those" don't.

GramActiva VIDEO

Want more help with demonstrative adjectives? Watch the **GramActiva** video.

Actividad 24 **Leer/Escribir**

En la tienda de ropa

Carmen y su amiga están en una tienda y hablan de la ropa que se están probando *(trying on)*. Escribe la forma correcta de *este(a)* o *estos(as)* para cada número.

Carmen: __1.__ botas son bonitas, ¿no?

Mariel: Sí, pero creo que __2.__ zapatos son bastante feos.

Carmen: ¿Qué piensas de __3.__ blusa? A mí me gusta mucho.

Mariel: A mí también. __4.__ jeans son demasiado cortos, ¿no?

Carmen: Tienes razón. Y pienso que __5.__ falda es muy corta también.

Mariel: Quizás. __6.__ suéter no cuesta mucho. ¡Qué bueno!

Hablar

¡Un día con tu hermanito!

Tienes que cuidar *(to take care of)* a tu hermanito. Tus padres tienen toda la ropa para él encima de la cama, pero ¡tu hermanito tiene sus propias ideas!

Modelo

A (tú) —*Tienes que llevar esta ropa.*
B (tu hermanito) —*¡No! No quiero llevar esa ropa. Prefiero esta ropa que está en el armario.*

Escribir/Hablar

Juego

¿Quién en tu clase sabe mejor cuánto cuestan diferentes cosas?

1. Trabaja con otro(a) estudiante. Escojan un objeto o una foto de un objeto. Puede ser ropa, algo de la casa, algo de la escuela, o de otro lugar. Escriban una descripción de ese objeto y determinen cuánto cuesta.

Modelo

Este suéter azul y amarillo es. . . . Puedes llevar este suéter a. . . . Puedes comprar este suéter en. . . . ¿Cuánto cuesta este suéter? (Cuesta 55 dólares.)

2. Ahora, trabajen con un grupo de cuatro parejas (ocho estudiantes). Lean la descripción de su objeto sin decir cuánto cuesta. La pareja que da el precio más aproximado *(closest)* sin exceder *(without exceeding)* el precio, gana.

Modelo

—Pensamos que el suéter cuesta 50 dólares.
—Daniel y Eva, Uds. ganan. El suéter cuesta 55 dólares.

Leer/Hablar

¡Muchos regalos!

Muchas personas en tu familia y unos amigos tienen cumpleaños este mes y tienes que comprar regalos. Tú y un(a) compañero(a) miran este anuncio para una tienda de ropa. Habla con tu compañero(a) sobre qué necesitas comprar.

Modelo

tu tía o tío

A —*Necesito un regalo para mi tía. Voy a buscar un suéter para ella.*

B —*Buena idea. ¿Te gusta este suéter rosado? Sólo cuesta 32 dólares.*

A —*Sí. Vamos a la tienda a buscar este suéter.*

1. tu hermano o amigo
2. tu hermana o amiga
3. tu abuelo o abuela
4. tu mamá o papá

La tienda de ropa Perfección

¡Sólo 1 día!

$35 orig. $50

$25 orig. $38

$18 orig. $30

$19 orig. $28

$11 orig. $18

$32 orig. $45

$16 orig. $24

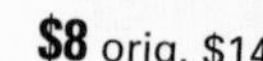

$8 orig. $14

Pensar/Hablar

Los descuentos

Conexiones
Las matemáticas

Estás ahora en la tienda de ropa Perfección de la Actividad 27.

1. Calcula el porcentaje de descuento de la ropa en el anuncio. La fórmula para calcular el porcentaje de descuento es:

   el precio original – el precio nuevo = la diferencia
   la diferencia ÷ el precio original = la respuesta
   la respuesta x 100 = el porcentaje de descuento

2. Habla con otro(a) estudiante de los descuentos que hay en la tienda. Una persona hace el papel *(plays the role)* de cliente, y la otra, un(a) dependiente(a). Pregunta y contesta según el modelo.

Modelo

A —*Perdón, señor (señorita). ¿Cuánto cuesta ese suéter rosado?*

B —*Hoy este suéter cuesta sólo 32 dólares. Es un descuento del 29 por ciento.*

A —*¡Genial! Quiero comprar el suéter. ¡Qué buen precio!*

Escribir/Hablar

Un desfile de modas

Trabaja con un grupo de tres. Una persona de los tres va a ser el/la modelo en un desfile de modas *(fashion show)*. Decidan qué va a llevar el/la modelo. En una hoja de papel, describan tres o más cosas que lleva el/la modelo. Pueden incluir los colores, cuánto cuesta, dónde pueden comprar la ropa y en qué ocasión o estación pueden llevar la ropa.

Su modelo va a participar con los/las otros(as) modelos de la clase en el desfile de modas. Los otros dos leen su descripción de la ropa.

Modelo

El (La) modelo que entra en este momento lleva . . .

Para decir más . . .

cómodo(a) comfortable
elegante elegant
de algodón cotton
de lana wool
de seda silk

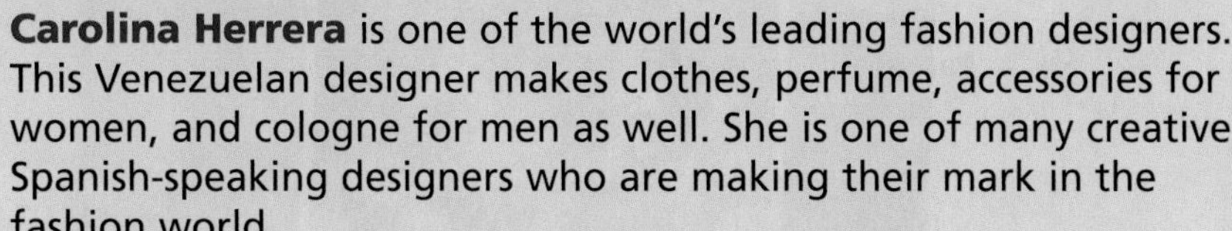

Carolina Herrera is one of the world's leading fashion designers. This Venezuelan designer makes clothes, perfume, accessories for women, and cologne for men as well. She is one of many creative Spanish-speaking designers who are making their mark in the fashion world.

- Think of the names of some fashion designers from the United States. In what ways do you think they influence everyday culture?

BOUTIQUE GUADALAJARA

Vestidos y accesorios para toda ocasión

Ropa sport y vaquera; sombreros, botas

- *Invitaciones y regalos*
- *Discos y casetes*
- *Libros y revistas*
- *Envío de dinero y tarjetas telefónicas*

1819 First Street Sonora, Arizona

El español en la comunidad

Locate a store in your community or on the Internet that sells products from Spanish-speaking countries. Visit the store or Web site and list the types of items you find there. Are they similar to the items listed in the ad? Bring your list to class and compare it with other students' lists. What are the most common types of items found in these stores?

Más práctica

- Practice Workbook, pp. 42–43: 7A-6, 7A-7
- WAV Wbk.: Writing, p. 51
- Guided Practice: Grammar, pp. 225–226
- *Real.* para hispanohablantes, pp. 258–261

¡Adelante!

Lectura

Objectives

- **Read about traditional clothing of Panama**
- **Learn what a *mola* is, and make one**
- **Create and perform a skit about buying an article of clothing**
- **Watch *¿Eres tú, María?*, Episodio 5**

Strategy

Predicting
Look at the maps and photos on these pages and read the title to predict what the reading will be about. This will help you anticipate the types of words and expressions you will encounter as you read.

Tradiciones de la ropa panameña

Mar Caribe
ISLAS DE SAN BLAS
COSTA RICA
Canal de Panamá
Ciudad de Panamá
Golfo de Panamá
PANAMÁ
Las Tablas
LOS SANTOS
OCÉANO PACÍFICO
COLOMBIA
Panama

Una tradición panameña de mucho orgullo[1] es llevar el vestido típico de las mujeres, "la pollera." Hay dos tipos de pollera, la pollera montuna[2] y la pollera de gala, que se lleva en los festivales. La pollera de gala se hace a mano y cuesta muchísimo por la cantidad de joyas[3] que adornan el vestido. ¿Cuánto cuesta una pollera de gala? Puede costar unos 1.850 dólares americanos, y requiere aproximadamente siete meses de trabajo. La pollera es tan importante que en la ciudad de Las Tablas celebran el Día Nacional de La Pollera el 22 de julio.

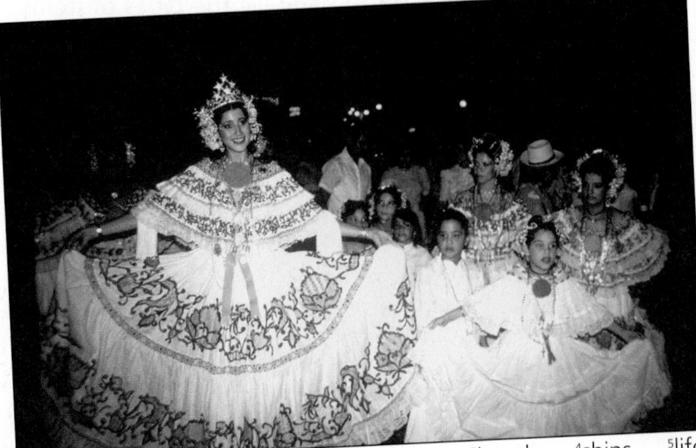

[1]pride [2]from the mountains [3]jewels [4]ships [5]life

Si quieres celebrar con los panameños, puedes visitar la ciudad de Las Tablas en la provincia de Los Santos. Las Tablas es famosa por ser el mejor lugar para celebrar los carnavales. Durante el carnaval y en otros festivales, puedes admirar los vestidos y los bailes tradicionales.

El Canal de Panamá conecta el océano Pacífico con el mar Caribe y el océano Atlántico.

El istmo de Panamá es la conexión entre dos continentes, y tiene costas sobre el océano Pacífico y el mar Caribe. Es famoso por el canal en el que navegan barcos[4] de todo el mundo. El folklore panameño es muy variado. La música, los bailes y los vestidos son importantes en la vida[5] social, especialmente en las provincias del centro del país.

Molas de colores brillantes con formas de animales

Otro tipo de ropa auténtica de Panamá viene de los indios Kuna, un grupo de indígenas que viven en las islas de San Blas. Las mujeres llevan una blusa hecha[6] de molas. Las molas son paneles decorativos que forman la parte de adelante y de atrás de las blusas.

Las mujeres demuestran[7] su talento y expresión personal con los diseños[8] originales de las molas. Los diseños representan formas humanas y animales. Hoy día, puedes ver y admirar molas como objetos de arte en muchos museos y colecciones.

[6]made [7]demonstrate [8]designs

Fondo cultural

Carnaval is a traditional celebration in many Latin American countries. It takes place in the weeks before the season of Lent. *Carnaval* normally includes the coronation of a beauty queen, parades, elaborate costumes, street music, and dancing. The *Carnaval* in Las Tablas, a town near the Pacific coast in Panama, is very popular and attracts thousands of visitors every year.

- What traditional parades or celebrations take place in your community? How do they compare to the celebration of *Carnaval*?

Una banda toca música durante el Carnaval.

¿Comprendes?

1. ¿Por qué es importante el Panamá en el comercio global?
2. ¿Cuáles son las dos formas de ropa auténtica de Panamá en el artículo?
3. ¿Qué puedes celebrar si visitas Las Tablas?
4. ¿Cuánto puede costar una pollera de gala? En tu opinión, ¿es mucho o poco dinero?
5. ¿Cómo se llama el grupo de indígenas que viven en las islas de San Blas?
6. ¿Quiénes llevan las molas, los hombres o las mujeres?
7. ¿Por qué es diferente cada mola?

Más práctica

- **WAV Wbk.: Writing, p. 52**
- **Guided Practice: *Lectura*, p. 227**
- ***Real.* para hispanohablantes, pp. 262–263**

For: Internet Activity
Web Code: jbd-0705

La cultura en vivo

Las molas

Molas are the bright fabric artwork created by the Kuna Indians of the San Blas Islands, a group of islands off the Panama coast in the Caribbean Sea. *Mola* is a Kuna word meaning "blouse." This art form was originally used to make clothing, but today the term *mola* refers to any piece of fabric made using this method.

Kuna women cut out a cloth pattern and sew it onto layers of cloth that have been sewn together. Pieces of the upper layers are cut away to expose the underlying colors and create a design. Later, the women embroider details. Many designs on *molas* represent nature or animals. Each *mola* may take many weeks to complete.

Try it out! Here's how you can make *molas* out of paper.

Figure 1

Materials:

- 2 pencils
- rubber bands
- construction paper
- paste or glue
- scissors

Figure 2

Directions:

Figure 3

1 Your teacher will provide a pattern to trace on a piece of construction paper. You may prefer to trace around a cookie cutter or draw a simple design found in nature (for example, a leaf, flower, or fir tree). *(Fig. 1)*

2 Double all the lines by drawing with two pencils fastened together with rubber bands. *(Fig. 2)*

3 Cut out all spaces that do NOT fall between the double lines. *(Fig. 3)*

4 Paste the cutout figure onto construction paper of a contrasting color.

5 Cut around the pasted figure, leaving a border of the second color. *(Fig. 4)*

6 Paste this cutout figure onto another piece of construction paper and cut around it, leaving a border of the new color. Paste the entire piece on a contrasting background.

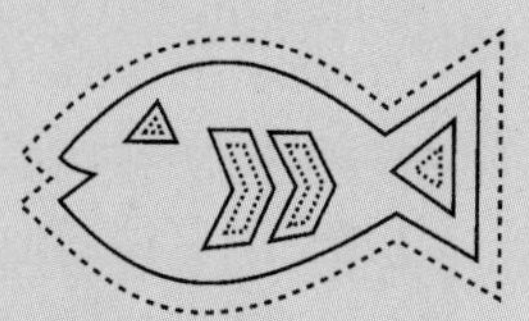

Figure 4

Think about it! Do you or anyone in your family practice a traditional handicraft? Do you have any clothes or outfits that you have made or customized to express your interests or personality?

Presentación oral

¿En qué puedo servirle?

Task

You and a partner will play the roles of a customer and a sales clerk in a clothing store. You will ask and answer questions about the articles of clothing sold in the store. The customer will then decide whether or not to buy the articles.

1. **Prepare** Work with a partner to prepare the skit. One of you will play the role of the salesperson, and the other will be the shopper. Be prepared to play both roles. Decide the type of clothing the store will sell and bring to class real articles of clothing or pictures from a magazine. Give the store a name.

   Cliente: Make a list of expressions and questions you can use to ask about, describe, and say whether you will buy an article of clothing.

   Dependiente(a): Make a list of expressions and questions you can use to help your client, answer his or her questions, and show him or her the clothing.

Seeking feedback
As you practice with a partner, seek his or her feedback to correct errors you have made and to improve your overall performance.

2. **Practice** Work with your partner and practice both roles. You might want to review *A primera vista,* the *Videohistoria,* and Actividad 14 for ideas. You can use your written notes when you practice, but not during the actual role-play.

3. **Present** Your teacher will assign the roles. The clerk will begin the conversation. Keep talking until the customer has made a decision to buy or not to buy the article of clothing.

4. **Evaluation** Your teacher may give you a rubric for how the presentation will be graded. You probably will be graded on:
   - how well you sustain a conversation
   - how complete your preparation is
   - how well you use new and previously learned vocabulary

Videomisterio

¿Eres tú, María? Episodio 5

Antes de ver el video

Personajes importantes

Rosalinda, una amiga de Carmela quien trabaja en el hospital San Carlos

Resumen del episodio

Lola y Carmela van al hospital para hablar con Rosalinda sobre doña Gracia y María. Aprenden más sobre el accidente de coche de María. Ocurrió entre María y otra joven, Julia. Las dos fueron llevadas[1] al Hospital San Carlos. Desafortunadamente,[2] Julia murió. Rosalinda va a los archivos para buscar los historiales clínicos de Julia y María. Pero hay un problema.

[1] were brought [2] unfortunately

Palabras para comprender

Estuvo aquí...	She was here...
¿Te acuerdas de ella?	Do you remember her?
Sí, me acuerdo de María.	Yes, I remember María.
Dos coches chocaron...	Two cars crashed...
la carretera	highway
murió	died
Las ayudó a las dos.	He helped the two of them.
No viene a trabajar.	He hasn't been coming to work.
el archivo	records
los historiales clínicos	medical records
los visitantes	visitors

"Primero, quiero hablar de una paciente que se llama María Requena. Estuvo aquí, en el hospital".

"Pues, no está su historial clínico. Ni un papel. Nada, absolutamente nada sobre María Requena".

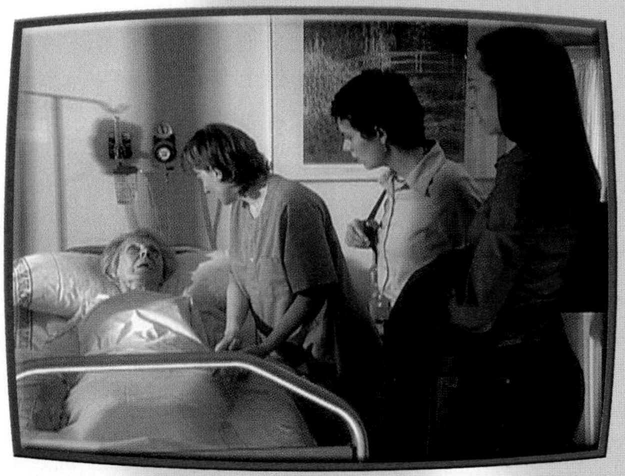

"¿Eres tú, María?".

Después de ver el video

¿Comprendes?

Lee las frases. Decide a quién(es) describe cada frase: Lola, Rosalinda, Carmela, doña Gracia, Julia, María o Luis Antonio.

1. Dos coches y dos chicas. Fue muy triste.
2. Ella murió en el accidente.
3. Hay un enfermero que ayudó a las dos.
4. Es muy simpática tu amiga.
5. No hay nada sobre ellas en los archivos.
6. Está bastante mal.
7. Las amigas de Carmela son amigas mías.

Nota gramatical Rosalinda uses two *vosotros* commands when she is talking with Carmela and Lola: *esperad* ("wait") and *venid* ("come"). You will hear this verb form often when you go to Spain.

For: More on *¿Eres tú, María?*
Web Code: jbd-0507

Chapter Review

Repaso del capítulo

To prepare for the test, check to see if you...

- know the new vocabulary and grammar
- can perform the tasks on p. 183

Vocabulario y gramática

jbd-0789 

to talk about shopping

buscar	to look for
comprar	to buy
el dependiente, la dependienta	salesperson
¿En qué puedo servirle?	How can I help you?
entrar	to enter
la tienda	store
la tienda de ropa	clothing store

to talk about clothing

el abrigo	coat
la blusa	blouse
las botas	boots
los calcetines	socks
la camisa	shirt
la camiseta	T-shirt
la chaqueta	jacket
la falda	skirt
la gorra	cap
los jeans	jeans
los pantalones	pants
los pantalones cortos	shorts
la sudadera	sweatshirt
el suéter	sweater
el traje	suit
el traje de baño	swimsuit
el vestido	dress
los zapatos	shoes
¿Cómo me/te queda(n)?	How does it (do they) fit (me/you)?
Me/Te queda(n) bien/mal.	It fits (They fit) me/you well/poorly.
llevar	to wear
nuevo, -a	new

other useful words

quizás	maybe
Perdón.	Excuse me.
¡Vamos!	Let's go!

to talk about prices

¿Cuánto cuesta(n)...?	How much does (do)... cost?
costar *(o → ue)*	to cost
el precio	price
tanto	so much
doscientos, -as	two hundred
trescientos, -as	three hundred
cuatrocientos, -as	four hundred
quinientos, -as	five hundred
seiscientos, -as	six hundred
setecientos, -as	seven hundred
ochocientos, -as	eight hundred
novecientos, -as	nine hundred
mil	a thousand

to indicate if someone is correct

tener razón	to be correct

to indicate specific items

los/las dos	both
este, esta	this
estos, estas	these
ese, esa	that
esos, esas	those

pensar *to think, to plan*

pienso	**pensamos**
piensas	**pensáis**
piensa	**piensan**

preferir *to prefer*

prefiero	**preferimos**
prefieres	**preferís**
prefiere	**prefieren**

querer *to want*

quiero	**queremos**
quieres	**queréis**
quiere	**quieren**

For *Vocabulario adicional,* see pp. 336–337.

Más práctica

- Practice Workbook: Puzzle, p. 44
- Practice Workbook: Organizer, p. 45

Go Online PHSchool.com
For: Test Preparation
Web Code: jbd-0706

Preparación para el examen

On the exam you will be asked to . . .	Here are practice tasks similar to those you will find on the exam . . .	If you need review . . .
jbd-0789  **1 Escuchar** Listen and understand why people are returning clothing items	Listen as people explain to the clerk in a department store why they are returning or exchanging clothing they received as gifts. Try to decide if the reason is: a) it doesn't fit well; b) it's the wrong color or style; c) it's too expensive; d) they just didn't like it.	**pp. 156–161** *A primera vista* **p. 163** Actividad 8 **p. 165** Actividad 12 **p. 167** Actividad 15 **p. 172** Actividad 24
 **2 Hablar** Describe what you are planning to buy with gift certificates from your favorite clothing store	You got gift certificates from your favorite clothing store for your birthday. Describe at least four items you would like to buy. You could say something like: *Me gustaría comprar un suéter rojo. Prefiero esos suéteres que me quedan grandes.*	**pp. 156–161** *A primera vista* **p. 164** Actividad 10 **p. 166** Actividad 14 **p. 169** Actividades 18–19 **p. 174** Actividad 27 **p. 179** *Presentación oral*
 **3 Leer** Read and understand an online order form for a popular department store	You want to apply for a job at a department store. They need someone who understands Spanish to interpret the online orders that come in. Read the entries to see if you can tell them: a) the description of the item ordered; b) the color; c) the price.	**pp. 156–161** *A primera vista* **p. 165** Actividad 12 **p. 174** Actividad 27

Artículo	Color	Precio
sudadera	rojo/azul	355 pesos
abrigo	negro	801 pesos
falda	blanco/marrón/verde	506 pesos

On the exam you will be asked to . . .	Here are practice tasks similar to those you will find on the exam . . .	If you need review . . .
 **4 Escribir** Fill in an order form for specific clothing items you might purchase as gifts	Order the following items using the online order form: a) black boots for your sister, who is very little; b) a blue-and-white baseball cap for your brother, who would need a small size; c) three pairs of gray socks for your dad, who has VERY big feet!	**pp. 156–161** *A primera vista* **p. 162** Actividades 6–7 **p. 164** Actividad 11 **p. 167** Actividad 16 **p. 169** Actividad 19

Descripción del artículo	Color	Tamaño

On the exam you will be asked to . . .	Here are practice tasks similar to those you will find on the exam . . .	If you need review . . .
5 Pensar Demonstrate an understanding of cultural perspectives and clothing	Give an example of American folk art that is handed down from generation to generation. How is it similar to or different from the *molas* made by the Kuna Indians?	**pp. 176–177** *Lectura* **p. 178** *La cultura en vivo*

Fondo cultural

Ñandutí, which means "spider web" in the Guaraní language, refers to the fine lace weavings from the South American country of Paraguay. Wall hangings and table linens are just a few of the intricately woven and multicolored items made from this fabric. *Ñandutí* looms are routinely found outside the doorways of houses in Itauguá, a small town where much of the country's *ñandutí* is made.

- Handmade items are usually more expensive than mass-produced ones. Why do you think some people are willing to pay more for these items?

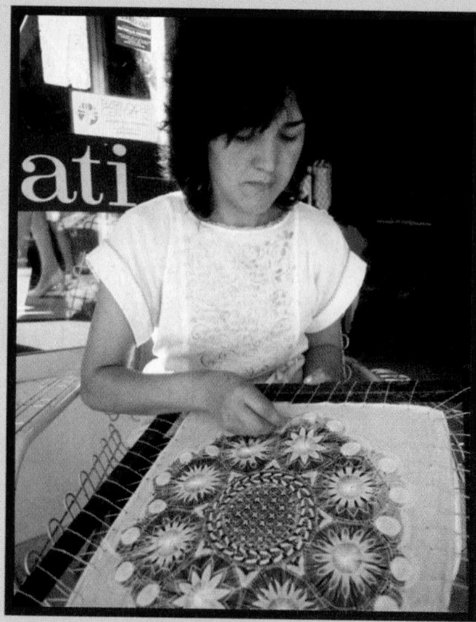

Capítulo 7B

¡Qué regalo!

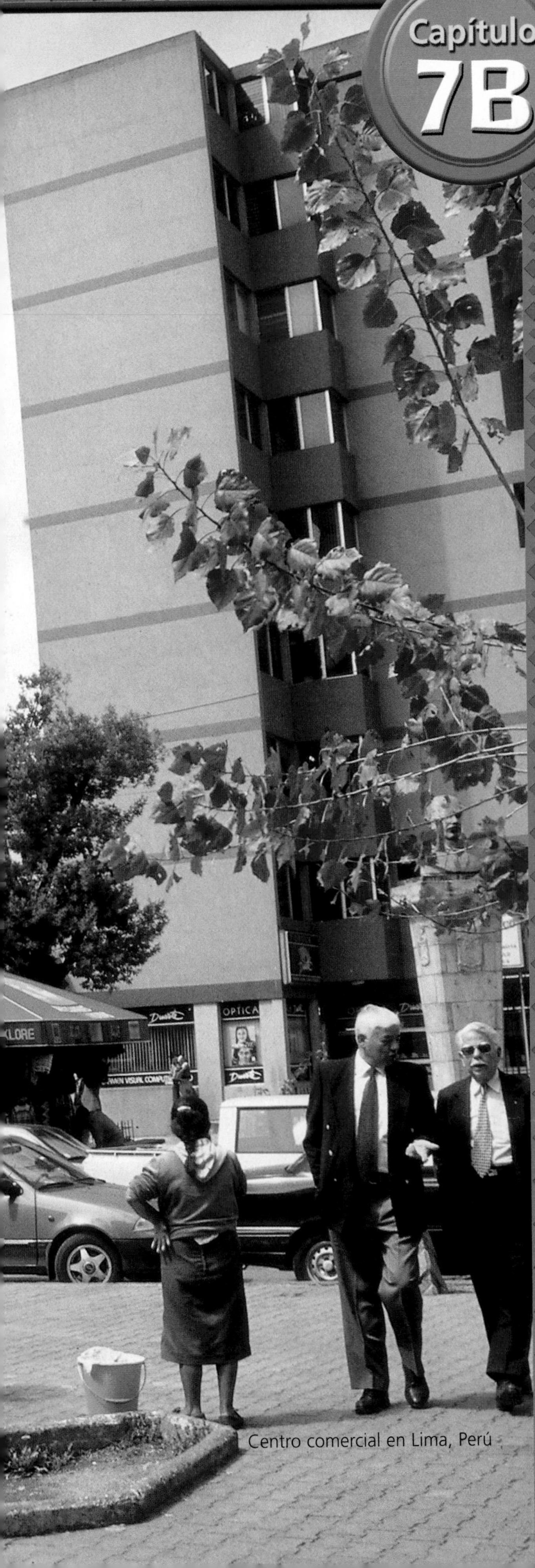

Centro comercial en Lima, Perú

Chapter Objectives

- Talk about buying gifts
- Tell what happened in the past
- Use direct object pronouns
- Understand cultural perspectives on gift-giving

Video Highlights

A primera vista: ***Un regalo especial***

GramActiva Videos: **the preterite of *-ar* verbs; the preterite of verbs ending in *-car* and *-gar*; direct object pronouns: *lo, la, los, las***

Videomisterio: ***¿Eres tú, María?*, Episodio 6**

Country Connection

As you learn about shopping and paying for gifts, you will make connections to these countries and places:

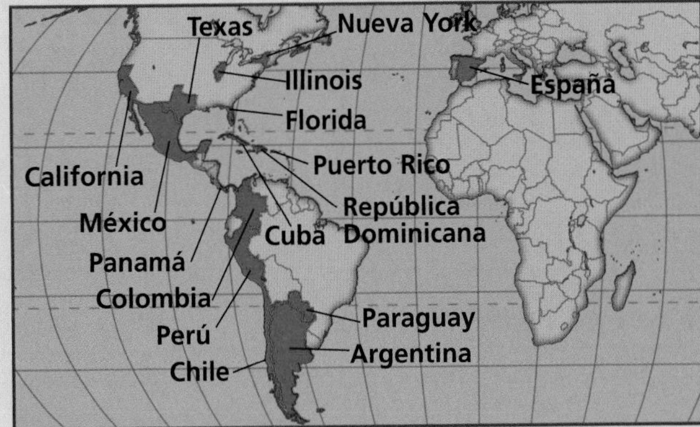

Más práctica

- ***Real.* para hispanohablantes, pp. 270–271**

Go Online PHSchool.com **For:** Online Atlas **Web Code:** jbe-0002

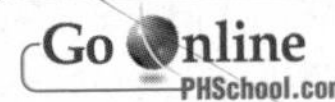

A primera vista

Vocabulario y gramática en contexto

jbd-0797

Objectives

Read, listen to, and understand information about
- stores
- shopping for gifts and accessories
- things done in the past

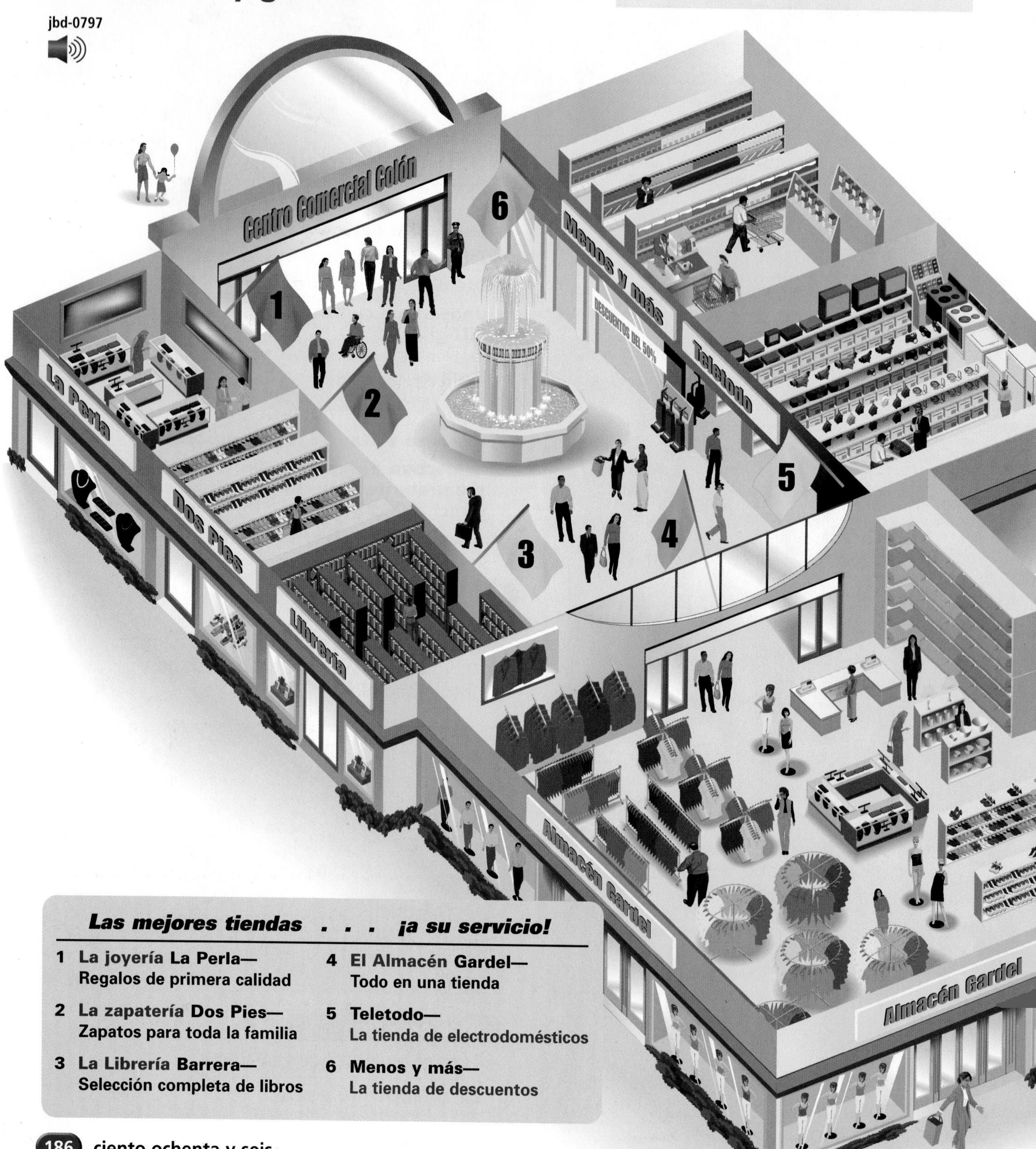

Las mejores tiendas . . . ¡a su servicio!

1 **La joyería La Perla—** Regalos de primera calidad

2 **La zapatería Dos Pies—** Zapatos para toda la familia

3 **La Librería Barrera—** Selección completa de libros

4 **El Almacén Gardel—** Todo en una tienda

5 **Teletodo—** La tienda de electrodomésticos

6 **Menos y más—** La tienda de descuentos

—**¡Mira!** Todo cuesta menos aquí. ¡Qué **barato!**

—¡No puede ser! Yo **compré** esta cartera en el Almacén Gardel **hace una semana** y **pagué** mucho más. **¡Uf!**

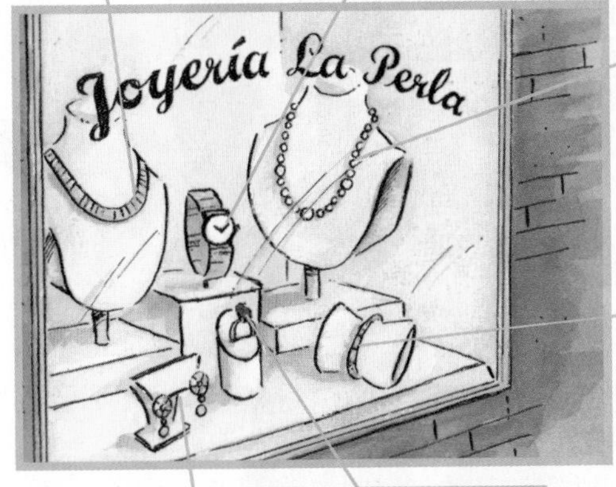

—Mi **novio** necesita un reloj pulsera.

—¿Por qué no **lo** compras? Cuesta 30 dólares. No es muy **caro.**

—¡Buena idea! Vamos a entrar.

jbd-0797

Escuchar

¿Qué vas a hacer?

Estás de compras con tu hermana en un centro comercial. Tu hermana te está diciendo todo lo que quiere hacer, o lo que necesita, en el centro comercial. Para cada cosa que dice, señala dónde en el centro comercial tiene que ir.

Actividad 2

jbd-0797

Escuchar

¿Dónde lo llevas?

Escucha cada una de estas frases. Señala la parte del cuerpo en la que una persona lleva cada artículo que se menciona.

Más práctica

- Practice Workbook, pp. 46–47: 7B-1, 7B-2
- WAV Wbk.: Writing, p. 59
- Guided Practice: Vocab. Flash Cards, pp. 229–232
- *Real.* para hispanohablantes, p. 272

For: Vocab. Practice
Web Code: jbd-0711

Videohistoria

jbd-0797 

Un regalo especial

¿Qué pasó cuando Manolo compró un regalo para su tía? Lee la historia.

Antes de leer

Using visuals Look at each picture before you read the text below it to help you understand the story.

- Look at photo 3. Can you guess what Claudia's reaction is to Manolo's suggestion to give his aunt computer software for her birthday?

1. Think about gifts that you've bought. Were they for friends or family? Of the people you know, for whom is it most difficult to buy gifts?
2. Skim the *Videohistoria* and make a list of the items that could be given as gifts. To whom would you give them? Which of those items would make a good gift for Manolo's aunt?

1 **Manolo:** Necesito comprar un regalo para mi tía. Mañana es su cumpleaños.

Claudia: ¿Qué compraste **el año pasado?**

Manolo: Compré un libro. Quizás otro libro.

Claudia: ¡Qué aburrido! Vamos al centro comercial . . .

2 **Manolo:** Aquí **venden** guantes, corbatas . . .

Claudia: ¿Corbatas para tu tía? ¿No tienes otra idea? Mira, aquí hay otras cosas . . .

3 **Manolo:** ¡Ah! Tengo una idea. **Anoche** compré un videojuego **en la Red** con mi computadora. ¿Quizás podemos comprar **software?**

Claudia: Para un amigo, sí, pero para tu tía, ¡no!

4 **Claudia:** Yo prefiero la joyería: una pulsera, un collar, un anillo. A ver. Señorita, ¿cuánto cuesta ese collar?

Dependienta: Cuesta 200 pesos con el descuento.

Claudia: ¡Qué barato! **La semana pasada** yo **pagué** 300 pesos **por** un collar.

5 *Claudia y Manolo están esperando el autobús. Tienen el regalo para la tía. A su derecha hay otra chica con un perro y otro regalo también.*

6 **Manolo:** ¡Vamos, Claudia! Aquí viene el autobús.

Claudia: Bueno . . . bueno.

7 **Manolo:** ¡Feliz cumpleaños, tía! Te compré este regalo **ayer.**

Tía: ¿Para mí? Ah, es muy bonito, pero . . . sabes que no tenemos un perro.

Manolo: ¡No entiendo . . . !

8 **Perro:** ¡Me gusta mucho este collar nuevo! Me queda bien, ¿no crees?

Leer/Pensar

¿Buena o mala idea?

Mira estos dibujos. Escribe los números del 1 al 6 en una hoja de papel. Para cada dibujo, escribe *buena idea* si según Claudia es un buen regalo para la tía de Manolo, o *mala idea* si no es un buen regalo.

1. 
2. 
3. 
4. 
5. 
6. 

Escribir

¿Qué compraron?

¿Qué compraron estas personas de la *Videohistoria?* Usa las palabras de la lista para completar sus frases. Escribe las frases completas en una hoja de papel.

Manolo: Yo compré ___, ___ y ___.

Claudia: Yo compré ___.

La chica: Yo compré ___.

un libro
un collar por 300 pesos
un collar por 200 pesos
un collar para un perro
un videojuego

Escribir/Hablar

¿Comprendes?

1. ¿Por qué van de compras Manolo y Claudia?
2. ¿Qué compró Manolo para su tía el año pasado?
3. ¿Qué piensa Claudia de comprar otro libro?
4. ¿Qúe regalo compran y cuánto pagan?
5. ¿A la tía le gusta el collar? ¿Por qué?
6. Al final *(At the end)*, ¿quién tiene el mejor collar?

Más práctica

- Practice Workbook, pp. 48–49: 7B-3, 7B-4
- WAV Wbk.: Video, pp. 53–55
- Guided Practice: Vocab. Check, pp. 233–236
- *Real.* para hispanohablantes, p. 273

For: Vocab. Practice
Web Code: jbd-0712

Manos a la obra

Vocabulario y gramática en uso

Objectives

- Talk about stores and where they are located
- Ask and tell about shopping and buying
- Talk about the past
- Learn to use the preterite of *-ar* verbs and verbs that end in *-car* and *-gar*
- Use the direct object pronouns *lo, la, los,* and *las*

jbd-0798

Escuchar/Escribir

Escucha y escribe

1. Vas a escuchar lo que unos jóvenes dicen de algunas tiendas. En una hoja de papel, escribe los números del 1 al 6. Escribe lo que escuchas.

2. Escribe frases para describir lo que crees que van a comprar los jóvenes en cada tienda.

Modelo

Creo que él (ella) va a comprar . . .

Escribir

En tu comunidad

Para cada tienda de la lista, piensa en una que está en tu comunidad. Escribe una frase para describir dos o más cosas que venden allí y explica dónde está la tienda.

Modelo

una tienda de ropa
En la tienda de ropa Ávila venden pantalones, camisas y corbatas. Está en el centro comercial Mill Valley.

1. una librería
2. una tienda de descuentos
3. una tienda de electrodomésticos
4. una joyería
5. un almacén
6. una zapatería

Fondo cultural

Centros comerciales **and** ***grandes almacenes*** are popular in Spanish-speaking countries, but many people still shop in traditional specialty stores. These stores are often owned and operated by families, and customer loyalty is built over generations.

- Why do you think small specialty stores continue to survive when large, one-stop superstores and malls are very popular? Where do you prefer to shop? Why?

Tienda en España

   **Hablar**

¿Sabes dónde ir para comprar . . . ?

Trabaja con otro(a) estudiante. Lee lo que escribiste en la Actividad 7, sin decir qué tipo de tienda es. Tu compañero(a) tiene que identificar qué tienda es.

Modelo

A —*Es una tienda que vende pantalones, camisas y corbatas. Está en el centro comercial Mill Valley.*

B —*Es una tienda de ropa. ¿Es la tienda Ávila?*

A —*Sí. Es la tienda de ropa Ávila.*

   **Dibujar/Escribir/Hablar**

¿Dónde está el almacén La Galería?

Habla con otro(a) estudiante sobre dónde están las tiendas en un centro comercial.

1. Haz un dibujo de un centro comercial. Incluye *(include)* estos lugares en tu dibujo y, para cada uno, inventa un nombre.

> una zapatería
> un almacén
> un restaurante
> una librería
> una tienda de descuentos
> una tienda de regalos
> una tienda de electrodomésticos
> una tienda de ropa
>
> **¡Respuesta personal!**

2. Muestra *(Show)* el dibujo a otro(a) estudiante. Usa las palabras en esta lista para hacer seis preguntas sobre su centro comercial. Tu compañero(a) debe contestar.

> vas/voy a . . .
> quieres/quiero . . .
> necesitas/necesito . . .
> te/me gustaría . . .
> piensas/pienso . . .
> comer . . .
> buscar . . .
> comprar . . .
> mirar . . .

¿Recuerdas?

To tell the location of something, use *está* . . . :

a la derecha de	**delante de**
a la izquierda de	**detrás de**
al lado de	**lejos de**
cerca de	

Para decir más . . .

entre between

enfrente de across from

Modelo

A —*¿Dónde está el restaurante La Mariposa?*

B —*Está detrás de la zapatería y la librería.*

A —*¿Por qué quieres ir allí?*

B —*Quiero comer con mi amigo.*

Hablar

Un buen regalo

Habla con otro(a) estudiante sobre los buenos regalos para diferentes personas.

Modelo

un señor que trabaja en una oficina

A —*¿Cuál es un buen* regalo para un señor que trabaja en una oficina?*

B —*Creo que una corbata es el mejor regalo para él.*

A —*¿Sabes dónde venden corbatas?*

B —*Por supuesto. En la tienda de ropa.*

Estudiante A

1. un(a) joven que no es puntual
2. un(a) joven que trabaja en un almacén
3. tu hermano(a) mayor (menor)
4. tu mejor amigo(a)
5. tu novio(a)
6. tu abuelo(a)

Estudiante B

¡Respuesta personal!

**Buen* is used in front of a masculine singular noun.

Leer/Escribir/Hablar

Vamos a la joyería

Lee el anuncio de una joyería en Tegucigalpa, Honduras y luego contesta las preguntas.

1. ¿Qué venden en la tienda?
2. Según el anuncio, ¿las cosas que venden en la tienda cuestan mucho o poco?
3. Además de *(In addition to)* vender, ¿qué otros servicios hay en la joyería?
4. Pregunta a dos personas diferentes: ¿Qué te gustaría comprar en una joyería? ¿Qué joyas tienes?

Strategy

Using cognates and context clues
Try to figure out the meanings of unknown words by looking for cognates or by seeing how other words are used in the sentence.

- Can you guess the meanings of *bajos, diamantes, piedras preciosas, baterías,* and *arreglos* in this ad?

JOYERÍA HERMANOS SILVA

Vendemos relojes variados y todo tipo de joyas para toda ocasión

- Anillos y collares de diamantes y otras piedras preciosas
- Baterías de reloj, incluyendo instalación
- Hacemos reparaciones y joyas nuevas de su oro* viejo
- Reparación de cadenas y arreglos de pulseras

¡Precios bajos todos los días!

MENCIONE ESTE ANUNCIO Y RECIBA UN DESCUENTO DEL 10%

Abierto lunes a sábado de 10:00 hs. a 18:00 hs.

*gold

Exploración del lenguaje

Nouns that end in *-ería*

The Spanish word ending, or suffix, *-ería* usually indicates a place where something is sold, made, or repaired. This suffix is added to a form of the word that names the specialty item. For example, if you know that *una joya* is a piece of jewelry, you understand that you can buy jewelry at *la joyería*.

Esta joyería vende pulseras, anillos y collares.

Try it out! You will often see these signs over stores. Tell what each one sells.

heladería	librería	pastelería
papelería	panadería	zapatería

Modelo

joyería
En la joyería venden joyas como anillos, pulseras y collares.

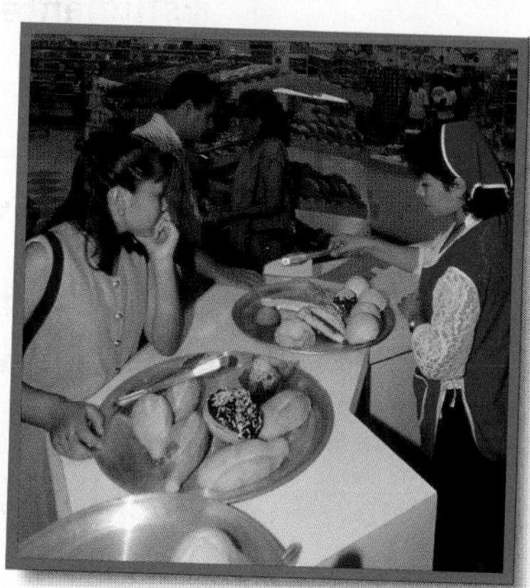

Muchos españoles compran pasteles en una pastelería.

Venden flores para todas las ocasiones en esta florería en Argentina.

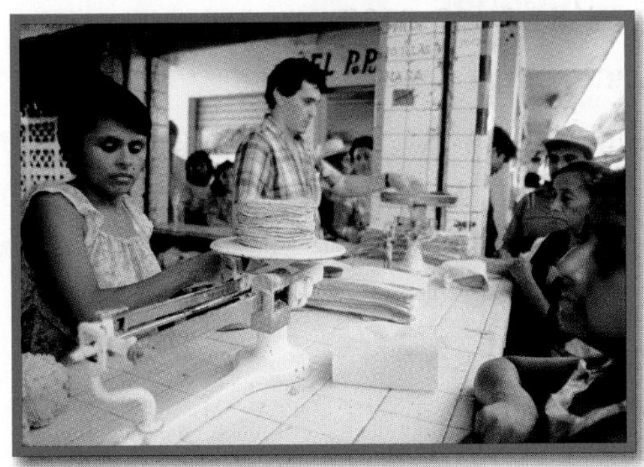

Muchos mexicanos compran tortillas frescas en una tortillería cerca de su casa.

Escribir/Hablar

Y tú, ¿qué dices?

1. ¿En qué tiendas vas de compras? ¿Qué te gusta comprar?
2. ¿Para quiénes compras regalos? ¿Qué tipo de regalos compras?
3. ¿Qué regalo compraste recientemente *(recently)*? ¿Cuándo y dónde compraste el regalo? ¿Pagaste mucho o poco dinero?

Gramática

The preterite of *-ar* verbs

To talk about actions that were completed in the past, use the preterite tense. To form the preterite tense of a regular *-ar* verb, add the preterite endings to the stem of the verb. Here are the preterite forms of *comprar:*

(yo)	**compré**	(nosotros) (nosotras)	**compramos**
(tú)	**compraste**	(vosotros) (vosotras)	**comprasteis**
Ud. (él) (ella)	**compró**	Uds. (ellos) (ellas)	**compraron**

Notice the accent marks on the endings *-é* and *-ó*.

The *nosotros* form is the same in the present and preterite tenses. You will need to look for other context clues to tell which tense is intended.

¿Recuerdas?
In Spanish, the endings of verbs identify both who is performing the action (the subject) and when it is being performed (the tense).

GramActiva VIDEO

Need more help with the preterite of *-ar* verbs? Watch the **GramActiva** video.

jbd-0798

Escuchar

¿El presente o el pasado?

En una hoja de papel, escribe los números del 1 al 8. Vas a escuchar ocho frases que describen los quehaceres de una familia. ¿Ocurren los quehaceres en el presente o el pasado *(past)*? Escribe *presente* o *pasado*.

Escribir/Hablar

El dinero es un buen regalo

Tus abuelos les regalaron *(gave)* a todos dinero y cada uno compró algo. Explica lo que compraron todos y cuándo compraron las cosas.

Modelo

Mi hermano ___ hace una semana.
Mi hermano compró un reloj pulsera hace una semana.

1.  Mi madre ___ ayer.
2.  Mis primos ___ anoche.
3.  Mi papá ___ el año pasado.
4.  Tú ___ hace tres días.
5.  Mis tíos ___ hace un mes.
6. 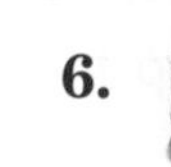 Mi hermana y yo ___ ayer.

   Hablar/GramActiva

Juego

1. Tu profesor(a) va a enseñar a todos cómo deben señalar *(point to)* a diferentes personas: *ella, nosotros, tú, ellos,* etc. Practica con tu profesor(a).

2. Trabaja en un grupo de cuatro. Una persona es líder y dice un infinitivo de la lista y un sujeto *(subject).* Por ejemplo: *cantar / ella*. Los otros tienen que señalar a la persona, o a las personas, y decir el verbo en el pretérito: *ella cantó.* Continúa así con tres sujetos más y el mismo verbo. Después, cambia de *(change)* líderes.

¿Recuerdas?

arreglar	cortar	hablar	nadar
bailar	dibujar	lavar	pasar
caminar	escuchar	levantar	patinar
cantar	esquiar	limpiar	trabajar
cocinar	estudiar	montar	usar

   Escribir/Hablar

Hace una semana

Usa el pretérito para escribir y hablar de tus actividades.

1. Copia la tabla *(chart)* en una hoja de papel. Usa los verbos de la lista de la Actividad 15 para escribir seis actividades que hiciste *(you did)* en el pasado. Indica cuándo hiciste cada actividad.

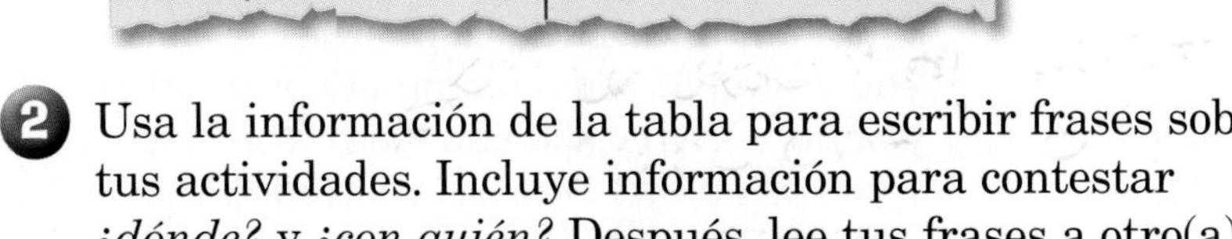

¿Qué?	¿Cuándo?
patiné	la semana pasada

2. Usa la información de la tabla para escribir frases sobre tus actividades. Incluye información para contestar *¿dónde?* y *¿con quién?* Después, lee tus frases a otro(a) estudiante y pregunta: *¿Y tú?* Tu compañero(a) debe contestar. Escribe la respuesta de tu compañero(a).

Modelo

A —*Patiné en el parque con mis amigos la semana pasada.¿Y tú?*
B —*Monté en monopatín con mi hermana la semana pasada.*

3. Escribe tres frases con la información del paso 2.

Modelo

Patiné en el parque con mis amigos la semana pasada, pero Luisa montó en monopatín con su hermana.

Nota

To say when something happened, use *hace* + a time expression. It's like saying "ago."

- Compré la pulsera **hace un año.**
  *I bought the bracelet **a year ago.***

Más práctica

- Practice Workbook, p. 50: 7B-5
- WAV Wbk.: Writing, p. 60
- Guided Practice: Grammar Acts., pp. 237–238
- *Real.* para hispanohablantes, pp. 274–277

Go Online PHSchool.com **For:** Regular Preterite *-ar* Verbs **Web Code:** jbd-0713

Gramática

The preterite of verbs ending in *-car* and *-gar*

Verbs that end in *-car* and *-gar* have a spelling change in the *yo* form of the preterite.

buscar: *c → qu* yo bus***qué***

Silvia y Rosa busc***aron*** aretes pero yo bus**qué** un collar.

pagar: *g → gu* yo pa***gué***

¿Cuánto pa***gaste*** por tu cadena? Pa***gué*** 13 dólares.

Verbs such as *jugar* that have a stem change in the present tense do not have a stem change in the preterite.

El sábado pasado **jugué** al tenis.
Mis hermanos **jugaron** al básquetbol.

¿Recuerdas?

You know these verbs that end in *-car* and *-gar:*

buscar	**practicar**
jugar	**sacar**
pagar	**tocar**

GramActiva VIDEO

Need more help with the preterite of verbs ending in *-car* and *-gar?* Watch the **GramActiva** video.

Actividad 17 Escribir

El viernes pasado

El viernes pasado Juan invitó a unos amigos a su casa. Completa la descripción de sus actividades con la forma apropiada del pretérito de los verbos *jugar, pagar, sacar* y *tocar.*

El viernes pasado mis amigos pasaron tiempo conmigo en mi casa. Tomás y Fernando __1.__ videojuegos en mi dormitorio pero yo no __2.__ con ellos. Yo __3.__ la guitarra en la sala y todos cantamos. Jorge __4.__ el piano un poco también. Después de cantar, nosotros __5.__ al vóleibol. Mi amiga Ana __6.__ fotos de nosotros. ¡Qué graciosas son las fotos! A las nueve fuimos por pizza y ¡mis padres __7.__ la cuenta! ¡Qué bueno porque nunca tengo mucho dinero! Yo __8.__ fotos de todos mis amigos en la pizzería. ¡Qué bien lo pasamos nosotros!

Fondo cultural

El Museo del Oro in Bogotá, Colombia, houses over 33,000 objects of gold, emeralds, and other precious stones made by pre-Columbian cultures—cultures that existed long before the arrival of Columbus in the Americas. These ancient civilizations viewed gold as life-giving energy from the sun.

- What kinds of specialized museums have you visited in your community or in other locations? What did you learn from the types of objects that were included there?

El Museo del Oro en Bogotá, Colombia

Pronunciación

The letter combinations *gue, gui, que,* and *qui* jbd-0798

You know that when the letter *g* appears before the letters *a, o,* or *u,* it is pronounced like the *g* in *go,* and that *g* before *e* and *i* is pronounced like the *h* in *he.*

To keep the sound of the *g* in *go* before *e* and *i*, add the letter *u: gue, gui.* Don't pronounce the *u*. Listen to and say these words:

Guillermo	guitarra	espaguetis
guisantes	hamburguesa	Miguel

You also know that the letter *c* before *a, o,* or *u* is pronounced like the *c* in *cat*, while the *c* before *e* and *i* is usually pronounced like the *s* in *Sally.*

To keep the sound of the *c* in "cat" before *e* and *i*, words are spelled with *qu: que, qui.* The *u* is not pronounced. Listen to and say these words:

queso	quince	quieres	riquísimo
quehacer	quinientos	quisiera	querer

Try it out! Listen to the first verse of this traditional song from Puerto Rico entitled *"El coquí." El coquí* is a little tree frog found in Puerto Rico, named for the *coquí, coquí* sound that it makes at night. Say the verse.

El coquí, el coquí siempre canta.
Es muy suave el cantar del coquí.
Por las noches a veces me duermo
con el dulce cantar del coquí.
Coquí, coquí, coquí, quí, quí, quí,
coquí, coquí, coquí, quí, quí, quí.

Escribir/Escuchar/Hablar/GramActiva

Juego

1. Escribe en una hoja de papel una o dos frases para indicar qué regalo compraste, para quién es, dónde lo compraste y cuánto pagaste.

Modelo

Compré un collar para mi novia en la Red. Pagué 45 dólares.

2. Trabaja con un grupo de cuatro. Pon tu hoja de papel en una bolsa *(bag)* con las otras hojas del grupo. Cada uno toma una hoja, que debe ser de otro(a) estudiante del grupo. Cambia una parte de la frase y lee la nueva frase al grupo. ¿Quién puede identificar el cambio?

Modelo

A —*Esta persona compró un collar para su madre en la Red. Pagó 45 dólares.*
B —*No es cierto. Compré un collar para mi novia.*

Leer/Pensar/Escribir/Hablar

Una lección de historia

Estudia la línea cronológica *(timeline)*, los eventos y el mapa. Luego usa el pretérito para emparejar estos eventos históricos con las personas en la linea cronológica.

Modelo

En 1492 Cristóbal Colón llegó (arrived) *a la República Dominicana.*

Nota

Here is how you say dates:

- **1500** mil quinientos
- **1898** mil ochocientos noventa y ocho
- **2005** dos mil cinco

Conexiones La historia

Los eventos

- **a.** fundar la misión de San Diego de Alcalá
- **b.** pagar 15 millones de dólares a México según el Tratado de Guadalupe Hidalgo
- **c.** empezar la construcción del canal de Panamá
- **d.** explorar la Florida
- **e.** ayudar a Cuba y Puerto Rico a declarar su independencia de España
- **f.** buscar las siete ciudades de Cibola en el suroeste de los Estados Unidos
- **g.** llegar a la República Dominicana

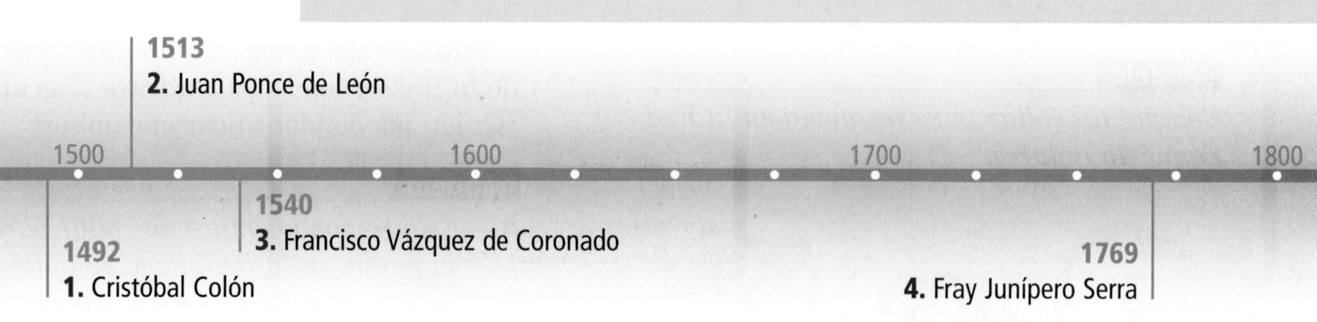

La misión de San Diego de Alcalá, California, fundada en 1769

Fray Junípero Serra

El edificio más antiguo de los Estados Unidos está en San Agustín, en la Florida.

OCÉANO ATLÁNTICO

Mar Caribe

1848
5. El presidente James K. Polk y los Estados Unidos

1900

1898
6. El presidente William McKinley y los Estados Unidos

1904
7. El presidente Theodore Roosevelt y los Estados Unidos

Escribir/Hablar

Y tú, ¿qué dices?

1. ¿Qué deportes practicaste el fin de semana pasado?
2. ¿Con quién practicaste el español la semana pasada?
3. ¿Qué cumpleaños celebraste el mes pasado? ¿Quién sacó fotos en la fiesta?
4. Para el cumpleaños de tu amigo(a) el año pasado, ¿qué compraste? ¿Cuánto pagaste?
5. Cuando celebraste tu quinto cumpleaños, ¿qué jugaste con tus amigos?

Más práctica

- **Practice Workbook, p. 51: 7B-6**
- **WAV Wbk.: Writing, p. 61**
- **Guided Practice: Grammar Activities, p. 239**
- ***Real.* para hispanohablantes, p. 278**

For: Preterite with *-car, -gar*
Web Code: jbd-0714

Gramática

Direct object pronouns

A direct object tells who or what receives the action of the verb.

Busco **una cadena.**
Compré **unos guantes.**

To avoid repeating a direct object noun, you can replace it with a direct object pronoun.

¿Dónde compraste **tus aretes?**
*Where did you buy **your earrings?***

Los compré en la joyería Sánchez.
*I bought **them** at Sánchez Jewelry.*

	SINGULAR		PLURAL	
M.	lo	*it*	los	*them*
F.	la	*it*	las	*them*

Direct object pronouns agree in gender and number with the nouns they replace.

¿Tienes **mi pulsera?** No, no **la** tengo.
¿Tienes **mis anillos?** No, no **los** tengo.

A direct object noun *follows* the conjugated verb. A direct object pronoun comes *before* the conjugated verb.

When an infinitive follows a conjugated verb, the direct object pronoun can either be placed before the conjugated verb or be attached to the infinitive.

¿Quieres comprar **el llavero?**
Sí, **lo** quiero comprar.
o: Sí, quiero comprar**lo.**

GramActiva VIDEO

For more help with direct object pronouns, watch the **GramActiva** video.

Leer/Escribir

Los regalos de José

Tu amigo, José, buscó regalos para su familia y sus amigos. Él está hablando de lo que compró. Escribe los números del 1 al 6 en una hoja de papel. Para cada cosa que buscó José, escribe la frase que explica dónde la compró.

1. Busqué unos discos compactos para mi papá.
2. Busqué un libro nuevo para mi hermana.
3. Busqué unos aretes para mi mamá.
4. Busqué unas revistas para mi amigo Juan.
5. Busqué un equipo de sonido para mi hermano.
6. Busqué una pulsera para mi novia.

a. La compré en la joyería.
b. Los compré en la tienda de música.
c. Lo compré en la librería.
d. Los compré en la joyería.
e. Las compré en la librería.
f. Lo compré en la tienda de música.

Escribir

¡No compraron nada!

Ayer muchas personas fueron *(went)* al centro comercial y miraron muchas cosas pero ¡no compraron nada! Escribe lo que no compraron.

Modelo

Carlos
Ayer Carlos miró unas carteras pero no las compró.

1. Juanita 
2. los novios 
3. tú 
4. nosotros 
5. el señor Miró 
6. yo  

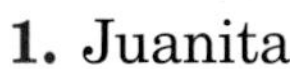

También se dice . . .

el anillo	= la sortija *(muchos países)*
los aretes	= los pendientes *(España)*; los aros *(Argentina, Uruguay)*
la pulsera	= el brazalete *(muchos países)*
el bolso	= la cartera *(Argentina)*; la bolsa *(Chile, México)*
los anteojos de sol	= las gafas de sol *(Argentina, España)*
la cartera	= la billetera *(Argentina, Uruguay, Bolivia)*

Leer/Pensar/Escribir

¿Quién compró qué?

¿Te gusta ser detective? ¡Vamos a ver si puedes descubrir lo que compraron las personas, dónde compraron las cosas y cuánto costó cada cosa!

1 Lee las pistas *(clues)*. Luego copia la tabla en una hoja de papel y completa la tabla.

Las pistas

1. José gastó *(spent)* $35 en la joyería.
2. El software costó $45.
3. Paco no compró una novela.
4. Isabel fue *(went)* de compras a la tienda de electrodomésticos.
5. Luisa gastó $20 en la librería.
6. Los guantes costaron $25.
7. Paco fue de compras al almacén, pero no compró el collar.

Nombre	¿Qué compró?	¿Dónde lo compró?	¿Cuánto costó?

2 Usa la información de la tabla y lee las frases completas.

Modelo

José compró . . . Los (Las / Lo / La) compró en . . . Costaron (Costó) . . .

Hablar

¡Demasiadas preguntas!

Tu hermanito te hace muchas preguntas. Trabaja con otro(a) estudiante y contesta todas sus preguntas con mucha paciencia.

Modelo

A —*¿Necesito llevar botas en el invierno?*
B —*Sí, necesitas llevarlas.*
o:—*No, no necesitas llevarlas.*

1. ¿Vas a comprar perritos calientes?
2. ¿Quieres leer este libro?
3. ¿Tienes que hacer la tarea?
4. ¿Quieres jugar videojuegos conmigo?
5. ¿Puedo comer este pastel?
6. ¿Vas a hacer mi cama?

Hablar

¡Qué barato! ¡Qué caro!

Compraste muchas cosas. Ahora un(a) amigo(a) quiere saber cuándo compraste todas estas cosas y cuánto pagaste.

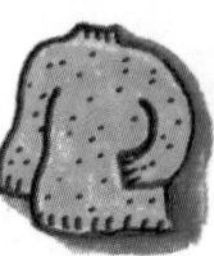

Modelo

A —*¿Cuándo compraste tu suéter nuevo?*
B —*Lo compré la semana pasada.*
A —*¿Cuánto pagaste?*
B —*Pagué 25 dólares.*
A —*¡Qué barato!*
o:—*¡Uf! ¡Qué caro!*

Estudiante A

Estudiante B

¡Respuesta personal!

Escribir/Hablar

¿Dónde lo compraste?

Haz una lista de cinco regalos que compraste recientemente *(recently)* y los nombres de las personas para quienes los compraste. Con un(a) compañero(a), habla de las cosas en tu lista y dónde las compraste. Si no compraste nada, habla de un amigo(a) o un miembro de tu familia que compró regalos.

Modelo

A —*¿Qué regalos compraste recientemente?*
B —*Compré unas botas nuevas para Emily.*
A —*¿Dónde las compraste?*
B —*Las compré en la zapatería Azuelo.*

Regalo	¿Para quién?
botas nuevas	Emily

Escribir/Hablar

¿Cuándo los compró?

1. Escribe cuatro frases para indicar lo que compró una persona y cuándo lo compró.

Modelo

Mi padre compró unos guantes la semana pasada.

2. Lee tus frases a otro(a) estudiante sin decir cuándo la persona compró el artículo. Tu compañero(a) va a preguntar cuándo lo compró.

Modelo

A —*Mi padre compró unos guantes.*
B —*¿Cuándo los compró?*
A —*Los compró la semana pasada.*

Fondo cultural

The Zapotecs and other indigenous groups in the Mexican state of Oaxaca have their own languages and cultures. However, every July they all gather to celebrate the *Guelaguetza*, a Zapotec word that means "offering" or "gift." The *Guelaguetza* was first celebrated more than 3,000 years ago with music, dance, and food products. Today the festivities last two weeks and celebrate regional dances, music, costumes, and foods.

- What celebration in your culture is similar?

La fiesta de la Guelaguetza en Oaxaca, México

Fondo cultural

Madrid's *El Rastro* is said to be the world's largest flea market. Located in one of the oldest sections of the city, *El Rastro* attracts thousands of visitors every Sunday of the year. Vendors line the streets with their stalls and offer everything from blue jeans to fine art. Everyone from teens to serious antiques collectors bargain with the vendors to get the best prices on the things they want to buy.

- Have you ever gone to a flea market in your community or state? What kind of things did you find there? How do you think that flea market would compare to Madrid's *el Rastro?*

El Rastro, en Madrid, España

Hablar

Juego

1. Each student in a group of five puts an object in the center of the group. They must be items for which you have learned the Spanish word. One student turns around and another hides one of the objects.

2. The student who turned around now guesses who has the object. Correct first guesses are worth five points; correct second guesses are worth three. If the second guess is wrong, the student who has the object must say that he or she has it. All take turns being the "guesser."

Modelo

A —*Marta, ¿tienes el llavero?*
B —*No, no lo tengo.*
A —*Carlos, ¿tienes el llavero?*
C —*No, no lo tengo.*
A —*¿Quién tiene el llavero?*
D —*¡Yo lo tengo!*

Escribir

Lo quiero porque . . .

Escribe una lista de cinco cosas que quieres comprar. Para cada cosa, escribe una frase para explicar por qué la quieres y una frase para explicar por qué la necesitas.

Modelo

Quiero comprar un disco compacto nuevo.
Lo quiero porque me gusta la música jazz.
Lo necesito para mi clase de música.

El español en el mundo del trabajo

Large stores and mail-order companies employ buyers who search the world over for goods to offer their customers. Buyers often need to rely on their language skills when looking for products in places where English may not be spoken, and when negotiating prices.

- What stores in your community might employ buyers who travel the world (or the Internet) in search of products from Spanish-speaking countries?

  **Hablar**

Pero mamá, necesito . . .

Quieres ir de compras, pero primero debes hablar con tu madre o padre. Trabaja con un(a) compañero(a) y usa tu lista de la Actividad 29 para explicar lo que necesitas y ¡pide *(ask for)* dinero! Tu madre o padre va a explicar por qué no necesitas comprar nada. Tu profesor(a) te dará el papel *(will assign the role)* que vas a hacer.

1. **Hijo(a):** Piensa en lo que quieres comprar y cómo vas a convencer *(convince)* a tu padre o madre.

   Padre (Madre): Tienes que decir a tu hijo(a) que no necesita lo que pide. Piensa en razones *(reasons)* para convencerle de esto.

2. Practica el drama con otro(a) estudiante.
3. Presenta el drama a tus compañeros. Ellos van a decidir quién tiene las mejores razones: los padres o los hijos.

Modelo

A —*Mamá, necesito dinero para comprar un disco compacto nuevo.*
B —*¿Y por qué lo quieres?*
A —*Lo quiero porque me gusta la música jazz.*
B —*No, no lo necesitas. Tienes muchos discos compactos.*
A —*Pero mamá, también lo necesito para mi clase de música.*
B —*Sí, pero lo tienen en la biblioteca, ¿verdad?*

  **Escribir/Hablar**

Y tú ¿qué dices?

1. ¿Qué ropa compraste recientemente? ¿Por qué la compraste?
2. ¿De qué color son tus zapatos favoritos? ¿Dónde los compraste?
3. ¿Qué ropa llevaste ayer? ¿Cuándo la compraste?
4. ¿Qué cosas buscaste recientemente en el centro comercial? ¿En qué tiendas las buscaste?

Más práctica

- Practice Workbook, p. 52: 7B-7
- Guided Practice: Grammar Acts., p. 240
- *Real.* para hispanohablantes, pp. 279–281

For: Direct Obj. Pronouns
Web Code: jbd-0715

¡Adelante!

Lectura

¡De compras!

Lee este artículo de una revista. A Luisa le encanta ir de compras. ¿Qué puede comprar en cada ciudad?

Objectives

- Read about shopping in four Hispanic communities in the United States
- Learn about differences between consumers in Chile and the United States
- Write a letter describing a gift that you bought
- Watch *¿Eres tú, María?*, Episodio 6

Strategy

Using prior experience
Think about a trip that you took to another city. Did you go shopping? What items did you find that were unique to that city?

De COMPRA$
con Luisa la compradora

¡Me encanta ir de compras! Hay muchos lugares donde me gusta ir de compras en los vecindarios[1] hispanos. Siempre es una experiencia divertida. Hay cosas que uno puede comprar que son muy baratas y que no hay en otros lugares. Voy a hablar de mis aventuras por las comunidades hispanas de Nueva York, Miami, Los Ángeles y San Antonio.

En el Barrio de Nueva York, en la calle[2] 116, venden ropa, comida típica del Caribe, discos compactos, libros y mucho más. Allí compré una camiseta con la bandera de Puerto Rico. En junio siempre hay una celebración grande que se llama el Festival de la calle 116. ¡Me encanta Nueva York!

La calle 116 en Nueva York

La Pequeña Habana y la calle Ocho son el corazón[3] de la comunidad cubana en Miami. Hay bodegas[4] que venden productos típicos cubanos: frijoles[5] negros y frutas tropicales como el maguey y la papaya. Allí compré pasta de guayaba, un dulce delicioso que los cubanos comen con queso blanco. ¡Qué rico!

Tienda en la Pequeña Habana, Miami

Pasta de guayaba

[1]neighborhoods [2]street [3]heart [4]grocery stores
[5]beans

De compras en la calle Olvera, Los Ángeles

El Mercado en San Antonio, Texas

La calle Olvera es la calle más antigua[6] de la ciudad de Los Ángeles y allí uno puede ver la cultura mexicana. Hay muchos restaurantes y muchos lugares para comprar artesanías[7]. Me encanta ir de compras en las joyerías porque las joyas me fascinan. En las joyerías de la calle Olvera, venden joyas de plata[8]: aretes, collares, anillos y mucho más. En una joyería de allí compré una pulsera muy bonita a un precio muy bajo.

¡Ahora vamos a hablar de San Antonio! ¡Qué compras! En esta ciudad bonita de Texas, hay tiendas de artesanías mexicanas que son fabulosas. Mis favoritas están en el Mercado o como dicen en inglés, *Market Square.* Allí compré una piñata para mi hermano, una blusa bordada[9] para mi madre, una cartera para mi padre y un sarape[10] para decorar mi dormitorio... ¡y no pagué mucho!

[6]oldest [7]handicrafts [8]silver [9]embroidered
[10]shawl; blanket

¿Comprendes?

1. De los cuatro lugares en *¡De compras!*, ¿adónde debe ir cada persona?

   Ana: Me gustaría comprar algo de Puerto Rico.
   Lorenzo: A mí me fascinan las artesanías mexicanas.
   Miguel: ¿Mi almuerzo favorito? El sándwich cubano.

2. ¿Qué compró Luisa en cada lugar?

Más práctica

- WAV Wbk.: Writing, p. 62
- Guided Practice: *Lectura*, p. 241
- *Real.* para hispanohablantes, pp. 282–283

For: Internet Activity
Web Code: jbd-0716

Fondo cultural

Las artesanías Handicrafts from Puerto Rico, Mexico, and other Spanish-speaking countries have been popular for years among tourists looking for gift ideas. Now these handicrafts are receiving recognition as museum-quality artwork. At the Mexican Fine Arts Center Museum in the Pilsen neighborhood of Chicago, visitors can see permanent collections of paintings, weavings, sculpture, pottery, and silver jewelry from all over Mexico. Other types of handmade items are for sale in the museum's gift shop.

- Do you think that handicrafts should be displayed in museums along with fine art? Why or why not?

Una caja pintada de El Salvador

Perspectivas del mundo hispano

¿Por qué vas al centro comercial?

Why do people go to the mall? Note the differences between consumers in Chile and the United States.

In the United States many people go to the mall to see what merchandise is available and to spend time. In Chile, many people go to the mall because they want to make a specific purchase. They decide where to go according to the merchandise they need to buy.

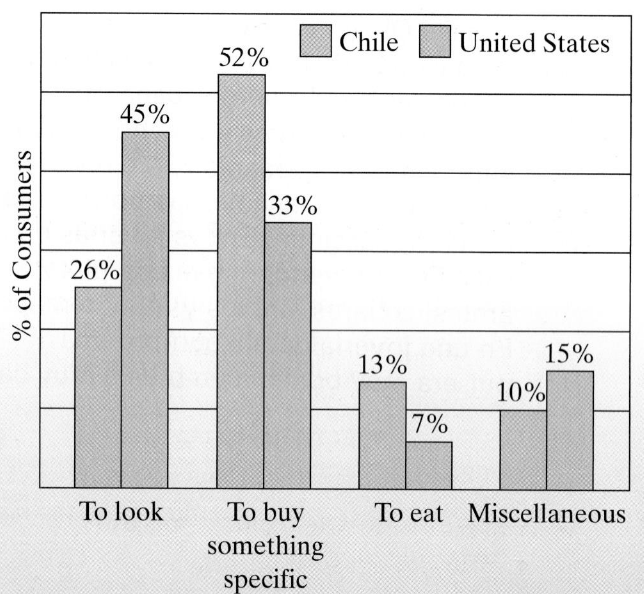

For many in the United States, going to the mall is more than going shopping. The mall offers an opportunity to eat and to spend time with friends. For 50% of U.S. consumers, the atmosphere of a mall is very important. Only 13% of Chilean consumers think that atmosphere is important.

Although their motivation for going to the mall is different, 80% of both Chilean and U.S. consumers make a purchase once they are in the stores.

Check it out! Interview at least three people your age and at least three adults that you know and find out what their main reasons for going to a mall are, how they decide which mall to go to, and if they usually make a purchase while at the mall. Compare what you find out with the results above for shoppers in the United States and Chile.

Think about it! Why might shoppers in the United States consider the mall atmosphere an important factor in their decision about where to shop? Given what you have read about the reasons Chileans go shopping, what do you think a store clerk in a mall in Chile might expect you to do if you entered his or her store? How might a Chilean exchange student feel if he or she went to the mall with you and your friends?

El centro comercial Galerías Pacífico en Buenos Aires, Argentina

Presentación escrita

Un regalo para mi . . .

Task
You recently bought a gift for a member of your family. Write a letter to a cousin or other relative about the gift so that he or she will not buy the same item.

1 Prewrite A member of your family is celebrating a special birthday. Think about the gift you bought. Answer the following questions to help organize your thoughts.

- ¿Para quién es el regalo?
- ¿Qué compraste?
- ¿Dónde compraste el regalo?
- ¿Por qué compraste ese regalo?
- ¿Cuánto pagaste por el regalo?
- ¿Cuándo es la fiesta de cumpleaños?

Organizing information
Thinking about the correct format and necessary information beforehand will help you write a better letter.

2 Draft Use the answers to the questions in Step 1 to help you write your letter. Write a first draft of your letter. Remember to use an appropriate salutation and closing. You may want to begin your letter with *Querido(a)* . . . or *Hola* . . . , and close it with *Tu primo(a)* . . . or *Saludos*, or *Hasta pronto.*

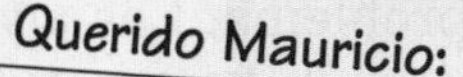

Querido Mauricio:

Compré un reloj pulsera para el abuelito. Lo compré en el almacén Génova que está en el centro comercial Plaza del Río. No pagué mucho por él. Creo que al abuelito le va a gustar. Voy a ver a toda la familia el 2 de octubre para la fiesta de cumpleaños del abuelito.

Tu primo,
Luis

3 Revise Read the letter and check spelling, vocabulary choice, verb forms, and agreement. Share the letter with your partner, who will check the following:

- Is the letter easy to read and understand?
- Does it provide all the necessary information?
- Did you use appropriate letter form?
- Are there any errors?

4 Publish Rewrite the letter, making any necessary changes or additions. Share your letter with your teacher. You may also want to add it to your portfolio.

5 Evaluation Your teacher may give you a rubric that will be used to grade the letter. You may be evaluated on:

- how easy the letter is to understand
- how much information is included about the gift
- how appropriate the greeting and closing are
- the accuracy of the use of the preterite

Videomisterio

¿Eres tú, María?

Episodio 6

Antes de ver el video

Resumen del episodio

Lola llega a su oficina y hay un recado de Pedro Requena. Él viene a hablar con ella sobre su abuela, doña Gracia. Necesita un detective privado y quiere la ayuda de Lola y Paco. Pedro explica que su abuela es una mujer muy rica y que tiene joyas preciosas. Pero hay un problema. Las joyas de doña Gracia no están en el piso. Pedro cree que un ladrón robó las joyas. Pero, ¿cómo sabe el ladrón que hay joyas en el piso de doña Gracia?

"Por favor, ¿por qué no me tuteas?"

Nota cultural In Spain, it is customary for adults to speak to new acquaintances using the formal *Ud.* In most cases, the other person will then invite you to address them informally using the *tú* form. This is called *tutear.* In this scene, Pedro invites Lola to speak to him informally. When you visit Spain, you should address new adult acquaintances in the *Ud.* form and wait to be invited to *tutear.*

Nota cultural Lola quotes Pedro a price for her agency's services in euros. The euro is the currency in Spain and many other countries in Europe that are part of the European Union.

Palabras para comprender

un recado	a message
una cita	an appointment
Acabo de venir del hospital.	I just came from the hospital.
Vi a su abuela.	I saw your grandmother.
necesito saber	I need to know . . .
el ladrón robó	the burglar stole
nosotros cobramos	we charge

"Mi abuela es una mujer rica. Tiene dinero y joyas de valor. Son de la familia".

"María va a recibir todo el dinero, todas las joyas, todo de mi abuela".

"Pedro, vamos a buscar las joyas".

Después de ver el video

¿Comprendes?

Termina las frases con la palabra más apropiada del recuadro.

fotos	sobrina
recado	abuela
joyas	teléfono
dinero	nieto

1. Lola, hay un ___ para ti de un tal Pedro Reteña, Resqueña o Retena. Algo así.
2. El ___ de doña Gracia viene a la una y media.
3. ¡Qué bueno! Un cliente con ___.
4. Acabo de venir del hospital. Vi a su ___.
5. Aquí tengo unas ___ de ella.
6. Mira, las ___ no están en el piso.
7. Aquí está el número de ___: 318-18-02.

For: More on *¿Eres tú, María?*
Web Code: jbd-0507

Repaso del capítulo

Chapter Review

To prepare for the test, check to see if you . . .

- know the new vocabulary and grammar
- can perform the tasks on p. 215

jbd-0799

Vocabulario y gramática 

to talk about places where you shop

el almacén, *pl.* **los almacenes**	department store
en la Red	online
la joyería	jewelry store
la librería	bookstore
la tienda de descuentos	discount store
la tienda de electrodomésticos	household appliance store
la zapatería	shoe store

to talk about gifts you might buy

el anillo	ring
los anteojos de sol	sunglasses
los aretes	earrings
el bolso	purse
la cadena	chain
la cartera	wallet
el collar	necklace
la corbata	tie
los guantes	gloves
el llavero	key chain
el perfume	perfume
la pulsera	bracelet
el reloj pulsera	watch
el software	software

to talk about who might receive a gift

el novio	boyfriend
la novia	girlfriend

For *Vocabulario adicional,* see pp. 336–337.

to talk about buying or selling

barato, -a	inexpensive, cheap
caro, -a	expensive
mirar	to look (at)
pagar (por)	to pay (for)
vender	to sell

to talk about time in the past

anoche	last night
el año pasado	last year
ayer	yesterday
hace + *time expression*	ago
la semana pasada	last week

other useful expressions

¡Uf!	Ugh! Yuck!

preterite of regular *-ar* verbs

compré	**compramos**
compraste	**comprasteis**
compró	**compraron**

preterite of *-car* and *-gar* verbs

These verbs have a spelling change in the *yo* form of the preterite.

buscar	*c* → *qu*	yo busqué
pagar	*g* → *gu*	yo pagué
jugar	*g* → *gu*	yo jugué

direct object pronouns

	Singular	Plural
M.	**lo** it	**los** them
F.	**la** it	**las** them

Más práctica

- Practice Workbook: Puzzle, p. 53
- Practice Workbook: Organizer, p. 54

Preparación para el examen

On the exam you will be asked to . . .	Here are practice tasks similar to those you will find on the exam . . .	If you need review . . .
jbd-0799  **1 Escuchar** Listen as someone describes what she bought as a gift and where she bought it	As a teenager tells what she bought for her friend's *quinceañera* (girl's fifteenth birthday party), see if you can tell: a) what she bought; b) where she bought it; c) how much she paid for it.	**pp. 186–191** *A primera vista* **p. 187** Actividad 1 **p. 192** Actividad 6
 **2 Hablar** Exchange opinions about whether certain items are expensive or inexpensive	Think about a gift you've bought. Tell your partner what you bought, for whom you bought it, and how much you paid. Then ask whether he or she thinks that it is expensive or inexpensive. Your partner will then share the same information and ask the same question about a gift he or she bought.	**p. 192** Actividad 7 **p. 193** Actividad 9 **p. 194** Actividad 10 **p. 203** Actividad 23 **p. 204** Actividad 25 **p. 205** Actividades 26–27
3 Leer Read and understand an online advertisement for a store you might find on the Internet	While surfing on the Internet, you find a Web site for a discount store in Mexico City. Can you list at least two advantages for customers who shop here?	**pp. 186–191** *A primera vista* **p. 194** Actividad 11

Tienda virtual de descuentos

Todos nuestros clientes reciben un descuento del 10%. Tenemos de todo; perfume para su novia, bolsos para su mamá, videojuegos para su hermano y software para Ud. Tenemos los mejores precios y descuentos en la Red. Si paga por algo en la Tienda virtual, va a recibir "ePesos". Puede usarlos en su próxima visita.

On the exam you will be asked to . . .	Here are practice tasks similar to those you will find on the exam . . .	If you need review . . .
 **4 Escribir** Write a short explanation about some items that you have bought this school year with your own money	As an entry for your class journal, explain how you spent your money last month. Describe: a) at least two new clothing items or accessories you bought; b) where you bought the items; c) how much you paid for them.	**p. 199** Actividad 18 **p. 203** Actividades 22–23 **p. 205** Actividad 27 **p. 211** *Presentación escrita*
 **5 Pensar** Demonstrate an understanding of cultural perspectives regarding shopping	Think about what you do when you go to a shopping mall. Based on what you've learned in this chapter, would these be the same things that Chileans do? What similarities and differences would you expect to see in shopping malls and in attitudes of shoppers in both countries?	**p. 210** *Perspectivas del mundo hispano*

Fondo cultural

Vista de Toledo is one of the most famous paintings by El Greco (the Greek). Born Doménikos Theotokópoulos in 1541 on the island of Crete, El Greco moved to Spain and settled in Toledo, a city south of Madrid. His amazing "View of Toledo", painted around 1597, was considered radical for its time because of its use of green, blue, and purple hues and its bold style. Instead of being realistic, the painting highlights the city's landmarks and its grandeur. El Greco's style has greatly influenced other painters.

- What would you highlight if you were painting your town or city?

"Vista de Toledo" (1597), El Greco

Oil on canvas.†Metropolitan Museum of Art, New York/Index/Bridgeman Art Library, London/New York

Vista de Toledo, España

De vacaciones

Chapter Objectives

- Talk about things to do on vacation
- Describe places to visit while on vacation
- Talk about events in the past
- Understand cultural perspectives on travel and vacations

Video Highlights

A primera vista: *¿Qué te pasó?*

GramActiva Videos: the preterite of *-er* and *-ir* verbs; preterite of *ir;* the personal *a*

Videomisterio: *¿Eres tú, María?*, Episodio 7

Country Connection

As you learn about travel and vacations, you will make connections to these countries and places:

Más práctica

- *Real.* para hispanohablantes, pp. 290–291

For: Online Atlas
Web Code: jbe-0002

A primera vista

jbd-0887

Objectives

Read, listen to, and understand information about

- **travel and vacations**
- **past events**

Vocabulario y gramática en contexto

—**Dime,** ¿adónde **fuiste** el mes pasado?

—**Fui de vacaciones** con mis padres a **un lugar fantástico.**

—¿Qué lugar **visitaste?**

—Fui a Barcelona. Me gusta mucho **viajar** a otros **países como** México, España, Guatemala . . .

—**¿Qué hiciste?**

—Pues, fui al zoológico con mi familia.

—**¿Te gustó?** ¿Qué **viste?**

—**Fue** fantástico. **Vi** muchos **animales** como osos y monos y también muchas otras **atracciones.** También compré **unos recuerdos:** una camiseta, unos aretes y un llavero.

—Y **¿saliste** de **la ciudad?**

—¡Por supuesto! **Salí*** muy **temprano** para ir al mar. **Durante** el día **aprendí a** bucear. Fue muy divertido. **Regresamos** al **hotel** muy **tarde,** como a las diez de la noche.

*The verb *salir* has an irregular *yo* form in the present tense: *salgo.*

el avión

el barco

el tren

el autobús

—¿Cómo prefieres viajar?

—**En** avión.

jbd-0887

Escuchar

El viaje de María Luisa

Vas a escuchar a María Luisa describir su viaje. Señala en tu libro cada lugar que ella menciona.

jbd-0887

Escuchar

¿Qué piensas? ¿Sí o no?

Vas a escuchar diez frases. Si la frase es lógica, haz el gesto del pulgar hacia arriba *("thumbs-up" sign)*. Si es ilógica, haz el gesto del pulgar hacia abajo *("thumbs-down" sign)*.

Más práctica

- **Practice Workbook, pp. 55–56: 8A-1, 8A-2**
- **WAV Wbk.: Writing, p. 69**
- **Guided Practice: Vocab. Flash Cards, pp. 243–248**
- ***Real.* para hispanohablantes, p. 292**

Videohistoria

jbd-0887

¿Qué te pasó?

¿Qué le pasó a Tomás durante su visita al parque nacional Sarapiquí en Costa Rica?

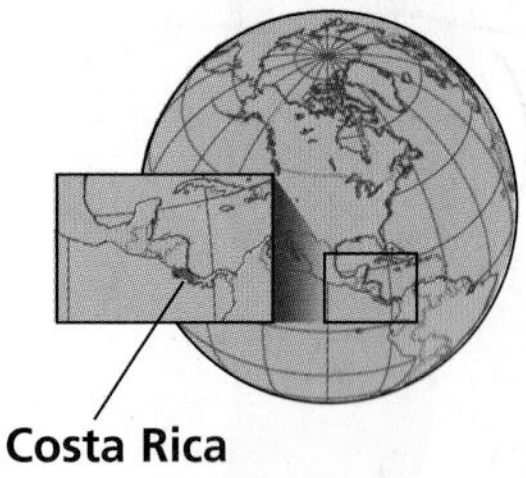

Antes de leer

Using visuals to make predictions Before you read the story, look at the pictures to try to predict what will happen. After you finish reading, see how your predictions compared with what you read.

- What do you think will happen to Raúl, Gloria, and Tomás?

1. Based on what you already know about rain forests, what kinds of things would you expect Raúl, Gloria, and Tomás to see on their visit to *el parque Sarapiquí?*
2. Look at photo 3. What animals do you think they are going to talk about?
3. Skim the *Videohistoria* and make a list of five cognates that will help you understand the story.

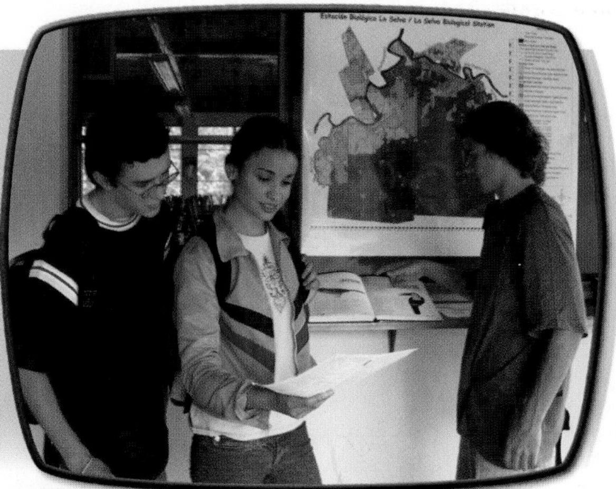

1 **Raúl:** Aquí están **los boletos** para el autobús.

Tomás: ¿Cuánto dura **el viaje?**

Gloria: El parque está a 82 kilómetros de San José. Es un viaje de hora y media.

2 **Gloria:** Mira este mapa del **parque nacional.** Es mi parque favorito y lo llamamos "bosque lluvioso."* No hace ni frío ni calor, pero llueve mucho.

Tomás: Aquí hay un libro sobre los animales del parque.

*rain forest

3 **Gloria:** ¿Lo ves? Allí en **el árbol.**

Tomás: No, no lo veo. ¿Qué es?

Gloria: Es **un pájaro.** Es un tucán. Hay más de cuatrocientas especies de pájaros en el parque.

4 **Raúl:** Tomás, **¿qué te pasó?**

Tomás: ¡Hay agua en las palmas! Eh... ¡no es nada divertido!

Raúl: Pero, Tomás, es un bosque lluvioso y llueve todo el tiempo. Siempre hay agua en las palmas. Pero sólo es un poco de agua.

Gloria: Estás aprendiendo muchas cosas, ¿verdad?

5 **Gloria:** Va a ser una foto fantástica, Tomás. Un momento . . . un poco más a la izquierda.

Tomás: ¿Aquí?

Gloria: No, un poco más. Uno, dos . . .

Tomás: ¡Ay!

Raúl: Tomás, ¿dónde estás? ¿Estás bien?

6 **Gloria:** Lo siento, Tomás. ¿Quieres regresar a casa?

Raúl: ¿Quieres **descansar** un poco?

Tomás: No. Estoy bien. ¡Vamos a la catarata* La Paz!

*waterfall

7 **Tomás:** Quiero una foto de la catarata. ¡Es **tremenda, impresionante!** Uno puede estar muy cerca de ella.

Raúl: No, creo que estar un poco lejos de ella es mejor. Voy a ayudarte, Tomás.

Gloria: Un poco más hacia atrás* y a la derecha . . .

*towards the back

8 **Mamá:** ¡Tomás! **¿Cómo lo pasaste?** ¿Qué te pasó?

Gloria: Pobre* Tomás . . . **fue un desastre.**

Tomás: No fue tan malo. **Me gustó.** Aprendí mucho y vi muchas cosas nuevas. ¡Pero hay mucha agua en el bosque lluvioso y en la catarata!

*Poor

Leer/Escribir

¿Cierto o falso?

Lee estas frases sobre el bosque lluvioso Sarapiquí. Escribe los números del 1 al 6 en una hoja de papel. Según la información en la *Videohistoria*, escribe *C* (cierto) si la frase es cierta o *F* (falso) si es falsa. Corrige *(Correct)* las frases falsas.

1. El parque Sarapiquí es un parque nacional.
2. El bosque lluvioso está a una hora y media de San José.
3. En el bosque lluvioso hay cuarenta especies de pájaros.
4. El tucán es un pájaro que vive en el bosque lluvioso.
5. Hace muchísimo calor en el bosque lluvioso.
6. Llueve todo el tiempo en el bosque lluvioso.

Leer/Escribir

¿Tomás, Gloria o Raúl?

Lee estas frases sobre las personas en la *Videohistoria*. Escribe los números del 1 al 6. Para cada frase, escribe el nombre de la persona a quien se refiere *(to whom it refers)*.

Raúl

Gloria

Tomás

1. Compró los boletos para el autobús.
2. Sacó fotos de los otros.
3. No vio el pájaro.
4. Sarapiquí es su parque favorito.
5. Ayudó a Tomás delante de la catarata La Paz.
6. Decidió no descansar.

Leer/Escribir

El diario de Tomás

Tomás está escribiendo en su diario sobre todo lo que le pasó en Costa Rica. Pon estas frases en orden según la *Videohistoria*. Escribe las frases en una hoja de papel para crear un párrafo *(paragraph)*.

29 de mayo: Hoy fui con Gloria y Raúl y pasé un día fantástico.

1. Hablé con la mamá de Raúl sobre el viaje al parque.
2. Vi un libro sobre los animales del parque.
3. Viajé una hora y media al parque.
4. Yo salí de San José para ir al parque nacional Sarapiquí.
5. Fui a la catarata de La Paz.
6. Me mojé* porque siempre hay agua en las palmas.

*I got wet

Más práctica

- Practice Workbook, pp. 57–58: 8A-3, 8A-4
- WAV Wbk.: Video, pp. 63–65
- Guided Practice: Vocab. Check, pp. 249–252
- *Real.* para hispanohablantes, p. 293

Manos a la obra

Vocabulario y gramática en uso

Objectives

- **Talk about vacations and trips**
- **Talk about places to visit and how to get there**
- **Learn the preterite tense of *-er* and *-ir* verbs and the preterite of *ir***
- **Learn to use the personal *a***

Escribir

Durante las vacaciones

El verano pasado, fuiste a muchos lugares interesantes y tus amigos quieren más información. En una hoja de papel, contesta estas preguntas usando las palabras de la lista.

el teatro	el lago
la ciudad	el estadio
el museo	el parque de diversiones
el zoológico	

Modelo

¿Adónde fuiste para ir a las tiendas y los restaurantes?
Fui a la ciudad.

1. ¿Adónde fuiste para ver esta obra de teatro?
2. ¿Adónde fuiste para ver el arte de Botero y Picasso?
3. ¿Adónde fuiste para nadar y descansar?
4. ¿Adónde fuiste para ver los monos y los osos?
5. ¿Adónde fuiste para ver las atracciones?
6. ¿Adónde fuiste para ver el partido de fútbol americano?

jbd-0888

Escuchar/Escribir

Escucha y escribe

Vas a escuchar a una persona describir su viaje a Puerto Rico. Uno de los lugares que visitó es El Yunque. En una hoja de papel, escribe los números del 1 al 6 y escribe las frases que escuchas.

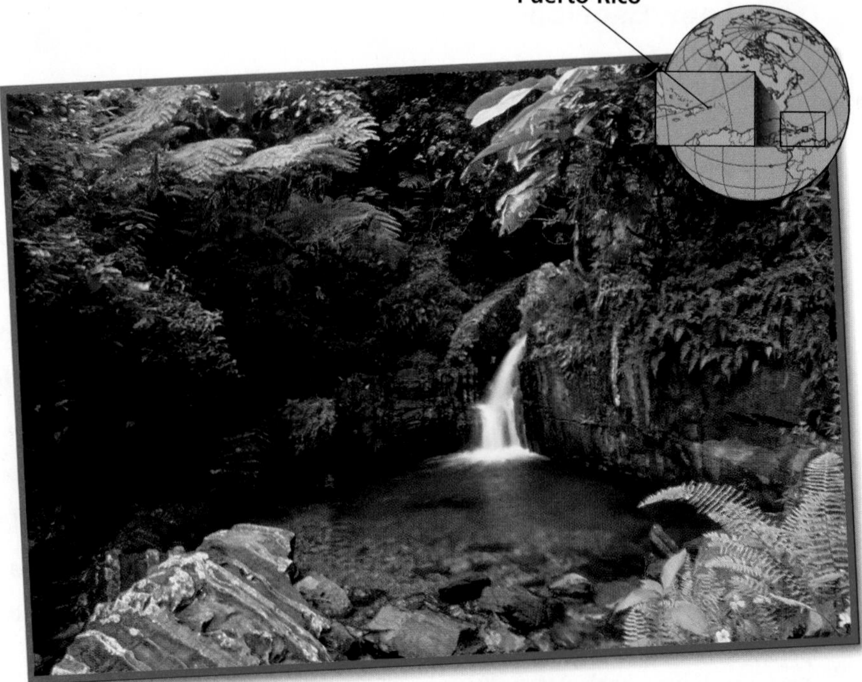

El Yunque, un parque nacional de Puerto Rico

Escribir/Hablar

Una lista de actividades

1 ¿Qué actividades te gusta hacer cuando vas de vacaciones? ¿Qué actividades no te gusta hacer? En una hoja de papel, haz tres columnas y escribe *me gusta mucho, me gusta* y *no me gusta nada.* Debajo de cada expresión, escribe estas actividades en la columna apropiada.

ver...

visitar...

sacar fotos de...

ir a...

ir a...

comprar...

2 Usa tu lista de actividades y habla con otro(a) estudiante. Pregunta y contesta según el modelo. Haz por lo menos *(at least)* cuatro preguntas.

Modelo

A —*Cuando vas de vacaciones, ¿qué te gusta más, ver una obra de teatro o ir al zoológico?*
B —*Me gusta más ir al zoológico.*

Hablar

¿Qué te gustaría hacer?

Habla con otro(a) estudiante sobre adónde les gustaría ir de vacaciones.

Modelo

A —*Dime, ¿te gustaría ir de vacaciones a una ciudad?*
B —*Sí, porque en una ciudad puedes ir de compras y comer en restaurantes fantásticos.*
o: *No, me gustaría más ir a un parque nacional porque puedes ir de cámping.*

Estudiante A

1. una ciudad
2. un parque nacional
3. un lago
4. el mar

Estudiante B

¡Respuesta personal!

Leer/Escribir

El delta del río[1] Paraná

Lee la descripción del delta del río Paraná, a 30 kilómetros de Buenos Aires, y completa las frases con las palabras apropiadas de la casilla. Después, contesta las preguntas.

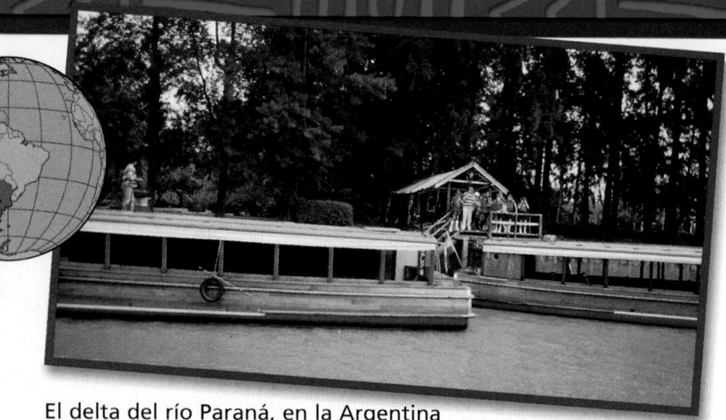

El delta del río Paraná, en la Argentina

tren	descansar	recuerdos
ciudad	regresar	lagos
país	pasear	pájaros
lugar	montar	árboles

Al norte de la **1.** de Buenos Aires, Argentina, está el delta del río Paraná, un laberinto de islas y canales con más de 2,500 kilómetros navegables. Es un **2.** favorito de los habitantes de Buenos Aires para ir de excursión. Para ir de Buenos Aires al delta, muchas personas viajan en **3.** hasta[2] el Tigre, un pueblo[3] pequeño.

Aquí las personas pueden **4.** en bote por los canales, **5.** y tomar el sol en la orilla,[4] **6.** a caballo o practicar el esquí acuático.

También pueden comprar comida y **7.** turísticos en los mercados.[5] Las personas siempre tienen sus cámaras en las excursiones al delta porque hay muchos tipos de animales y **8.** que viven en los **9.** muy altos.

[1]river [2]as far as [3]town [4]riverbank [5]markets

- Para ti, ¿es el delta del río Paraná un buen lugar para ir de vacaciones? ¿Por qué?
- ¿Qué actividades te gustaría hacer en este lugar?

Hablar

Cómo puedes viajar

Mira los mapas en las páginas xii–xxv. Dile a tu compañero(a) que te gustaría viajar de un lugar o país a otro. Tu compañero(a) debe decir cómo puedes viajar entre los dos lugares.

Modelo

A —*Me gustaría viajar de la República Dominicana a Puerto Rico.*
B —*Pues, entonces, puedes viajar en barco o en avión.*

También se dice . . .

el autobús = el camión *(México);* el colectivo, el ómnibus *(Argentina, Bolivia);* la guagua *(Puerto Rico, Cuba);* el micro *(Perú)*

Estudiante A

¡Respuesta personal!

Estudiante B

Leer/Escribir/Hablar

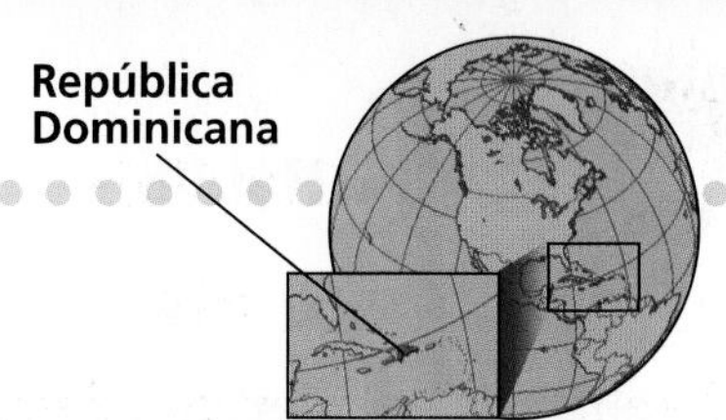

¿Quieres aprender a bucear?

Lee el anuncio y contesta las preguntas.

Escuela de buceo "Flor del mar"

Puerto Plata, República Dominicana

Cursos de buceo "Flor del mar"

¡Aprende a bucear en sólo tres cursos!
Ve peces impresionantes y otros animales del mar.
Practica un deporte interesante y divertido.
Pasa tiempo con amigos en un lugar fantástico.

Si quieres información sobre un curso de buceo en la República Dominicana, comunícate al 555-19-19 con la Dra. María Elena Santos o al 555-02-28 con Marcos Morelos.

Señales de buceo

Hay un lenguaje especial que permite a los buzos comunicarse en el agua con señales. En los cursos de buceo, puedes aprender estas señales. Así no vas a tener ningún problema practicando este deporte. Algunas de las señales más importantes son:

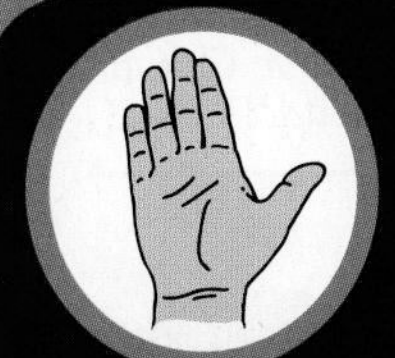
Alto

Ir hacia arriba

Ir hacia abajo

Preguntar si estás bien

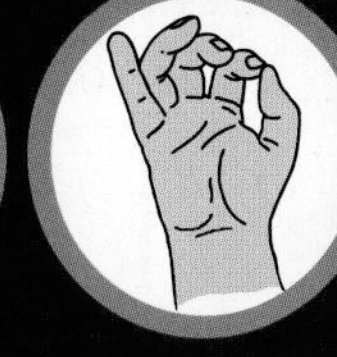
Contestar OK o sí

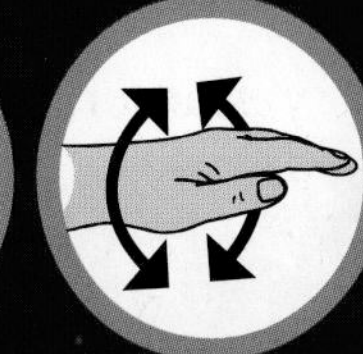
Hay un problema

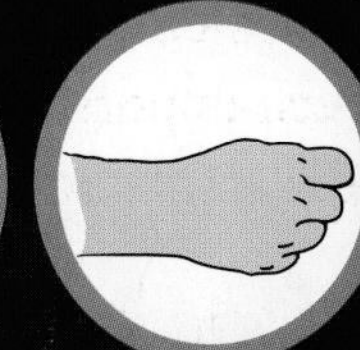
¡Peligro!

1. ¿Por qué debes estudiar buceo en la escuela "Flor del mar"?
2. Practica las señales con otro(a) estudiante. ¿Qué puedes comunicar?

Hablar

¿Dónde aprendiste a bucear?

Habla con otro(a) estudiante sobre dónde aprendió a hacer las actividades de la lista.

1. bucear
2. montar a caballo
3. esquiar
4. montar en bicicleta
5. patinar
6. tocar la guitarra

Modelo

nadar
A —*¿Dónde aprendiste a nadar?*
B —*Aprendí a nadar en California.*
o: —*No aprendí a nadar nunca, pero me gustaría aprender.*
o: —*No aprendí a nadar nunca y no quiero aprender.*

Hablar

¿Adónde fuiste?

La primavera pasada fuiste de vacaciones a la Ciudad de México. Ahora tienes tus fotos y hablas con otro(a) estudiante. En la Ciudad de México viste estas cosas:

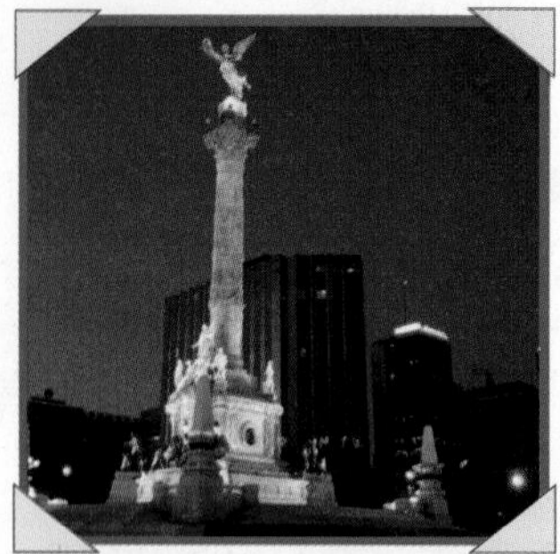

El Paseo de la Reforma con el monumento del Ángel de la Independencia ¡Impresionante!

Modelo

A —*¿Adónde fuiste?*
B —*Fui al Paseo de la Reforma.*
A —*¿Qué viste?*
B —*Vi el monumento del Ángel de la Independencia.*
A —*¿Cómo lo pasaste allí? ¿Te gustó?*
B —*Fue impresionante. Me gustó mucho.*

- un partido de fútbol
- el monumento del Ángel de la Independencia
- muchas atracciones
- animales como osos y monos
- una obra de teatro
- muchos cuadros interesantes

1. 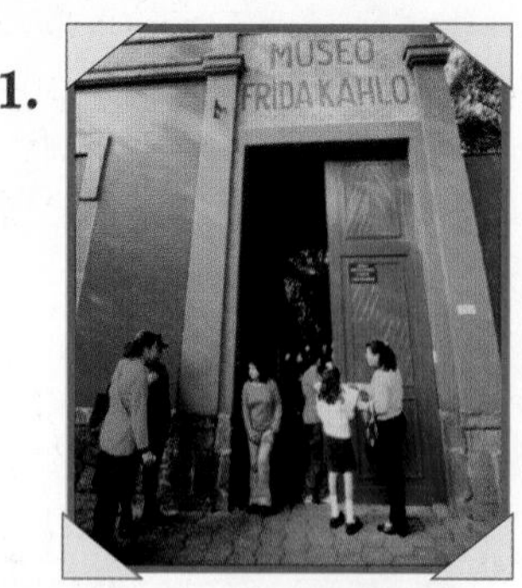

Museo de arte de Frida Kahlo ¡Fantástico!

2. 
El Zoológico del Parque Chapultepec ¡Tremendo!

3. 
El parque de diversiones en el Parque Chapultepec ¡Muy divertido!

4. 
El Teatro del Auditorio ¡Fenomenal!

5. 
El Estadio Azteca ¡Genial!

Fondo cultural

Mexico City's *Metro* is one of the most advanced subway systems in the world. It is fast, modern, and very inexpensive. In addition, an extensive bus service crosses the whole city, with even-numbered lines running east-west and odd-numbered lines running north-south. Smaller green and gray minibuses, called *peseros,* also serve passengers along major routes.

- Why do you think Mexico City has such an advanced and varied public transportation system?

Pronunciación

Diphthongs

jbd-0888

In Spanish, there are two groups of vowels, "strong" *(a, e,* and *o)* and "weak" *(i* and *u)*. The strong vowels are *a, e,* and *o*.

When a weak vowel is combined with any other vowel, the individual vowel sounds become blended to form a single sound called a diphthong *(un diptongo)*. Listen to and say these words:

limpiar	cuarto	seis	piensas
fuimos	siete	aire	ciudad
baile	juego	estadio	autobús

When two strong vowels are together, each vowel is pronounced as a separate sound. Listen to and say these words:

teatro	museo	pasear	bucear
cereal	video	leer	zoológico
traer	idea	tarea	cumpleaños

If there is an accent mark over a weak vowel, it causes that letter to be pronounced as though it were a strong vowel. Listen to and say these words:

día	frío	tíos	zapatería
joyería	país	esquío	gustaría

Try it out! Listen to some of the lines of *"Cielito lindo,"* a song from Mexico that is very popular with mariachi bands. Can you identify the diphthongs in the lyrics? Try saying the words and then singing the song.

De la sierra morena,
cielito lindo, vienen bajando
un par de ojitos negros,
cielito lindo, de contrabando.
¡Ay, ay, ay, ay!
Canta y no llores,
porque cantando se alegran,
cielito lindo, los corazones.

Actividad 15 **Escribir/Hablar**

Y tú, ¿qué dices?

1. ¿Adónde te gustaría ir de vacaciones en los Estados Unidos? ¿Cómo quieres viajar? ¿Qué te gustaría hacer?
2. ¿Qué ciudades te gustaría visitar? ¿Qué lugares en esas ciudades quieres ver?
3. Cuando viajas, ¿prefieres salir temprano o tarde?
4. Durante un viaje, ¿descansas mucho o regresas a casa muy cansado(a)?

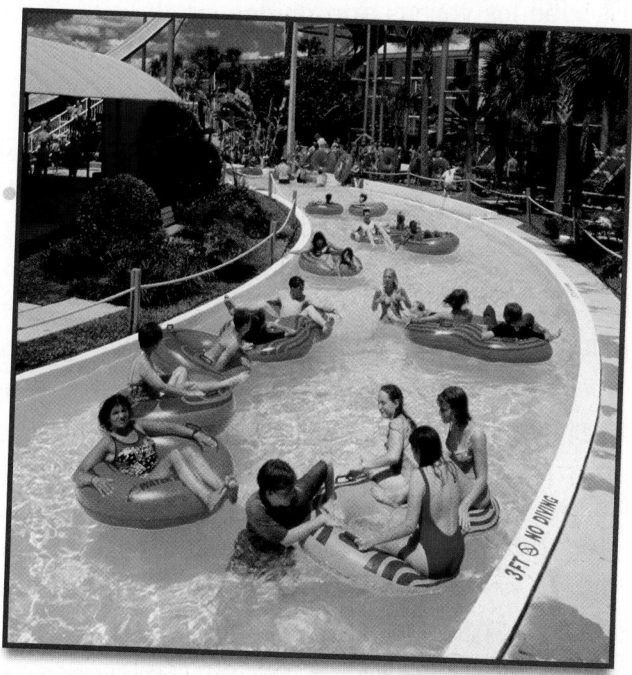

En un parque acuático de Kissimmee, en la Florida

Gramática

The preterite of *-er* and *-ir* verbs

Regular *-er* and *-ir* verbs are similar to one another in the preterite. Here are the preterite forms of *aprender* and *salir.* Notice the accent marks on the endings *-í* and *-ió:*

¿Recuerdas?

You have already learned to talk about completed past actions using regular *-ar* verbs.

(yo)	**aprendí**	(nosotros) (nosotras)	**aprendimos**
(tú)	**aprendiste**	(vosotros) (vosotras)	**aprendisteis**
Ud. (él) (ella)	**aprendió**	Uds. (ellos) (ellas)	**aprendieron**

(yo)	**salí**	(nosotros) (nosotras)	**salimos**
(tú)	**saliste**	(vosotros) (vosotras)	**salisteis**
Ud. (él) (ella)	**salió**	Uds. (ellos) (ellas)	**salieron**

The verb *ver* is regular in the preterite but does not have accent marks in any of its forms:

vi viste vio vimos visteis vieron

GramActiva VIDEO

Want more help with the preterite of *-er* and *-ir* verbs? Watch the **GramActiva** video.

Leer/Escribir

Ricitos de Oro y los tres osos

Escribe los verbos apropiados en el pretérito para completar cada frase del cuento de *Ricitos de Oro y los tres osos.*

Un día los tres osos __1.__ *(salir / beber)* temprano de su casa para caminar. Ricitos de Oro, una chica muy bonita, __2.__ *(comer / ver)* la casa de los tres osos y __3.__ *(recibir / abrir)* la puerta. Ella no __4.__ *(ver / comprender)* que era[1] la casa de los tres osos y __5.__ *(comer / aprender)* toda la comida del oso chiquito. Luego ella __6.__ *(beber / decidir)* dormir un poco. Poco después, los tres osos regresaron a su casa, __7.__ *(abrir / salir)* la puerta y __8.__ *(deber / ver)* a Ricitos de Oro en la cama del osito. Cuando Ricitos de Oro __9.__ *(viajar / ver)* a los osos __10.__ *(abrir / salir)* de la casa rápidamente. __11.__ *(Comer / Correr)* hasta llegar[2] a su propia casa.

[1]it was [2]until she arrived

  **Escribir**

Durante las vacaciones

Escribe seis frases para decir qué hicieron *(did)* estas personas durante las vacaciones. Usa las palabras de la lista.

Modelo

Durante las vacaciones, mi hermana y yo corrimos en la playa de Punta Cana.

1. mi familia y yo
2. mis amigos
3. yo
4. mis padres
5. mi hermano(a)
6. mi amigo(a) *(nombre)*

comer en . . .	aprender a . . .
compartir una casa en . . .	ver . . .
escribir . . .	salir de casa temprano para . . .
correr en . . .	salir con . . .

   **Hablar/Escribir**

Tú y yo

1. Trabaja con otro(a) estudiante. Lee una frase de la Actividad 17. Tu compañero(a) va a contestar si tiene una idea similar en su hoja de papel.

Modelo

A —*Mi hermana y yo corrimos en la playa de Punta Cana.*
B —*Mi amigo y yo también corrimos, pero nosotros corrimos en un estadio.*
o: —*Yo no corrí en las vacaciones. Escribí cuentos todos los días.*

2. Escribe seis frases para comparar lo que hicieron tú y tu compañero(a) durante las vacaciones.

Modelo

Adela y yo corrimos durante las vacaciones. Ella corrió en un estadio con su amigo. Yo corrí en la playa con mi hermana.

Vacaciones en las playas de la República Dominicana

Más práctica

- Practice Workbook, p. 59: 8A-5
- WAV Wbk.: Writing, p. 70
- Guided Practice: Grammar Acts., pp. 253–254
- *Real.* para hispanohablantes, pp. 294–297

For: Preterite *-er*, *-ir* Verbs
Web Code: jbd-0803

Gramática

The preterite of *ir*

Ir is irregular in the preterite. Notice that the preterite forms of *ir* do not have accent marks:

(yo)	**fui**	(nosotros) (nosotras)	**fuimos**
(tú)	**fuiste**	(vosotros) (vosotras)	**fuisteis**
Ud. (él) (ella)	**fue**	Uds. (ellos) (ellas)	**fueron**

The preterite of *ir* is the same as the preterite of *ser*. The context makes the meaning clear.

José **fue** a Barcelona. — *José **went** to Barcelona.*
El viaje **fue** un desastre. — *The trip **was** a disaster.*

Strategy

Using memory devices
Here's a memory tip to help you remember the subjects of *fui* and *fue:*

The "I" form ends in *-i (fui).*

The "he" and "she" form ends in *-e (fue).*

GramActiva VIDEO

Want more help with the preterite of *ir*? Watch the **GramActiva** video.

Escribir

Mis amigos y yo fuimos a . . .

En una hoja de papel, escribe cinco frases para decir adónde fueron tú y tus amigos.

1. yo
2. mi mejor amigo(a)
3. mis amigos
4. mis amigos y yo
5. uno(a) de mis compañeros de clase

¡Respuesta personal!

Hablar

¿Adónde fueron?

Con otro(a) estudiante, di adónde y cómo fueron estas personas a estos lugares.

Óscar y Lourdes

Modelo

A —*¿Adónde fueron Óscar y Lourdes?*
B —*Fueron al teatro.*
A —*¿Cómo fueron?*
B —*Fueron en coche.*

1. 
los Sánchez

2. 
tus amigos y tú

3. 

Liliana

4. 

Uds.

5. 
Gregorio

6. **¡Respuesta personal!**
tú

Hablar

¿Cómo fuiste tú?

El mes pasado fuiste a muchos lugares, unos cerca y otros más lejos. Trabaja con otro(a) estudiante para hablar de cómo fueron Uds. a cada uno de estos lugares.

Modelo

A —*¿Cómo fuiste de tu casa a tu restaurante favorito?*
B —*Fui en el coche de mis padres.*

Estudiante A

1. de tu casa a tu escuela
2. de tu escuela al centro comercial
3. de tu ciudad a tu lugar favorito
4. de Miami a Puerto Rico
5. de la Ciudad de México a Cancún
6. de Nueva York a la República Dominicana

Estudiante B

   **Escribir/Hablar/GramActiva**

Juego

1 Play in groups of four. Each person cuts a sheet of paper to form a perfect square. Fold that square into four smaller squares. Unfold the paper and label the squares *a, b, c,* and *d.* Follow Step a below for the *a* square. Fold the corner of that little square so it covers what you have written. Pass the paper to the person on your left. Follow Step b for the *b* square on the paper you receive from the person on your right, fold down the corner, and pass it to your left. Continue until all the squares have been filled. Do not look at what is written on the paper you receive. Write all of your answers in Spanish.

a. Write a subject plus the correct preterite form of *ir.*

b. Write a destination or place *(a / al / a la . . .).*

c. Write a mode of transportation.

d. Write a reason *(para* + infinitive) for going somewhere.

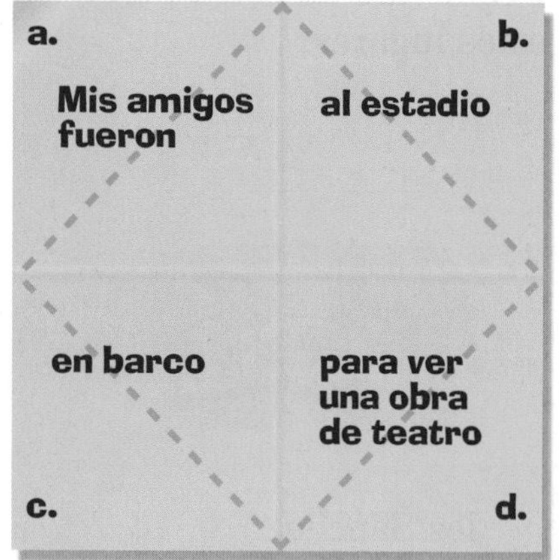

2 When you get your original paper back, unfold each square and read the complete sentence to your group. Let the group decide, *¿Cuál es la frase más tonta* (silly)? Read your silliest sentence to the class. Then make changes to the sentence so it makes sense.

  **Escribir**

En mis vacaciones . . .

Inventa unas vacaciones fantásticas. En una hoja de papel, escribe una carta en que hablas de dónde fuiste y qué hiciste. Necesitas responder a estas preguntas.

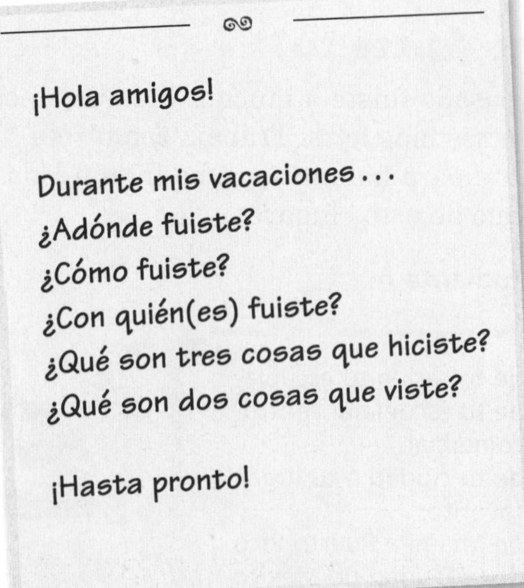

Hablar

Hablando de nuestras experiencias

Con otro(a) estudiante, usa la información en la Actividad 23 para hablar de lo que hiciste en tus vacaciones.

Modelo

A —*¿Adónde fuiste de vacaciones?*
B —*Fui a Argentina.*
A —*¿Qué hiciste allí?*
B —*Visité Patagonia y vi mucha nieve.*
A —*¿Cómo lo pasaste?*
B —*¡Fantástico!*

Escribir/Hablar

Las mejores vacaciones

Con tu compañero(a) de la Actividad 24, escribe una comparación *(comparison)* de sus vacaciones. Después, trabaja con otra pareja. Lee su comparación y decide quién en el grupo pasó las mejores vacaciones *(who had the best vacation)*.

Modelo

Yo fui a la Argentina y Pedro fue a San Antonio. Él fue a unos restaurantes mexicanos, y vio muchos monumentos, y yo vi mucha nieve. Pedro y yo aprendimos mucho en nuestras vacaciones...

Fondo cultural

Patagonia is a vast, windy region of diverse climates and terrains at the southern tip of South America. It lies east of the Andes and spans parts of Chile and nearly a quarter of Argentina. A sparsely populated area, it is home to many species, including a large colony (400,000 breeding pairs) of Magellanic penguins, whose breeding grounds are the eastern and western coasts of Chile and Argentina, as well as offshore islands.

- What regions of the United States can be compared to Patagonia? What types of animals live in those regions?

Más práctica

- Practice Workbook, p. 60: 8A-6
- WAV Wbk.: Writing, p. 71
- Guided Practice: Grammar Acts., p. 255
- *Real.* para hispanohablantes, p. 298

For: Preterite of *ir*
Web Code: jbd-0804

Gramática

The personal *a*

You know that the direct object is the person or thing that receives the action of a verb. When the direct object is a person or group of people, you usually use the word *a* before the object. This is called the "personal *a*."

Visité **a mi abuela.**	*I visited **my grandmother**.*
Vimos **a Juan y Gloria.**	*We saw **Juan and Gloria**.*

You can also use the personal *a* when the direct object is a pet.

Busco **a mi perro,** Capitán.

To ask who receives the action of a verb, use *¿A quién?*

¿A quién visitaron Uds.?

GramActiva VIDEO

Watch the **GramActiva** video for more help with the personal *a*.

Leer/Escribir/Hablar

Don Pepito y don José

1 Lee esta rima tradicional.

—Hola, don Pepito.
—Hola, don José.
—¿Pasó* Ud. por mi casa?
—Por su casa no pasé.
—¿Vio Ud. a mi abuela?
—A su abuela no la vi.
—Adiós, don Pepito.
—Adiós, don José.

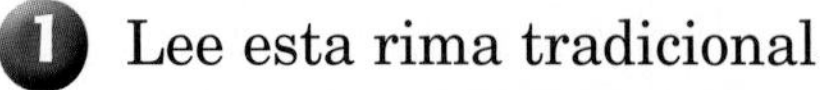

*Did you stop by

Nota

You have learned the direct object pronouns *lo*, *la*, *los*, and *las*. These direct object pronouns can refer to people as well as to things. Note that the direct object pronouns do not take the personal *a*.

- ¿Viste **a tus primos** durante tus vacaciones?
- Sí, **los** vi.

2 Ahora escribe las líneas *¿Vio Ud. a mi abuela?* y *A su abuela no la vi* y sustituye estos miembros de la familia por "abuela". Usa el pronombre *(pronoun)* apropiado.

1. tíos
2. hermano
3. primas
4. hermanita

3 Con otro(a) estudiante, lee la rima. Un(a) estudiante va a ser don Pepito y el/la otro(a), don José. Lean la rima cuatro veces, cada vez con un miembro diferente de la familia.

En Barcelona, España

Actividad 27 — **Escribir/Hablar**

De visita el año pasado

1. ¿Visitaste a muchas personas o muchos lugares el año pasado? Copia esta tabla en una hoja de papel y complétala *(complete it)* con la información apropiada.

Personas y lugares	¿Cuándo?	¿Dónde?
1. tus abuelos	el verano pasado	en Puerto Rico
2. un(a) amigo(a) que no vive aquí		
3. un parque de diversiones		
4. tus primos		
5. una nueva ciudad		
6. un museo de arte		

2. Usa la información en tu tabla para hablar con un(a) compañero(a) sobre tus visitas del año pasado.

Modelo

A —*¿Visitaste a tus abuelos durante las vacaciones?*
B —*Sí, los visité el verano pasado.*
o: —*No, no los visité.*
A —*¿Dónde los visitaste?*
B —*Los visité en Puerto Rico.*

El español en la comunidad

Your community may have some of the tourist destinations you learned about in this chapter, such as *un museo, un teatro, un zoológico,* or *un parque de diversiones.* Think of different opportunities to use your Spanish at each of the locations. As you learn more Spanish, perhaps you could provide tours to visitors who speak Spanish. You could help write brochures and maps in Spanish to assist Spanish-speaking visitors. Can you think of other opportunities?

- Visit one of these locations in person or online and see what resources are available in Spanish. Bring them to share with the class.

Leer/Pensar

Juego de geografía: Las Américas

¿Conoces[1] bien los países de las Américas? Empareja las descripciones con los países apropiados.

Conexiones La geografía

1. Este país es el más grande de América Central. En el suroeste hay un lago muy grande que tiene el mismo nombre que el país. El lago está muy cerca de la frontera[2] con Costa Rica. En el este del país está el mar Caribe donde el clima es tropical y llueve mucho.
2. Este país pequeño tiene dos regiones tropicales, en el este y en el oeste, con montañas en el centro. Un cuarto de las personas en el país son de origen indígena y hablan quechua, el idioma[3] de los incas. Su nombre viene de la línea imaginaria que cruza el país.
3. Las ciudades más grandes de este país, como la capital, están en el centro del país donde hay montañas y volcanes. En el norte hay desiertos extensos y en el sur hay selvas[4] tropicales. Este país comparte una frontera con los Estados Unidos.
4. Este país es el más grande de América del Sur, con el río más grande del mundo.[5] Una gran parte del país es selva tropical con miles de especies de plantas, árboles y animales como monos, jaguares y tucanes. No hablan español aquí; hablan portugués.
5. Es el único[6] país de América del Sur que tiene playas en el mar Caribe y el océano Pacífico. Es un país famoso por su café, que viene de los valles fértiles.

[1]Do you know [2]border [3]language [4]forests [5]world [6]only

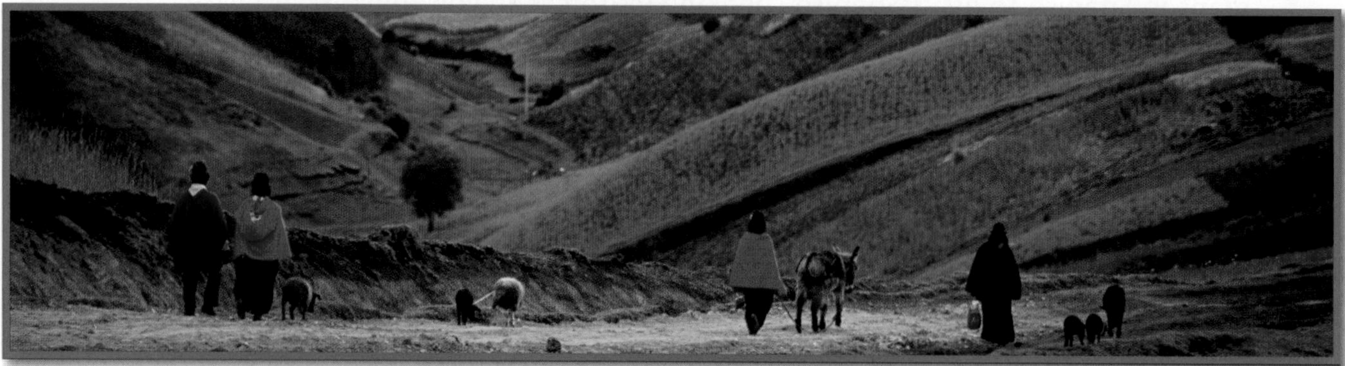

Exploración del lenguaje

Nouns that end in *-io* and *-eo*

Latin words for buildings and places have carried into many modern languages, including Spanish. In many place names the Latin ending *-um* (which remains in a number of words in English today) changed to an *-io* or *-eo* in Spanish. You know some of these words: *el estadio, el museo, el gimnasio.*

El Acuario de Madrid, España

Try it out! Based on your knowledge of English and what you have learned about Spanish place names from Latin, match the definitions with the Spanish words in the list.

1. where you stand to deliver a speech
2. usually found in a cemetery
3. where you can see all kinds of sea life
4. where you sit when you see school plays or concerts
5. where you go to learn about stars and planets
6. where the ancient Romans went to see sporting events

a. el auditorio
b. el podio
c. el acuario
d. el planetario
e. el coliseo
f. el mausoleo

Escribir/Hablar

Y tu, ¿qué dices?

1. ¿Qué puedes visitar en tu comunidad? ¿Hay museos, parques de diversiones o monumentos? ¿Cuál prefieres visitar?
2. El año pasado, ¿fuiste a ver una obra de teatro en tu comunidad o en tu escuela? ¿Te gustó? ¿Por qué?
3. El año pasado, ¿visitaste un museo o un zoológico en tu comunidad? ¿Cómo lo pasaste?
4. ¿Prefieres viajar a otros países o ciudades, o prefieres visitar lugares en tu comunidad?

El Museo del Prado en Madrid, España

Más práctica

- **Practice Workbook, p. 61: 8A-7**
- **Guided Practice: Grammar Acts., p. 256**
- ***Real.* para hispanohablantes, pp. 299–301**

For: Personal *a*
Web Code: jbd-0805

¡Adelante!

Lectura

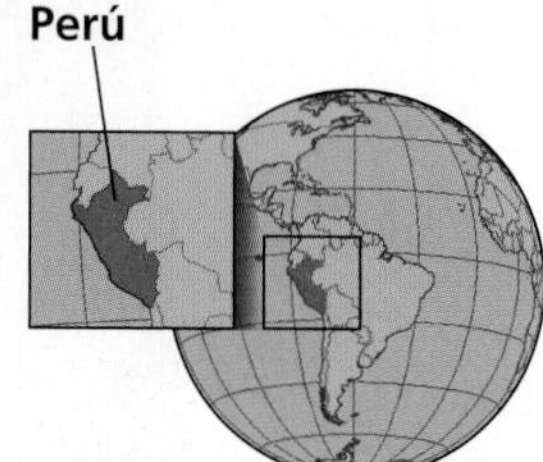

Objectives

- **Read journal entries about a trip to Peru**
- **Learn about *los ojos de Dios***
- **Describe a trip you have taken**
- **Watch *¿Eres tú, María?*, Episodio 7**

Álbum de mi viaje al Perú

Por Sofía Porrúa

Strategy

Using context clues
If you don't recognize a word, use the other words in the sentence to help you guess its meaning. Use context clues to guess the meaning of words such as *antigua, altura, construyeron,* and *nivel.*

domingo, 25 de julio
Estoy en el Perú con mis amigos Beto y Carmen. Vamos en autobús al Cuzco, antigua capital del imperio inca. Hoy día es una ciudad pequeña y una atracción turística. Beto está sacando muchas fotos con su cámara digital. Carmen está dibujando todo lo que ve. Las montañas son fantásticas.

miércoles, 28 de julio
Hoy es el Día de la Independencia peruana. En esta fecha en 1821, José de San Martín proclamó la independencia del Perú. En Lima, una gran ciudad moderna y capital del país, hay grandes celebraciones.

jueves, 29 de julio
Hoy estamos en Machu Picchu, ruinas impresionantes de una ciudad antigua de los incas. A más de 2.000 metros de altura en los Andes, los incas construyeron calles, casas, acueductos, palacios, templos y terrazas para cultivar. Hiram Bingham, un arqueólogo de la Universidad de Yale, descubrió[1] Machu Picchu en 1911.

[1]discovered

sábado, 31 de julio
Estamos paseando en bote por el lago Titicaca, en la frontera del Perú y Bolivia. Es el lago más grande de estos países y el más alto del mundo.[2] ¡Estamos a más de 3.800 metros sobre el nivel del mar!

miércoles, 4 de agosto
Ahora estamos en un avión pequeño. Sobre la tierra[3] podemos ver algo muy misterioso: hay un desierto donde vemos enormes dibujos de animales y figuras geométricas. Estos dibujos se llaman las Líneas de Nazca. Miden[4] más de 300 metros y tienen más de dos mil años. ¿Quiénes los dibujaron, y por qué? Es necesario estar en un avión para verlos. ¿Cómo dibujaron los artistas algo tan[5] grande sin poder verlo?

Mañana regresamos al Cuzco y el domingo salimos de Perú. ¡Un viaje muy interesante! Beto tiene sus fotos y Carmen, sus dibujos. Yo no soy ni fotógrafa ni artista, por eso voy a comprar tarjetas postales[6] como recuerdos.

[2]world [3]ground [4]They measure [5]so [6]postcards

¿Comprendes?

1. ¿Cómo va a recordar Sofía su viaje al Perú? ¿Y Beto y Carmen?
2. Pizarro y los españoles descubrieron muchas de las ciudades de los incas. ¿Por qué piensas que no descubrieron Machu Picchu? ¿Quién lo descubrió?
3. Para muchos turistas que visitan el lago Titicaca es difícil caminar y respirar *(to breathe)*. ¿Por qué piensas que tienen estos problemas?
4. ¿Cuáles son los misterios de las Líneas de Nazca?
5. Copia la tabla en una hoja de papel. Usa la información de la lectura para comparar el Perú con los Estados Unidos.

	Perú	Estados Unidos
a. Dos lugares históricos y turísticos		
b. Día de la Independencia		
c. Año de la proclamación de la independencia		
d. Capital del país hoy		
e. Héroe nacional		

Más práctica
- **WAV Wbk.: Writing, p. 72**
- **Guided Practice: *Lectura*, p. 257**
- ***Real.* para hispanohablantes, pp. 302–303**

For: Internet Activity
Web Code: jbd-0806

La cultura en vivo

El ojo de Dios

Mujer tarahumara en San Rafael, México

Traveling in the Spanish-speaking world you will encounter a marvelous variety of artwork and crafts, many of which have their origins in the time before the Spaniards came to the Americas. One form of art that is popular among visitors to parts of Mexico is the *ojo de Dios.*

The *ojo de Dios* is a diamond-shaped weaving. As a gift, it symbolizes good wishes from one person to another. *Ojos de Dios* may have originated in Peru about 300 B.C. The people best known for making these today are the Indians of Mexico's Sierra Madre region. The Cora, Huichol, Tarahumara, and Tepehuane all make and use these weavings in their daily lives.

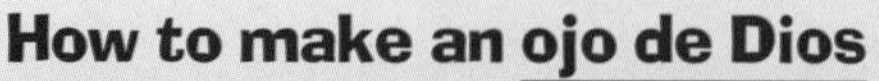

How to make an ojo de Dios

Materials

- yarn
- scissors
- two sticks of the same size
- optional: feathers, beads, or tassels for finishing touches

Figure 1

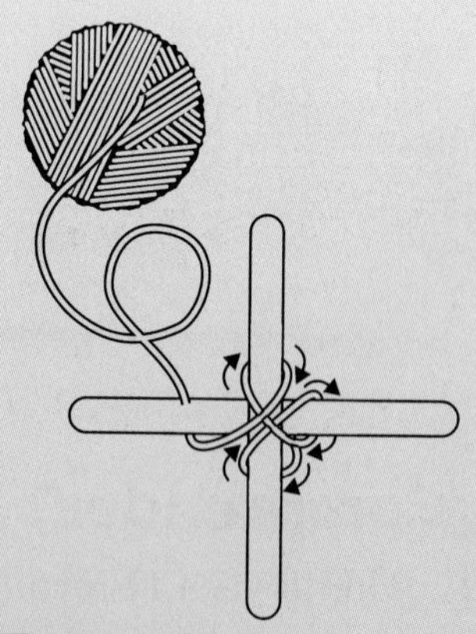
Figure 2

Directions

1 Tie the sticks together to form a cross. *(Fig. 1)*

2 Tie the end of the yarn to the center of the cross.

3 Weave the yarn over and around each stick, keeping the yarn pulled tight. *(Fig. 2)* To change color, knot together two ends of different-colored yarn. The knot should fall on the back side. Continue wrapping until the sticks are covered with yarn. Tie a small knot at the back and leave enough yarn to make a loop for hanging.

4 You may want to add feathers, beads, or tassels to the ends of the sticks. Hang your decorative piece for everyone to enjoy.

Think about it! What are some of the traditional handicrafts in the United States? What is the ethnic heritage of these crafts?

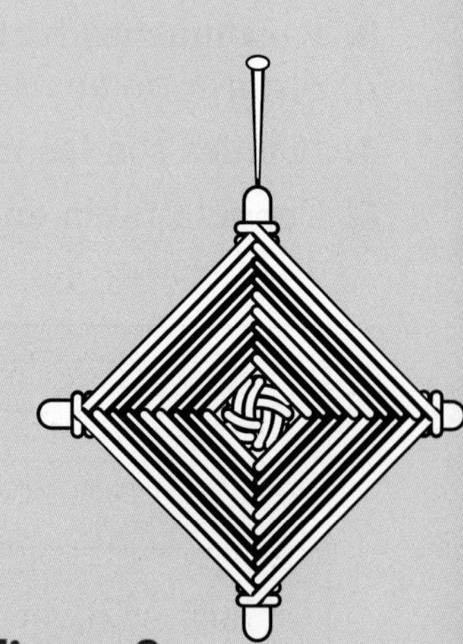
Figure 3

Presentación oral

Mi viaje

Task

Tell a friend about a trip you took. It could be a vacation or a trip to visit family members, or you can make up a trip. Use photographs or drawings to make your talk more interesting.

1 Prepare Use the word web to help you think about what you did on your trip. Think of information and events to include in each circle. Bring in photos from the trip or draw pictures to illustrate each part of the trip represented on the word web. Design the illustration of your trip so it looks appealing.

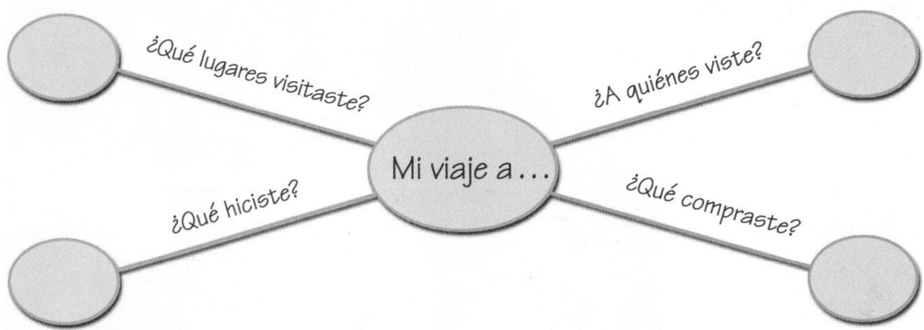

2 Practice Work with a partner and use the information in your word web to tell about your trip. Go through your story several times using the photographs or illustrations. You can use your notes in practice, but not when you present. End your presentation by saying how you felt about the trip.

Strategy

Using graphic organizers
Using a graphic organizer such as a word web will help you think through what you want to say in your presentation.

Modelo

En marzo, fui a Florida para visitar a mi abuelita y a mis primos. Tomamos el sol en la playa y nadamos mucho. Aprendí a bucear y vi animales muy interesantes en el mar. Me gusta mucho Florida. Es un lugar fantástico. El viaje fue muy divertido.

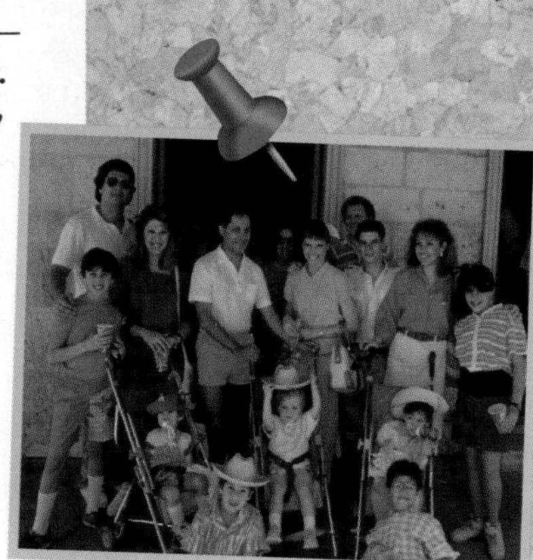

3 Present Talk about your trip to a small group or the whole class. Use your photos or drawings to help you present.

4 Evaluation Your teacher may give you a rubric for how the presentation will be graded. You may be evaluated on:

- how much information you provide
- how well you use photographs or visuals to illustrate your story
- how well you are understood

Videomisterio

¿Eres tú, María?

Episodio 7

Antes de ver el video

Resumen del episodio

Lola y Pedro visitan el piso elegante de doña Gracia. Entran en la habitación[1] de María. Hay ropa, libros, unas fotos y una tarjeta postal. Lola y Pedro leen algo muy interesante en la tarjeta postal. Después, van al piso de Julia. Allí vive un hombre que no conoce a Julia. Pero antes vivía[2] una chica en el piso. Todavía hay unas cosas de esa chica: ropa, unas cartas y unos papeles. ¿Y qué más?

[1] bedroom [2] used to live

Nota cultural Addresses in Spain are written differently than in the United States. For example, the name of Julia's street is Calle Norte. The building number is 23. The 1° *(primero)* indicates the apartment is on the first floor (not the ground floor, but what we would call the second floor), and Julia lives in apartment D.

"Lola, te llamo porque tengo información sobre la otra chica en el accidente. Tengo la dirección de su piso. Es Calle Norte, 23, 1°, D".

Palabras para comprender

¡Suerte!	Good luck!
No la conozco.	I don't know her.
tenía un secretario	had a secretary
tuvo problemas con él	had problems with him
¡Qué casualidad!	What a coincidence!

"¿A quién buscáis? Antes aquí vivía una chica . . . ".

"Mira esta tarjeta postal. Interesante, ¿no?".

"¿Sabes, Pedro? En mi profesión la casualidad no existe".

Después de ver el video

¿Comprendes?

Pon las frases en orden según el episodio.

1. Pedro recuerda el nombre de Luis Antonio Llamas, un secretario de su papá.
2. Leen la tarjeta postal de Luis Antonio.
3. Pedro llama a Lola para invitarla a visitar el piso de su abuela.
4. El joven en el piso de Julia no está nada contento.
5. Rosalinda llama a Lola para darle la dirección de Julia.
6. Quieren ver la habitación de María.
7. Deciden visitar el piso de Julia.

Nota gramatical In this episode you will hear a few more examples of the *vosotros* form: *queréis, sois, podéis, buscáis.* Remember that you use *vosotros* or *vosotras* when talking to more than one person whom you would address individually as *tú.*

For: More on *¿Eres tú, María?*
Web Code: jbd-0507

Repaso del capítulo

Chapter Review

To prepare for the test, check to see if you . . .

- know the new vocabulary and grammar
- can perform the tasks on p. 247

Vocabulario y gramática

jbd-0889 

to talk about places to visit on vacation

la ciudad	city
el estadio	stadium
el lago	lake
el lugar	place
el mar	sea
el monumento	monument
el museo	museum
el país	country
el parque de diversiones	amusement park
el parque nacional	national park
el teatro	theater
la obra de teatro	play
el zoológico	zoo

to talk about things to see on vacation

el animal	animal
el árbol	tree
la atracción, *pl.* **las atracciones**	attraction(s)
el mono	monkey
el oso	bear
el pájaro	bird

to talk about things to do on vacation

aprender (a)	to learn
bucear	to scuba dive / snorkel
(comprar) recuerdos	(to buy) souvenirs
descansar	to rest, to relax
montar a caballo	to ride horseback
pasear en bote	to go boating
tomar el sol	to sunbathe
visitar	to visit

to talk about ways to travel

en	by
el autobús	bus
el avión	airplane
el barco	boat, ship
el tren	train

For *Vocabulario adicional*, see pp. 336–337.

to talk about your vacation

el boleto	ticket
como	like, as
¿Cómo lo pasaste?	How was it (for you)?
dime	tell me
fantástico, -a	fantastic
Fue un desastre.	It was a disaster.
el hotel	hotel
impresionante	impressive
ir de vacaciones	to go on vacation
Me gustó.	I liked it.
¿Qué hiciste?	What did you do?
¿Qué te pasó?	What happened to you?
regresar	to return
salir	to leave, to go out
¿Te gustó?	Did you like it?
tremendo, -a	tremendous
viajar	to travel
el viaje	trip
vi	I saw
¿Viste . . . ?	Did you see . . . ?

to express time

durante	during
tarde	late
temprano	early

preterite of *-er* and *-ir* verbs

aprendí **salí**	**aprendimos** **salimos**
aprendiste **saliste**	**aprendisteis** **salisteis**
aprendió **salió**	**aprendieron** **salieron**

preterite of *ir*

fui	**fuimos**
fuiste	**fuisteis**
fue	**fueron**

Más práctica

- Practice Workbook: Puzzle, p. 62
- Practice Workbook: Organizer, p. 63

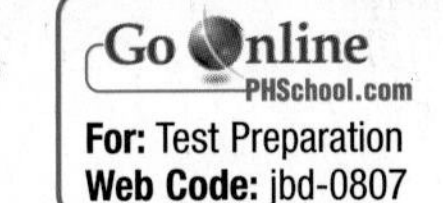

Preparación para el examen

On the exam you will be asked to . . .	Here are practice tasks similar to those you will find on the exam . . .	If you need review . . .
jbd-0889  **1 Escuchar** Listen and understand what people say they did and where they went during their last vacation	As part of a presentation in Spanish class, a student talked about his last vacation. As you listen, see if you can determine: a) where he went; b) one thing he did; c) one thing he saw.	**pp. 218–223** *A primera vista* **p. 219** Actividad 1 **p. 224** Actividad 7 **p. 225** Actividades 8–9
 **2 Hablar** Tell about your best trip or vacation	Find out where your partner went on his or her best vacation, and what he or she did and saw. As you listen, make a drawing that includes details of the trip. Then your partner will ask you to describe your best vacation. Do your drawings match the descriptions?	**p. 226** Actividad 11 **p. 228** Actividad 14 **p. 233** Actividad 20 **p. 237** Actividad 27 **p. 243** *Presentación oral*
 **3 Leer** Read and understand a vacation postcard	Read the postcard Javier sent to his friend last summer during his family vacation. Which things does he say he liked? Was there anything he didn't like? ¡Hola! Salí de vacaciones la semana pasada y ahora estamos aquí en Puerto Rico. Visitamos a nuestra tía en San Juan. Ayer fuimos al Viejo San Juan, donde vi muchos monumentos. También vi El Morro, un lugar muy famoso. ¡Fue fabuloso! Hoy fui a la playa de Luquillo y tomé el sol. Los otros bucearon por tres horas, pero a mí no me gusta el mar. Después, comimos arroz con pollo en un restaurante. ¡Uf! ¡Siempre arroz con pollo aquí! Regreso el sábado. ¡Hasta luego! Javier	**p. 226** Actividad 10 **p. 227** Actividad 12 **p. 238** Actividad 28 **pp. 240–241** *Lectura*
4 Escribir Write a brief narrative about an imaginary character's trip	A first-grade teacher has asked you to write a story in Spanish for her students. You decide to write about a stuffed bear, *el Oso Teo,* and his trip. Tell where he went, what he did, what he saw, and what he ate. Begin with something like, *"El Oso Teo fue de viaje a su parque favorito . . ."*	**p. 225** Actividad 8 **p. 231** Actividades 17–18 **p. 237** Actividad 27 **p. 239** Actividad 29 **pp. 240–241** *Lectura*
 **5 Pensar** Demonstrate an understanding of cultural perspectives regarding artwork and crafts.	Think about a gift you might give someone to symbolize good luck and good fortune in our culture. Compare it to a traditional craft from Mexico that is given for the same reason. Describe its significance and history in the Spanish-speaking world.	**p. 242** *La cultura en vivo*

Fondo cultural

The United States Peace Corps has programs in countries throughout the world. The volunteer in this photo is working on a project in Guatemala, where more than 4,000 United States volunteers have served since the establishment of the Peace Corps program. Since 1963, Peace Corps volunteers have been helping rural communities through projects in agriculture, the environment, health, and business development.

- How do you think your language skills could help you serve other people? What types of projects might you want to work on if you were a Peace Corps volunteer?

Un proyecto del Cuerpo de Paz, en Guatemala

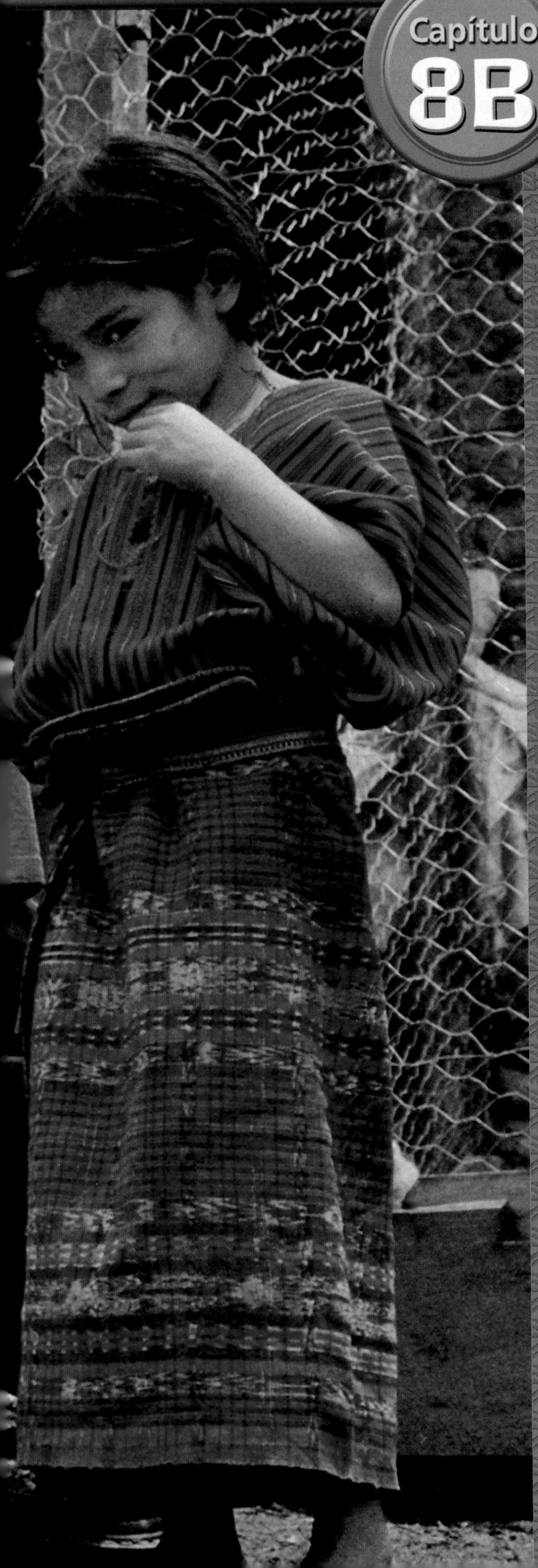

Capítulo 8B

Ayudando en la comunidad

Chapter Objectives

- **Discuss volunteer work and ways to protect the environment**
- **Talk about what people say**
- **Talk about what people did for others**
- **Understand cultural perspectives on volunteer work**

Video Highlights

A primera vista: ***Cómo ayudamos a los demás***

GramActiva Videos: the present tense of *decir*; indirect object pronouns; the preterite of *hacer* and *dar*

Videomisterio: *¿Eres tú, María?*, Episodio 8

Country Connection

As you learn about volunteer work and ways to protect the environment, you will make connections to these countries and places:

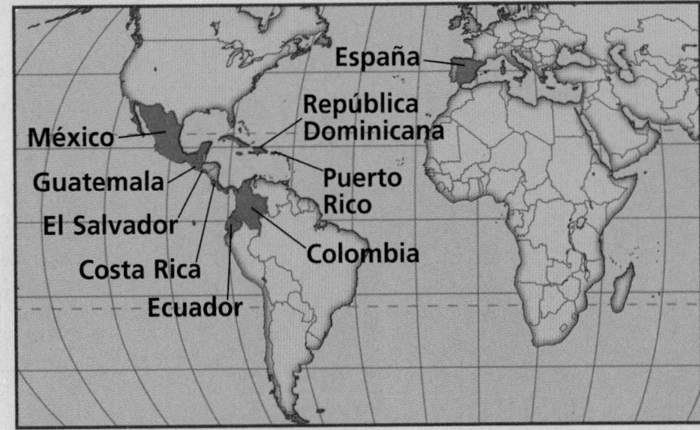

Más práctica

- ***Real.* para hispanohablantes, pp. 310–311**

Go Online PHSchool.com **For:** Online Atlas **Web Code:** jbe-0002

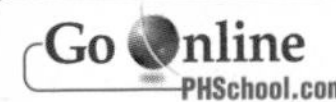

A primera vista

jbd-0897

Vocabulario y gramática en contexto

Objectives

Read, listen to, and understand information about
- volunteer work
- community-service tasks
- what people did to help others

¿Quieres ayudar a los demás?

¡Trabaja como voluntario en tu comunidad!

ayudar en un jardín de verduras

trabajar en un proyecto de construcción

¡Habla con los Amigos del barrio hoy! ¡Tú puedes ser la diferencia!

hacer trabajo voluntario en una escuela primaria

trabajar en un campamento de deportes

—Mira el cartel. Hay **problemas*** en nuestra comunidad. Debemos trabajar como voluntarios.

—Tienes razón. ¿Cómo puedes **decidir** qué hacer? Es la primera **vez** que trabajo como voluntario.

—Quiero enseñar**les** a **los niños** a leer. **Es necesario** poder leer, ¿no crees?

*Even though *problema* ends in *-a,* it is a masculine noun: *Tengo un problema.*

—¿Me ayudas a **reciclar** la basura del río y de las calles? Son cosas que pueden usar **otra vez. Dicen** que tenemos que **separar**las.

—Bueno, te ayudo. ¿Adónde vamos a **llevar**las?

—Al centro de reciclaje en la calle Bolívar.

Actividad 1

jbd-0897

Escuchar

El trabajo voluntario

Gloria investiga *(is researching)* los trabajos voluntarios en la comunidad. Señala cada lugar que ella menciona.

Actividad 2

jbd-0897

Escuchar

¿Qué puedes reciclar?

Estás separando unos artículos en dos cajas: una es para el papel y la otra es para todos los demás artículos. Levanta una mano si debes poner el artículo en la caja para papel. Levanta dos manos si debes ponerlo en la otra caja.

Más práctica

- Practice Workbook, pp. 64–65: 8B-1, 8B-2
- WAV Wbk.: Writing, p. 79
- Guided Practice: Vocab. Flash Cards, pp. 259–264
- *Real.* para hispanohablantes, p. 312

Videohistoria

jbd-0897

Cómo ayudamos a los demás

Gloria, Raúl y Tomás hacen trabajos voluntarios. ¿Por qué les gusta ser voluntarios?

Costa Rica

Raúl Gloria Tomás

Antes de leer

Activating prior knowledge Before you read the *Videohistoria,* think about what you know about the topic of volunteer work.

- In what ways can someone volunteer in your community? How do you think Gloria, Tomás, and Raúl might help their communities?

1. Look at the photos and make a list of the kinds of volunteer work that you see Gloria, Tomás, and Raúl doing.
2. Look at photo 7. What kinds of things are Raúl, Gloria, and Tomás recycling?

1 **Gloria:** Raúl y yo trabajamos como voluntarios en **el Hospital** Nacional de Niños. ¿Quieres venir con nosotros?

Tomás: Sí. Me encanta el trabajo voluntario. Es **increíble** la satisfacción que **nos** da cuando ayudamos a los demás.

2 **Papá:** Un momento. ¿Pueden Uds. reciclar este papel y estas botellas?

Tomás: ¡Por supuesto! Dame la bolsa de plástico.

3 **Tomás:** ¿Y qué hacen Uds. en el hospital?

Gloria: Ayudamos con los niños. Leemos libros y cantamos y jugamos con ellos. **A menudo** les traemos **juguetes.**

4 **Gloria:** A veces es difícil porque los niños están muy enfermos. Pero es **una experiencia inolvidable.**

5 **Raúl:** El año pasado yo trabajé en un centro para **ancianos.** Pasé mucho tiempo con ellos.

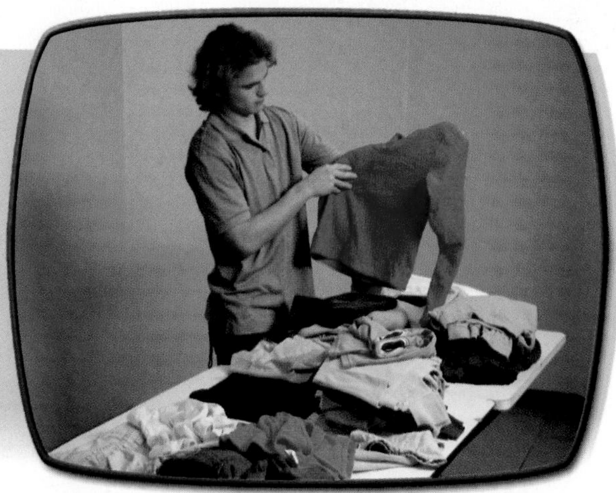

6 **Tomás:** Soy miembro de un club que se llama "Casa Latina". El año pasado recogimos ropa **usada.** ¿Sabes que **hay que** separar la ropa y después lavarla?

Gloria: **¿Qué más hicieron** Uds.?

Tomás: Luego le **dimos** la ropa a **la gente pobre**.

7 **Raúl:** Aquí podemos reciclar el papel y las botellas.

Gloria: Mira, para el plástico, el papel y el vidrio.

Tomás: En mi comunidad también reciclamos.

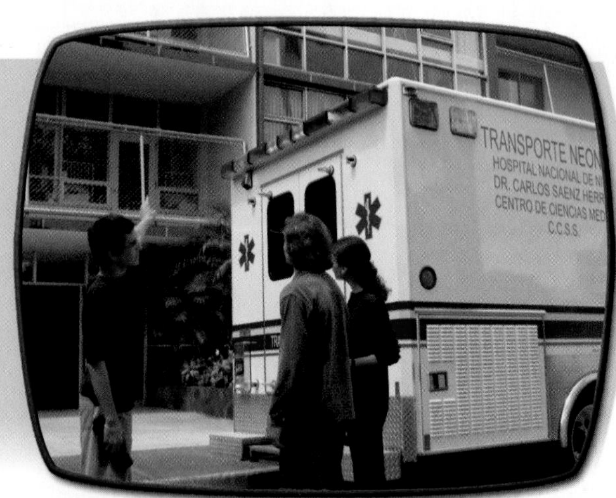

8 **Raúl:** Mira. Aquí está el hospital. ¿Entramos?

Leer/Escribir

¿"Casa Latina" u Hospital Nacional de Niños?

Escribe los números del 1 al 6 en una hoja de papel. Lee cada frase. Si una frase describe una actividad que los jóvenes hacen en el Hospital Nacional de Niños, escribe las letras *HNN*. Si la frase describe una actividad que hacen en el club "Casa Latina", escribe las letras *CL*.

1. Recoge ropa usada de sus compañeros de clase.
2. Lee un libro a María y Juanito.
3. Canta una canción de niños.
4. Trae un traje y dos camisas blancas al Sr. Mendoza.
5. Compra unos juguetes para dos chicas enfermas.
6. Separa la ropa blanca de la ropa de colores.

Leer/Escribir

¿Quién es?

¿Quién diría *(would say)* estas frases: Gloria, Tomás o Raúl? Escribe los números del 1 al 6 y escribe el nombre de la persona quien diría cada frase. ¡Ojo! Una frase puede ser de más de una persona.

Gloria

Tomás

Raúl

1. Me gusta mucho el trabajo voluntario.
2. Trabajo en un hospital para niños.
3. Ayudar a los demás me da mucha satisfacción.
4. Trabajo con los niños y les traigo juguetes.
5. Me gusta pasar tiempo con los ancianos. Les leo el periódico y hablo con ellos.
6. Recojo* la ropa usada.

Recoger is a regular *-er* verb with a spelling change in the *yo* form of the present tense: *recojo.*

Leer/Escribir

¿Comprendes?

1. Para Gloria, ¿es fácil trabajar en el hospital? ¿Por qué sí o por qué no?
2. ¿Por qué quiere ir Tomás con Raúl y Gloria al hospital?
3. ¿Dónde hace Tomás su trabajo voluntario?
4. ¿Qué hace Tomás antes de dar ropa a la gente pobre?
5. ¿Qué cosas necesita reciclar el papá de Gloria y Raúl?

Más práctica

- Practice Workbook, pp. 66–67: 8B-3, 8B-4
- WAV Wbk.: Video, pp. 73–75
- Guided Practice: Vocab. Check, pp. 265–268
- *Real.* para hispanohablantes, p. 313

Go Online PHSchool.com — **For:** Vocab. Practice **Web Code:** jbd-0812

Manos a la obra

Vocabulario y gramática en uso

Objectives

- Talk about helping your community
- Ask and tell about recycling
- Ask and tell about volunteering
- Learn the present tense of *decir* and the preterite of *hacer* and *dar*
- Learn to use indirect object pronouns

Actividad 6

jbd-0898

Escuchar/Escribir

Escucha y escribe

En la región de Cataluña en España, hay un sistema para reciclar que usan muchas personas. En una hoja de papel, escribe los números del 1 al 6. Escucha la descripción de este sistema y escribe las frases.

También se dice . . .

la lata = el bote *(España, Puerto Rico)*

España

En España separan el vidrio del papel para reciclarlos.

Actividad 7

Leer/Escribir

Lo que podemos hacer todos

Lee el cartel que dice cómo puedes ayudar en la comunidad. En una hoja de papel, escribe los números del 1 al 8 y escribe las palabras apropiadas para completar cada frase.

ancianos	vidrio
calle	separar
escuela primaria	comunidad
problemas	voluntario

Todos queremos:

Una comunidad que ayuda

Para ayudar a la __1.__, tenemos que hacer muchas cosas. Por ejemplo, podemos trabajar en un hospital con los __2.__, o en una __3.__ con los niños. El trabajo __4.__ es muy importante para toda la gente de la comunidad.

Una comunidad limpia

Podemos ayudar cuando recogemos la basura de la __5.__. El reciclaje es importante también. Debemos __6.__ el papel, el plástico y el __7.__ de la basura y traerlos al centro de reciclaje.

Cuando todos ayudan, tenemos menos __8.__ y más soluciones.

Para aprender más de cómo ayudar en la comunidad, Ud. debe venir al:
Centro de la Comunidad este viernes entre las 6:00 P.M. y las 9:00 P.M.

Pensar/Escribir

Un cartel para ayudar en la comunidad

En una hoja de papel, escribe tu propio cartel con cuatro o más cosas que uno puede hacer para ayudar a la comunidad. Usa el cartel en la Actividad 7 como modelo.

Hablar

El reciclaje

Habla con otro(a) estudiante sobre el reciclaje.

Modelo

A —*En nuestra comunidad, ¿hay que reciclar el papel?*
B —*¡Por supuesto! Lo separamos y lo ponemos en una caja azul.*
o: —*No sé. Nosotros no lo reciclamos.*

¿Recuerdas?
The direct object pronouns *lo, la, los,* and *las* replace nouns. They have the same gender and number as the nouns they replace.

1. 
2. 
3. 
4. 
5. 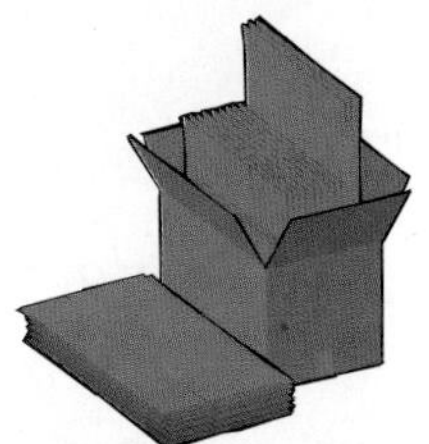
6. 

Fondo cultural

El reciclaje Spain is one of the leading European countries in recycling. Spain's glass recycling program is called *Ecovidrio,* from the Spanish words for *ecology (ecología)* and *glass (vidrio). Ecovidrio* started in the late 1990s and has been very successful. Glass recycling is an excellent way of reducing waste and protecting the environment.

- How do efforts in your community compare to glass recycling in Spain? What other efforts are available in your community?

Reciclaje en Cataluña, España

Leer/Pensar/Escribir/Hablar

El trabajo voluntario

Según las preferencias de los jóvenes de las fotos, explica dónde debe trabajar cada uno de ellos.

Modelo

Samuel debe trabajar en un hospital.

Teresa: Prefiero los trabajos al aire libre,* como un proyecto de construcción. Me encanta trabajar con las manos.

*outdoors

Rafael: Mi trabajo voluntario favorito es estar con niños en un campamento o una escuela primaria. Para mí es una experiencia inolvidable ver cómo aprenden tanto.

Samuel: Me gusta mucho ayudar a la gente pobre o a las víctimas de los desastres. Sus problemas son muy importantes para mí.

Bárbara: Me gusta mucho pasar tiempo con los ancianos. Son muy interesantes y simpáticos y me enseñan muchas cosas.

1. 
2. 
3. 
4. 
5. 
6. 

Hablar

¿Dónde quieres hacer el trabajo voluntario?

Escoge dos de los lugares de la Actividad 10 donde te gustaría hacer el trabajo voluntario. Con otro(a) estudiante, explica por qué prefieres estos lugares.

Modelo

A —*¿Dónde quieres hacer trabajo voluntario?*
B —*Me gustaría hacer trabajo voluntario en un hospital.*
A —*Y, ¿por qué?*
B —*Porque me gusta trabajar con los ancianos. Siempre ayudo a mis abuelos.*

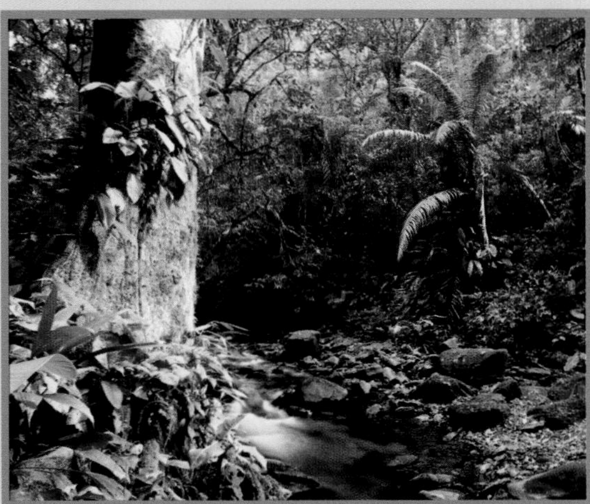
El bosque lluvioso

Fondo cultural

La Asociación Conservacionista de Monteverde in Costa Rica helps protect the rain forest around the Monteverde Cloud Forest Preserve. Young people from around the world come to help preserve the natural forest. Volunteers maintain trails and help in preservation projects. They also get the chance to make friends with local families while enjoying one of the most impressive landscapes in the world.

- What programs in your community or state are similar to the program in Costa Rica?

Escribir

Una experiencia inolvidable

Hay un proyecto voluntario en tu escuela. Los miembros van a viajar a Costa Rica este verano para trabajar en un pueblo en Guanacaste y necesitan voluntarios. Escribe un párrafo de cinco frases para explicar por qué te gustaría ir con ellos y por qué vas a ser un(a) buen(a) voluntario(a). Si nunca haces el trabajo voluntario, puedes inventarlo *(invent it)*.

Modelo

Me gustaría ir a Costa Rica porque me encanta el trabajo voluntario. El año pasado yo trabajé en un hospital y ayudé a los ancianos.

Exploración del lenguaje

Nouns that end in *-dad, -tad, -ción,* and *-sión*

You know that *actividad* means "activity" and that *comunidad* means "community." In Spanish, nouns that end in *-dad* or *-tad* usually correspond to nouns in English that end in *-ty*. Nouns that end in *-dad* or *-tad* are feminine.

In a similar way, nouns in Spanish that end in *-ción* or *-sión* frequently correspond to nouns in English that end in *-tion* or *-sion*. These nouns are also feminine. You know that *construcción* means "construction" and that *posesión* means "possession."

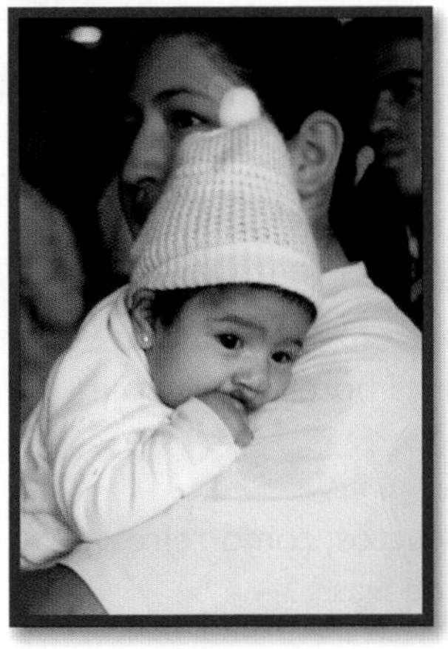
Los médicos *(doctors)* de Interplast, una organización voluntaria, ayudan a la comunidad ecuatoriana de Azogues, en los Andes del Ecuador.

Try it out! Figure out the meanings of these Spanish words.

la generosidad	la comunicación
la responsabilidad	la comisión
la variedad	la vegetación
la tranquilidad	la información
la libertad	la organización
la universidad	la presentación

Leer/Escribir

La cadena de reciclaje

Todos estamos de acuerdo en que la protección del medio ambiente *(environment)* es importantísima. Una cosa que hacemos es reciclar el vidrio. Pero, después de poner las botellas y otros objetos de vidrio en los contenedores de reciclaje, ¿qué pasa? Mira esta "Cadena de reciclaje", y contesta las preguntas en una hoja de papel.

Conexiones — Las ciencias

1 Consumidor[1] responsable
¡Eres muy importante! Si no ayudas, es imposible empezar la cadena de reciclaje. Hay que poner las botellas de vidrio en los contenedores de reciclaje.

2 Recoger el vidrio
Recogen el vidrio de los contenedores y lo llevan a una planta de tratamiento[2].

3 Planta de tratamiento
En la planta de tratamiento limpian las botellas de vidrio y las trituran[3].

4 Fábrica[4] de botellas
Con el vidrio que trituraron, hacen nuevas botellas que son como las botellas originales.

5 Envasador[5]
El envasador pone productos, como refrescos y jugos, en las botellas nuevas.

6 Tiendas
En las tiendas venden productos en botellas que tienen el símbolo: 

7 Consumidor
Si compras estos productos, completas la cadena de reciclaje. Ahora, ¡puedes empezar otra vez!

[1]consumer [2]treatment plant [3]crush and grind [4]factory [5]bottler

1. ¿Reciclas las botellas de vidrio a menudo? ¿Cuántas veces a la semana?
2. ¿Dónde está un centro de reciclaje donde tú vives?
3. ¿Dónde están los contenedores de reciclaje en tu escuela o en tu comunidad?
4. ¿Qué hacen con el vidrio que trituran?
5. ¿En cuáles de los pasos *(steps)* de la "Cadena de reciclaje" puedes participar tú?

Leer/Escribir/Hablar

Las 3 Rs

Lee el anuncio que está abajo *(below)*. Habla de Puerto Rico y la importancia de la conservación. Luego contesta las preguntas.

Puerto Rico

¡Tú puedes ser parte de la solución del problema de la basura en nuestra isla!

Recuerda esta guía práctica de las 3 Rs

Reduce: Cuando vas de compras, decide no comprar cosas que no son necesarias.

Reúsa: Usa un producto, objeto o material varias veces.[1] No debes tirar[2] a la basura las cosas que puedes usar otra vez.

Recicla: Usa los mismos materiales otra vez o usa un proceso natural o industrial para hacer el mismo o nuevos productos.

Lo que compras, comes, cultivas o tiras puede ser la diferencia entre un buen futuro o un futuro de destrucción para Puerto Rico.

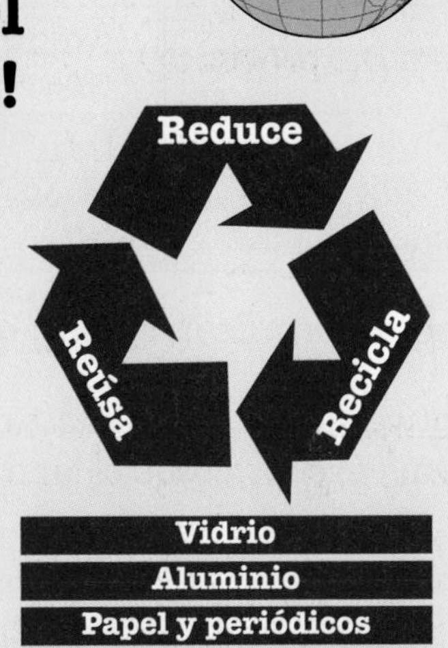

[1]several times [2]throw away

1. ¿Cómo puedes "reducir"? ¿Qué cosas compras o usas a veces que no son necesarias?
2. ¿Cómo puedes reciclar o reusar cosas en casa o en la escuela?
3. Según las frases que escribiste para la Actividad 11, escribe tres recomendaciones para cuidar *(take care of)* más tu comunidad.

Fondo cultural

Arte de vidrio Mexico is known for its production of beautiful glassware. Many of these works of art—including a wonderful variety of drinking glasses, bowls, and vases—are made from recycled bottles or car windshields. The glass is melted and hand-blown into new forms. Artisans also make trays and decorative windows by cutting different pieces of colored glass into a collage, then melting them together into a single piece. Each recycled glass artwork is unique.

- What everyday items or art objects are you familiar with that are made from recycled materials?

Gramática

The present tense of *decir*

The verb *decir* means "to say" or "to tell." Here are its present-tense forms:

(yo)	**digo**	(nosotros) (nosotras)	**decimos**
(tú)	**dices**	(vosotros) (vosotras)	**decís**
Ud. (él) (ella)	**dice**	Uds. (ellos) (ellas)	**dicen**

The *yo* form is irregular: ***digo.***

Notice that the *e* of *decir* changes to *i* in all forms except *nosotros* and *vosotros.*

¿Recuerdas?

You have used forms of *decir* in the questions *¿Cómo se dice?* and *Y tú, ¿qué dices?*

GramActiva VIDEO

Need more help with the verb *decir?* Watch the **GramActiva** video.

Actividad 15 **Escribir**

Hay que reciclar

En una hoja de papel, escribe las formas apropiadas del verbo *decir* para completar las opiniones de diferentes personas sobre cómo tener una comunidad limpia.

1. Mis padres ___ que es necesario recoger la basura en las calles.
2. La gente ___ que es importante llevar los periódicos a un centro de reciclaje.
3. Las personas en mi comunidad ___ que tenemos que separar la basura.
4. Mi profesor de biología ___ que es necesario reciclar el vidrio y el plástico.
5. Nosotros ___ que debemos limpiar nuestro barrio y comunidad.
6. Yo ___ que el reciclaje es muy importante.
7. ¿Qué ___ tú?

Nota

Use the *él/ella* form of the verb with *la gente.*

To tell *what* people say, use ***que*** after *decir:*

- La gente dice **que**...

Escribir/Hablar

¿Qué dices sobre . . . ?

1. Copia esta tabla en una hoja de papel. En la segunda columna, escribe *muy importante, importante* o *no es importante* para decir tu opinión de cada actividad. En la tercera columna, escribe *a menudo, a veces* o *nunca* para decir con qué frecuencia *(how often)* haces estas actividades para ayudar a tu comunidad.

2. Usa la información en tu tabla para hablar con otro(a) estudiante de lo que haces para ayudar en tu comunidad.

Actividad	¿Importante o no?	¿Con qué frecuencia?
recoger la basura de las calles o ríos	muy importante	a veces
separar el vidrio y el plástico de la basura para reciclar		
llevar los periódicos al centro de reciclaje		
ser voluntario(a)		
ayudar a la gente pobre		

Modelo

A —*Yo digo que recoger la basura de las calles y ríos es muy importante y a veces lo hago. Y tú, ¿qué dices?*

B —*Yo digo que es importante pero sólo lo hago a veces.*

Hablar/Escribir

¿Cómo podemos ayudar más?

Con tu compañero(a) de la Actividad 16, trabaja con otro grupo para decidir lo que pueden hacer para ayudar más en la comunidad. En una hoja de papel, escriban sus ideas y luego presenten sus ideas a la clase.

Modelo

A —*Yo digo que es muy importante recoger la basura de las calles y ríos. Juan dice que es importante, pero Luisa y Rafael dicen que no es importante. Todos lo hacemos a veces.*

B —*¿Qué más podemos hacer?*

C —*Yo digo que podemos limpiar el barrio dos veces al mes.*

D —*Bueno, también podemos recoger el plástico cerca del río y reciclarlo.*

Más práctica

- Practice Workbook, p. 68: 8B-5
- WAV Wbk.: Writing, p. 80
- Guided Practice: Grammar Acts., p. 269
- *Real.* para hispanohablantes, pp. 314–316

For: Present-tense *Decir*
Web Code: jbd-0813

Gramática

Indirect object pronouns

An indirect object tells *to whom* or *for whom* an action is performed. Indirect object pronouns are used to replace an indirect object noun.

Les doy dinero.	*I give money* ***to them.***
Te llevo el vidrio y las latas.	*I'll bring* ***you*** *the glass and the cans.*
¿**Nos** reciclas estas botellas?	*Will you recycle these bottles* ***for us?***

The indirect object pronoun comes right before the conjugated verb. Here are the different indirect object pronouns:

SINGULAR		PLURAL	
me	(to/for) me	**nos**	(to/for) us
te	(to/for) you	**os**	(to/for) you
le	(to/for) him, her; you *(formal)*	**les**	(to/for) them; you *(formal)*

When an infinitive follows a conjugated verb, the indirect object pronoun can be attached to the infinitive or be placed before the conjugated verb.

Quiero **darle** un juguete al niño.
o: Le quiero dar un juguete al niño.

Because *le* and *les* have more than one meaning, you can make the meaning clear, or show emphasis, by adding *a* + the corresponding name, noun, or pronoun.

Les damos lecciones **a Miguel y a Felipe.**
Les damos lecciones **a los niños.**
Les damos lecciones **a ellos.**

GramActiva VIDEO

Need more help with indirect object pronouns? Watch the **GramActiva** video.

Leer/Escribir

Las Olimpíadas Especiales

Unos jóvenes ayudan con las Olimpíadas Especiales. En una hoja de papel, escribe *me, te, le, nos* o *les* para completar cada frase.

Modelo

___ ayudan a los padres de los niños.
Les ayudan a los padres de los niños.

1. ___ dan naranjas y jugo a los participantes.
2. ___ hacen una donación a la señora que organizó el evento.
3. ___ traen agua a mis compañeros porque tienen sed.
4. ___ dan lecciones de varios deportes a los participantes.
5. ___ dicen a nosotros que debemos preparar los concursos *(contests)*.
6. ___ traen a mí un sándwich porque tengo hambre.
7. ___ dicen a nosotros que necesitan más ayuda.

Lanzador de bala *(shot-putter)*

Hablar/GramActiva

Juego

1. Tu profesor(a) va a dividir a los estudiantes en grupos de cinco. Cada grupo forma una fila *(line)*. Las primeras personas de cada fila van al frente de la clase y el/la profesor(a) les dice una frase.

2. Las personas regresan a sus grupos y le dicen a la primera persona en la fila, *"Me dice que..."* y repite la frase del (de la) profesor(a). Luego la primera persona repite la frase a la segunda persona de la fila.

3. Cada grupo continúa hasta decir la frase a la última *(last)* persona. Esta persona escribe la frase que escucha en una hoja de papel. El grupo más rápido y que dice la frase más correcta gana *(wins)* el juego.

Escribir

¿Cómo ayuda la gente a los demás?

Escribe frases para decir cómo la gente ayuda a los demás. Usa las palabras de las listas y *a menudo, a veces* o *nunca.*

Modelo

A veces la gente les lleva comida a los ancianos.

dar	dinero	ropa usada	los pobres
enseñar	flores	juguetes	los niños
comprar	cuentos	periódicos	las personas enfermas
llevar	comida	revistas	los ancianos
leer	una lección de...		

Escribir/Hablar

Regalos

1. En una hoja de papel, haz dos listas. En la primera, escribe los nombres de cinco personas. En la segunda, describe un regalo que vas a comprar para cada una de estas personas.

2. Habla con otro(a) estudiante sobre los regalos que vas a comprar.

Modelo

A —*¿Para quién vas a comprar un regalo?*
B —*Le voy a comprar un regalo a mi abuela.*
A —*¿Qué le vas a comprar?*
B —*Le voy a comprar flores.*

Más práctica

- Practice Workbook, p. 69: 8B-6
- WAV Wbk.: Writing, p. 81
- Guided Practice: Grammar Acts., pp. 270–271
- *Real.* para hispanohablantes, pp. 317–318

For: Indirect Obj. Pronouns
Web Code: jbd-0815

Gramática

The preterite of *hacer* and *dar*

Hacer and *dar* are irregular verbs in the preterite. Notice that these verbs do not have any accent marks in the preterite.

- The preterite stem for *hacer* is *hic-*. In the *Ud./él/ella* form, the *c* changes to a *z* so that it still has an "s" sound: *hizo.*
- The preterite stem for *dar* is *di-*. The same stem is used for all the preterite forms.

(yo)	**hice**	(nosotros) (nosotras)	**hicimos**
(tú)	**hiciste**	(vosotros) (vosotras)	**hicisteis**
Ud. (él) (ella)	**hizo**	Uds. (ellos) (ellas)	**hicieron**

(yo)	**di**	(nosotros) (nosotras)	**dimos**
(tú)	**diste**	(vosotros) (vosotras)	**disteis**
Ud. (él) (ella)	**dio**	Uds. (ellos) (ellas)	**dieron**

¿Recuerdas?
You used the preterite *tú* form of *hacer* when you asked, *¿Qué hiciste?*

GramActiva VIDEO

Watch the **GramActiva** video to learn more about the preterite of *hacer* and *dar.*

Pensar/Escribir

Ayudando a los pobres

Los estudiantes en tu escuela recogieron latas de comida para los pobres. Lee la gráfica para saber cuántas latas dieron estas personas. Escribe las frases en una hoja de papel.

Modelo

José y David
Ellos dieron 60 latas.

1. Guillermo
2. Lupita y yo
3. yo
4. Marta, Lupita y Raquel
5. José
6. David, Marta y yo

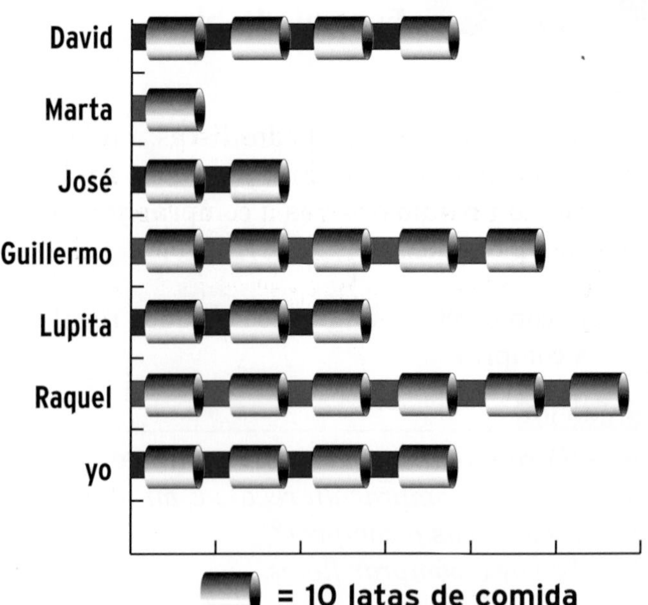

Fondo cultural

El Hospital de la Caridad, a hospice in Seville, Spain, was founded in the 1600s by the monks of *la Hermandad de la Caridad* (Charity Brotherhood). Today, the brothers still look after people who are old or poor as part of a long tradition of caring for the needy.

- What programs in your community or state provide support for people in need?

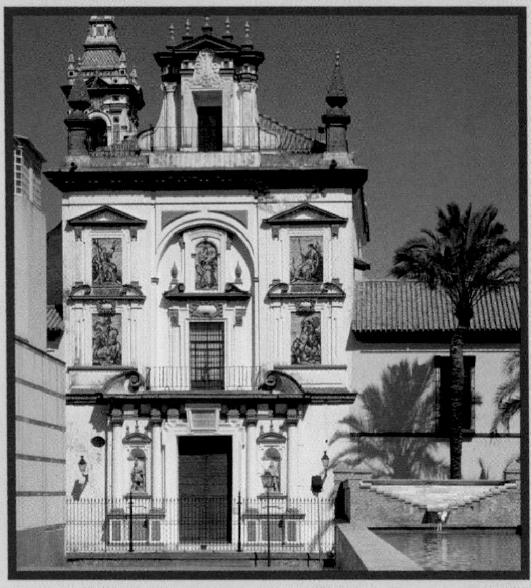

El Hospital de la Caridad en Sevilla, España

Actividad 23 Leer/Escribir

En un hospital

Una joven habla de su experiencia como voluntaria en un hospital. Escribe los verbos en el pretérito para completar las frases.

Mis amigos y yo __1.__ *(dar / decidir)* hacer un trabajo voluntario en un hospital. Nosotros __2.__ *(ir / hacer)* dibujos para los ancianos en el hospital. La semana pasada una amiga y yo __3.__ *(llevar / hablar)* los dibujos al hospital. La enfermera[1] nos __4.__ *(dar / decidir)* permiso para entrar en los cuartos de varios ancianos. Nosotros __5.__ *(llevar / visitar)* a los ancianos y les __6.__ *(decidir / dar)* los dibujos. Los ancianos nos __7.__ *(hablar / llevar)* de sus familias y nos __8.__ *(decidir / dar)* abrazos.[2] Ésta fue la primera vez que yo __9.__ *(hacer / llevar)* un trabajo voluntario. Fue una experiencia inolvidable para nosotros. Vamos a regresar al hospital otra vez.

[1] nurse [2] hugs

Actividad 24 jbd-0898

Escuchar/Escribir

Las donaciones

Vas a escuchar cómo varias personas y organizaciones, como la Cruz Roja, ayudaron a las víctimas de un desastre en El Salvador. En una hoja de papel, escribe los números del 1 al 6. Escribe las frases que escuchas.

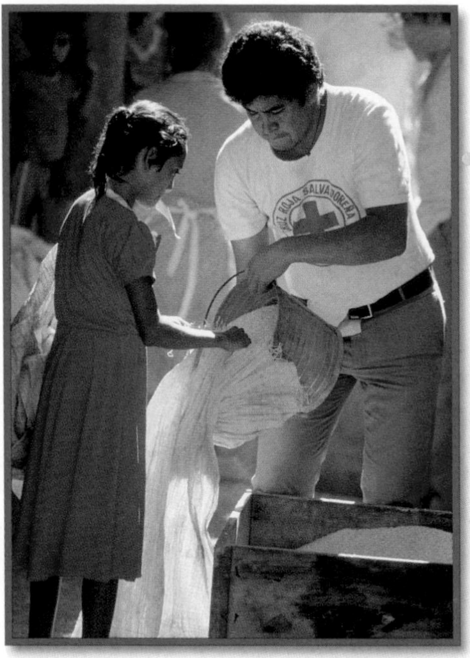

La Cruz Roja ayuda en El Salvador.

Leer/Escribir

¿Dónde hicieron trabajo voluntario?

Lee estas frases que describen el trabajo voluntario de varias personas. En una hoja de papel, escribe frases que dicen dónde lo hicieron.

- el barrio
- el centro de la comunidad
- el centro de reciclaje
- la escuela primaria
- el jardín de la comunidad
- el hospital

Modelo

Antonio trabajó con los niños.
Antonio hizo trabajo voluntario en la escuela primaria.

1. Mis amigos pasaron tiempo con los ancianos enfermos.
2. Yo separé las botellas de plástico y las botellas de vidrio de la basura.
3. Un chico en la clase cultivó *(grew)* flores.
4. Mi compañero de clase y yo recogimos basura de la calle.
5. Los demás recogieron ropa usada para los pobres.

Hablar

¿Qué les dieron?

Trabaja con otro(a) estudiante para hablar de lo que tú y tus amigos les dieron a las organizaciones voluntarias el año pasado.

Modelo

A —*¿Qué le diste tú a una organización voluntaria?*
B —*Yo les di flores a los ancianos en el hospital.*

Estudiante A

tú
tú y tus amigos
tu mejor amigo(a)
tus compañeros de clase
tu profesor(a)

¡Respuesta personal!

Estudiante B

ropa usada
juguetes para niños pobres
comida
regalos
flores
libros
latas y botellas para reciclar
periódicos

¡Respuesta personal!

   **Escribir/Hablar**

¿Qué hicieron el sábado pasado?

1. Escribe lo que hicieron estas personas el fin de semana pasado.

tu mejor amigo(a)	tu profesor(a) de...
tu madre (padre)	tus amigos(as)
tú y tus amigos	tú

2. Habla con otro(a) estudiante sobre lo que hicieron las personas.

Modelo

tus amigos
A —*¿Qué hicieron tus amigos el fin de semana pasado?*
B —*Mis amigos fueron al río. Y tus amigos, ¿qué hicieron ellos?*
A —*Vieron una película en el cine.*
o:—*No sé qué hicieron ellos.*

Una voluntaria de *The Mobility Project* de Colorado Springs conversando con dos amigos en Villa Guerrero, México.

 **Escribir/Hablar**

Juego

1. En grupos de cuatro, deben pensar en diferentes premios *(prizes)* que reciben las personas: por ejemplo, el premio Nobel, el Heisman, el Óscar, el Emmy, el Golden Globe o el Grammy. Cada uno escribe una pregunta que tu grupo va a hacerle a otro grupo sobre los premios que dieron el año pasado.

2. Tu grupo debe leer una de las preguntas a otro grupo, que tiene 30 segundos para contestarla. Si el grupo contesta bien la primera vez, recibe tres puntos. Si contesta bien la segunda vez, recibe un punto. Si contesta mal, tu grupo debe decirles la respuesta.

Modelo

A —*¿A quién le dieron el Óscar por ser la mejor actriz el año pasado?*
B —*Le dieron el premio a...*

Para decir más...

la actriz actress
el actor actor
el/la cantante singer
el/la atleta athlete

Al autor colombiano Gabriel García Márquez le dieron el premio Nobel de Literatura.

Pronunciación

The letter *x*

jbd-0898 

The letter *x* is pronounced several ways in Spanish. When it is between vowels or at the end of a word, it is pronounced /ks/. Listen to and say these words:

examen	*taxi*	*aproximadamente*
exactamente	*dúplex*	*éxito*

When the *x* is at the beginning of a word, it is usually pronounced /s/. At the end of a syllable, the *x* can be pronounced /s/, /ks/, or /gs/. Listen to and say these words:

xilófono	*explicar*	*experiencia*
exploración	*experimento*	*experto*

Try it out! Work with a partner to ask and answer these questions, paying special attention to how you pronounce the letter *x*.

1. ¿En qué clase son más difíciles los exámenes?
2. ¿Qué clase tienes durante la sexta hora?
3. ¿En qué clase haces experimentos? ¿Qué tipo de experimentos haces?
4. ¿En qué clase hablas o escribes mucho de tus experiencias personales?

In the 1500s, the *x* represented the "h" sound of the Spanish letter *j*. That is why you see some words, like *México, Oaxaca,* and *Texas* written with *x,* even though they are pronounced like the letter *j*. In words from indigenous languages of present-day Mexico and Central America, the *x* has the "sh" sound, as with the Mayan cities of Xel-há and Uxmal.

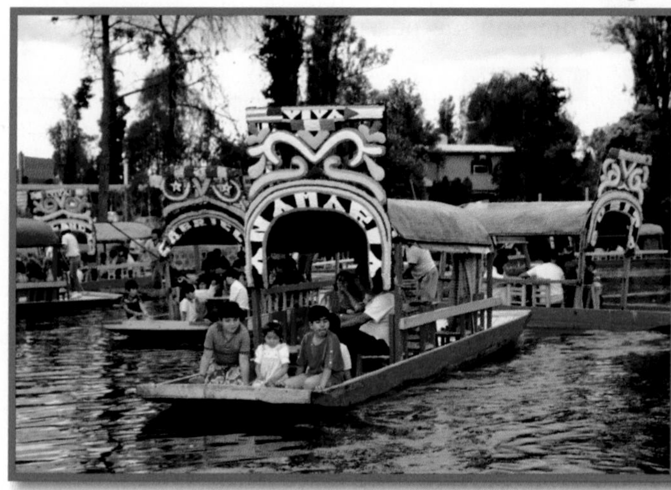

Una familia en Xochimilco, México

Actividad 29 **Escribir/Hablar**

Y tú, ¿qué dices?

1. ¿Qué hiciste el viernes pasado? ¿Qué hicieron tus amigos?
2. ¿Qué hizo tu familia el verano pasado?
3. ¿Qué les diste a tus hermanos o a tus amigos para su cumpleaños? ¿Qué te dieron a ti?
4. ¿Qué hizo la gente de tu comunidad el año pasado para ayudar a los pobres o a las víctimas de un desastre?
5. ¿Hizo tu barrio algo para ayudar a los ancianos o a los niños? ¿Qué?

Más práctica

- Practice Workbook, p. 70: 8B-7
- Guided Practice: Grammar Acts., p. 272
- *Real.* para hispanohablantes, pp. 319–320

Leer/Escribir/Hablar

Las tortugas tinglar

Lee esta información sobre las tortugas tinglar. Luego contesta las preguntas.

¡La tortuga tinglar es enorme! Es la tortuga marina más grande del mundo[1]. Los tinglares adultos pueden ser de hasta siete pies de largo y pesar[2] hasta 1.400 libras[3]. Cada año, entre febrero y julio, esta tortuga sale del mar en la noche y pone sus huevos en playas tropicales, como las de la República Dominicana, Costa Rica o de la isla de Culebra cerca de Puerto Rico. Después regresa a aguas frías.

Desde 1970 el tinglar está en peligro[4] de extinción. Por eso, en la primavera voluntarios de diferentes países van a las playas como las de la isla de Culebra. Llevan trajes de baño, jeans, sudaderas, camisetas, cámaras, binoculares, linternas[5], repelente contra mosquitos y muchas ganas de[6] ayudar a las tortugas. Patrullan[7] las playas buscando las tortugas.

Después de poner las tortugas los huevos, los voluntarios los llevan a un nido artificial. Aproximadamente 60 días después, las tortuguitas salen de los huevos. Los voluntarios llevan a las tortuguitas al mar donde nadan contínuamente por unas 28 horas. Estos voluntarios son muy importantes para la preservación de la tortuga tinglar.

[1]in the world [2]weigh [3]pounds [4]danger [5]flashlights [6]the desire [7]They patrol

1. Para ti, ¿cuáles son los hechos *(facts)* más increíbles sobre la tortuga tinglar?
2. Escribe una lista, en orden, del trabajo que hacen los voluntarios en la playa.
3. ¿Te gustaría trabajar como voluntario en una de las playas donde están las tortugas tinglar? ¿Por qué?

El español en el mundo del trabajo

There may be community service organizations in your neighborhood where knowing Spanish is helpful. These organizations include medical clinics, food kitchens, senior centers, career counseling and job training, and after-school programs. Volunteering your skills for these agencies is the first step to find out if you would be interested in pursuing work in the nonprofit sector.

- Check with local agencies to find out which ones offer services in Spanish (or in other languages). Develop a class list of volunteer opportunities in your community in which you could use your Spanish skills.

¡Adelante!

Lectura

Objectives

- Read about an international volunteer organization
- Learn about volunteer work in Spanish-speaking countries
- Create a poster announcing a community-service project
- Watch *¿Eres tú, María?,* Episodio 8

Lee este artículo sobre una organización que hace proyectos de construcción en muchos países del mundo.

Strategy

Recognizing cognates
Recognizing cognates in the following article can help improve your understanding of the reading.

Hábitat para la Humanidad Internacional

Hábitat es una organización internacional que ayuda a la gente pobre a tener casa. Su objetivo es construir casas seguras[1] que no cuestan mucho para las personas que no tienen mucho dinero. Hábitat trabaja con las familias pobres, con los grupos de voluntarios y con las personas que les dan dinero. Esta organización tiene más de 2.500 proyectos en muchas comunidades de los Estados Unidos y otros 1.600 proyectos en más de 83 países diferentes. Hábitat ha construido[2] unas 175.000 casas en todo el mundo.

Guatemala tiene catorce afiliados de Hábitat. Cada afiliado tiene su propio dinero y hace su plan de construcción y sus proyectos. Los afiliados de Guatemala tienen mucho éxito.[3] Han construido más de 10.000 casas y tienen planes para construir 15.000 más en los años que vienen. Según Hábitat, las personas pobres tienen que ayudar a construir sus casas. Es una manera positiva de ayudar a los demás. Hábitat les da los materiales de construcción y los trabajadores voluntarios. Cuando la casa está construida, el nuevo propietario[4] paga una pequeña hipoteca[5] cada mes. Después, los nuevos propietarios tienen que ayudar a otros futuros propietarios a construir sus casas.

[1] safe [2] has built [3] success [4] owner [5] mortgage

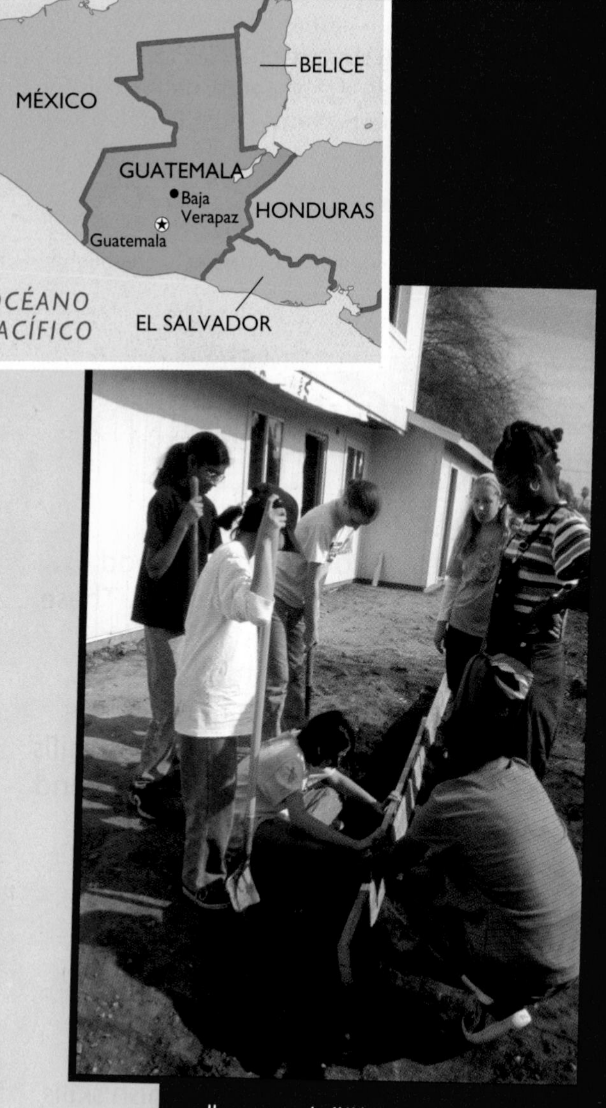

Un proyecto de Hábitat para la Humanidad Internacional

Para todos, es una experiencia increíble.

Trabajadores de Hábitat para la Humanidad Internacional

—Ayer fue mi cumpleaños y recibí el mejor regalo de mi vida, mi propia casa —dijo una señora de la comunidad de Baja Verapaz.

La mayoría[6] del dinero viene de donaciones privadas y del trabajo voluntario de muchísimas personas.

¿Sabes que el expresidente Jimmy Carter y su esposa Rosalynn son dos de los primeros miembros voluntarios de Hábitat? Los grupos de voluntarios son una parte fundamental del éxito de la organización.

—Es una experiencia inolvidable para ayudar a los demás —dijo un voluntario en Guatemala.

[6] the majority

¿Comprendes?

1. ¿Qué hace Hábitat?
2. ¿Con quiénes trabaja Hábitat?
3. ¿En cuántos países está Hábitat?
4. ¿Cuántas casas construyeron los afiliados de Guatemala?
5. ¿Qué tienen que pagar los nuevos propietarios?
6. ¿Qué tienen que hacer los nuevos propietarios?
7. ¿De dónde viene el dinero para construir las casas?
8. Y a ti, ¿te gustaría trabajar con Hábitat? ¿Por qué?

Más práctica

- **WAV Wbk.: Writing, p. 82**
- **Guided Practice: *Lectura*, p. 273**
- ***Real.* para hispanohablantes, pp. 322–323**

For: Internet Activity
Web Code: jbd-0816

Fondo cultural

El trabajo voluntario AmeriCorps is an organization of volunteers who work in urban and rural communities throughout the United States. They teach children to read, assist victims of natural disasters, and participate in other activities that benefit needy people.

One of the advantages of serving as an AmeriCorps volunteer is learning skills that can be used later in the workplace.

- What are some of the skills a volunteer might learn? Why are they important?

Doctores de las Naciones Unidas en Santa Cruz, Perú

Perspectivas del mundo hispano

¿Trabajas como voluntario?

Throughout the Spanish-speaking world students are involved in volunteer activities and organizations. In many private schools students are encouraged to serve their community for two to three hours per week to help them learn responsibilities that will make them good citizens. Community service also provides a good occasion to explore different professions such as education, medicine, or social work. For example, many young people work with local branches of the *Cruz Roja* (Red Cross) and learn how to respond in times of emergency. Courses are offered by the organization, and some students even study for a degree in health services.

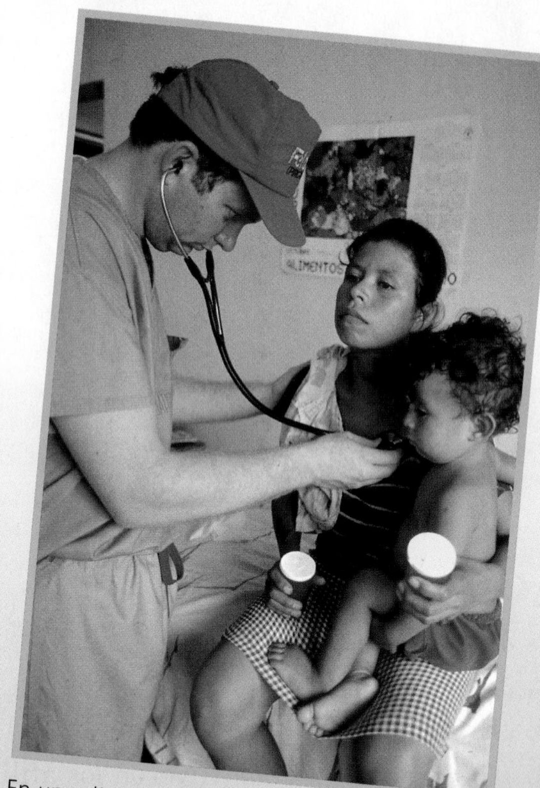

En una clínica en Trinidad, Honduras

In many Spanish-speaking countries, students are involved in causes dealing with the environment. In many countries, the natural beauty of the land is not only a source of national pride, it is also an economic resource and important to the well-being of the country. Students work at recycling centers collecting paper, glass, and plastic and collect trash along roadsides and in parks.

Check it out! Survey the students in your class. Who does volunteer work? What kind of work do they do? How often are they involved in community service activities?

Think about it! How does the involvement in volunteerism among teenagers in many Spanish-speaking countries compare with the involvement in your community?

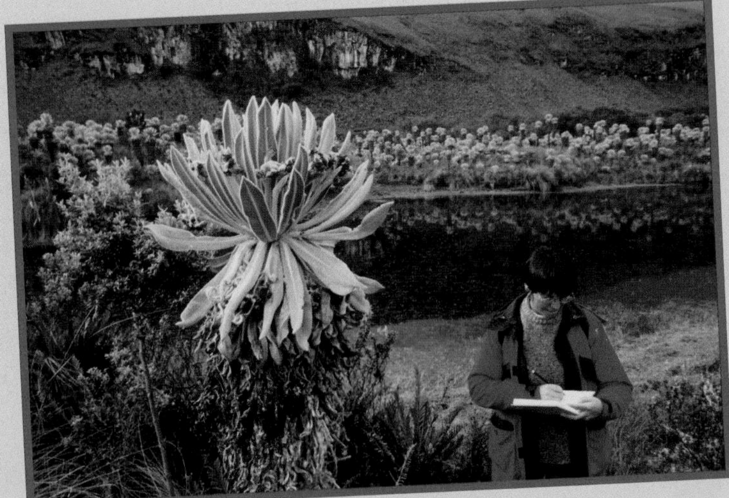

En la Reserva Ecológica El Ángel, en el Ecuador

Presentación escrita

¿Puedes ayudarnos?

Task
Your school sponsors community-service projects every year, so you want to organize a clean-up campaign for a park, recreation center, school playground, or other place in your community. Make a poster announcing the project and inviting students to participate.

1. **Prewrite** Answer the following questions about your project:
   - ¿Qué van a limpiar?
   - ¿Qué tienen que hacer?
   - ¿Dónde está el lugar?
   - ¿Cuándo van a trabajar?
   - ¿Cuántas horas van a trabajar?
   - ¿Quién(es) puede(n) participar?

Using key questions
Answering key questions can help you think of ideas for writing.

2. **Draft** Prepare a first draft using the answers to the questions. Organize the information in a clear and logical manner. Remember that you want students to stop and read the poster.

3. **Revise** Check your poster idea for spelling, accent marks, punctuation, and vocabulary usage. Share your work with a partner, who will check the following:
   - Is the information presented clearly and is it easy to understand?
   - Is it arranged logically?
   - Is there anything that you should add or change?
   - Are there any errors?

4. **Publish** Prepare a final version of the poster making any necessary changes. Add visuals to make the poster appealing. Display it in the classroom, cafeteria, or school library, or add it to your portfolio.

5. **Evaluation** Your teacher may give you a rubric for grading the poster. You may be evaluated on:
   - how complete the information is
   - the accuracy of the language in the poster
   - the visual presentation

Videomisterio

¿Eres tú, María?

Episodio 8

Antes de ver el video

"A ver. Esta foto. Yo conozco a este hombre. Pero no sé de qué. ¡Qué problema!".

Resumen del episodio

Después de visitar el piso de Julia, Lola y Pedro van a un café a tomar unos refrescos. Hablan de las cosas de Julia que el joven acaba de darles:[1] la ropa, las fotos, los papeles. Cuando Lola llega a su piso en la noche, ve que una mujer entra en el edificio número 8. Lola cree que es María. Sale rápidamente de su piso y espera[2] enfrente. Una mujer sale del edificio y Lola le pregunta, "¿Eres tú, María?".

[1] just gave them [2] waits

Palabras para comprender

María tenía las llaves.	María had the keys.
Ella las perdió.	She lost them.
¡No me sigas!	Don't follow me!
Acabo de ver . . .	I just saw . . .
Acabo de hablar con . . .	I just spoke with . . .

—¿Eres María Requena?
—¿Por qué quieres saberlo?

—Acabo de hablar con María Requena delante del piso de doña Gracia.

—Srta. Lago, esto es cosa de la policía.

Después de ver el video

¿Comprendes?

A. ¿Quién lo dice: Lola, Carmela, Pedro, el Inspector Gil, la camarera o María?

1. ¿Qué desean Uds.?
2. Y yo, un agua mineral.
3. ¿Cómo es que tienes las llaves del piso de Julia?
4. ¿Sabes algo más sobre el caso de doña Gracia?
5. Las diez y media. ¡Por fin!
6. ¿Qué quieres? ¿Quién eres?
7. ¡No me sigas! ¡No me sigas!
8. Acabo de ver a María Requena.
9. Ahora trabajo para Pedro Requena, el nieto de doña Gracia.
10. Hay que decirlo todo a la policía.

B. Escribe dos frases que describan cada foto de esta página.

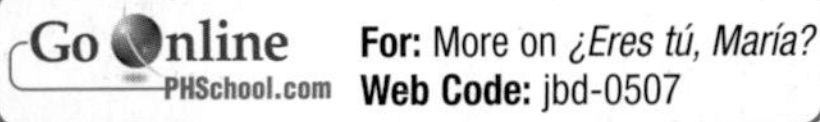

Repaso del capítulo

Chapter Review

To prepare for the test, check to see if you . . .

- know the new vocabulary and grammar
- can perform the tasks on p. 279

Vocabulario y gramática

jbd-0899

to talk about recycling

la bolsa	bag, sack
la botella	bottle
la caja	box
el cartón	cardboard
el centro de reciclaje	recycling center
la lata	can
llevar	to take; to carry
el periódico	newspaper
el plástico	plastic
reciclar	to recycle
recoger	to collect; to gather
separar	to separate
usado, -a	used
el vidrio	glass

to talk about places in a community

el barrio	neighborhood
la calle	street, road
la comunidad	community
el jardín	garden, yard
el río	river

to discuss possibilities for volunteer work

los ancianos	older people
el anciano	older man
la anciana	older woman
el campamento	camp
los demás	others
la escuela primaria	primary school
la gente	people
el hospital	hospital
el juguete	toy
los niños	children
el niño	young boy
la niña	young girl
pobre	poor
el problema	problem
el proyecto de construcción	construction project
el trabajo voluntario	volunteer work
el voluntario, la voluntaria	volunteer

other useful words and expressions

a menudo	often
decidir	to decide
Es necesario.	It's necessary.
la experiencia	experience
Hay que . . .	One must . . .
increíble	incredible
inolvidable	unforgettable
¿Qué más?	What else?
la vez, *pl.* **las veces**	time
otra vez	again

decir *to say, to tell*

digo	**decimos**
dices	**decís**
dice	**dicen**

indirect object pronouns

SINGULAR	PLURAL
me (to/for) me	**nos** (to/for) us
te (to/for) you	**os** (to/for) you
le (to/for) him, her; you *(formal)*	**les** (to/for) them; you *(formal)*

preterite of *dar*

di	**dimos**
diste	**disteis**
dio	**dieron**

preterite of *hacer*

hice	**hicimos**
hiciste	**hicisteis**
hizo	**hicieron**

For *Vocabulario adicional,* see pp. 336–337.

Más práctica

- Practice Workbook: Puzzle, p. 71
- Practice Workbook: Organizer, p. 72

Preparación para el examen

On the exam you will be asked to . . .	Here are practice tasks similar to those you will find on the exam . . .	If you need review . . .
jbd-0899  **1 Escuchar** Listen and understand as someone describes what he did in his community	A radio station is sponsoring a contest to encourage people to help in the community. Listen as a teen tells the announcer what he did. Identify whether he: a) helped older people; b) worked on a recycling project; c) contributed money; d) volunteered in a hospital or school.	**pp. 250–255** *A primera vista* **p. 251** Actividades 1–2 **p. 256** Actividad 6 **p. 267** Actividad 24
 **2 Hablar** Ask and answer questions about what you or someone you know did to help others in the past few months	Many organizations offer scholarships to students who help others. With a partner, practice asking and answering the following questions for the scholarship interviews with a local agency that works in the Spanish-speaking community: a) What did you do to help others? b) Why did you decide to do volunteer work?	**p. 257** Actividad 9 **p. 258** Actividad 10
 **3 Leer** Read and understand what people gave as donations to various people or groups	The Spanish Club treasurer's report about contributions to various organizations and individuals in the community is ready for the members. Read one line from the report. Indicate whether the member(s) donated: a) cash; b) lessons for an individual group; c) clothing; d) furniture. For example, you might read: *Scott y Jamie le dieron una cama y una cómoda a una familia pobre.*	**p. 267** Actividad 23 **p. 271** Actividad 30 **pp. 272–273** *Lectura*
 **4 Escribir** Write a list of things teenagers can do to help in their communities	To encourage your classmates to participate in *La semana de la comunidad,* make a poster for your classroom with at least five suggestions for activities. For example: *Recicla las botellas. Ayuda a los niños de la escuela primaria.*	**p. 260** Actividad 13 **p. 261** Actividad 14 **p. 263** Actividad 17 **p. 267** Actividad 23 **p. 275** *Presentación escrita*
5 Pensar Demonstrate an understanding of cultural perspectives regarding volunteer work	Think about the volunteer activities in which you and your friends participate. Based on what you've learned in this chapter, compare these to the type of work teenage volunteers do in Spanish-speaking countries.	**p. 248** *Fondo cultural* **pp. 250–255** *A primera vista* **p. 267** *Fondo cultural* **pp. 272–273** *Lectura* **p. 274** *Perspectivas del mundo hispano*

Tema 9 • Medios de comunicación

Fondo cultural

Luis Buñuel (1900–1983) was a Spanish-born film director. He made films in Spain, the United States, Mexico, and France. His films were often controversial because of their strong imagery and difficult topics. Buñuel made two surrealist films with artist Salvador Dalí (1904–1989), Spain's most famous Surrealist painter. The films mixed reality and dreams. This portrait of Buñuel was painted by Dalí in 1924 when the painter was 20 years old and Buñuel was 24.

- Who are some young directors today whose films are considered to be "cutting edge"?

"Retrato de Luis Buñuel" (1924), Salvador Dalí

Oil on canvas, .70 x .60 m. Coll. Luis Buñuel, Mexico City, D.F., Mexico. © 2004 Salvador Dalí, Gala-Salvador Dalí Foundation/Artists Rights Society (ARS), NY. Photo credit: Bridgeman-Giraudon / Art Resource, NY.

El cine y la televisión

Presentadoras de *Primer Impacto,* un programa de Univisión

Chapter Objectives

- Describe movies and television programs
- Express opinions about entertainment
- Talk about things you have done recently
- Understand cultural perspectives on common gestures

Video Highlights

A primera vista: ***¿Qué dan en la tele?***
GramActiva Videos: ***acabar de*** **+ infinitive;** ***gustar*** **and similar verbs**
Videomisterio: ***¿Eres tú, María?*****, Episodio 9**

Country Connection

As you learn about movies and TV programs, you will make connections to these countries and places:

Más práctica

- *Real.* para hispanohablantes, pp. 330–331

For: Online Atlas
Web Code: jbe-0002

A primera vista

jbd-0987 

Vocabulario y gramática en contexto

Objectives

Read, listen to, and understand information about
- **movies and television programs**
- **opinions on media entertainment**

¿Qué le interesa? Un programa...

¿...de entrevistas?

Entre tú y yo
Pablo Ramírez habla con personas fascinantes.

¿...educativo?

Nuestro planeta
Explora el mundo de los animales.

¿...de concursos?

¡Una fortuna para ti!
¡Los participantes pueden recibir mucho dinero!

¿...de noticias?

Las noticias de hoy
Presentamos todo lo que necesita saber del mundo en 30 minutos.

¿...deportivo?

Fútbol hoy
Hay fútbol, fútbol y mas fútbol.

¿...una telenovela?

Secretos de amor
¿Qué va a pasar con Rosario y Felipe en este programa **emocionante**?

¿...musical?

Ritmos latinos
Le presenta música de **más de** 20 países diferentes.

¿...de dibujos animados?

Patito y Paquito
Una presentación cómica para todos los niños.

—¿Qué quieres ver en la tele?

—¿La verdad? **Me aburre** la televisión. No me interesan nada los programas que **dan.**

—No estoy de acuerdo. Pienso que la televisión presenta muchos programas interesantes y divertidos.

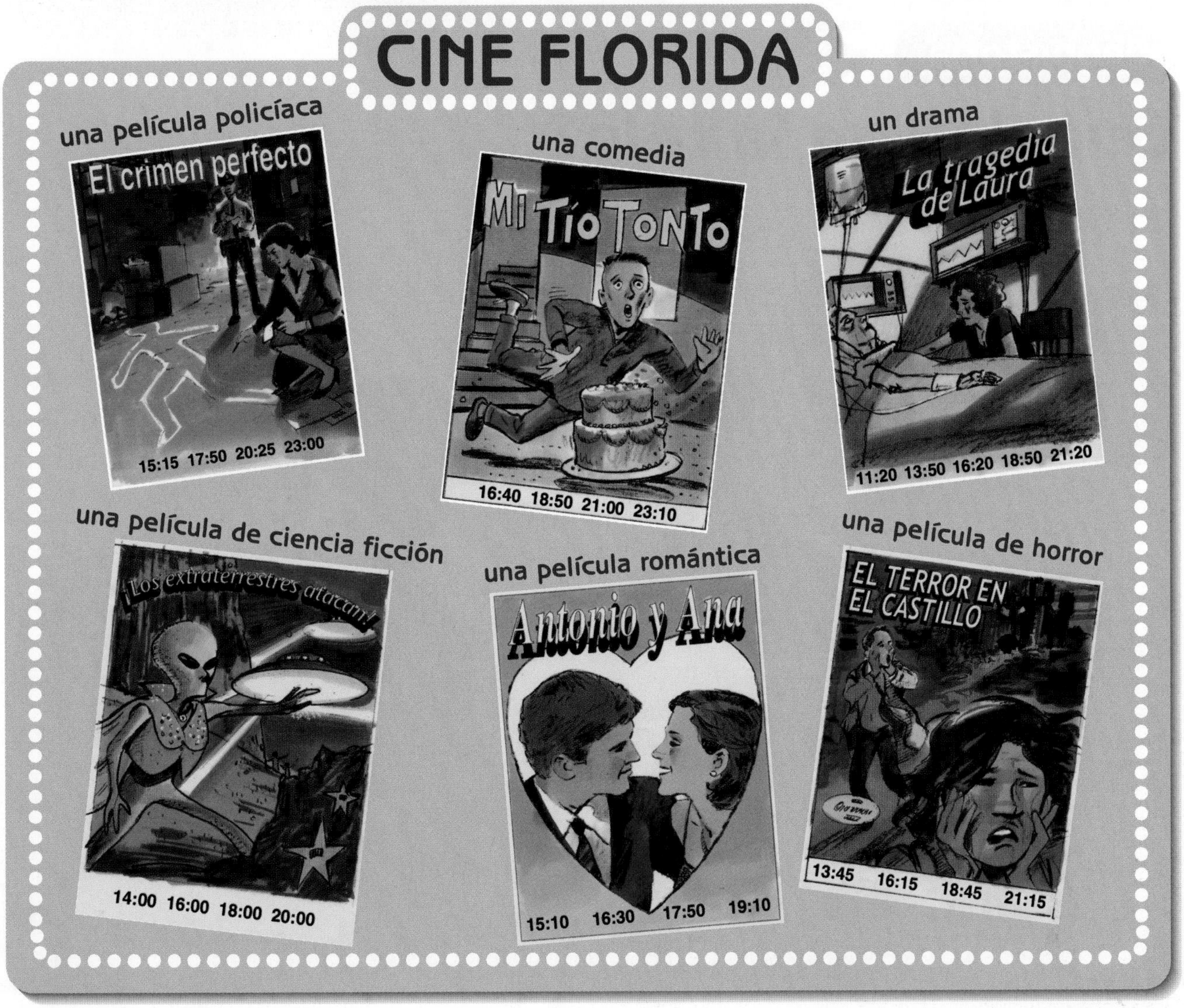

CINE FLORIDA

una película policíaca

El crimen perfecto

15:15 17:50 20:25 23:00

una comedia

Mi Tío Tonto

16:40 18:50 21:00 23:10

un drama

La tragedia de Laura

11:20 13:50 16:20 18:50 21:20

una película de ciencia ficción

¡Los extraterrestres atacan!

14:00 16:00 18:00 20:00

una película romántica

Antonio y Ana

15:10 16:30 17:50 19:10

una película de horror

EL TERROR EN EL CASTILLO

13:45 16:15 18:45 21:15

—¿Qué dan en el Cine Florida?

—Hay seis películas. Mis amigos dicen que esta película policíaca es muy **violenta.** No quiero verla. Me interesan más las películas románticas como *Antonio y Ana.*

—Yo también quiero verla. ¿A qué hora va a **empezar?**

—**Empieza** a las cuatro y media, y **termina antes de** las seis. **Dura menos de** una hora y **media.**

—**¿De veras?** Son **casi** las cuatro. ¡Vamos ahora!

Más práctica

- Practice Workbook, pp. 73–74: 9A-1, 9A-2
- WAV Wbk.: Writing, p. 89
- Guided Practice: Vocab. Flash Cards, pp. 275–280
- *Real.* para hispanohablantes, p. 332

For: Vocab. Practice
Web Code: jbd-0901

jbd-0987

Escuchar

¿Qué dan en la tele hoy?

Vas a escuchar información sobre ocho programas del Canal 9. Señala cada tipo de programa en tu libro.

jbd-0987

Escuchar

¿Qué película vamos a ver?

Vas a escuchar siete frases sobre las películas que dan en el Cine Florida. Si una frase es lógica, haz el gesto del pulgar hacia arriba. Si no es lógica, haz el gesto del pulgar hacia abajo.

Videohistoria

jbd-0987 

¿Qué dan en la tele?

¿Qué programa de televisión van a ver los chicos? Lee la historia.

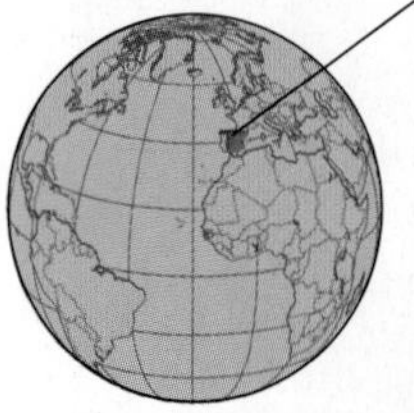

España

Ignacio

Javier

Jorgito

Elena

Ana

Antes de leer

Scanning Scanning the text for key concepts is important for reading comprehension. Look over the *Videohistoria* and find at least two instances where people are disagreeing about something.

- What do they disagree about and what are the expressions they use?

1. Elena and her friends are trying to agree on what to watch on television. Look at the captions for photos 7 and 8 to predict what they decide to do.
2. Make a list of the cognates in the *Videohistoria*. Which ones can you use to help you understand the types of movies that Elena and her friends like to watch?

1 **Ignacio:** ¿Qué dan en la televisión? Elena, ¿dónde está el mando a distancia?*

Elena: Está encima de la mesita, al lado de la lámpara.

Ignacio: ¡Ah, sí! Lo veo. Vamos a ver lo que hay . . .

*remote control

2 **Ana:** ¡Fabuloso! Mi telenovela favorita.

Elena: Sí, me encanta. Es muy emocionante. **El actor** y **la actriz** principales son muy guapos.

Ignacio: ¡No! Me aburren las telenovelas. Vamos a ver otro canal.

Ana y Elena: Ignacio, ¡nuestra telenovela, por favor!

3 **Elena:** ¿Qué más hay? Mmmm. **¿Qué clase de** programa es éste?

Ana: Es **un programa de la vida real.** Es muy **realista.**

Ignacio: No son realistas. Pienso que son **tontos.** ¿Verdad, Javier?

Javier: Pues, no sé mucho **sobre** esta clase de programas.

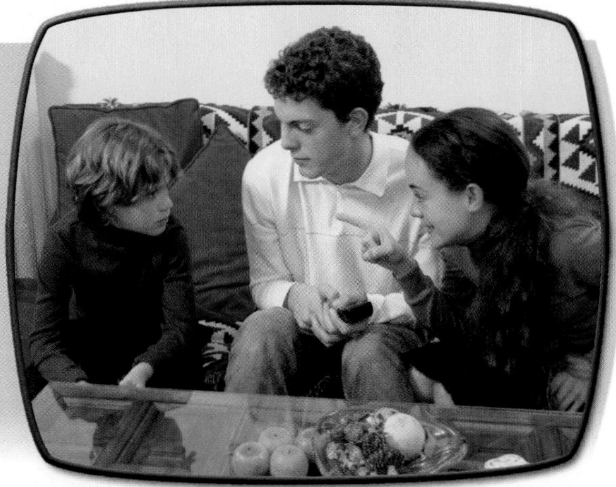

4 **Jorgito:** Elena, quiero ver dibujos animados. **Ya** son las cuatro.

Elena: Jorgito, ¿no ves que estoy con mis amigos? Tú puedes ver la tele más tarde. Mira, puedes escuchar música en mi cuarto.

Jorgito: Está bien, pero sólo hoy.

Todos: Adiós, Jorgito.

5 **Ignacio:** No me gustan estos programas **infantiles.** ¿Qué más hay?

Elena: Un momento ... este programa de entrevistas es mi favorito. Hablan de todo. Ohhh, **¡acaban de** hablar con mi actor favorito!

Ignacio: Sí, y ya terminaron. **Por eso** no tenemos que verlo.

6 **Ignacio:** Podemos ver un programa de concursos.

Javier: ¿O un programa educativo? ¿O las noticias?

Todos: ¡Nooo!

Ignacio: ¡Tantos canales y no hay nada que ver!

Ana: ¿Por qué no vamos al cine?

7 **Ana:** Quiero ver una comedia.

Elena: Yo prefiero ver una película romántica.

Ignacio: No, son tontas. ¿Qué tal una película de ciencia ficción?

Todos: ¡Nooo!

Javier: Dan un drama nuevo en el Cine Capitol.

Todos: ¡Nooo!

8 **Jorgito:** Ahora puedo ver los dibujos animados, **especialmente** mi favorito, *Rin, ran, run.* ¡Qué bien!

Leer

¿Cierto o falso?

Escribe los números del 1 al 6 en una hoja de papel. Lee estas frases. Si una frase es cierta según la *Videohistoria,* escribe *C.* Si es falsa, escribe *F.*

1. El mando a distancia está encima de la mesita.
2. El actor principal en la telenovela favorita de Ana es muy guapo.
3. Jorgito va a ver la tele cuando Elena y sus amigos están en la sala.
4. Jorgito va a escuchar música en el cuarto de Elena.
5. En el Cine Capitol dan una película de ciencia ficción.
6. Los amigos deciden ver un programa de televisión.

Leer

¿En qué canal?

Según las preferencias de Elena y sus amigos, ¿cuál de estos programas les gustaría ver o no les gustaría ver? Lee la lista de programas y en una hoja de papel, escribe el número del canal que mejor completa cada una de estas frases.

1. A Jorgito le gustaría ver el Canal ___ porque es su programa favorito.
2. A Ana y Elena les gustaría mucho ver el Canal ___.
3. A Ignacio no le gustaría nada ver el Canal ___ porque piensa que es tonto.
4. A Elena le gustaría ver el Canal ___ porque hablan con sus actores favoritos.
5. A Javier le gustaría ver el Canal ___ o un programa educativo.
6. A Ignacio le gustaría ver el Canal ___ pero a los otros no.

Canal 5	Noticias Tele-5
Canal 7	La telenovela del amor
Canal 8	Rin, ran, run
Canal 11	¡Dime más! Entrevistas de Hollywood
Canal 13	Ciencia ficción 3000
Canal 15	La vida real: Un invierno en Antártica

Más práctica

- Practice Workbook, pp. 75–76: 9A-3, 9A-4
- WAV Wbk.: Video, pp. 83–85
- Guided Practice: Vocab. Check, pp. 281–284
- *Real.* para hispanohablantes, p. 333

Manos a la obra

Vocabulario y gramática en uso

Objectives

- Talk about different kinds of movies and television programs
- Express opinions and preferences about entertainment
- Use *acabar de* + infinitive to talk about things you have just done
- Tell why you don't do something
- Learn to use *gustar* and similar verbs

Leer/Escribir

Mis amigos ven . . .

Completa estas frases con el nombre de uno(a) de tus amigos y una de las palabras de la lista. Escribe las frases en una hoja de papel.

tonto	drama
dibujos animados	deportivo
educativo	policíaca

1. Mi amigo(a) ___ prefiere las películas ___. Le encantan los detectives.
2. Mi amigo(a) ___ ve los programas ___ porque siempre le gusta aprender más.
3. Mi amigo(a) ___ ve ___ porque le gustan las cosas infantiles.
4. Mi amigo(a) ___ prefiere ver un programa emocionante como un ___.
5. Mi amigo(a) ___ prefiere ver un programa ___ como una comedia.
6. Mi amigo(a) ___ es muy deportista y le interesan los programas ___.

jbd-0988

Escuchar/Escribir/Hablar

Muchas opiniones

Un programa de radio les pregunta a sus oyentes *(listeners)* qué piensan de los diferentes programas de televisión.

1 En una hoja de papel copia la gráfica y escribe los números del 1 al 6. Vas a escuchar las opiniones de unas personas. Escribe la clase de programa en la primera columna y la descripción en la segunda columna. Luego escribe frases para expresar tu opinión.

Programa de televisión	Descripción
1. las comedias	muy cómicas

Modelo

Me encantan las comedias porque son muy cómicas.

2 Habla con otro(a) estudiante. Di si estás de acuerdo con sus opiniones.

Modelo

Estoy de acuerdo. Las comedias son muy cómicas.

o: *No estoy de acuerdo. Las comedias son muy tontas.*

Escribir

Buenos ejemplos

Escoge seis de los siguientes programas de televisión. Luego escribe frases para dar un buen ejemplo de los diferentes programas.

Modelo

Chica Graciosa *es una comedia.*

Filmando una película

Hablar

¿Te gustaría ver . . . ?

Usa la información que escribiste en la Actividad 7 y habla con otro(a) estudiante sobre qué clase de programas le gustaría ver. Él o ella puede usar las siguientas palabras.

me aburren	tontos, -as	fascinantes
me gustan	emocionantes	cómicos, -as
me interesan	violentos, -as	infantiles
me encantan	realistas	**¡Respuesta personal!**

Modelo

A —*¿Te gustaría ver* una comedia *como* Chica graciosa*?*
B —*¡Uf!* Me aburren las comedias. *Son* tontas.
o:—*¡Por supuesto!* Me encantan las comedias. *Son* cómicas.

Las telenovelas Venezuela, Mexico, Argentina, and Spain produce many soap operas that are popular with people of all ages. Unlike soap operas in the United States that continue for years with the same characters, the *telenovelas* frequently last only a matter of months. They are then replaced with new shows and different characters.

- What are the advantages of stories that continue for years versus stories that are new every several months? Which would you prefer?

El juego de la vida, una telenovela popular de Televisa (México)

jbd-0988

Escucha y escribe

Escucha y luego escribe en una hoja de papel lo que dice un joven sobre un programa de televisión que ve.

Escribir/Hablar

¿Qué programa ves tú?

1. Usa la descripción del programa de televisión de la Actividad 9 como modelo y escribe sobre un programa que tú ves. No debes nombrar el programa en la descripción.

2. Lee tu descripción a otros(as) estudiantes de la clase. Ellos deben identificar el programa que describes.

Escribir/Hablar

Mis actores y actrices favoritos

Haz una lista de tres actores o actrices que te gustan y los nombres de las películas en que trabajaron. Con otro(a) estudiante, habla de los actores y sus películas.

Modelo

A —*¿Quién es tu actor favorito?*
B —*Para mí el mejor actor es Rafael Montenegro. ¿Viste* Cuando el amor llega?
A —*Sí, creo que es un actor muy talentoso y la película es fascinante.*
o: —*No me gustan las películas románticas y tampoco me gusta este actor.*

Leer/Hablar

¿Qué dicen los críticos?

Lee el artículo de abajo que escribieron los críticos Guillo y Nadia. Luego trabaja con otro(a) estudiante para decidir qué película van a ver. Contesta las preguntas en la casilla.

Nota

Use *más/menos* **de** with numbers.

- más **de** tres horas
- menos **de** diez personas

¿Qué clase de película es?
¿De veras? ¿Cómo es?
¿Sí? ¿Qué pasa en la película?
¿Cuánto tiempo dura?
¿Quiénes son los actores principales?
Pues, ¿quieres verla?

Modelo

A —*Acabo de leer un artículo sobre la película. . . . ¿Te gustaría verla?*
B —*¿Qué clase de película es?*

En nuestra opinión

¿Piensas ir al cine este fin de semana? Guillo y Nadia te dan sus impresiones de tres nuevas películas.

Guillo

Nadia

★★★ **recomendable**
★★ **más o menos**
★ **no la recomiendo**

Cuando el amor llega Con Cristina Campos y Rafael Montenegro. Una película romántica sobre un joven rico enamorado de una chica pobre. Ante la oposición de sus padres, el amor de los jóvenes es imposible. Esta película, de dos horas y media, es similar a las viejas fórmulas de las telenovelas—un poco tonta y aburrida. Los protagonistas son buenos, pero los actores secundarios son demasiado dramáticos. Recomendable para personas que no tienen nada que hacer. (★)

Mis padres son de otro planeta Unos chicos descubren que sus padres son originarios de otra galaxia y que están en este planeta para explorar y planear una invasión. Una producción para toda la familia que combina elementos de comedia y ciencia ficción. Es tan fascinante y cómica que no puedes creer que estás en el cine por más de tres horas. Los actores principales, Javier Zaragoza y Miguel Vilar, son fantásticos. (★★★)

Mi perro es mi héroe Un drama para toda la familia—no es violenta y es bastante realista. Un poco infantil, pero con mucha acción y emoción. El mejor amigo del hombre, el perro, con inteligencia y valor, le salva la vida* a toda la familia. La película es divertida pero un poco corta (menos de dos horas). Tiene muy buenos actores, como Ana Jiménez y Antonio Barrera. Es una buena película. (★★★)

*saves the life

Pensar/Hablar/Escribir

¿Cuántas horas de tele?

Vas a calcular el promedio *(average)* de horas que tus compañeros ven la tele.

Conexiones — Las matemáticas

1. Escribe el número de horas que viste la tele cada día de la semana pasada. Suma *(Add up)* estas horas. Calcula el promedio de horas para cada día.

   ____ *(total de horas)* dividido por 7

2. Trabaja con un grupo de cuatro personas. Pregunta a tus compañeros(as) el tiempo promedio que vieron la televisión cada día. Escribe la información que recibes de tu grupo.

Modelo

A —*Como promedio, ¿cuántas horas viste la tele cada día?*
B —*La vi casi dos horas y media cada día.*

3. Calcula el promedio de horas que tu grupo vio la tele cada día la semana pasada. Escribe una frase para presentar la información a la clase.

Pensar/Leer/Hablar

La tele en tu vida

En un estudio reciente, se dio a conocer que, como promedio, las personas de los Estados Unidos ven casi cuatro horas de tele al día. ¡La suma de estas horas equivale a casi dos meses al año frente a la televisión!

Los principales países adictos a la pantalla chica

País	Horas (1 hr. – 4 hr.)
Estados Unidos	3 horas y 58 minutos
Grecia	3 horas y 39 minutos
Italia y Gran Bretaña	3 horas y 36 minutos
España	3 horas y 31 minutos
Canadá e Irlanda	3 horas y 14 minutos

Los siete países que ven más televisión al día

Fuente: Red de los que apagan la tele

1. Usa el promedio de horas de tu grupo de la Actividad 13 y calcula el número total de horas que vieron la tele en un año.
   - 365 días al año por *(promedio de horas)* son *(total de horas)* al año.

2. Usa el total de horas al año para contestar estas preguntas. *(Nota: Hay aproximadamente 720 horas en un mes.)*

   1. ¿Tu grupo ve la tele más de un mes al año o menos?
   2. ¿La ven Uds. más que el promedio de personas en los Estados Unidos o menos? ¿Y de las personas en los otros países de la gráfica?
   3. ¿Crees que las personas en los países de la gráfica ven demasiada tele? ¿Por qué?

Pronunciación

jbd-0988

Linking words 

In Spanish just as in English, you don't pronounce a sentence as completely separate words. Instead, the words flow together in phrases. That is why it often seems that phrases or sentences sound as if they are one long word.

How the words flow together depends on the last sound of a word and the beginning sound of the following word. The flow of sounds is usually created by two of the same vowels, two different vowels, or a consonant followed by a vowel. Listen to and say these word combinations:

Me‿encanta	de‿entrevistas	le‿aburre
nos‿interesa	dibujos‿animados	de‿horror

Try it out! Listen to and say these sentences. Be careful not to break the flow of sound where you see "‿".

Me‿interesa‿ese programa de‿entrevistas.

A‿Ana le‿aburre‿ese programa‿educativo.

La película de‿horror dura‿una‿hora‿y media.

Vamos‿a ver lo que‿hay‿en la tele.

Me‿encanta‿el‿actor y la‿actriz de‿esa telenovela.

Actividad 15 **Escribir/Hablar**

Y tú, ¿qué dices?

1. ¿Qué piensas de los programas de entrevistas? ¿Y de los programas de la vida real?
2. En tu opinión, ¿cómo son los programas policíacos que dan en la televisión? ¿Cómo son las telenovelas?
3. ¿Te interesan o te aburren las películas románticas? ¿Y las películas de ciencia ficción? ¿Por qué?
4. ¿Qué dicen tus amigos y tú sobre las películas de horror? ¿Las ven Uds. a menudo?

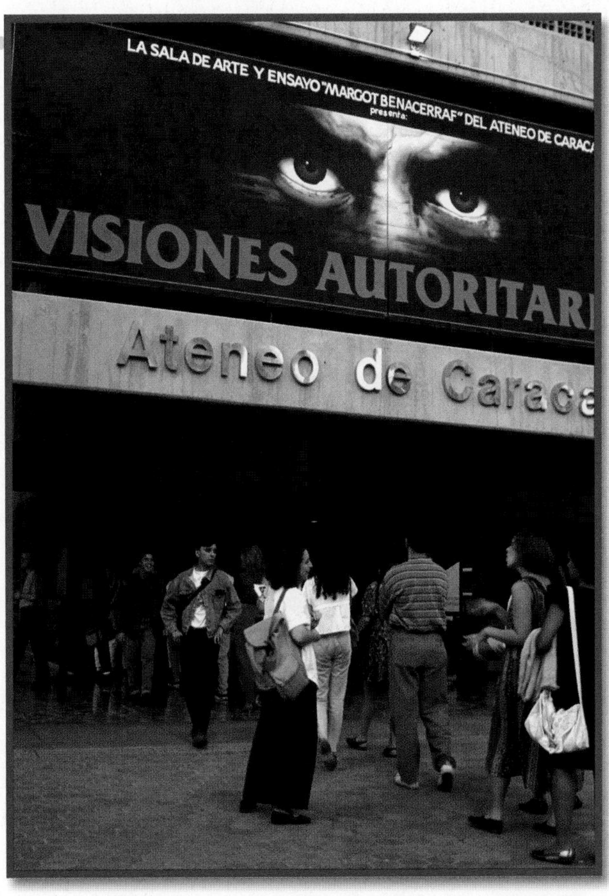

Gramática

Acabar de + infinitive

When you want to say that something just happened, use the present tense of *acabar de* + infinitive.

Acabo de ver un programa musical.	***I just saw*** *a music program.*
Mis padres **acaban de ir** al cine.	*My parents* ***just went*** *to the movies.*
Acabamos de hablar de esa película.	***We just talked*** *about that movie.*

Although the action took place in the past, the present-tense forms of *acabar* are used.

GramActiva VIDEO

Want more help with *acabar de* + infinitive? Watch the **GramActiva** video.

Escribir

¡Acaban de hacer muchas cosas!

La familia Martínez acaba de hacer muchas cosas esta mañana antes de ir a estudiar y trabajar. Lee la lista y escribe quién acaba de hacer qué cosa.

Modelo

mamá/preparar el desayuno para sus hijos
Mamá acaba de preparar el desayuno para sus hijos.

Quehaceres...

1. mamá / preparar el desayuno para sus hijos ✓
2. Carlitos / comer el desayuno ✓
3. Mariel / limpiar su dormitorio ✓
4. Ezequiel / sacar la basura ✓
5. Ezequiel, Carlitos y Mariel / terminar su tarea ✓
6. papá / pasar la aspiradora en la sala ✓
7. Elena / dar de comer al gato ✓
8. todos / buscar sus abrigos ✓

Fondo cultural

Sábado Gigante is one of the longest-running shows in television history. Its popular host, Don Francisco, started this unique variety program in his native Chile in 1962. It now airs from Miami every Saturday night and brings comedy, celebrity guests, musical performances, games, and contests to its more than 100 million viewers in 42 countries. In June, 2005, the program celebrated its 1000th episode on the Miami-based Univisión network.

- What television shows do you know that have enjoyed continued success over the years?

El famosísimo Don Francisco

Escribir/Hablar

Acabo de ver . . .

¿Recuerdas?
Some adverbs you can use in descriptions are:

bastante muy
demasiado un poco

1. Copia la gráfica en una hoja de papel. Escribe los títulos de tres programas de televisión, obras de teatro o películas que acabas de ver. Da el nombre y haz una descripción.

Acabo de ver . . .	Nombre	Descripción
una película romántica	¡No puedo vivir sin ti!	demasiado triste

2. Trabaja con otro(a) estudiante para hablar sobre lo que acaban de ver.

Modelo

A —*Acabo de ver una película romántica.*
B —*¿De veras? ¿Cómo se llama?*
A —¡No puedo vivir sin ti!
B —*¿Te gustó?*
A —*No, no me gustó porque es demasiado triste.*

Más práctica

- Practice Workbook, p. 77: 9A-5
- WAV Wbk.: Writing, p. 90
- Guided Practice: Grammar Acts., pp. 285–286
- *Real.* para hispanohablantes, pp. 334–337

For: *Acabar de*
Web Code: jbd-0903

Exploración del lenguaje

Words of Greek and Arabic origin

Languages change when regions and nations interact with, or are conquered or colonized by, people who speak a different language. Long before the Romans brought Latin to Spain, certain Greek words had entered the Latin language. Words such as *el problema, el programa,* and *el drama* originally were masculine nouns in Greek. When they came into Latin and then Spanish, they kept their masculine gender even though they end in *a*.

Try it out! Which of these new words would you use in the following sentences?

el clima el sistema el poema

1. No comprendo ___ de clasificación de películas en ese país.
2. Me gustaría visitar Panamá porque ___ allí es tropical.
3. Me gusta ___ que acabo de leer.

Arabic also had a large influence on Spanish. Around A.D. 700, the Arabic-speaking Moors invaded Spain from northern Africa. They ruled for 800 years and played a major role in the development of the Spanish language and culture. Words that came from Arabic often begin with the letters *al-*. Many words in Spanish that have a *z* or a *j* in them are also of Arabic origin. You know these words that came from Arabic: *alfombra, azúcar, naranja.*

Try it out! You also know these words that are from Arabic. On your paper, fill in the missing letters.

a_ul ___macén _anahoria

Gramática

Gustar and similar verbs

Even though we usually translate the verb *gustar* as "to like," it literally means "to please." So when you say, *Me gustan los programas deportivos,* you're actually saying, "Sports programs are pleasing to me." *Programas deportivos* is the subject of the sentence, and *me* is the indirect object. Here's the pattern:

indirect object + form of *gustar* + subject

The subject in a sentence with *gustar* usually follows the verb. You need to know if the subject is singular or plural to know which form of *gustar* to use. If the subject is singular, use *gusta.* If it's plural, use *gustan.* If it's an infinitive, use *gusta.*

Me gusta **el actor** en la telenovela pero no me gust**an** **las actrices.**

A mis amigos les gusta **ver** películas.

To emphasize or clarify *who* is pleased, you can use an additional *a* + pronoun:

A mí me gustan los dibujos animados, pero **a él** no le gustan.

Here are the other verbs you know that are similar to *gustar:*

aburrir	A mí **me aburren** las películas románticas.
doler *(o→ue)*	A Fernando **le duelen** los pies.
encantar	A mis padres **les encanta** el teatro.
faltar	**Me faltan** un cuchillo y un tenedor.
interesar	**Nos interesan** mucho los programas musicales.
quedar	¿No **te queda** bien el vestido?

¿Recuerdas?

You have used *me gusta(n), te gusta(n),* and *le gusta(n)* to talk about what a person likes.

- A mí **me gusta** el cine pero a mi hermano **le gusta** más la televisión.

GramActiva VIDEO

Want more help with *gustar* and similar verbs? Watch the **GramActiva** video.

jbd-0988

Escuchar/Escribir

Escucha y escribe

Escucha las opiniones de la familia Linares sobre los programas que dan en la televisión. En una hoja de papel, escribe los números del 1 al 6 y escribe las frases que escuchas.

Nos gustan las películas cómicas.

Escribir/Hablar

A mí y a ti

1. Trabaja con otro(a) estudiante. Copia el diagrama Venn en una hoja de papel. Escribe el nombre de tu compañero(a) encima del óvalo a la derecha. En el óvalo indicado con *A mí* escribe cinco clases de películas o programas de televisión que te gustan.

2. Pregunta a tu compañero(a) si le gustan las clases de programas y películas que tú escribiste. Si a él o a ella le gusta la clase de programa o película, escribe el nombre en el óvalo de la derecha. (Vas a usar el diagrama Venn en la Actividad 20.)

Modelo

A mí — A nosotros — A Rosa

A mí: los programas policíacos; las películas de horror

A Rosa: las películas de horror

Modelo

A —*¿Te gustan los programas policíacos?*
B —*A ver . . . no, no me gustan mucho.*
A —*Pues, ¿te gustan las películas de horror?*
B —*Sí, me gustan mucho.*

Escribir

A nosotros nos gusta . . .

Compara los dos lados de tu diagrama. Escribe las clases de programas y películas que a los dos les gustan en el centro de ese diagrama. Escribe al menos cinco frases completas para describir qué les gusta a Uds.

Modelo

A nosotros nos gustan las películas de horror.
A mí me gustan los programas policíacos pero a Rosa no le gustan.

Modelo

A mí — A nosotros — A Rosa

A mí: los programas policíacos; las películas de horror

A nosotros: las películas de horror

A Rosa: las películas de horror

Fondo cultural

La televisión The cable and satellite television industry in Latin America has grown tremendously. Hundreds of channels are available to viewers. Some cable channels specialize in news or sports, and offer their programming to other countries as well. Among the sports, soccer is the one that attracts the most viewers. The World Cup is enormously popular in Latin America and around the world.

- What Latin American programs can you find in your local cable or satellite listings? Watch some of them to see what countries the shows are produced in.

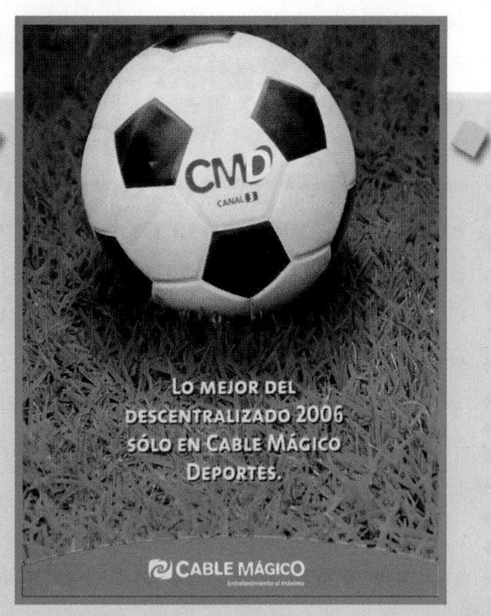

Escribir/Hablar/GramActiva

Juego

1. Copia esta tabla en una hoja de papel. Escribe siete cosas que te interesan y siete cosas que te aburren. Puedes escribir los nombres de actores, películas, música, programas de televisión, actividades, etc.

2. Con tu lista en la mano, pregúntales a tus compañeros de clase si les interesan o les aburren las mismas que a ti. Si un(a) estudiante responde *sí,* escribe su nombre a lado de esa cosa en tu lista, si responde *no,* tienes que preguntarle a otro(a) estudiante. La primera persona que tiene un nombre diferente a lado de cada cosa en su lista gana *(wins).*

Cosas que me interesan	Cosas que me aburren
1. los programas de concursos Jaime	1. las telenovelas Ana
2.	2.
3.	3.
4.	4.
5.	5.

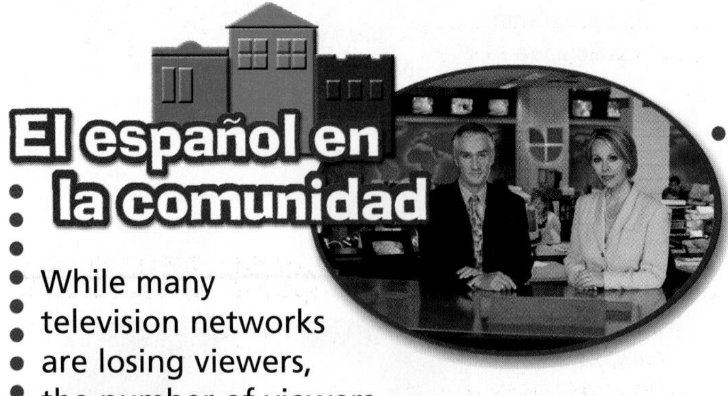

El español en la comunidad

While many television networks are losing viewers, the number of viewers watching Spanish-language networks is growing. Look in your newspaper's TV guide and find listings for a Spanish-language network. Find the name of a program for each kind of show on p. 282. Watch a few minutes of one of the programs. Although you might find it difficult to understand, tune in from time to time. You'll be amazed at how much you'll learn!

- How are the listings similar to or different from those for the networks you usually watch? Write your impressions of the television show you watched.

Escribir/Hablar

¿Qué hay en la tele?

A veces decimos, "¡Hay tantos canales y programas en la tele pero no hay nada interesante!" Ahora tienes la oportunidad de planear seis horas de televisión para el sábado, desde las 17.00 horas hasta las 23.00 horas, para un concurso que se llama "Tus propias seis horas en la tele."

1. Trabaja con un grupo de tres. Escriban una lista de programas o películas que les gustaría incluir *(to include)* en las seis horas. Den esta información para cada programa o película:
   - la clase de programa
   - el nombre
   - cómo es
   - cuánto tiempo dura
   - para quiénes es recomendable
   - por qué le va a interesar al público

2. Preparen una presentación para la clase. Pueden hacer algo visual para acompañar su presentación.

3. Después de escuchar a los diferentes grupos, cada grupo va a votar por la mejor presentación. ¡No pueden votar por la suya *(your own)*! Los grupos tienen que escribir cuatro frases para explicar su decisión. El grupo que recibe más votos gana *(wins)* el concurso.

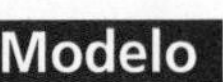

Modelo

Nosotros votamos por la presentación del grupo de Ana, David y Laura. Tienen muchos programas que nos interesan a nosotros.

Escribir/Hablar

Y tú, ¿qué dices?

1. En tu familia, ¿a quién le interesan más las películas de horror? ¿Los dramas? ¿Las comedias?
2. ¿Qué programas de televisión te aburren? ¿Por qué?
3. ¿Qué programas de televisión te encantan? ¿Por qué?
4. ¿A cuáles de tus amigos les gusta ir al cine? ¿Qué tipo de películas les gusta ver?
5. ¿A cuáles de tus amigos no les gusta nada ir al cine? ¿Por qué?

Más práctica

- Practice Workbook, pp. 78–79: 9A-6, 9A-7
- WAV Wbk.: Writing, p. 91
- Guided Practice: Grammar Acts., pp. 287–288
- *Real.* para hispanohablantes, pp. 338–341

For: Verbs Like *gustar*
Web Code: jbd-0904

¡Adelante!

Lectura

Objectives

- Read about TV-watching habits of young people
- Learn to use gestures
- Present a summary of a movie or TV show
- Watch *¿Eres tú, María?*, Episodio 9

Strategy

Reading for comprehension
You don't need to understand every word in a reading to comprehend the key information. Try reading without stopping at unknown words. Then go back and decide if the words are important to the reading, and see if you can guess their meanings.

Una semana sin televisión

¿Sabes que los niños estadounidenses pasan más horas al año pegados a la pantalla de su televisión que haciendo cualquier otra cosa, a excepción de dormir?

Hay estudios que dicen que ver demasiado la televisión puede causar malos hábitos de comida, falta de ejercicio y obesidad. En cuatro horas de dibujos animados el sábado por la mañana los niños pueden ver 202 anuncios sobre refrescos, dulces y cereales azucarados. Esta comida combinada con las horas frente a la pantalla resulta en que uno de cada ocho niños estadounidenses tenga exceso de peso.

También hay estudios que dan nuevas pruebas de la relación entre la televisión y la violencia. Uno de estos estudios indica que niños que ven más de una hora de televisión al día tienen más probabilidad de ser violentos y agresivos de adultos.

¿Quieres participar en una solución? Durante el mes de abril millones de personas en más de doce países apagan la tele por una semana. En vez de ver la tele los participantes van con sus familias o con amigos al campo, o a caminar, montar en bicicleta o visitar un parque.

¿Y qué pasa después de unos días sin televisión? Una niña de diez años dice: —¿Para qué necesito la tele? Hay muchas cosas más interesantes que puedo hacer.

¿Comprendes?

Prepara información para un debate sobre la cuestión: ¿Es bueno o malo ver la televisión?

1. Escribe una lista de cuatro razones *(reasons)* en favor de no ver la tele. Usa información que leíste en el artículo.
2. Escribe una lista de cuatro razones en favor de ver la tele.

Y tú, ¿qué dices?

1. Usa la información en tu lista para expresar tu opinión: ¿Es bueno o malo ver la televisión? ¿Por qué?
2. Para ti, ¿va a ser fácil o difícil pasar una semana sin ver la televisión? ¿Por qué?
3. En Chile, a una persona que ve mucha televisión se le llama "un(a) tevito(a)". ¿Qué puedes decirle a un(a) tevito(a) para persuadirlo(a) a hacer otras cosas que son mejores para la salud?

Más práctica

- WAV Wbk.: Writing, p. 92
- Guided Practice: *Lectura*, p. 289
- *Real.* para hispanohablantes, pp. 342–343

For: Internet Activity
Web Code: jbd-0905

La cultura en vivo

Comunicación sin palabras

Every culture has gestures that communicate a message. You've already seen gestures for *¡ojo!* and *más o menos.* Here are a few more gestures used in many Spanish-speaking countries to communicate a message.

mucha gente

¡Hay mucha gente en la fiesta!

(Place your fingertips together, then open your hand. Repeat this motion in a rhythmic gesture.)

un poco

Por favor, un poquito de postre.

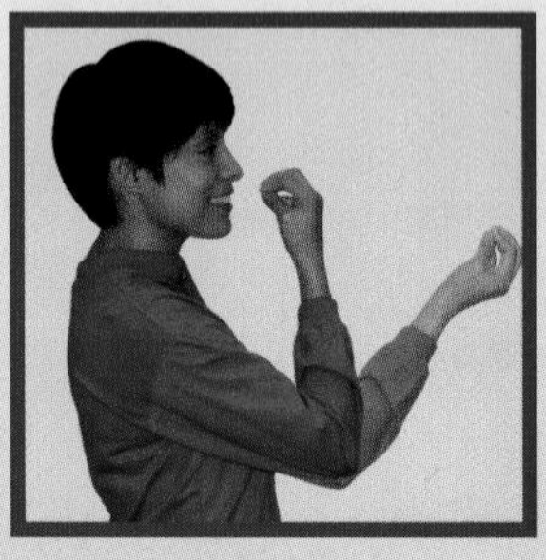

¡a comer!

¡Vamos a comer!

(With your fingertips bunched, bring your hand up close to your mouth, then extend it forward, bending your arm at the elbow. Repeat the motion two or three times.)

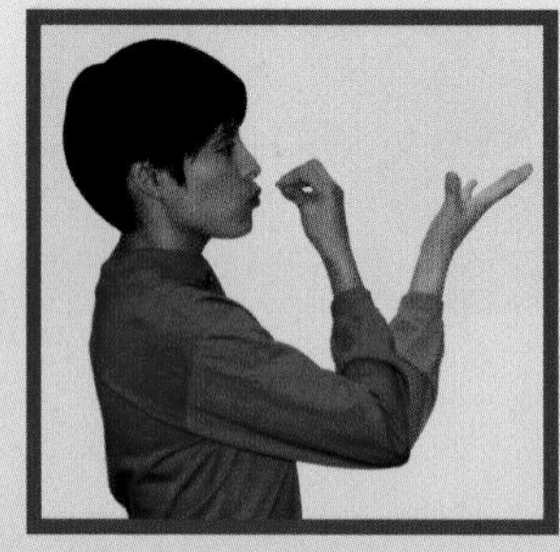

¡qué rico!

¡Este plato está muy rico!

(Kiss the bunched fingertips of one hand, then quickly pull your hand away, extending your fingers.)

no sé

No sé dónde está el libro.

nada

No tengo nada.

Try it out! Work with a partner and create a short skit in which you use one of these gestures. Present it for the class.

Think about it! What gestures do you use most often? Do you ever use gestures that are the same as or similar to the ones shown on this page? Do you think you would understand some of the gestures on this page even without explanation?

Presentación oral

¿Qué dan esta semana?

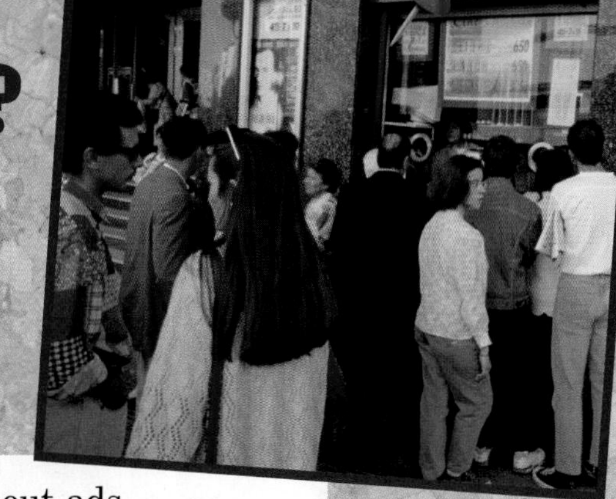

Task
You are reviewing a movie or television show you have just seen for your school's closed-circuit TV system. Prepare a summary of the movie or show.

1 Prepare Choose a movie or TV show to talk about. Cut out ads or photos about it from a newspaper or TV guide or download them from the Internet. Copy the chart below on a sheet of paper and provide the information for the movie or show you have chosen.

Nombre	
Clase de película o programa	
Actor / actores	
Actriz / actrices	
Cómo es	
Cuánto tiempo dura	
Para quiénes es	
Tus impresiones	

Strategy

Using charts
Create a chart to help you think through the key information you will want to talk about. This will help you speak more effectively.

2 Practice Use your notes from the chart for your presentation. Create a poster with the visuals you have collected. Go through your presentation several times. You may use your notes in practice, but not when you present. Try to:

- provide all key information about the film or show
- use complete sentences in your presentation
- speak clearly

3 Present Present your chosen movie or television show to a small group or the class. Use your poster to help guide you through the presentation.

4 Evaluation Your teacher may give you a rubric for how the presentation will be graded. You probably will be graded on:

- how complete your presentation is
- how much information you communicate
- how easy it is to understand you

Videomisterio

¿Eres tú, María? Episodio 9

Antes de ver el video

"Paco, te digo que te necesito ahora mismo. Por favor, rápido. Y a Margarita, también."

Nota gramatical What's a good mystery without an expression like "Follow her!"? In this episode you'll hear several uses of the verb *seguir* ("to follow," "to continue").

sigo	**seguimos**
sigues	**seguís**
sigue	**siguen**

Resumen del episodio

Al día siguiente Lola va a su trabajo, cuando ve a María. ¡Qué suerte! Lola la sigue y llama a Paco y a Margarita. Ella necesita a los dos ahora mismo para ayudarla. Vigilan[1] a María y a un hombre en el café, y Margarita muestra[2] sus talentos de detective. Es evidente que María y el hombre no están nada contentos. Pero, ¿quién es este hombre misterioso y por qué quiere irse de Madrid?

[1] They watch [2] shows

Palabras para comprender

¡Venid!	Come!
ve a sentarte	go sit
aparece	appears
quiere irse	wants to go away
vengan en seguida	come right away
sigue vigilando	continue watching

—¡Ay de mí!
—Cálmate, Lola.

"Lola, ¿quién es ese hombre? ¿De qué están hablando?"

"Ahora lo comprendo todo. Voy a llamar al Inspector Gil."

Después de ver el video

¿Comprendes?

A. Contesta las preguntas.

1. ¿Quiénes ayudan a Lola con la investigación?
2. ¿Quién va al café para escuchar a María y al hombre?
3. ¿Está Lola tranquila o nerviosa? ¿Por qué?
4. Según Lola, ¿quién es el hombre en el café?
5. Según Margarita, ¿quién es la chica en el café?
6. Según Margarita, ¿el hombre quiere quedarse *(stay)* en Madrid o quiere irse?

B. Lola dice: "Ahora lo comprendo todo". En tu opinion, ¿qué comprende Lola? ¿Cuál es la solución del misterio?

For: More on *¿Eres tú, María?*
Web Code: jbd-0507

Chapter Review

Repaso del capítulo

To prepare for the test, check to see if you . . .

- know the new vocabulary and grammar
- can perform the tasks on p. 307

Vocabulario y gramática

jbd-0989 

to talk about television shows

el canal	channel
el programa de concursos	game show
el programa deportivo	sports show
el programa de dibujos animados	cartoon show
el programa de entrevistas	interview program
el programa de la vida real	reality program
el programa de noticias	news program
el programa educativo	educational program
el programa musical	musical program
la telenovela	soap opera

to talk about movies

la comedia	comedy
el drama	drama
la película de ciencia ficción	science fiction movie
la película de horror	horror movie
la película policíaca	crime movie, mystery
la película romántica	romantic movie

to give your opinion of a movie or program

cómico, -a	funny
emocionante	touching
fascinante	fascinating
infantil	for children; childish
realista	realistic
tonto, -a	silly, stupid
violento, -a	violent
me aburre(n)	it bores me (they bore me)
me interesa(n)	it interests me (they interest me)

to ask and tell about movies or programs

el actor	actor
la actriz	actress
dar	to show
durar	to last
empezar *(e→ie)*	to begin
terminar	to end
más / menos de	more / less than
medio, -a	half
¿Qué clase de . . . ?	What kind of . . . ?

to talk about what has just happened

acabar de + *infinitive*	to have just . . .

verbs similar to *gustar*

aburrir	to bore
doler *(o→ue)*	to hurt, to ache
encantar	to please very much, to love
faltar	to be missing
interesar	to interest
quedar	to fit

other useful words and expressions

antes de	before
casi	almost
¿De veras?	Really?
especialmente	especially
por eso	therefore, for that reason
sobre	about
ya	already

For *Vocabulario adicional,* see pp. 336–337.

Más práctica

- Practice Workbook: Puzzle, p. 80
- Practice Workbook: Organizer, p. 81

Go Online PHSchool.com
For: Test Preparation
Web Code: jbd-0906

Preparación para el examen

	On the exam you will be asked to . . .	Here are practice tasks similar to those you will find on the exam . . .	If you need review . . .
jbd-0989	**1 Escuchar** Listen and understand as people express opinions about movies and TV programs	Listen as you hear a phone pollster ask people about TV programs they have watched on the new Spanish-language cable station. For each viewer, decide if the show(s): a) was (were) boring; b) was (were) interesting; c) was (were) too violent; d) was (were) too childish or silly.	**pp. 282–287** *A primera vista* **p. 288** Actividad 6 **p. 289** Actividad 8 **p. 290** Actividad 9 **p. 295** Actividad 17
	**2 Hablar** Ask and answer questions about the types of movies and TV programs people prefer	Tell your partner about a movie or TV program you just saw and express your opinion about it. Ask if your partner saw the same thing and what he or she thought of it. If your partner didn't see it, ask him or her to tell about something he or she just saw. You might say: *Acabo de ver una película fantástica con Tom Cruise . . .*	**pp. 282–287** *A primera vista* **p. 288** Actividad 6 **p. 289** Actividad 8 **p. 291** Actividad 12 **p. 295** Actividad 17 **p. 297** Actividad 19 **p. 303** *Presentación oral*
	**3 Leer** Read and understand what an entertainment critic writes about a new TV program	Before class begins, you grab a Spanish-language magazine and turn to the entertainment section. After reading part of the entertainment critic's review, see if you can determine his opinion of a new soap opera series, *Mi secreto.* Does he like it? Why or why not? En el primer episodio de Mi secreto, nos aburren con una historia infantil y con actores sin talento que quieren ser emocionantes pero no pueden. ¡Pienso que este programa es para las personas que no tienen nada que hacer!	**pp. 282–287** *A primera vista* **p. 291** Actividad 12
	**4 Escribir** Write about a movie you recently saw	You are keeping a journal to practice writing in Spanish. Today you are going to write about a movie you saw recently. Mention the name of the movie, the type of movie it is, and what you liked or disliked about it.	**p. 290** Actividad 10 **p. 295** Actividad 17 **p. 297** Actividades 19–20 **p. 303** *Presentación oral*
	**5 Pensar** Demonstrate an understanding of common gestures	You learned that almost all cultures can communicate without words. With a partner, try making the gestures shown in this chapter from the Spanish-speaking world. Are these similar to those in our culture?	**p. 302** *La cultura en vivo*

Fondo cultural

Reading the Letter is from painter Pablo Picasso's Neo-Classical period, when he was influenced by ancient Roman sculpture. He used simplified color and heavy lines. For instance, the thickness of the hand over the man's shoulder on the right can remind you of weighty, unmoving, ancient statues.

- What other characteristics of statues do you see in the painting?

"Reading the Letter" (1921), Pablo Picasso
Oil on canvas, 184 x 105 cm. Photo: J.G. Berizzi. Musée Picasso, Paris, France.

Photo credit: Réunion des Musées Nationaux/Art Resource, NY.

La tecnología

Edificio de Correos, Madrid, España

Chapter Objectives

- Talk about computers and the Internet
- Learn to ask for something and to tell what something is used for
- Talk about knowing people or knowing how to do things
- Understand cultural perspectives on using technology

Video Highlights

A primera vista: ***¿Cómo se comunica?***

GramActiva Videos: **the present tense of** ***pedir*** **and** ***servir; saber*** **and** ***conocer***

Videomisterio: ***¿Eres tú, María?*****, Episodio 10**

Country Connection

As you learn about different means of communication and how technology changes people's lives, you will make connections to these countries and places:

Más práctica

- ***Real.*** **para hispanohablantes, pp. 350–351**

For: Online Atlas
Web Code: jbe-0002

A primera vista

Vocabulario y gramática en contexto

jbd-0997

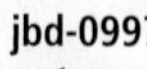

Objectives

Read, listen to, and understand information about
- computers and ways to use computers
- ways to communicate

"En **el laboratorio** en nuestra escuela, los estudiantes **saben** usar las computadoras para hacer muchas cosas. A muchos estudiantes les gusta . . .

. . . **crear documentos** o escribir **una composición**,

. . . hacer **gráficos**,

la diapositiva

la computadora portátil

. . . y preparar **presentaciones** con diapositivas.

Otros estudiantes **están en línea** para **navegar en la Red.** Pueden **buscar un sitio Web** o **bajar información** para **un informe.**

una canción

A otros les interesa **grabar un disco compacto.** Esta chica graba canciones".

—Nunca **me comunico** con **el correo electrónico.** ¿Es **complicado?** ¿Debo **tomar un curso** para aprender?

—No, abuelito, puedes aprender fácilmente. No debes **tener miedo de** usar la computadora. Y siempre me puedes **pedir** ayuda. ¿Cómo **te comunicas** con tus amigos que no viven cerca?

—Prefiero **enviarles** una carta o una tarjeta o puedo visitarlos para hablar cara a cara. Es mucho más personal.

la carta

la tarjeta

hablar cara a cara

jbd-0997

Escuchar

¿Sí o no?

Vas a escuchar siete frases. Si la frase es cierta, haz el gesto del pulgar hacia arriba. Si una frase es falsa, haz el gesto del pulgar hacia abajo.

Más práctica

- Practice Workbook, pp. 82–83: 9B-1, 9B-2
- WAV Wbk.: Writing, p. 98
- Guided Practice: Vocab. Flash Cards, pp. 291–294
- *Real.* para hispanohablantes, p. 352

Go Online PHSchool.com
For: Vocab. Practice
Web Code: jbd-0911

jbd-0997

Escuchar

¿Es lógico?

Primero lee las respuestas. Luego escucha cada conversación y escoge el comentario más lógico.

1. **a.** Al papá le gusta usar la Red.
   b. El papá no sabe usar la Red.
2. **a.** El estudiante quiere grabar un disco compacto.
   b. El estudiante quiere bajar información.
3. **a.** Va a enviarle una carta.
   b. Va a enviarle una tarjeta.

Videohistoria

jbd-0997

¿Cómo se comunica?

Ana sabe usar una cámara digital y una computadora. Ella puede navegar en la Red y tiene su propia página Web. ¿Qué le va a enseñar a Javier?

También se dice ...

la computadora = el ordenador *(España)*

España

Javier

Ana

Antes de leer

Recognizing cognates Recognizing cognates when you read can help improve your understanding.

- Skim the *Videohistoria* and make a list of the cognates. Which words on your list help you understand what types of technology Javier and Ana are talking about?

1. Look at what Javier and Ana are holding in photo 1. Who do you think feels more comfortable with new technology? Why?
2. Think about what you know about computers and the Internet. How would you explain to someone why computers are useful?

1 **Javier:** Hola, Ana. ¿Cómo estás?

Ana: Muy bien, ¿y tú? Mira. Acabo de comprar esta **cámara digital.** Es fascinante. ¿La **conoces?**

Javier: A ver. No **conozco** ese tipo de cámara. ¡Qué interesante!

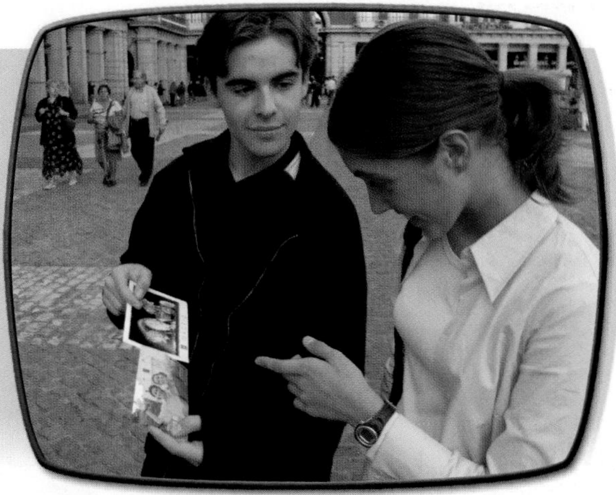

2 **Ana:** ¿Adónde vas?

Javier: Voy a enviar una tarjeta a Esteban, mi amigo en San Antonio. Mira, tengo una foto de él.

Ana: Mmmm. Es muy simpático, ¿no? Si quieres, te acompaño.

3 **Ana:** Vamos, Javier. Uno, dos, tres. Y mira, aquí estás. **¿Qué te parece?**

Javier: Muy bien. Sacaste las fotos muy **rápidamente.** Veo que no es complicado.

4 **Javier:** Un momento, voy a enviar mi tarjeta.

Ana: ¿Por qué no te comunicas con Esteban por correo electrónico?

Javier: Porque no tengo ordenador.

Ana: No importa. En Madrid hay muchos cibercafés. Vamos a uno.

5 **Ana:** Aquí puedes navegar en la Red o **visitar salones de chat.** Mira, mi **página Web.** Yo la hice.

Javier: ¿Tú la hiciste? ¡Qué bien! Pero . . . **¿para qué sirve?**

Ana: El Internet **sirve para** mucho. Puedes **escribir por** correo electrónico, buscar información, jugar juegos . . .

6 **Ana:** Tengo una idea. Tu amigo Esteban tiene **dirección electrónica,** ¿no?

Javier: Creo que sí. ¡Ah! Aquí está en su carta.

7 **Javier:** Hola, Esteban. Saludos desde un cibercafé en Madrid . . .

Ana: ¡Eso es! Tú vas a escribirle por correo electrónico. Y le vamos a enviar esta foto de nosotros.

8 **Javier:** . . . y aquí estoy con mi buena amiga, Ana. ¿Qué tal la familia? Y el cumpleaños de Cristina, ¿cómo lo pasaste?

Esteban: Es evidente que Javier está muy contento en Madrid.

Leer

¿Quién es?

Decide cuál de las personas de la *Videohistoria* diría *(would say)* cada frase. Escribe su nombre en una hoja de papel.

1. ¿Por qué no sacamos fotos con mi cámara digital?
2. Tengo su dirección electrónica en esta carta.
3. Yo hice mi propia página Web.
4. Mis amigos me enviaron fotos a mi dirección electrónica.
5. No tengo mi propia computadora.
6. Sé mucho de computadoras.

Javier

Ana

Esteban

Leer/Pensar/Escribir

Las computadoras sirven para mucho

Ana da muchas razones *(reasons)* de por qué las computadoras sirven para mucho, pero hay otras también. Lee estas frases y escribe en una hoja de papel sólo las razones que da Ana.

1. Una persona puede navegar la Red.
2. Es fácil escribir por correo electrónico.
3. Puedes grabar un disco compacto.
4. Puedes escribir una composición.
5. Una persona puede buscar información.
6. Es posible mandar fotos.
7. Puedes hacer una presentación.
8. Una persona puede jugar juegos.
9. Puedes visitar salones de chat.
10. Es posible hacer una página Web.

Leer/Escribir

¿Comprendes?

En cada frase hay un error. Lee la frase y después escribe la frase con la información correcta.

1. Ana acaba de comprar una computadora portátil.
2. Javier quiere enviarle a Esteban una carta.
3. Javier no le escribe por correo electrónico porque no le gusta usar las computadoras.
4. Según Ana, la Red no sirve para mucho.
5. Ana le escribe a Esteban por correo electrónico.
6. Javier le pregunta a Esteban sobre el cumpleaños de Angélica.

Más práctica

- Practice Workbook, pp. 84–85: 9B-3, 9B-4
- WAV Wbk.: Video, pp. 93–95
- Guided Practice: Vocab. Check, pp. 295–298
- *Real.* para hispanohablantes, p. 353

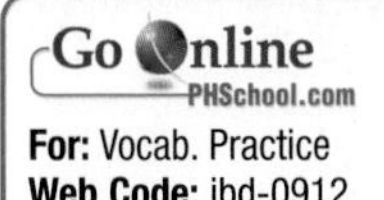

Manos a la obra

Vocabulario y gramática en uso

Objectives

- **Talk about traditional and electronic forms of communication**
- **Talk about how computers are used**
- **Express opinions about computers**
- **Learn e → *i* stem-changing verbs: *pedir* and *servir***
- **Know when to use *saber* and *conocer***

Leer/Escribir

Definiciones

Lee las definiciones y escribe la palabra correspondiente.

Modelo

Es cómo puedes enviar una carta por computadora.
el correo electrónico

1. Es una foto transparente que podemos proyectar durante una presentación.
2. Es una composición musical que podemos cantar.
3. Es una forma de comunicación que usa bolígrafo y papel. *(Hay dos posibilidades).*
4. Es un lugar en la Red que da información sobre una organización o una persona.
5. Es una computadora pequeña que puedes llevar a diferentes lugares.
6. Es un lugar en la escuela donde hay muchas computadoras que los estudiantes pueden usar.
7. Es una forma de comunicación bonita o cómica que le envías* a una persona para su cumpleaños.
8. Es algo visual que puedes crear o ver en la computadora.
9. Es algo que escribes sobre un tema para una clase. *(Hay dos posibilidades).*

**Enviar* has an accent mark on the *i* in all present-tense forms except *nosotros* and *vosotros.*

Fondo cultural

La Real Academia Española was founded in Spain in 1713 to preserve the quality, elegance, and purity of the Spanish language. There are now *Academias* in all the Spanish-speaking countries, including the Philippines and the United States. Today the *Academias* ensure that changes in Spanish reflect the needs of all of its more than 360 million native speakers. *La Real Academia Española* publishes the most complete and authoritative dictionary of the Spanish language.

- Why do you think that it's important to preserve the quality and purity of a language?

La Real Academia Española, en Madrid

jbd-0998

Escuchar/Escribir

Opiniones diferentes

1. Vas a escuchar las opiniones de cuatro personas sobre cómo prefieren comunicarse. En una hoja de papel, escribe los números del 1 al 4 y escribe lo que escuchas.

2. Después de escuchar sus opiniones, indica si crees que las personas que tienen estas opiniones están en la sala de clases o en el laboratorio de computadoras.

Leer/Pensar/Hablar

La computadora y tú

1. Toma esta prueba *(test)* sobre cómo usas la computadora. Determina tu evaluación y lee la recomendación del Centro de Computación.

2. Pregunta a otro(a) estudiante qué curso debe tomar según los resultados de la prueba. Tiene que darte tres razones *(reasons)* para justificar el curso.

Modelo

A —*¿Qué curso debes tomar?*
B —*Debo tomar un curso avanzado.*
A —*¿Por qué?*
B —*Porque ya navego en la Red y busco sitios Web. Sé crear un sitio Web.*

La computadora y tú

1. ¿Cómo te comunicas más con otras personas?
   - **a.** Les hablo cara a cara.
   - **b.** Les envío cartas o tarjetas.
   - **c.** Les escribo por correo electrónico.
   - **d.** Visito salones de chat.
2. ¿Cómo buscas información cuando escribes informes?
   - **a.** Voy a la biblioteca por un libro.
   - **b.** Les pido ayuda a mis amigos.
   - **c.** Navego en la Red y busco sitios Web.
   - **d.** Bajo documentos que me sirven mucho.
3. ¿Qué sabes hacer en la computadora?
   - **a.** Sé encender* la computadora.
   - **b.** Sé escribir una composición.
   - **c.** Sé crear una presentación usando diapositivas.
   - **d.** Sé crear un sitio Web.
4. ¿Para qué te sirve la computadora?
   - **a.** No me sirve para nada.
   - **b.** Me sirve para jugar juegos.
   - **c.** Me sirve para navegar en la Red.
   - **d.** Me sirve para buscar y bajar información.
5. ¿Cuál es tu opinión de las computadoras?
   - **a.** Tengo miedo de las computadoras.
   - **b.** Las computadoras son demasiado complicadas.
   - **c.** Las computadoras me ayudan a hacer cosas más rápidamente.
   - **d.** Las computadoras son necesarias para la comunicación.

Evaluación

Cada a = 1 punto
Cada b = 3 puntos
Cada c = 4 puntos
Cada d = 6 puntos

El Centro de Computación tiene cursos ideales para ti. Según el resultado de la prueba, debes tomar uno de estos cursos:

Puntos	Tu curso ideal
de 5 a 10	Básico 1
de 11 a 16	Básico 2
de 17 a 23	Intermedio
de 24 a 30	Avanzado

*to turn on

Leer/Escribir/Hablar

¿Quiénes están en línea?

Lee el anuncio y luego contesta estas preguntas.

1. ¿Quiénes usan más el Internet: los estadounidenses o los españoles? ¿Los estadounidenses o los suecos?
2. ¿Usas tú el Internet a menudo, a veces o nunca?
3. Entre *(Among)* las personas que conoces, ¿quién usa más el Internet? ¿Para qué lo usa?

¡A sus teclados[1], listos ... a navegar!

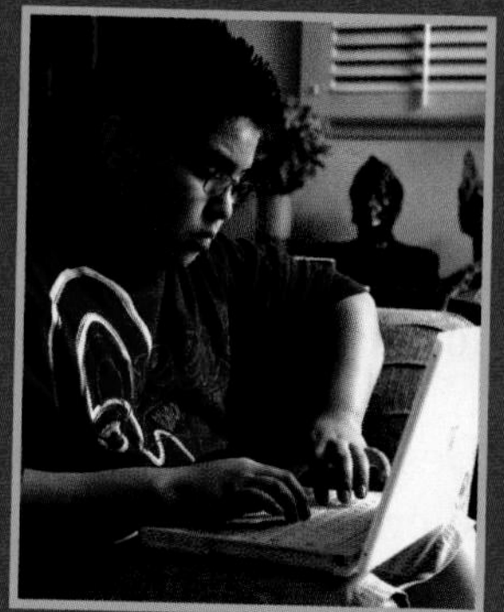

¿Usas el Internet? En el mundo hay más de 600 millones de internautas. El récord lo tienen los suecos:[2] siete de cada diez personas usan la Red. En los Estados Unidos, seis de cada diez estadounidenses[3] la usan. En España la gente está muy lejos de esa cifra.[4] Sólo dos de cada diez españoles están conectados al Internet.

[1] keyboards [2] Swedes [3] Americans [4] figure

Exploración del lenguaje

Using *-mente* to form an adverb

Adverbs are words that describe verbs. They often tell *how* an action is performed. Many adverbs in English end in the letters *-ly: slowly, frequently, happily,* and so on. To form similar adverbs in Spanish, you add the ending *-mente* to the feminine singular form of an adjective. This *-mente* ending is equivalent to the *-ly* ending in English.

rápida → rápidamente
práctica → prácticamente
fácil → fácilmente
feliz → felizmente
general → generalmente
especial → especialmente

Note that if the adjective has a written accent, as with *rápida, fácil,* and *práctica,* the accent appears in the same place in the adverb form.

Try it out! Give the adverb for each of the adjectives in the list. Then use each adverb in one of the sentences. Some sentences have more than one possible answer.

normal total completo
frecuente reciente

1. El laboratorio de nuestra escuela es _____ nuevo.
2. _____ les escribo a mis amigos por correo electrónico pero hoy les envío una carta.
3. _____ mis padres nos compraron una nueva computadora.
4. Mi hermano está _____ contento cuando está usando la computadora.
5. _____ grabamos canciones en un disco compacto.

Escribir/Hablar

¿Cómo te comunicas?

1 Mira cada dibujo y escribe qué forma de comunicación es. Luego escribe por qué se usa esta forma de comunicación.

Modelo

hablar por teléfono
Casi todos tienen teléfonos. Es fácil.

1. 
2. 
3. 
4. 

2 Trabaja con un grupo de cinco personas y pregunta a tus compañeros cómo se comunican con otras personas y por qué. Escriban sus respuestas.

Modelo

A —*¿Cómo te comunicas con otras personas?*
B —*Les hablo por teléfono.*
A —*¿Por qué?*
B —*Porque casi todos tienen teléfonos y es fácil.*

3 Una persona de cada grupo va a escribir en la pizarra la forma preferida de comunicación de su grupo. Según esta información, ¿cuál es la forma de comunicación preferida de la clase?

¿Recuerdas?
You use the indirect object pronoun *les* to mean "to them" or "for them."

Para decir más . . .
eficiente efficient
íntimo, -a personal
rápido, -a quick, fast

Escribir/Hablar

Y tú, ¿qué dices?

1. ¿Tienes tú, o tiene tu familia o un(a) amigo(a), una computadora portátil? ¿Qué te parece?
2. ¿A veces tienes miedo de las computadoras? ¿Por qué?
3. ¿Tienes tu propia dirección electrónica? Crea una nueva dirección electrónica "inolvidable" para las personas que nunca recuerdan *(remember)* tu dirección.
4. ¿Qué sabes crear en la computadora?
5. ¿Qué sitio Web conoces mejor? ¿Qué te parece?

Fondo cultural

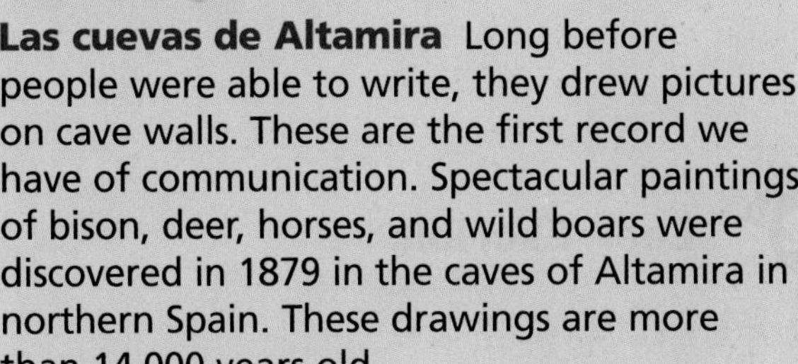

Las cuevas de Altamira Long before people were able to write, they drew pictures on cave walls. These are the first record we have of communication. Spectacular paintings of bison, deer, horses, and wild boars were discovered in 1879 in the caves of Altamira in northern Spain. These drawings are more than 14,000 years old.

- Why do you think the cave dwellers drew pictures of animals? What would you draw?

Un bisonte en las cuevas de Altamira

Gramática

The present tense of *pedir* and *servir*

Pedir and *servir* are stem-changing verbs in which the *e* in the stem of the infinitive changes to *i* in all forms except *nosotros* and *vosotros.*

Here are the present-tense forms of *pedir* and *servir:*

(yo)	**pido**	(nosotros) (nosotras)	**pedimos**
(tú)	**pides**	(vosotros) (vosotras)	**pedís**
Ud. (él) (ella)	**pide**	Uds. (ellos) (ellas)	**piden**

(yo)	**sirvo**	(nosotros) (nosotras)	**servimos**
(tú)	**sirves**	(vosotros) (vosotras)	**servís**
Ud. (él) (ella)	**sirve**	Uds. (ellos) (ellas)	**sirven**

Pedir means "to ask for."

Juan **pide** la dirección electrónica.
Pedimos más información sobre la Red.

Servir means "to serve" or "to be useful for."

Servimos refrescos después de la clase.
Las computadoras **sirven** para mucho.

GramActiva VIDEO

Need more help with *pedir* and *servir?* Watch the **GramActiva** video.

Leer/Escribir

En el cibercafé

Completa esta descripción de un cibercafé con la forma apropiada de *servir* o *pedir*. Escribe los verbos en una hoja de papel.

Tecnocapuccino

En el cibercafé Tecnocapuccino no hay solo computadoras. Nosotros __1.__ café, refrescos y todo tipo de sándwiches. Si tú __2.__ un café con leche yo te __3.__ el mejor café de la ciudad. Cuando nuestros clientes __4.__ un sándwich, nuestros camareros les __5.__ uno de nuestros riquísimos sándwiches con papas fritas y un refresco. Nuestras computadoras te __6.__ para todo: navegar en la Red, escribir por correo electrónico y visitar salones de chat. Si uno __7.__ ayuda, nosotros podemos ayudarle sin problemas.

¡Reserva tu computadora hoy!

  **Escribir**

Les piden a los profesores

Tú y tus amigos tienen problemas y necesitan pedirles ayuda a los profesores. Usa los nombres de tus amigos y los profesores de tu escuela para decir a quién(es) le(s) piden ayuda. Escribe las frases en una hoja de papel.

Modelo

Mi amigo(a) *(nombre)* no puede bajar los gráficos para hacer su sitio Web.
Mi amiga Lupita le pide ayuda a la Sra. Márquez, la profesora de tecnología.

1. Mi amigo(a) *(nombre)* no puede grabar un disco compacto de música.
2. *(Nombre)* y tú no comprenden por qué hay un error en su tarea de matemáticas.
3. Tú no sabes todas las palabras en una página Web en español.
4. *(Nombre)* y *(nombre)* no pueden abrir un documento sobre un monumento.
5. Yo quiero crear un cuadro de unos árboles.

¿Recuerdas?

The indirect object pronouns *le* and *les* mean "to him, her, you *(pl.)*, them." With *pedir,* they refer to the person whom you ask for something. If you mention that person by name or title, you need to use *a.*

- **Le pido** dinero **a** mi hermano Juan.

Nota

In English you say that you ask *for* help. In Spanish, "for" is implied in the meaning of *pedir* and a separate word is *not* used.

   **Hablar**

¿Pides muchas cosas?

Habla con otro(a) estudiante sobre las cosas que les pides a diferentes personas.

Modelo

dinero
A —*¿A quién le pides dinero?*
B —*Le pido dinero a mi mejor amiga, Luisa.*
o: —*Les pido dinero a mis padres.*

1. ropa nueva
2. tiempo libre sin tarea
3. ayuda con . . .
4. tu propio(a) . . .
5. tiempo libre sin quehaceres
6. **¡Respuesta personal!**

   **Hablar/Escribir**

Los mejores restaurantes

1. Piensa en los restaurantes que conoces. ¿Qué sirven allí que te gusta? Con otro(a) estudiante, habla sobre los restaurantes y la comida que sirven.

Modelo

A —*¿En qué restaurante comes?*
B —*Como en el restaurante.... A menudo pido... allí. Es muy.... Lo sirven con....*

2. Ahora hablen con otra pareja de los restaurantes donde Uds. comen, lo que piden y con qué sirven las comidas. Preparen tres o más recomendaciones de restaurantes para presentar a la clase.

Modelo

Si Uds. quieren comer bien, recomendamos el restaurante Las Palmeras. Siempre pedimos el pescado... ¡es delicioso! Lo sirven con arroz....

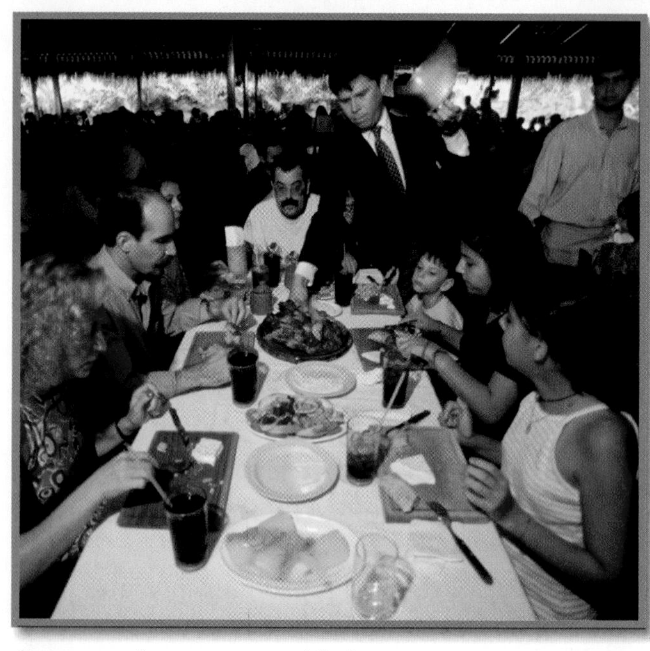

Siempre pedimos carne y enchiladas.

   **Escribir/Hablar**

Juego

Con otro(a) estudiante, escriban descripciones de tres cosas y expliquen para qué sirven. Lean las frases a otra pareja para ver si ellos pueden identificar las cosas.

Modelo

A —*Es una cosa bastante pequeña. Puede estar en tu mochila o pupitre. No cuesta mucho dinero.*
B —*¿Para qué sirve?*
A —*Sirve para escribir cartas o composiciones.*
B —*Es un bolígrafo.*

Pronunciación

jbd-0998

Dividing words into syllables 

Knowing how to divide words into syllables will help you sound out a new word. Just as in English, all syllables in Spanish include a vowel. When there is a consonant between two vowels, you divide the word into syllables before the consonant. The letter combinations *ch, ll,* and *rr* are never divided in Spanish. Listen to and say these words:

ju-gar	pá-gi-na	la-bo-ra-to-rio	na-ve-gar
ca-lle	no-ti-cias	co-mu-ni-dad	a-bu-rri-do

When there are two consonants between vowels, you divide the word between the consonants. Exceptions are the blends *pr, pl, br, bl, fr, fl, tr, dr, cr, cl, gr,* and *gl.* These blends are never divided and go with the following vowel: *pro-ble-ma.* Listen to and say these words:

car-ta	in-fan-til	con-cur-sos	jar-dín
par-que	a-bri-go	des-can-sar	pa-dres

When there are three or more consonants between vowel sounds, the first two go with the vowel that precedes them and the third goes with the vowel that follows them: *trans-por-te.* When the second and third consonants form a blend, however, the first consonant goes with the vowel before it and the other consonants go with the vowel that follows them: *en-tre.* Listen to and say these words:

es-cri-to-rio	com-pli-ca-do
en-tre-vis-tas	com-pras-te

Try it out! See if you can separate the following words into the correct syllables.

1. emocionante
2. rápidamente
3. computadora
4. anaranjado
5. electrónico
6. comunicamos

Escribir/Hablar

Y tú, ¿qué dices?

1. ¿A quién le pides ayuda con la computadora? ¿Le pides ayuda a menudo o sólo a veces?
2. ¿Qué haces cuando tus amigos te piden ayuda con la computadora? ¿Para qué cosas te piden ayuda?
3. ¿Para qué sirve una clase de tecnología? ¿Qué te gustaría aprender en una clase de tecnología?
4. ¿Para qué sirve una computadora portátil? ¿Te gustaría tener una computadora portátil? ¿Por qué sí o por qué no?

Más práctica

- Practice Workbook, p. 86: 9B-5
- WAV Wbk.: Writing, p. 99
- Guided Practice: Grammar Acts., pp. 299–300
- *Real.* para hispanohablantes, pp. 354–357

For: *e* → *i* Verbs
Web Code: jbd-0913

Gramática

Saber and *conocer*

Sé and *sabes* come from the verb *saber,* "to know." There is another verb in Spanish that also means "to know": *conocer.* Use *conocer* to talk about people, places, and things that you are familiar with.

Here are the present-tense forms of *saber* and *conocer.* Except for the *yo* forms, they are regular in the present tense.

¿Recuerdas?

You have used *(yo) sé* and *(tú) sabes* to talk about knowing a fact and to say what you know how to do.

- **¿Sabes** dónde está la biblioteca?
- Yo **sé** esquiar bastante bien.

(yo)	**sé**	(nosotros) (nosotras)	**sabemos**
(tú)	**sabes**	(vosotros) (vosotras)	**sabéis**
Ud. (él) (ella)	**sabe**	Uds. (ellos) (ellas)	**saben**

(yo)	**conozco**	(nosotros) (nosotras)	**conocemos**
(tú)	**conoces**	(vosotros) (vosotras)	**conocéis**
Ud. (él) (ella)	**conoce**	Uds. (ellos) (ellas)	**conocen**

Conocer is followed by the personal *a* when the direct object is a person. Direct object pronouns can also be used with *conocer.*

¿Conocen Uds. **a la señora** que trabaja en el laboratorio?

Sí, **la** conocemos bien. ¿Quieres **conocerla**?

GramActiva VIDEO

Watch the **GramActiva** video to learn more about using the verbs *saber* and *conocer.*

Escribir

¿Qué lugares y a qué personas conoces?

Si una persona visita tu comunidad y tu escuela, ¿puedes ayudarla a conocer a diferentes personas y lugares? Escribe la forma apropiada del verbo *conocer* y la información apropiada para cada frase. Escribe las frases en una hoja de papel.

1. (Yo) ___ a muchos de los estudiantes en la clase de ___ .
2. Mis amigos y yo ___ al (a la) secretario(a) de la escuela. Es el (la) Sr. (Sra.) ___ .
3. Mi hermano(a)/amigo(a) ___ bastante bien al (a la) profesor(a) de ___ .
4. Mis amigos ___ bien el parque de diversiones ___ .
5. (Yo) ___ la tienda ___ donde me gusta comprar ___ .
6. Mi padre (madre) ___ bien el monumento de ___ .

  **Hablar**

¿Conocemos a las mismas personas y los mismos lugares?

Trabaja con otro(a) estudiante y lee tus frases de la Actividad 18. Habla de las personas y los lugares que Uds. conocen.

Modelo

A —*Conozco a Jaime, que está en mi clase de matemáticas.*

B —*Yo también lo conozco. Está en mi clase de historia.*

o:—*No lo conozco. ¿Cómo es?*

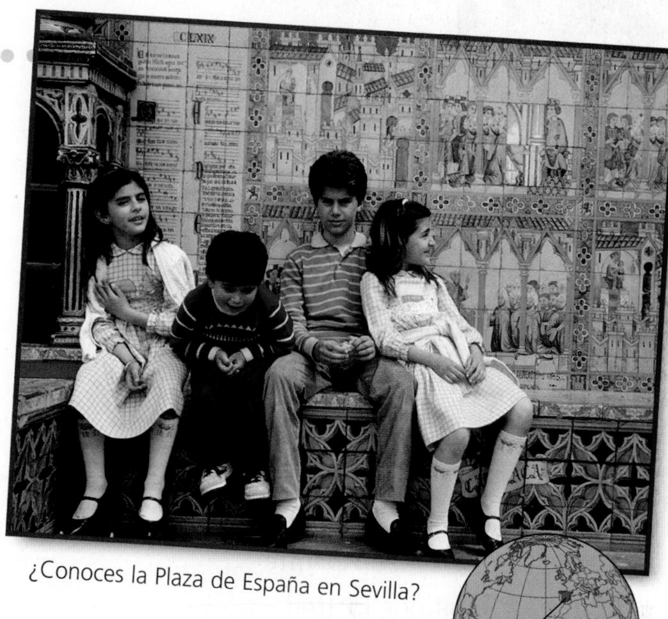

¿Conoces la Plaza de España en Sevilla?

España

  **Hablar**

Lo que sabemos hacer

Habla con otro(a) estudiante sobre quiénes saben hacer las diferentes actividades en los dibujos.

Modelo

A —*¿Quién sabe grabar un disco compacto?*

B —*Mi hermano Mario sabe grabar un disco compacto. Lo hace a menudo.*

o:—*No sé quién sabe grabar un disco compacto.*

¿Recuerdas?

When you say that you know how to do something, you don't need a separate word for "how."

- **Sabemos crear** presentaciones con diapositivas.

1. 

2. 

3. 

4. 

5. 

6. 

Actividad 21 Hablar

¿Saber o conocer?

Trabaja con otro(a) estudiante para ver lo que sabe y conoce.

1. la hermana de...
2. bajar información de la Red
3. el nombre de una canción en español
4. las cámaras digitales
5. España o México
6. la dirección electrónica de...
7. un sitio Web interesante
8. enviar fotos por la Red

Modelo

la persona que trabaja en la biblioteca de la escuela
A —*¿Conoces a la persona que trabaja en la biblioteca de la escuela?*
B —*Sí, la conozco. Es muy simpática. Es la Sra. Wilton.*
o: —*No, no la conozco.*

bailar salsa
A —*¿Sabes bailar salsa?*
B —*Sí, sé bailar salsa. Me encanta.*
o: —*No, no sé bailar salsa.*

Actividad 22 Leer/Escribir

Los tres cerditos

Lee el anuncio y contesta las preguntas.

1. ¿Conocen los cerditos a la "persona" que está en la puerta? ¿Saben ellos lo que quiere?
2. ¿Tiene tu familia un servicio de identificación de llamadas en su teléfono? ¿Te gusta este servicio, o te gustaría tener este servicio? ¿Por qué?
3. ¿Te parece bien saber quién llama por teléfono? ¿Por qué?
4. ¿Te gusta hablar por teléfono? ¿Con quién te gusta hablar más?

¿Sabes quién es?

Pide el servicio de identificación de llamadas.
Si eres cliente de Teléfonos Caribe, es completamente gratis.

Así, siempre vas a saber quién está llamando.
¡Pídelo hoy! Llama al teléfono 20-05-617.

Leer/Pensar/Escribir/Dibujar

¿Qué inventos conoces?

Mucho antes de la invención de la computadora, había *(there were)* otros inventos que nos ayudaron a comunicarnos y que seguimos *(keep)* usando. Mira la línea cronológica y lee la lista de inventos. Luego contesta las preguntas.

Conexiones La tecnología

1800 | 1829 | 1837 | 1839 | 1840 | 1850 | 1868 | 1878 | 1884 | 1900 | 1910 | 1926 | 1939 | 1950 | 1953 | 1980 | 1988 | 1999 | 2000

la máquina	el televisor	la primera película con sonido	el código Morse
el teléfono celular	el televisor de color	el telégrafo	el teléfono
el alfabeto Braille	la pluma	el sello	el walkie talkie
	el reproductor MP3[1]		la Red (World Wide Web)

[1] compressed audio tapes

1. Identifica cada invento según el año en que se inventó y explica qué impacto tiene sobre la comunicación.
2. Busca información en la Red o en la biblioteca para identificar los inventores de cada invento de la lista.
3. ¿Cuál de estos inventos te parece el más importante? ¿Por qué?
4. Piensa en un invento que quieres hacer. ¿Para qué sirve? Escribe un párrafo y haz un dibujo para explicar tu invento.

El español en el mundo del trabajo

The need to share information will be crucial in the twenty-first century. Innovations from medicine, science, technology, engineering, manufacturing, and social services need to be communicated across the globe. With a partner, make a list of six ways in which information can be spread. For each, tell how knowing Spanish would be beneficial. Share your ideas with the class.

Más práctica

- Practice Workbook, pp. 87–88: 9B-6, 9B-7
- WAV Wbk.: Writing, p. 100
- Guided Practice: Grammar Acts., pp. 301–302
- *Real.* para hispanohablantes, pp. 358–361

For: *Saber* vs. *conocer*
Web Code: jbd-0914

¡Adelante!

Lectura

Objectives

- Read about the Internet and its impact on the Spanish language
- Learn about *cibercafés*
- Write an e-mail message defending your use of the computer
- Watch *¿Eres tú, María?*, Episodio 10

La invasión del ciberspanglish

Lee este artículo sobre el Internet. El Internet sirve para muchas cosas aquí en los Estados Unidos y también en los otros países donde hablan español. Pero no es siempre fácil traducir[1] los términos técnicos.

Strategy

Using prior knowledge
Use what you know about a topic to help you understand what you read. This article is on the Internet and its impact on the Spanish language. List five things you know about the Internet that might help you with this reading.

La invasión del ciberspanglish

¿Te gusta usar el Internet? Actualmente[2] hay gente en todos los países del mundo que usan el Internet. Sirve para muchas cosas: para hacer compras, divertirse, educarse, trabajar, buscar información, hacer planes para un viaje y mucho más. Hoy en día uno no puede pensar en una vida sin computadoras o el Internet.

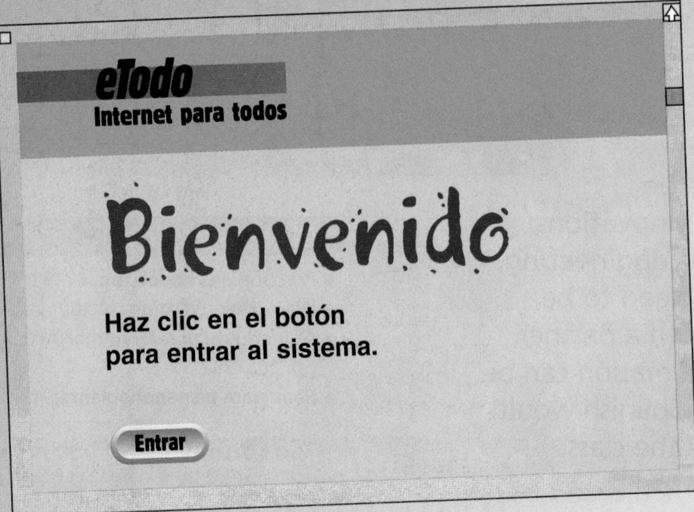

Si quieres explorar el Internet en español, hay una explosión de portales (sitios que sirven como puerta al Internet) en los Estados Unidos, España y América Latina. Como puedes imaginar, hay una rivalidad[3] grande entre estos portales para atraer[4] a los hispanohablantes. Algunos portales dan la misma información en inglés y español; sólo tienes que hacer clic para cambiarla.

[1]to translate [2]Nowadays [3]rivalry
[4]to attract

Juntos,[5] el inglés y el español en el Internet dieron origen al "ciberspanglish". A algunas personas no les gusta nada este nuevo "idioma"[6]. Piensan que el español es suficientemente rico para poder traducir los términos del inglés. Hay otros que dicen que no hay problema con mezclar[7] los idiomas para comunicarse mejor. Piensan que el "ciberspanglish" es más fácil y lógico porque los términos técnicos vienen del inglés y expresarlos en español es bastante complicado.

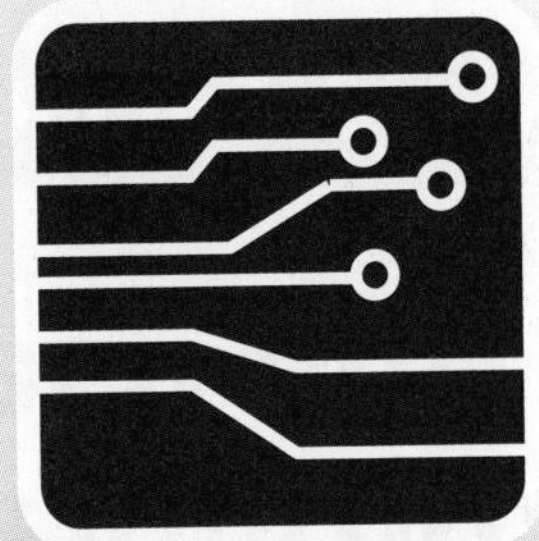

Éste es un debate que va a durar[8] mucho tiempo, y no presenta grises.

Términos de ciberspanglish	Términos en español
emailear	mandar por correo electrónico
espam	mandar por un bombardeo de grandes cantidades de correo
chatear	conversar
hacer clic	picar con el ratón
hacer doble clic	picar dos veces con el ratón
rebootear	rearrancar
linkear	enlazar con una página en Internet
crashear	quebrar o chocar
formatear	hacer un formato
programar	escribir un programa
escanear	rastrear o digitalizar
surfear	explorar o navegar
hacer un upgrade	actualizar o subir un grado
el clipart	dibujos artísticos
hacer un exit	salir
printear	imprimir

[5]Together [6]language [7]mixing [8]to last

¿Comprendes?

1. Look at the list you created for the Strategy "Using prior knowledge." Place a check mark next to any pieces of information mentioned in the article.
2. According to the article, how could the Internet help you learn more Spanish?
3. Summarize briefly the two sides of the argument related to *ciberspanglish.*
4. What do you think the statement *Éste es un debate que . . . no presenta grises* means? Why is it appropriate as the closing statement for this article?

Más práctica

- WAV Wbk.: Writing, p. 101
- Guided Practice: *Lectura*, p. 303
- *Real.* para hispanohablantes, pp. 362–363

Perspectivas del mundo hispano

¿Para qué usas una computadora?

In many Spanish-speaking countries, the use of computers and access to the Internet are often not as widespread as in the United States. Many homes don't have telephones, computers cost more money, and in many cases, the Internet is not as accessible. Schools and libraries may not have the computers and access to the Internet as they do in most communities in the United States. For these reasons, many cybercafés *(los cibercafés)* have opened. Cybercafés are nice places for students to meet after school and work on assignments, do research, or e-mail friends. They offer very inexpensive access to the Internet.

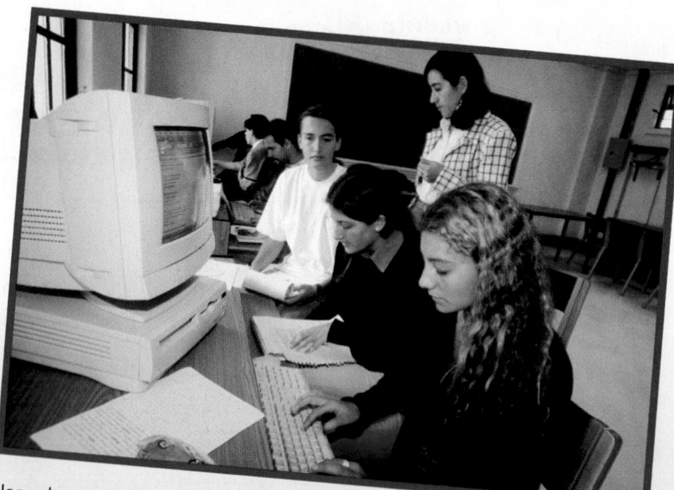

Usando computadoras para estudiar en Quito, Ecuador

In recent years, the number of *portales* (portals) that serve as access points to the Internet has increased and many of these are offered in Spanish as well as English. The number of *buscadores* (search engines) has also increased, making it easier for Spanish speakers to search for information or just surf the Internet.

Check it out! Survey your friends. Over the course of one week, how much time do they spend using a computer and for what reasons?

Think about it! Name three ways that you think Spanish-language Internet sites could help you learn more Spanish and understand the perspectives of Spanish speakers.

Haciendo la tarea en la computadora

Presentación escrita

La computadora en mi vida

Task
Your parents think that you are spending too much time on the computer and you disagree. Send an e-mail message (of course!) to your best friend in Mexico explaining your position and how you plan to defend your computer use to your parents.

1 Prewrite Create a chart. In the first column, list at least three ways you use the computer. In the second column, write the benefit *(la ventaja)* to you.

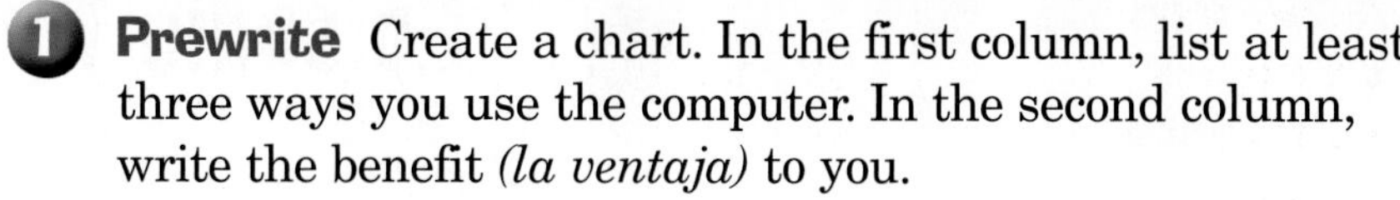

Cómo uso la computadora	La ventaja
Busco información para mis clases en Internet.	Aprendo mucho y es muy interesante.

2 Draft Use the information from the chart to write the first draft of your e-mail. Here are some expressions you might include:

pienso que . . . tengo que . . .
creo que . . . primero, segundo, tercero, . . .

3 Revise Check for spelling, accent marks, verb forms, pronouns, and vocabulary use. Share the e-mail with a partner. Your partner should check the following:

- Is the paragraph easy to read and understand?
- Does it provide good reasons and support for your position?
- Is there anything that you could add to give more information or change to make it more understandable?
- Are there any errors?

4 Publish Rewrite the e-mail, making necessary changes. Make a copy for your teacher and add it to your portfolio.

5 Evaluation Your teacher may give you a rubric for grading the paragraph. You may be evaluated on:

- the amount of information provided
- how well you presented each reason and its benefit
- use of vocabulary and accuracy of spelling and grammar

Strategy

Using supporting examples
When preparing a persuasive argument, you should first clearly state your position and then provide examples to support it. Making a list of your arguments will help you make a strong statement.

Videomisterio

¿Eres tú, María?

Episodio 10

Antes de ver el video

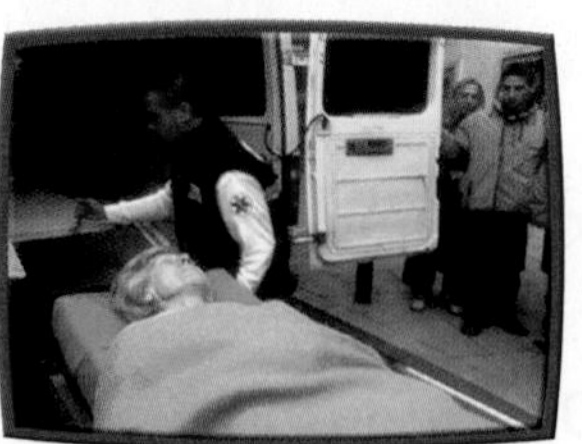

Resumen del episodio

Es el último episodio y Lola y el Inspector Gil van a solucionarlo todo. En realidad, ¿quién es María? ¿Qué importancia tiene Luis Antonio? ¿Quién tiene las joyas? ¿Cómo y por qué ocurrió el crimen? ¿Quién va a la cárcel? ¿Quién va a necesitar un buen abogado? ¿Qué pasa cuando Pedro ve a su abuela por primera vez?

Palabras para comprender

Deténgala.	Arrest her.
No quería.	I didn't want to.
las reconoció	recognized them
los novios	boyfriend and girlfriend
tomó	took
mucha suerte	a lot of luck
robarlas	to steal them
no quería esperar	didn't want to wait
Parece que . . .	It seems like . . .
la cárcel	jail
un abogado	lawyer

Y tú, ¿qué piensas?

¿Sabes lo que va a pasar en este episodio? Escribe tus respuestas a las preguntas en el *Resumen del episodio.* Ahora, mira el episodio y compara tus respuestas con lo que pasó. ¿Tenías razón?

Después de ver el video

¿Comprendes?

A. ¿A quién(es) describe cada frase: Lola, María, Julia, Luis Antonio, Pedro o doña Gracia?

1. Pues, señorita, es evidente que Ud. sabe mucho.
2. Las reconoció en el hospital.
3. Es evidente en la foto que son novios.
4. Murió en el hospital.
5. No puede ver muy bien.
6. Viene a Madrid para vivir con ella.
7. Tiene ochenta y cinco años y está en buena salud.
8. Entra en el piso y ataca a la señora.
9. Ud. no va a París, señor. Ud. va a la cárcel.
10. La mejor detective de Madrid.

B. Con un grupo de tres o cuatro estudiantes, escoge una escena del video. Tu profesor(a) les va a dar el guión *(script)* de la escena. Representen la escena para la clase. Hay que aprender de memoria el papel *(the part),* llevar la ropa del personaje y representar la escena de una manera bien profesional.

Go Online PHSchool.com **For:** More on *¿Eres tú, María?* **Web Code:** jbd-0507

Chapter Review

Repaso del capítulo

To prepare for the test, check to see if you . . .

- know the new vocabulary and grammar
- can perform the tasks on p. 335

Vocabulario y gramática

jbd-0999 

to talk about communication

cara a cara	face-to-face
la carta	letter
comunicarse **(yo) me comunico** **(tú) te comunicas**	to communicate (with)
enviar	to send
la tarjeta	card

to talk about computer-related activities

bajar	to download
buscar	to search (for)
la cámara digital	digital camera
la canción, *pl.* **las canciones**	song
la composición, *pl.* **las composiciones**	composition
la computadora portátil	laptop computer
crear	to create
el curso **tomar un curso**	course to take a course
la diapositiva	slide
la dirección electrónica	e-mail address
el documento	document
escribir por correo electrónico	to send an e-mail message
estar en línea	to be online
grabar un disco compacto	to burn a CD
los gráficos	graphics
la información	information
el informe	report
el laboratorio	laboratory
navegar en la Red	to surf the Web
la página Web	Web page
la presentación, *pl.* **las presentaciones**	presentation
el sitio Web	Web site
visitar salones de chat	to visit chat rooms

For *Vocabulario adicional,* see pp. 336–337.

other useful words and expressions

complicado, -a	complicated
¿Para qué sirve?	What's it (used) for?
¿Qué te parece?	What do you think?
rápidamente	quickly
Sirve para . . .	It's used for . . .
tener miedo (de)	to be afraid (of)

pedir *(e → i) to ask for*

pido	**pedimos**
pides	**pedís**
pide	**piden**

servir *(e → i) to serve, to be useful*

sirvo	**servimos**
sirves	**servís**
sirve	**sirven**

saber *to know (how)*

sé	**sabemos**
sabes	**sabéis**
sabe	**saben**

conocer *to know, to be acquainted with*

conozco	**conocemos**
conoces	**conocéis**
conoce	**conocen**

Más práctica

- Practice Workbook: Puzzle, p. 89
- Practice Workbook: Organizer, p. 90

Go Online PHSchool.com
For: Test Preparation
Web Code: jbd-0916

Preparación para el examen

	On the exam you will be asked to . . .	Here are practice tasks similar to those you will find on the exam . . .	If you need review . . .
jbd-0999 	**1 Escuchar** Listen and understand as people talk about how they use computers	You overhear some people expressing their opinions about computers. Tell whether each person likes or dislikes using computers.	**pp. 310–315** *A primera vista* **p. 311** Actividades 1–2 **p. 317** Actividad 7
	2 Hablar Ask and answer questions about what you know about computers and the Internet	A local Internet company wants to interview you to work as a telephone tech support assistant. To prepare, you and your partner take turns interviewing each other. Ask if your partner: a) knows how to surf the Web; b) is familiar with Web sites for teens; c) knows how to use the computer to create music; d) knows how to make graphics. Then switch roles.	**pp. 310–315** *A primera vista* **p. 317** Actividad 8 **p. 319** Actividad 11 **p. 323** Actividad 17 **p. 325** Actividad 20 **p. 326** Actividad 21
	**3 Leer** Read and understand part of an online conversation in a chat room	A teen in the chat room *Mis padres y yo* is upset. According to the teenager, what do his parents not understand? What is his parents' opinion? ¡Yo soy muy impaciente! Para hacer la tarea, me gusta tener la información que necesito rápidamente. Mis padres dicen que puedo ir a la biblioteca y buscar libros allí para hacer mi tarea, pero me gustaría tener mi propia computadora. Ellos piensan que las computadoras sólo sirven para jugar juegos. ¿Qué hago?	**pp. 310–315** *A primera vista* **p. 316** Actividad 6 **p. 317** Actividad 8 **p. 318** Actividad 9 **pp. 328–329** *Lectura*
	**4 Escribir** Write your personal profile *(perfil)* for a Web survey	You are completing a Web survey online for *MundoChat.* Provide answers to the following: a) what you like to do; b) your favorite Web site; c) how often you visit chat rooms; d) how much time you spend online each day.	**p. 321** Actividad 13 **p. 323** Actividad 17 **p. 324** Actividad 18 **p. 331** *Presentación escrita*
	**5 Pensar** Demonstrate an understanding of cultural perspectives regarding technology	Explain why cybercafés are so popular in many Spanish-speaking countries. Compare how you use computers to the way in which teenagers might use them in these countries. If you lived in one of these countries, how might you approach homework differently?	**p. 330** *Perspectivas del mundo hispano*

Vocabulario adicional

Los animales

el conejillo de Indias guinea pig
el conejo rabbit
el gerbo gerbil
el hámster, *pl.* **los hámsters** hamster
el hurón, *pl.* **los hurones** ferret
el loro parrot
el pez, *pl.* **los peces** fish
la serpiente snake
la tortuga turtle

Los miembros de la familia

el bisabuelo, la bisabuela great-grandfather, great-grandmother
el nieto, la nieta grandson, granddaughter
el sobrino, la sobrina nephew, niece

Las descripciones de personas

llevar anteojos to wear glasses
ser
- **calvo, -a** bald
- **delgado, -a** thin
- **gordo, -a** fat

tener
- **la barba** beard
- **el bigote** moustache
- **las pecas** freckles
- **el pelo lacio** straight hair
- **el pelo rizado** curly hair
- **las trenzas** braids

Las partes de la casa y cosas en la casa

el balcón, *pl.* **los balcones** balcony
la estufa stove
el jardín, *pl.* **los jardines** garden
el lavadero laundry room
la lavadora washing machine
el lavaplatos, *pl.* **los lavaplatos** dishwasher
el microondas, *pl.* **los microondas** microwave oven
los muebles furniture
el patio patio
el refrigerador refrigerator
la secadora clothes dryer
el sillón, *pl.* **los sillones** armchair
el sofá sofa
el tocador dressing table

Los quehaceres

quitar
- **la nieve con la pala** to shovel snow
- **los platos de la mesa** to clear the table

rastrillar las hojas to rake leaves

Los colores

(azul) claro light (blue)
(azul) marino navy (blue)
(azul) oscuro dark (blue)

Las expresiones para las compras

ahorrar to save
el dinero en efectivo cash
gastar to spend
la(s) rebaja(s) sale(s)
regatear to bargain
se vende for sale

La ropa

la bata bathrobe
el chaleco vest
las pantimedias pantyhose
el paraguas, *pl.* **los paraguas** umbrella
el pijama pajamas
la ropa interior underwear
el saco loose-fitting jacket
los tenis tennis shoes
las zapatillas slippers
los zapatos atléticos athletic shoes
los zapatos de tacón alto high-heeled shoes

Las expresiones para los viajes

el aeropuerto airport

la agencia de viajes travel agency

los cheques de viajero travelers' checks

el equipaje luggage

hacer una reservación to make a reservation

el lugar de interés place of interest

el pasaporte passport

volar *(o → ue)* to fly

Los animales del zoológico

el ave *(f.), pl.* **las aves** bird

el canguro kangaroo

la cebra zebra

el cocodrilo crocodile

el delfín, *pl.* **los delfines** dolphins

el elefante elephant

la foca seal

el gorila gorilla

el hipopótamo hippopotamus

la jirafa giraffe

el león, *pl.* **los leones** lion

el oso bear

el oso blanco polar bear

el pingüino penguin

el tigre tiger

Las expresiones para las computadoras

la búsqueda search

comenzar *(e → ie)* **la sesión** to log on

el disco duro hard disk

la impresora printer

imprimir to print

el marcapáginas, *pl.* **los marcapáginas** bookmark

multimedia multimedia

la página inicial home page

la tecla de borrar delete key

la tecla de intro enter key

Resumen de gramática

Grammar Terms

Adjectives describe nouns: *a* ***red*** *car.*

Adverbs usually describe verbs; they tell when, where, or how an action happens: *He read it* ***quickly.*** Adverbs can also describe adjectives or other adverbs: ***very*** *tall,* ***quite well.***

Articles are words in Spanish that can tell you whether a noun is masculine, feminine, singular, or plural. In English, the articles are ***the, a,*** and ***an.***

Commands are verb forms that tell people to do something: ***Study!, Work!***

Comparatives compare people or things.

Conjugations are verb forms that add endings to the stem in order to tell who the subject is and what tense is being used: *escrib****o****, escrib****iste.***

Conjunctions join words or groups of words. The most common ones are ***and, but,*** and ***or.***

Direct objects are nouns or pronouns that receive the action of a verb: *I read* ***the book.*** *I read* ***it.***

Gender in Spanish tells you whether a noun, pronoun, or article is masculine or feminine.

Indirect objects are nouns or pronouns that tell you to whom / what or for whom / what something is done: *I gave* ***him*** *the book.*

Infinitives are the basic forms of verbs. In English, infinitives have the word "to" in front of them: ***to walk.***

Interrogatives are words that ask questions: ***What*** *is that?* ***Who*** *are you?*

Nouns name people, places, or things: ***students, Mexico City, books.***

Number tells you if a noun, pronoun, article, or verb is **singular** or **plural.**

Prepositions show relationship between their objects and another word in the sentence: *He is* ***in*** *the classroom.*

Present tense is used to talk about actions that always take place, or that are happening now: *I always* ***take*** *the bus; I* ***study*** *Spanish.*

Present progressive tense is used to emphasize that an action is happening *right now: I* ***am doing*** *my homework; he* ***is finishing*** *dinner.*

Preterite tense is used to talk about actions that were completed in the past: *I* ***took*** *the train yesterday; I* ***studied*** *for the test.*

Pronouns are words that take the place of nouns: ***She*** *is my friend.*

Subjects are the nouns or pronouns that perform the action in a sentence: ***John*** *sings.*

Superlatives describe which things have the most or least of a given quality: *She is the* ***best*** *student.*

Verbs show action or link the subject with a word or words in the predicate (what the subject does or is): *Ana* ***writes;*** *Ana* ***is*** *my sister.*

Nouns, Number, and Gender

Nouns refer to people, animals, places, things, and ideas. Nouns are singular or plural. In Spanish, nouns have gender, which means that they are either masculine or feminine.

Singular Nouns	
Masculine	**Feminine**
libro	carpeta
pupitre	casa
profesor	noche
lápiz	ciudad

Plural Nouns	
Masculine	**Feminine**
libros	carpetas
pupitres	casas
profesores	noches
lápices	ciudades

Definite Articles

El, la, los, and *las* are definite articles and are the equivalent of "the" in English. *El* is used with masculine singular nouns; *los* with masculine plural nouns. *La* is used with feminine singular nouns; *las* with feminine plural nouns. When you use the words *a* or *de* before *el,* you form the contractions *al* and *del: Voy **al** centro; Es el libro **del** profesor.*

Masculine	
Singular	Plural
el libro	los libros
el pupitre	los pupitres
el profesor	los profesores
el lápiz	los lápices

Feminine	
Singular	Plural
la carpeta	las carpetas
la casa	las casas
la noche	las noches
la ciudad	las ciudades

Indefinite Articles

Un and *una* are indefinite articles and are the equivalent of "a" and "an" in English. *Un* is used with singular masculine nouns; *una* is used with singular feminine nouns. The plural indefinite articles are *unos* and *unas.*

Masculine	
Singular	Plural
un libro	unos libros
un escritorio	unos escritorios
un baile	unos bailes

Feminine	
Singular	Plural
una revista	unas revistas
una mochila	unas mochilas
una bandera	unas banderas

Pronouns

Subject pronouns tell who is doing the action. They replace nouns or names in a sentence. Subject pronouns are often used for emphasis or clarification: *Gregorio escucha música.*
***Él** escucha música.*

A direct object tells who or what receives the action of the verb. To avoid repeating a direct object noun, you can replace it with a *direct object pronoun*. Direct object pronouns have the same gender and number as the nouns they replace: *¿Cuándo compraste **el libro? Lo** compré ayer.*

An indirect object tells to whom or for whom an action is performed. *Indirect object pronouns* are used to replace an indirect object noun: ***Les** doy dinero. (I give money to them.)* Because *le* and *les* have more than one meaning, you can make the meaning clear, or show emphasis, by adding *a* + the corresponding name, noun, or pronoun: ***Les** doy el dinero **a ellos.***

After most prepositions, you use *mí* and *ti* for "me" and "you." The forms change with the preposition *con: conmigo, contigo.* For all other persons, you use subject pronouns after prepositions.

The personal a

When the direct object is a person, a group of people, or a pet, use the word *a* before the object. This is called the "personal *a*": *Visité **a** mi abuela. Busco **a** mi perro, Capitán.*

Subject Pronouns		Direct Object Pronouns		Indirect Object Pronouns		Objects of Prepositions	
Singular	Plural	Singular	Plural	Singular	Plural	Singular	Plural
yo	nosotros, nosotras	me	nos	me	nos	(para) mí, conmigo	nosotros, nosotras
tú	vosotros, vosotras	te	os	te	os	(para) ti, contigo	vosotros, vosotras
usted (Ud.)	ustedes (Uds.)	lo, la	los, las	le	les	Ud.	Uds.
él, ella	ellos, ellas					él, ella	ellos, ellas

Adjectives

Words that describe people and things are called adjectives. In Spanish, most adjectives have both masculine and feminine forms, as well as singular and plural forms. Adjectives must agree with the noun they describe in both gender and number. When an adjective describes a group including both masculine and feminine nouns, use the masculine plural form.

Masculine	
Singular	**Plural**
alto	altos
inteligente	inteligentes
trabajador	trabajadores
fácil	fáciles

Feminine	
Singular	**Plural**
alta	altas
inteligente	inteligentes
trabajadora	trabajadoras
fácil	fáciles

Shortened Forms of Adjectives

When placed before masculine singular nouns, some adjectives change into a shortened form.

bueno	buen chico
malo	mal día
primero	primer trabajo
tercero	tercer plato
grande	gran señor

One adjective, ***grande,*** changes to a shortened form before any singular noun: *una gran señora, un gran libro.*

Possessive Adjectives

Possessive adjectives are used to tell what belongs to someone or to show relationships. Like other adjectives, possessive adjectives agree in number with the nouns that follow them.

Only *nuestro* and *vuestro* have different masculine and feminine endings. *Su* and *sus* can have many different meanings: *his, her, its, your,* or *their.*

Singular	Plural
mi	mis
tu	tus
su	sus
nuestro, -a	nuestros, -as
vuestro, -a	vuestros, -as
su	sus

Demonstrative Adjectives

Like other adjectives, demonstrative adjectives agree in gender and number with the nouns that follow them. Use *este, esta, estos, estas* ("this" / "these") before nouns that name people or things that are close to you. Use *ese, esa, esos, esas* ("that" / "those") before nouns that name people or things that are at some distance from you.

Singular	Plural
este libro	estos libros
esta casa	estas casas

Singular	Plural
ese niño	esos niños
esa manzana	esas manzanas

Interrogative Words

You use interrogative words to ask questions. When you ask a question with an interrogative word, you put the verb before the subject. All interrogative words have a written accent mark.

¿Adónde?	¿Cuándo?	¿Dónde?
¿Cómo?	¿Cuánto, -a?	¿Por qué?
¿Con quién?	¿Cuántos, -as?	¿Qué?
¿Cuál?	¿De dónde?	¿Quién?

Comparatives and Superlatives

Comparatives Use *más . . . que* or *menos . . . que* to compare people or things: *más interesante que . . . , menos alta que . . .*

When talking about number, use *de* instead of *que: Tengo **más de** cien monedas en mi colección.*

Superlatives Use this pattern to express the idea of "most" or "least."

el / la / los / las + *noun* + más / menos + *adjective*

*Es la chica **más seria de** la clase.*
*Son los perritos **más pequeños.***

Several adjectives are irregular when used with comparisons and superlatives.

mayor	older
menor	younger
mejor	better
peor	worse

Affirmative and Negative Words

To make a sentence negative in Spanish, *no* usually goes in front of the verb or expression. To show that you do not like either of two choices, use *ni . . . ni.*

Alguno, alguna, algunos, algunas and *ninguno, ninguna* match the number and gender of the noun to which they refer. *Ningunos* and *ningunas* are rarely used. When *alguno* and *ninguno* come before a masculine singular noun, they change to *algún* and *ningún.*

Affirmative	Negative
algo	nada
alguien	nadie
algún	ningún
alguno, -a, -os, -as	ninguno, -a, -os, -as
siempre	nunca
también	tampoco

Adverbs

To form an adverb in Spanish, *-mente* is added to the feminine singular form of an adjective. This *-mente* ending is equivalent to the "-ly" ending in English. If the adjective has a written accent, such as *rápida, fácil,* and *práctica,* the accent appears in the same place in the adverb form.

general → generalmente
especial → especialmente
fácil → fácilmente
feliz → felizmente
rápida → rápidamente
práctica → prácticamente

Verbos

Regular Present and Preterite Tenses

Here are the conjugations for regular *-ar, -er,* and *-ir* verbs in the present and preterite tense.

Infinitive	Present		Preterite	
estudiar	estudio estudias estudia	estudiamos estudiáis estudian	estudié estudiaste estudió	estudiamos estudiasteis estudiaron
correr	corro corres corre	corremos corréis corren	corrí corriste corrió	corrimos corristeis corrieron
escribir	escribo escribes escribe	escribimos escribís escriben	escribí escribiste escribió	escribimos escribisteis escribieron

Present Progressive

When you want to emphasize that an action is happening *right now,* you use the present progressive tense.

estudiar	estoy estás está	estudiando estudiando estudiando	estamos estáis están	estudiando estudiando estudiando
correr	estoy estás está	corriendo corriendo corriendo	estamos estáis están	corriendo corriendo corriendo
escribir	estoy estás está	escribiendo escribiendo escribiendo	estamos estáis están	escribiendo escribiendo escribiendo

Affirmative tú Commands

When telling a friend, a family member, or a young person to do something, use an affirmative *tú* command. To give these commands for most verbs, use the same present-tense forms that are used for *Ud., él, ella.* Some verbs have an irregular affirmative *tú* command.

Regular	Irregular	
¡Estudia!	decir	di
¡Corre!	hacer	haz
¡Escribe!	ir	ve
	poner	pon
	salir	sal
	ser	sé
	tener	ten
	venir	ven

Stem-changing Verbs

Here is an alphabetical list of the stem-changing verbs. You will learn the verb forms that are in italic type next year.

Infinitive and Present Participle	Present		Preterite	
costar (o → ue) costando	cuesta	cuestan	costó	costaron
doler (o → ue) doliendo	duele	duelen	dolió	dolieron
dormir (o → ue) *durmiendo*	duermo duermes duerme	dormimos dormís duermen	dormí dormiste *durmió*	dormimos dormisteis *durmieron*
empezar (e → ie) empezando	empiezo empiezas empieza	empezamos empezáis empiezan	*empecé* empezaste empezó	empezamos empezasteis empezaron
jugar (u → ue) jugando	juego juegas juega	jugamos jugáis juegan	jugué jugaste jugó	jugamos jugasteis jugaron
llover (o → ue) lloviendo	llueve		llovió	
nevar (e → ie) nevando	nieva		nevó	
pedir (e → i) *pidiendo*	pido pides pide	pedimos pedís piden	pedí pediste *pidió*	pedimos pedisteis *pidieron*
pensar (e → ie) pensando	pienso piensas piensa	pensamos pensáis piensan	pensé pensaste pensó	pensamos pensasteis pensaron
preferir (e → ie) *prefiriendo*	prefiero prefieres prefiere	preferimos preferís prefieren	preferí preferiste *prefirió*	preferimos preferisteis *prefirieron*
sentir (e → ie) *sintiendo*	*See* preferir			
servir (e → i) *sirviendo*	*See* pedir			

Spelling-changing Verbs

These verbs have spelling changes in different tenses. The spelling changes are indicated in black.

You will learn the verb forms that are in italic type next year.

Infinitive and Present Participle	Present		Preterite	
buscar (c → qu) **buscando**	*See regular verbs*		**busqué** **buscaste** **buscó**	**buscamos** **buscasteis** **buscaron**
comunicarse (c → qu) ***comunicándose***	*See reflexive verbs*		*See reflexive verbs and* **buscar**	
conocer (c → zc) **conociendo**	**conozco** **conoces** **conoce**	**conocemos** **conocéis** **conocen**	*See regular verbs*	
creer (i → y) ***creyendo***	*See regular verbs*		**creí** **creíste** ***creyó***	**creímos** **creísteis** ***creyeron***
empezar (z → c) **empezando**	*See stem-changing verbs*		**empecé** **empezaste** **empezó**	**empezamos** **empezasteis** **empezaron**
enviar (i → í) **enviando**	**envío** **envías** **envía**	**enviamos** **enviáis** **envían**	*See regular verbs*	
esquiar (i → í) **esquiando**	*See* **enviar**		*See regular verbs*	
jugar (g → gu) **jugando**	*See stem-changing verbs*		**jugué** **jugaste** **jugó**	**jugamos** **jugasteis** **jugaron**
leer (i → y) **leyendo**	*See regular verbs*		*See* **creer**	
pagar (g → gu) **pagando**	*See regular verbs*		*See* **jugar**	
parecer (c → zc) **pareciendo**	*See* **conocer**		*See regular verbs*	
practicar (c → qu) **practicando**	*See regular verbs*		*See* **buscar**	
recoger (g → j) **recogiendo**	**recojo** **recoges** **recoge**	**recogemos** **recogéis** **recogen**	*See regular verbs*	
sacar (c → qu) **sacando**	*See regular verbs*		*See* **buscar**	
tocar (c → qu) **tocando**	*See regular verbs*		*See* **buscar**	

Irregular Verbs

These verbs have irregular patterns. You will learn the verb forms that are in italic type next year.

Infinitive and Present Participle	Present		Preterite	
dar dando	doy das da	damos dais dan	di diste dio	dimos disteis dieron
decir *diciendo*	digo dices dice	decimos decís dicen	*dije* *dijiste* *dijo*	*dijimos* *dijisteis* *dijeron*
estar estando	estoy estás está	estamos estáis están	*estuve* *estuviste* *estuvo*	*estuvimos* *estuvisteis* *estuvieron*
hacer haciendo	hago haces hace	hacemos hacéis hacen	hice hiciste hizo	hicimos hicisteis hicieron
ir *yendo*	voy vas va	vamos vais van	fui fuiste fue	fuimos fuisteis fueron
poder *pudiendo*	puedo puedes puede	podemos podéis pueden	*pude* *pudiste* *pudo*	*pudimos* *pudisteis* *pudieron*
poner poniendo	pongo pones pone	ponemos ponéis ponen	*puse* *pusiste* *puso*	*pusimos* *pusisteis* *pusieron*
querer queriendo	quiero quieres quiere	queremos queréis quieren	*quise* *quisiste* *quiso*	*quisimos* *quisisteis* *quisieron*
saber sabiendo	sé sabes sabe	sabemos sabéis saben	*supe* *supiste* *supo*	*supimos* *supisteis* *supieron*
salir saliendo	salgo sales sale	salimos salís salen	salí saliste salió	salimos salisteis salieron
ser siendo	soy eres es	somos sois son	fui fuiste fue	fuimos fuisteis fueron
tener teniendo	tengo tienes tiene	tenemos tenéis tienen	*tuve* *tuviste* *tuvo*	*tuvimos* *tuvisteis* *tuvieron*

Irregular Verbs (continued) You will learn the verb forms that are in italic type next year.

Infinitive and Present Participle	Present		Preterite	
traer *trayendo*	traigo traes trae	traemos traéis traen	*traje* *trajiste* *trajo*	*trajimos* *trajisteis* *trajeron*
venir *viniendo*	vengo vienes viene	venimos venís vienen	*vine* *viniste* *vino*	*vinimos* *vinisteis* *vinieron*
ver viendo	veo ves ve	vemos veis ven	vi viste vio	vimos visteis vieron

Reflexive Verbs You will learn the verb forms that are in italic type next year.

Infinitive and Present Participle	Present	
comunicarse *comunicándose*	me comunico te comunicas *se comunica*	*nos comunicamos* *os comunicáis* *se comunican*
Affirmative Familiar *(tú)* Command	**Preterite**	
comunícate	me comuniqué te comunicaste *se comunicó*	*nos comunicamos* *os comunicasteis* *se comunicaron*

Expresiones útiles para conversar

The following are expressions that you can use when you find yourself in a specific situation and need help to begin, continue, or end a conversation.

Greeting Someone

Buenos días. Good morning.

Buenas tardes. Good afternoon.

Buenas noches. Good evening. Good night.

Making Introductions

Me llamo . . . My name is . . .

Soy . . . I'm . . .

¿Cómo te llamas? What's your name?

Éste es mi amigo *m.* **. . .** This is my friend . . .

Ésta es mi amiga *f.* **. . .** This is my friend . . .

Se llama . . . His / Her name is . . .

¡Mucho gusto! It's a pleasure!

Encantado, -a. Delighted.

Igualmente. Likewise.

Asking How Someone Is

¿Cómo estás? How are you?

¿Cómo andas? How's it going?

¿Cómo te sientes? How do you feel?

¿Qué tal? How's it going?

Estoy bien, gracias. I'm fine, thank you.

Muy bien. ¿Y tú? Very well. And you?

Regular. Okay. All right.

Más o menos. More or less.

(Muy) mal. (Very) bad.

¡Horrible! Awful!

¡Excelente! Great!

Talking on the Phone

Aló. Hello.

Diga. Hello.

Bueno. Hello.

¿Quién habla? Who's calling?

Habla . . . It's [name of person calling].

¿Está . . . , por favor? Is . . . there, please?

¿De parte de quién? Who is calling?

¿Puedo dejar un recado? May I leave a message?

Un momento. Just a moment.

Llamo más tarde. I'll call later.

¿Cómo? No le oigo. What? I can't hear you.

Making Plans

¿Adónde vas? Where are you going?

Voy a . . . I'm going to . . .

¿Estás listo, -a? Are you ready?

Tengo prisa. I'm in a hurry.

¡Date prisa! Hurry up!

Sí, ahora voy. OK, I'm coming.

Todavía necesito . . . I still need . . .

¿Te gustaría . . . ? Would you like to . . . ?

Sí, me gustaría . . . Yes, I'd like to . . .

¡Claro que sí (no)! Of course (not)!

¿Quieres . . . ? Do you want to . . . ?

Quiero . . . I want to . . .

¿Qué quieres hacer hoy? What do you want to do today?

¿Qué haces después de las clases? What do you do after school (class)?

¿Qué estás haciendo? What are you doing?

Te invito. It's my treat.

¿Qué tal si . . . ? What about . . . ?

Primero . . . First . . .

Después . . . Later . . .

Luego . . . Then . . .

Making an Excuse

Estoy ocupado, -a. I'm busy.

Lo siento, pero no puedo. I'm sorry, but I can't.

¡Qué lástima! What a shame!

Ya tengo planes. I already have plans.

Tal vez otro día. Maybe another day.

Being Polite

Con mucho gusto. With great pleasure.

De nada. You're welcome.

Disculpe. Excuse me.

Lo siento. I'm sorry.

Muchísimas gracias. Thank you very much.

Te (Se) lo agradezco mucho. I appreciate it a lot.

Muy amable. That's very kind of you.

Perdón. Pardon me.

¿Puede Ud. repetirlo? Can you repeat that?

¿Puede Ud. hablar más despacio? Can you speak more slowly?

Keeping a Conversation Going

¿De veras? Really?

¿Verdad? Isn't that so? Right?

¿En serio? Seriously?

¡No lo puedo creer! I don't believe it!

¡No me digas! You don't say!

Y entonces, ¿qué? And then what?

¿Qué hiciste? What did you do?

¿Qué dijiste? What did you say?

¿Crees que . . . ? Do you think that . . . ?

Me parece bien. It seems all right.

Perfecto. Perfect.

¡Qué buena idea! What a good idea!

¡Cómo no! Of course!

De acuerdo. Agreed.

Está bien. It's all right.

Giving a Description When You Don't Know the Name of Someone or Something

Se usa para . . . It's used to / for . . .

Es la palabra que significa . . . It's the word that means . . .

Es la persona que . . . It's the person who . . .

Ending a Conversation

Bueno, tengo que irme. Well, I have to go.

Chao. (Chau.) Bye.

Hasta pronto. See you soon.

Hasta mañana. See you tomorrow.

Vocabulario español-inglés

The *Vocabulario español-inglés* contains all active vocabulary from the text, including vocabulary presented in the grammar sections.

A dash (—) represents the main entry word. For example, **pasar la —** after **la aspiradora** means **pasar la aspiradora.**

The number following each entry indicates the chapter in which the word or expression is presented. Remember that Temas 1–4 appeared in Level A. The letter *P* following an entry refers to the *Para empezar* section of Level A.

The following abbreviations are used in this list: *adj.* (adjective), *dir. obj.* (direct object), *f.* (feminine), *fam.* (familiar), *ind. obj.* (indirect object), *inf.* (infinitive), *m.* (masculine), *pl.* (plural), *prep.* (preposition), *pron.* (pronoun), *sing.* (singular).

A

a to *(prep.)* (4A)
- **— . . . le gusta(n)** he / she likes (5A)
- **— . . . le encanta(n)** he / she loves (5A)
- **— casa** (to) home (4A)
- **— la derecha (de)** to the right (of) (6A)
- **— la izquierda (de)** to the left (of) (6A)
- **— la una de la tarde** at one (o'clock) in the afternoon (4B)
- **— las ocho de la mañana** at eight (o'clock) in the morning (4B)
- **— las ocho de la noche** at eight (o'clock) in the evening / at night (4B)
- **— menudo** often (8B)
- **— mí también** I do (like to) too (1A)
- **— mí tampoco** I don't (like to) either (1A)
- **¿— qué hora?** (At) what time? (4B)
- **— veces** sometimes (1B)
- **— ver** Let's see (2A)

al *(a + el),* **a la,** to the (4A)
- **al lado de** next to (2B)

el **abrigo** coat (7A)
abril April (P)
abrir to open (5A)
la **abuela, el abuelo** grandmother, grandfather (5A)
los **abuelos** grandparents (5A)
aburrido, -a boring (2A)
me **aburre(n)** it bores me (they bore me) (9A)
aburrir to bore (9A)
acabar de + *inf.* to have just . . . (9A)
el **actor** actor (9A)
la **actriz,** *pl.* **las actrices** actress (9A)
acuerdo:
- **Estoy de —.** I agree. (3B)
- **No estoy de —.** I don't agree. (3B)

¡Adiós! Good-bye! (P)
¿Adónde? (To) where? (4A)
agosto August (P)
el **agua** *f.* water (3A)
ahora now (5B)
al *(a + el),* **a la,** to the (4A)
- **al lado de** next to (2B)

la **alfombra** rug (6A)
algo something (3B)
- **¿— más?** Anything else? (5B)

allí there (2B)
el **almacén,** *pl.* **los almacenes** department store (7B)
el **almuerzo** lunch (2A)
- **en el —** for lunch (3A)

alto, -a tall (5B)
amarillo, -a yellow (6A)
el **amigo** male friend (1B)
la **amiga** female friend (1B)
anaranjado, -a orange (6A)
la **anciana, el anciano** older woman, older man (8B)
los **ancianos** older people (8B)
el **anillo** ring (7B)
el **animal** animal (8A)
anoche last night (7B)
los **anteojos de sol** sunglasses (7B)
antes de before (9A)
el **año** year (P)
- **el — pasado** last year (7B)
- **¿Cuántos años tiene(n) . . . ?** How old is / are . . . ? (5A)
- **Tiene(n) . . . años.** He / She is / They are . . . (years old). (5A)

el **apartamento** apartment (6B)
aprender (a) to learn (to) (8A)
aquí here (2B)
el **árbol** tree (8A)
los **aretes** earrings (7B)
el **armario** closet (6A)
arreglar el cuarto to straighten up the room (6B)
el **arroz** rice (3B)
el **arte:**
- **la clase de —** art class (2A)

artístico, -a artistic (1B)
asco:
- **¡Qué —!** How awful! (3A)

la **atracción,** *pl.* **las atracciones** attraction (8A)
atrevido, -a daring (1B)
el **autobús,** *pl.* **los autobuses** bus (8A)
el **avión,** *pl.* **los aviones** airplane (8A)
¡Ay! ¡Qué pena! Oh! What a shame / pity! (4B)
ayer yesterday (7B)
ayudar to help (6B)
el **azúcar** sugar (5B)
azul blue (6A)

B

bailar to dance (1A)
el **baile** dance (4B)
bajar (información) to download (9B)
bajo, -a short *(stature)* (5B)
la **bandera** flag (2B)
el **baño** bathroom (6B)
- **el traje de —** swimsuit (7A)

barato, -a inexpensive, cheap (7B)

el **barco** boat, ship (8A)
el **barrio** neighborhood (8B)
el **básquetbol: jugar al —** to play basketball (4B)
bastante enough, rather (6B)
beber to drink (3A)
las **bebidas** beverages (3B)
béisbol: jugar al — to play baseball (4B)
la **biblioteca** library (4A)
bien well (P)
el **bistec** beefsteak (3B)
blanco, -a white (6A)
la **blusa** blouse (7A)
la **boca** mouth (P)
el **boleto** ticket (8A)
el **bolígrafo** pen (P)
la **bolsa** bag, sack (8B)
el **bolso** purse (7B)
bonito, -a pretty (6A)
las **botas** boots (7A)
el **bote: pasear en —** to go boating (8A)
la **botella** bottle (8B)
el **brazo** arm (P)
bucear to scuba dive, to snorkel (8A)
bueno (buen), -a good (1B)
Buenas noches. Good evening. (P)
Buenas tardes. Good afternoon. (P)
Buenos días. Good morning. (P)
buscar to look for (7A); to search (for) (9B)

C

el **caballo: montar a —** to ride horseback (8A)
la **cabeza** head (P)
cada día every day (3B)
la **cadena** chain (7B)
el **café** coffee (3A); café (4A)
la **caja** box (8B)
los **calcetines** socks (7A)
la **calculadora** calculator (2A)
la **calle** street, road (8B)
calor:
Hace —. It's hot. (P)
tener — to be warm (5B)
la **cama** bed (6A)
hacer la — to make the bed (6B)
la **cámara** camera (5A)
la — digital digital camera (9A)
el **camarero, la camarera** waiter, waitress (5B)
caminar to walk (3B)
la **camisa** shirt (7A)
la **camiseta** T-shirt (7A)
el **campamento** camp (8B)
el **campo** countryside (4A)
el **canal** (TV) channel (9A)
la **canción,** *pl.* **las canciones** song (9B)
canoso: pelo — gray hair (5B)
cansado, -a tired (4B)
cantar to sing (1A)
cara a cara face-to-face (9B)
la **carne** meat (3B)
caro, -a expensive (7B)
la **carpeta** folder (P)
la — de argollas three-ring binder (2A)
la **carta** letter (9B)
el **cartel** poster (2B)
la **cartera** wallet (7B)
el **cartón** cardboard (8B)
la **casa** home, house (4A)
a — (to) home (4A)
en — at home (4A)
casi almost (9A)
castaño: pelo — brown (chestnut) hair (5B)
catorce fourteen (P)
la **cebolla** onion (3B)
celebrar to celebrate (5A)
la **cena** dinner (3B)
el **centro:**
el — comercial mall (4A)
el — de reciclaje recycling center (8B)
cerca (de) close (to), near (6B)
el **cereal** cereal (3A)
cero zero (P)
la **chaqueta** jacket (7A)
la **chica** girl (1B)
el **chico** boy (1B)
cien one hundred (P)
las **ciencias:**
la clase de — naturales science class (2A)
la clase de — sociales social studies class (2A)
cinco five (P)
cincuenta fifty (P)
el **cine** movie theater (4A)
la **ciudad** city (8A)
la **clase** class (2A)
la sala de clases classroom (P)
¿Qué — de . . . ? What kind of . . . ? (9A)
el **coche** car (6B)
la **cocina** kitchen (6B)
cocinar to cook (6B)
el **collar** necklace (7B)
el **color,** *pl.* **los colores** (6A)
¿De qué — . . . ? What color . . . ? (6A)
la **comedia** comedy (9A)
el **comedor** dining room (6B)
comer to eat (3A)
cómico, -a funny, comical (9A)
la **comida** food, meal (3A)
como like, as (8A)
¿Cómo?:
¿— eres? What are you like? (1B)
¿— es? What is he / she like? (1B)
¿— está Ud.? How are you? *formal* (P)
¿— estás? How are you? *fam.* (P)
¿— lo pasaste? How was it (for you)? (8A)

¿— **se dice . . . ?** How do you say . . . ? (P)

¿— **se escribe . . . ?** How is . . . spelled? (P)

¿— **se llama?** What's his / her name? (1B)

¿— **te llamas?** What is your name? (P)

¿— **me / te queda(n)?** How does it (do they) fit (me / you)? (7A)

la cómoda dresser (6A)

compartir to share (3A)

complicado, -a complicated (9B)

la composición, *pl.* **las composiciones** composition (9B)

comprar to buy (7A)

comprar recuerdos to buy souvenirs (8A)

comprender to understand (3A)

la computadora computer (2B)

la — portátil laptop computer (9B)

usar la — to use the computer (1A)

comunicarse to communicate (9B)

(tú) te comunicas you communicate (9B)

(yo) me comunico I communicate (9B)

la comunidad community (8B)

con with (3A)

— mis / tus amigos with my / your friends (4A)

¿— **quién?** With whom? (4A)

el concierto concert (4B)

conmigo with me (4B)

conocer to know, to be acquainted with (9B)

contento, -a happy (4B)

contigo with you (4B)

la corbata tie (7B)

correr to run (1A)

cortar el césped to cut / to mow the lawn (6B)

las cortinas curtains (6A)

corto, -a short *(length)* (5B)

los pantalones cortos shorts (7A)

la cosa thing (6A)

costar (o → ue) to cost (7A)

¿Cuánto cuesta(n) . . . ? How much does (do) . . . cost? (7A)

crear to create (9B)

creer:

Creo que . . . I think . . . (3B)

Creo que no. I don't think so. (3B)

Creo que sí. I think so. (3B)

el cuaderno notebook (P)

el cuadro painting (6A)

¿Cuál? Which?, What? (3A)

¿— **es la fecha?** What is the date? (P)

¿Cuándo? When? (4A)

¿Cuánto?: ¿— cuesta(n) . . . ? How much does (do) . . . cost? (7A)

¿Cuántos, -as? How many? (P)

¿Cuántos años tiene(n) . . . ? How old is / are . . . ? (5A)

cuarenta forty (P)

cuarto, -a fourth (2A)

el cuarto room (6B)

y — quarter past *(in telling time)* (P)

menos — *(time)* quarter to (P)

cuatro four (P)

cuatrocientos, -as four hundred (7A)

la cuchara spoon (5B)

el cuchillo knife (5B)

la cuenta bill (5B)

el cumpleaños birthday (5A)

¡Feliz —! Happy birthday! (5A)

el curso: tomar un curso to take a course (9B)

D

dar to give (6B)

— + *movie or TV program* to show (9A)

— de comer al perro to feed the dog (6B)

de of (2B); from (4A)

¿— **dónde eres?** Where are you from? (4A)

— la mañana / la tarde / la noche in the morning / afternoon / evening (4B)

— nada. You're welcome. (5B)

— plato principal as a main dish (5B)

— postre for dessert (5B)

¿— **qué color . . . ?** What color . . . ? (6A)

¿— **veras?** Really? (9A)

debajo de underneath (2B)

deber should, must (3B)

decidir to decide (8B)

décimo, -a tenth (2A)

decir to say, to tell (8B)

¿Cómo se dice . . . ? How do you say . . . ? (P)

dime tell me (8A)

¡No me digas! You don't say! (4A)

¿Qué quiere — . . . ? What does . . . mean? (P)

Quiere — . . . It means . . . (P)

Se dice . . . You say . . . (P)

las decoraciones decorations (5A)

decorar to decorate (5A)

el dedo finger (P)

delante de in front of (2B)

delicioso, -a delicious (5B)

los demás, las demás others (8B)

demasiado too (4B)

el dependiente, la dependienta salesperson (7A)

deportista athletic, sports-minded (1B)

derecha: a la — (de) to the right (of) (6A)

el desayuno breakfast (3A)

en el — for breakfast (3A)

descansar to rest, to relax (8A)

los descuentos: la tienda de — discount store (7B)

desear to wish (5B)

¿Qué desean (Uds.)? What would you like? (5B)
desordenado, -a messy (1B)
el **despacho** office (home) (6B)
el **despertador** alarm clock (6A)
después (de) after (4A)
después afterwards (4A)
detrás de behind (2B)
el **día** day (P)
Buenos —s. Good morning. (P)
cada — every day (3B)
¿Qué — es hoy? What day is today? (P)
todos los —s every day (3A)
la **diapositiva** slide (9B)
dibujar to draw (1A)
el **diccionario** dictionary (2A)
diciembre December (P)
diecinueve nineteen (P)
dieciocho eighteen (P)
dieciséis sixteen (P)
diecisiete seventeen (P)
diez ten (P)
difícil difficult (2A)
digital: la cámara — digital camera (9B)
dime tell me (8A)
el **dinero** money (6B)
la **dirección electrónica** e-mail address (9B)
el **disco compacto** compact disc (6A)
grabar un disco compacto to burn a CD (9B)
el **disquete** diskette (2B)
divertido, -a amusing, fun (2A)
doce twelve (P)
el **documento** document (9B)
doler (o → ue) to hurt (9A)
domingo Sunday (P)
dónde:
¿—? Where? (2B)
¿De — eres? Where are you from? (4A)
dormir (o → ue) to sleep (6A)
el **dormitorio** bedroom (6A)
dos two (P)
los / las dos both (7A)
doscientos, -as two hundred (7A)
el **drama** drama (9A)
los **dulces** candy (5A)
durante during (8A)
durar to last (9A)

E

educación física: la clase de — physical education class (2A)
el **ejercicio: hacer —** to exercise (3B)
el the *m. sing.* (1B)
él he (1B)
los **electrodomésticos: la tienda de —** household appliance store (7B)
electrónico, -a: la dirección — e-mail address (9B)
ella she (1B)
ellas they *f. pl.* (2A)
ellos they *m. pl.* (2A)
emocionante touching (9A)
empezar (e → ie) to begin, to start (9A)
en in, on (2B)
— + *vehicle* by, in, on (8A)
— casa at home (4A)
— la . . . hora in the . . . hour (class period) (2A)
— la Red online (7B)
¿— qué puedo servirle? How can I help you? (7A)
encantado, -a delighted (P)
encantar to please very much, to love (9A)
a él / ella le encanta(n) he / she loves (5A)
me / te encanta(n) . . . I / you love . . . (3A)
encima de on top of (2B)
enero January (P)
enfermo, -a sick (4B)
la **ensalada** salad (3A)
la — de frutas fruit salad (3A)
enseñar to teach (2A)
entonces then (4B)
entrar to enter (7A)
enviar (i → í) to send (9B)
el **equipo de sonido** sound (stereo) system (6A)
¿Eres . . . ? Are you . . . ? (1B)
es is (P); (he / she / it) is (1B)
— el *(number)* **de** *(month)* it is the . . . of . . . *(in telling the date)* (P)
— el primero de *(month)*. It is the first of . . . (P)
— la una. It is one o'clock. (P)
— necesario. It's necessary. (8B)
— un(a) . . . it's a . . . (2B)
la **escalera** stairs, stairway (6B)
escribir:
¿Cómo se escribe . . . ? How is . . . spelled? (P)
— cuentos to write stories (1A)
— por correo electrónico to write e-mail (9B)
Se escribe . . . It's spelled . . . (P)
el **escritorio** desk (2B)
escuchar música to listen to music (1A)
la **escuela primaria** primary school (8B)
ese, esa that (7A)
eso: por — that's why, therefore (9A)
esos, esas those (7A)
los **espaguetis** spaghetti (3B)
el **español: la clase de —** Spanish class (2A)
especialmente especially (9A)
el **espejo** mirror (6A)
la **esposa** wife (5A)
el **esposo** husband (5A)
esquiar (i → í) to ski (1A)
la **estación,** *pl.* **las estaciones** season (P)
el **estadio** stadium (8A)
el **estante** shelf, bookshelf (6A)
estar to be (2B)

¿Cómo está Ud.? How are you? *formal* (P)

¿Cómo estás? How are you? *fam.* (P)

— + *present participle* to be + *present participle* (6B)

— en línea to be online (9B)

Estoy de acuerdo. I agree. (3B)

No estoy de acuerdo. I don't agree. (3B)

este, esta this (7A)

esta noche this evening (4B)

esta tarde this afternoon (4B)

este fin de semana this weekend (4B)

el **estómago** stomach (P)

estos, estas these (7A)

¿Qué es esto? What is this? (2B)

Estoy de acuerdo. I agree. (3B)

el/la **estudiante** student (P)

estudiar to study (2A)

estudioso, -a studious (1B)

la **experiencia** experience (8B)

F

fácil easy (2A)

la **falda** skirt (7A)

faltar to be missing (9A)

fantástico, -a fantastic (8A)

fascinante fascinating (9A)

favorito, -a favorite (2A)

febrero February (P)

la **fecha: ¿Cuál es la —?** What is the date? (P)

¡Feliz cumpleaños! Happy birthday! (5A)

feo, -a ugly (6A)

la **fiesta** party (4B)

el **fin de semana:**

este — this weekend (4B)

los fines de semana on weekends (4A)

la **flor,** *pl.* **las flores** flower (5A)

la **foto** photo (5A)

las **fresas** strawberries (3A)

frío:

Hace —. It's cold. (P)

tener — to be cold (5B)

fue it was (8A)

— un desastre. It was a disaster. (8A)

el **fútbol: jugar al —** to play soccer (4B)

el **fútbol americano: jugar al —** to play football (4B)

G

la **galleta** cookie (3A)

el **garaje** garage (6B)

el **gato** cat (5A)

generalmente generally (4A)

¡Genial! Great! (4B)

la **gente** people (8B)

el **gimnasio** gym (4A)

el **globo** balloon (5A)

el **golf: jugar al —** to play golf (4B)

la **gorra** cap (7A)

grabar un disco compacto to burn a CD (9B)

gracias thank you (P)

gracioso, -a funny (1B)

los **gráficos** computer graphics (9B)

grande large (6A)

gris gray (6A)

los **guantes** gloves (7B)

guapo, -a good-looking (5B)

los **guisantes** peas (3B)

gustar:

a él / ella le gusta(n) he / she likes (5A)

(A mí) me gusta . . . I like to . . . (1A)

(A mí) me gusta más . . . I like to . . . better (I prefer to . . .) (1A)

(A mí) me gusta mucho . . . I like to . . . a lot (1A)

(A mí) no me gusta . . . I don't like to . . . (1A)

(A mí) no me gusta nada . . . I don't like to . . . at all. (1A)

Le gusta . . . He / She likes . . . (1B)

Me gusta . . . I like . . . (3A)

Me gustaría . . . I would like . . . (4B)

Me gustó. I liked it. (8A)

No le gusta . . . He / She doesn't like . . . (1B)

¿Qué te gusta hacer? What do you like to do? (1A)

¿Qué te gusta hacer más? What do you like better (prefer) to do? (1A)

Te gusta . . . You like . . . (3A)

¿Te gusta . . . ? Do you like to . . . ? (1A)

¿Te gustaría . . . ? Would you like . . . ? (4B)

¿Te gustó? Did you like it? (8A)

H

hablar to talk (2A)

— por teléfono to talk on the phone (1A)

hacer to do (3B)

hace + *time expression* ago (7B)

Hace calor. It's hot. (P)

Hace frío. It's cold. (P)

Hace sol. It's sunny. (P)

— ejercicio to exercise (3B)

— la cama to make the bed (6B)

— un video to videotape (5A)

haz *(command)* do, make (6B)

¿Qué estás haciendo? What are you doing? (5B)

¿Qué hiciste? What did you do? (8A)

¿Qué tiempo hace? What's the weather like? (P)

(yo) hago I do (3B)

(tú) haces you do (3B)

hambre: Tengo —. I'm hungry. (3B)

la **hamburguesa** hamburger (3A)

hasta:

— luego. See you later. (P)

— **mañana.** See you tomorrow. (P)

Hay There is, There are (2B)

— **que** one must (8B)

el **helado** ice cream (3B)

el **hermano, la hermana** brother, sister (5A)

el **hermanastro, la hermanastra** stepbrother, stepsister (5A)

los **hermanos** brothers; brother(s) and sister(s) (5A)

el **hijo, la hija** son, daughter (5A)

los **hijos** children; sons (5A)

la **hoja de papel** sheet of paper (P)

¡Hola! Hello! (P)

el **hombre** man (5B)

la **hora:**

en la . . . — in the . . . hour (class period) (2A)

¿A qué —? (At) what time? (4B)

el **horario** schedule (2A)

horrible horrible (3B)

el **horror: la película de —** horror movie (9A)

el **hospital** hospital (8B)

el **hotel** hotel (8A)

hoy today (P)

los **huevos** eggs (3A)

I

la **iglesia** church (4A)

igualmente likewise (P)

impaciente impatient (1B)

importante important (6A)

impresionante impressive (8A)

increíble incredible (8B)

infantil childish (9A)

la **información** information (9B)

el **informe** report (9B)

el **inglés: la clase de —** English class (2A)

inolvidable unforgettable (8B)

inteligente intelligent (1B)

interesante interesting (2A)

interesar to interest (9A)

me interesa(n) it interests me (they interest me) (9A)

el **invierno** winter (P)

ir to go (4A)

— **a** + *inf.* to be going to + *verb* (4B)

— **a la escuela** to go to school (1A)

— **de cámping** to go camping (4B)

— **de compras** to go shopping (4A)

— **de pesca** to go fishing (4B)

— **de vacaciones** to go on vacation (8A)

¡Vamos! Let's go! (7A)

izquierda: a la — (de) to the left (of) (6A)

J

el **jardín,** *pl.* **los jardines** garden, yard (8B)

los **jeans** jeans (7A)

el **joven, la joven** young man, young woman (5B)

joven *adj.* young (5B)

la **joyería** jewelry store (7B)

las **judías verdes** green beans (3B)

jueves Thursday (P)

jugar (a) (u → ue) to play *(games, sports)* (4B)

— **al básquetbol** to play basketball (4B)

— **al béisbol** to play baseball (4B)

— **al fútbol** to play soccer (4B)

— **al fútbol americano** to play football (4B)

— **al golf** to play golf (4B)

— **al tenis** to play tennis (4B)

— **al vóleibol** to play volleyball (4B)

— **videojuegos** to play video games (1A)

el **jugo:**

— **de manzana** apple juice (3A)

— **de naranja** orange juice (3A)

el **juguete** toy (8B)

julio July (P)

junio June (P)

L

la the *f. sing.* (1B); it, her *f. dir. obj. pron.* (7B)

el **laboratorio** laboratory (9B)

lado: al — de next to, besides (2B)

el **lago** lake (8A)

la **lámpara** lamp (6A)

el **lápiz,** *pl.* **los lápices** pencil (P)

largo, -a long (5B)

las the *f. pl.* (2B); them *f. dir. obj. pron.* (7B)

— **dos, los dos** both (7A)

la **lata** can (8B)

lavar to wash (6B)

— **el coche** to wash the car (6B)

— **la ropa** to wash the clothes (6B)

— **los platos** to wash the dishes (6B)

le (to / for) him, her, *(formal)* you *sing. ind. obj. pron.* (8B)

— **gusta . . .** He / She likes . . . (1B)

— **traigo . . .** I will bring you . . . (5B)

No — gusta . . . He / She doesn't like . . . (1B)

la **lección,** *pl.* **las lecciones de piano** piano lesson (class) (4A)

la **leche** milk (3A)

la **lechuga** lettuce (3B)

el **lector DVD** DVD player (6A)

leer revistas to read magazines (1A)

lejos (de) far (from) (6B)

les (to / for) them, *(formal)* you *pl. ind. obj. pron.* (8B)

levantar pesas to lift weights (3B)

la **librería** bookstore (7B)

el **libro** book (P)

la **limonada** lemonade (3A)

limpiar el baño to clean the bathroom (6B)

limpio, -a clean (6B)

línea: estar en — to be online (9B)

llamar:

¿Cómo se llama? What's his / her name? (1B)

¿Cómo te llamas? What is your name? (P)

Me llamo . . . My name is . . . (P)

el **llavero** key chain (7B)

llevar to wear (7A); to take, to carry, to bring (8B)

llover (o → ue): Llueve. It's raining. (P)

lo it, him *m. dir. obj. pron.* (7B)

— siento. I'm sorry. (4B)

los the *m. pl.* (2B); them *m. dir. obj. pron* (7B)

— dos, las dos both (7A)

— fines de semana on weekends (4A)

— lunes, los martes . . . on Mondays, on Tuesdays . . . (4A)

el **lugar** place (8A)

lunes Monday (P)

los lunes on Mondays (4A)

la **luz,** *pl.* **las luces** light (5A)

M

la **madrastra** stepmother (5A)

la **madre (mamá)** mother (5A)

mal bad, badly (4B)

malo, -a bad (3B)

la **mano** hand (P)

mantener: para — la salud to maintain one's health (3B)

la **mantequilla** butter (3B)

la **manzana** apple (3A)

el jugo de — apple juice (3A)

mañana tomorrow (P)

la **mañana:**

a las ocho de la — at eight (o'clock) in the morning (4B)

de la — in the morning (4B)

el **mar** sea (8A)

marrón, *pl.* **marrones** brown (6A)

martes Tuesday (P)

los martes on Tuesdays (4A)

marzo March (P)

más:

¿Qué —? What else? (8B)

— . . . que more . . . than (2A)

— de more than (9A)

— o menos more or less (3A)

las **matemáticas: la clase de —** mathematics class (2A)

mayo May (P)

mayor older (5A)

me (to / for) me *ind. obj. pron.* (8B)

— aburre(n) it / they bore(s) me (9A)

— falta(n) . . . I need . . . (5B)

— gustaría I would like (4B)

— gustó. I liked it. (8A)

— interesa(n) it / they interest(s) me (9A)

— llamo . . . My name is . . . (P)

— queda(n) bien / mal. It / They fit(s) me well / poorly. (7A)

— quedo en casa. I stay at home. (4A)

¿— trae . . . ? Will you bring me . . . ? (5B)

media, -o half (P)

y — thirty, half past *(in telling time)* (P)

mejor:

el / la —, los / las —es the best (6A)

—(es) que better than (6A)

menor younger (5A)

menos:

más o — more or less (3A)

— . . . que less / fewer . . . than (6A)

— de less / fewer than (9A)

el **menú** menu (5B)

menudo: a — often (8B)

el **mes** month (P)

la **mesa** table (2B)

poner la — to set the table (6B)

la **mesita** night table (6A)

la **mezquita** mosque (4A)

mi, mis my (2B, 5A)

mí:

a — también I do (like to) too (1A)

a — tampoco I don't (like to) either (1A)

para — in my opinion, for me (6A)

miedo: tener — (de) to be scared (of), to be afraid (of) (9B)

miércoles Wednesday (P)

mil a thousand (7A)

mirar to look (at) (7B)

mismo, -a same (6A)

la **mochila** bookbag, backpack (2B)

el **momento: un —** a moment (6B)

el **mono** monkey (8A)

las **montañas** mountains (4A)

montar:

— a caballo to ride horseback (8A)

— en bicicleta to ride a bicycle (1A)

— en monopatín to skateboard (1A)

el **monumento** monument (8A)

morado, -a purple (6A)

mucho a lot (2A)

— gusto pleased to meet you (P)

muchos, -as many (3B)

la **mujer** woman (5B)

el **museo** museum (8A)

muy very (1B)

— bien very well (P)

N

nada nothing (P)

(A mí) no me gusta — . . . I don't like to . . . at all. (1A)

De —. You're welcome. (5B)

nadar to swim (1A)

la **naranja: el jugo de —** orange juice (3A)

la **nariz,** *pl.* **las narices** nose (P)

navegar en la Red to surf the Web (9B)

necesario: Es —. It's necessary. (8B)

necesitar:

(yo) necesito I need (2A)

(tú) necesitas you need (2A)

negro, -a black (6A)

el pelo — black hair (5B)

nevar (e → ie) Nieva. It's snowing. (P)

ni . . . ni neither . . . nor, not . . . or (1A)

el **niño, la niña** young boy, young girl (8B)

los **niños** children (8B)

No estoy de acuerdo. I don't agree. (3B)

¡No me digas! You don't say! (4A)

noche:

a las ocho de la — at eight (o'clock) in the evening, at night (4B)

Buenas —s. Good evening. (P)

de la — in the evening, at night (4B)

esta — this evening (4B)

nos (to / for) us *ind. obj. pron.* (8B)

¡— vemos! See you later! (P)

nosotros, -as we (2A)

novecientos, -as nine hundred (7A)

noveno, -a ninth (2A)

noventa ninety (P)

noviembre November (P)

el **novio, la novia** boyfriend, girlfriend (7B)

nuestro(s), -a(s) our (5A)

nueve nine (P)

nuevo, -a new (7A)

nunca never (3A)

O

o or (1A)

la **obra de teatro** play (8A)

ochenta eighty (P)

ocho eight (P)

ochocientos, -as eight hundred (7A)

octavo, -a eighth (2A)

octubre October (P)

ocupado, -a busy (4B)

el **ojo** eye (P)

once eleven (P)

ordenado, -a neat (1B)

os (to / for) you *pl. fam. ind. obj. pron.* (8B)

el **oso** bear (8A)

el **otoño** fall, autumn (P)

otro, -a other, another (5B)

otra vez again (8B)

¡Oye! Hey! (4B)

P

paciente patient (1B)

el **padrastro** stepfather (5A)

el **padre (papá)** father (5A)

los **padres** parents (5A)

pagar (por) to pay (for) (7B)

la **página Web** Web page (9B)

el **país** country (8A)

el **pájaro** bird (8A)

el **pan** bread (3A)

el — tostado toast (3A)

la **pantalla** (computer) screen (2B)

los **pantalones** pants (7A)

los — cortos shorts (7A)

las **papas** potatoes (3B)

las — fritas French fries (3A)

el **papel picado** cut-paper decorations (5A)

la **papelera** wastepaper basket (2B)

para for (2A)

— + *inf.* in order to + *inf.* (4A)

— la salud for one's health (3B)

— mantener la salud to maintain one's health (3B)

— mí in my opinion, for me (6A)

¿— qué sirve? What's it (used) for? (9B)

— ti in your opinion, for you (6A)

la **pared** wall (6A)

el **parque** park (4A)

el — de diversiones amusement park (8A)

el — nacional national park (8A)

el **partido** game, match (4B)

pasar:

¿Cómo lo pasaste? How was it (for you)? (8A)

— la aspiradora to vacuum (6B)

— tiempo con amigos to spend time with friends (1A)

¿Qué pasa? What's happening? (P)

¿Qué te pasó? What happened to you? (8A)

pasear en bote to go boating (8A)

el **pastel** cake (5A)

los **pasteles** pastries (3B)

patinar to skate (1A)

pedir (e → i) to order (5B); to ask for (9B)

la **película:** film, movie (9A)

la — de ciencia ficción science fiction movie (9A)

la — de horror horror movie (9A)

la — policíaca crime movie, mystery (9A)

la — romántica romantic movie (9A)

ver una — to see a movie (4A)

pelirrojo, -a red-haired (5B)

el **pelo** hair (5B)

el — canoso gray hair (5B)

el — castaño brown (chestnut) hair (5B)

el — **negro** black hair (5B)
el — **rubio** blond hair (5B)
pensar (e → ie) to plan, to think (7A)
peor:
el / la —, los / las —es the worst (6A)
—**(es) que** worse than (6A)
pequeño, -a small (6A)
Perdón. Excuse me. (7A)
perezoso, -a lazy (1B)
el **perfume** perfume (7B)
el **periódico** newspaper (8B)
pero but (1B)
el **perrito caliente** hot dog (3A)
el **perro** dog (5A)
la **persona** person (5A)
pesas: levantar — to lift weights (3B)
el **pescado** fish (3B)
el **pie** foot (P)
la **pierna** leg (P)
la **pimienta** pepper (5B)
la **piñata** piñata (5A)
la **piscina** pool (4A)
el **piso** story, floor (6B)
primer — second floor (6B)
segundo — third floor (6B)
la **pizza** pizza (3A)
la **planta baja** ground floor (6B)
el **plástico** plastic (8B)
el **plátano** banana (3A)
el **plato** plate, dish (5B)
de — principal as a main dish (5B)
el — principal main dish (5B)
la **playa** beach (4A)
pobre poor (8B)
poco: un — (de) a little (4B)
poder (o → ue) to be able (6A)
(yo) puedo I can (4B)
(tú) puedes you can (4B)
policíaca: la película — crime movie, mystery (9A)

el **pollo** chicken (3B)
poner to put, to place (6B)
pon *(command)* put, place (6B)
— **la mesa** to set the table (6B)
(yo) pongo I put (6B)
(tú) pones you put (6B)
por:
— **eso** for that reason, therefore (9A)
— **favor** please (P)
¿— qué? Why? (3B)
— **supuesto** of course (3A)
porque because (3B)
la **posesión,** *pl.* **las posesiones** possession (6A)
el **postre** dessert (5B)
de — for dessert (5B)
practicar deportes to play sports (1A)
práctico, -a practical (2A)
el **precio** price (7A)
preferir (e → ie) to prefer (7A)
(yo) prefiero I prefer (3B)
(tú) prefieres you prefer (3B)
preparar to prepare (5A)
la **presentación,** *pl.* **las presentaciones** presentation (9B)
la **primavera** spring (P)
primer (primero), -a first (2A)
— **piso** second floor (6B)
el **primo, la prima** cousin (5A)
los **primos** cousins (5A)
el **problema** problem (8B)
el **profesor, la profesora** teacher (P)
el **programa** program, show (9A)
el — de concursos game show (9A)
el — de dibujos animados cartoon (9A)
el — de entrevistas interview program (9A)
el — de la vida real reality program (9A)
el — de noticias news program (9A)
el — deportivo sports program (9A)
el — educativo educational program (9A)
el — musical musical program (9A)
propio, -a own (6A)
el **proyecto de construcción** construction project (8B)
puedes: (tú) — you can (4B)
puedo: (yo) — I can (4B)
la **puerta** door (2B)
pues well *(to indicate pause)* (1A)
la **pulsera** bracelet (7B)
el reloj — watch (7B)
el **pupitre** student desk (P)

Q

que who, that (5A)
qué:
¿Para — sirve? What's it (used) for? (9B)
¡— + *adj.*! How . . . ! (5B)
¡— asco! How awful! (3A)
¡— buena idea! What a good / nice idea! (4B)
¿— clase de . . . ? What kind of . . . ? (9A)
¿— desean (Uds.)? What would you like? (5B)
¿— día es hoy? What day is today? (P)
¿— es esto? What is this? (2B)
¿— hiciste? What did you do? (8A)
¿— hora es? What time is it? (P)
¿— más? What else? (8B)
¿— pasa? What's happening? (P)
¡— pena! What a shame / pity! (4B)
¿— quiere decir . . . ? What does . . . mean? (P)
¿— tal? How are you? (P)
¿— te gusta hacer? What do you like to do? (1A)

¿— **te gusta hacer más?** What do you like better (prefer) to do? (1A)
¿— **te parece?** What do you think (about it)? (9B)
¿— **te pasó?** What happened to you? (8A)
¿— **tiempo hace?** What's the weather like? (P)
quedar to fit (9A)
los **quehaceres (de la casa)** (household) chores (6B)
querer (e → ie) to want (7A)
¿Qué quiere decir . . . ? What does . . . mean? (P)
Quiere decir . . . It means . . . (P)
quisiera I would like (5B)
(yo) quiero I want (4B)
(tú) quieres you want (4B)
¿Quién? Who? (2A)
quince fifteen (P)
quinientos, -as five hundred (7A)
quinto, -a fifth (2A)
quisiera I would like (5B)
quitar el polvo to dust (6B)
quizás maybe (7A)

R

rápidamente quickly (9B)
el **ratón,** *pl.* **los ratones** (computer) mouse (2B)
razón: tener — to be correct (7A)
realista realistic (9A)
recibir to receive (6B)
reciclar to recycle (8B)
la **Red:**
en la — online (7B)
navegar en la — to surf the Web (9B)
recoger (g → j) to collect, to gather (8B)
los **recuerdos** souvenirs (8A)
comprar — to buy souvenirs (8A)
el **refresco** soft drink (3A)
el **regalo** gift, present (5A)
regresar to return (8A)
regular okay, so-so (P)
el **reloj** clock (2B)
el — pulsera watch (7B)
reservado, -a reserved, shy (1B)
el **restaurante** restaurant (4A)
rico, -a rich, tasty (5B)
el **río** river (8B)
rojo, -a red (6A)
romántico, -a: la película — romantic movie (9A)
romper to break (5A)
la **ropa: la tienda de —** clothing store (7B)
rosado, -a pink (6A)
rubio, -a blond (5B)

S

sábado Saturday (P)
saber to know (how) (9B)
(yo) sé I know (how to) (4B)
(tú) sabes you know (how to) (4B)
sabroso, -a tasty, flavorful (3B)
el **sacapuntas,** *pl.* **los sacapuntas** pencil sharpener (2B)
sacar:
— fotos to take photos (5A)
— la basura to take out the trash (6B)
la **sal** salt (5B)
la **sala** living room (6B)
la **sala de clases** classroom (P)
la **salchicha** sausage (3A)
salir to leave, to go out (8A)
la **salud:**
para la — for one's health (3B)
para mantener la — to maintain one's health (3B)
el **sándwich de jamón y queso** ham and cheese sandwich (3A)
sé: (yo) — I know (how to) (1B)
sed: Tengo —. I'm thirsty. (3B)
según according to (1B)
— mi familia according to my family (1B)
segundo, -a second (2A)
— piso third floor (6B)
seis six (P)
seiscientos, -as six hundred (7A)
la **semana** week (P)
este fin de — this weekend (4B)
la — pasada last week (7B)
los fines de — on weekends (4A)
señor (Sr.) sir, Mr. (P)
señora (Sra.) madam, Mrs. (P)
señorita (Srta.) miss, Miss (P)
separar to separate (8B)
septiembre September (P)
séptimo, -a seventh (2A)
ser to be (3B)
¿Eres . . . ? Are you . . . ? (1B)
es he / she is (1B)
fue it was (8A)
no soy I am not (1B)
soy I am (1B)
serio, -a serious (1B)
la **servilleta** napkin (5B)
servir (e → i) to serve, to be useful (9B)
¿En qué puedo servirle? How can I help you? (7A)
¿Para qué sirve? What's it (used) for? (9B)
Sirve para . . . It's used for . . . (9B)
sesenta sixty (P)
setecientos, -as seven hundred (7A)
setenta seventy (P)
sexto, -a sixth (2A)
si if, whether (6B)
sí yes (1A)
siempre always (3A)
siento: lo — I'm sorry (4B)
siete seven (P)
la **silla** chair (2B)

simpático, -a nice, friendly (1B)
sin without (3A)
la **sinagoga** synagogue (4A)
el **sitio Web** Web site (9B)
sobre about (9A)
sociable sociable (1B)
el **software** software (7B)
el **sol:**
Hace —. It's sunny. (P)
los anteojos de — sunglasses (7B)
tomar el — to sunbathe (8A)
sólo only (5A)
solo, -a alone (4A)
Son las . . . It's . . . *(time)* (P)
la **sopa de verduras** vegetable soup (3A)
el **sótano** basement (6B)
soy I am (1B)
su, sus his, her, your *formal,* their (5A)
sucio, -a dirty (6B)
la **sudadera** sweatshirt (7A)
sueño: tener — to be sleepy (5B)
el **suéter** sweater (7A)
supuesto: por — of course (3A)

T

tal: ¿Qué — ? How are you? (P)
talentoso, -a talented (1B)
también also, too (1A)
a mí — I do (like to) too (1A)
tampoco: a mí — I don't (like to) either (1A)
tanto so much (7A)
tarde late (8A); afternoon (4B)
a la una de la — at one (o'clock) in the afternoon (4B)
Buenas —s. Good afternoon. (P)
de la — in the afternoon (4B)
esta — this afternoon (4B)
la **tarea** homework (2A)
la **tarjeta** card (9B)
la **taza** cup (5B)
te (to / for) you *sing. ind. obj. pron.* (8B)
¿— gusta . . . ? Do you like to . . . ? (1A)
¿— gustaría . . . ? Would you like . . . ? (4B)
¿— gustó? Did you like it? (8A)
el **té** tea (3A)
el — helado iced tea (3A)
el **teatro** theater (8A)
el **teclado** (computer) keyboard (2B)
la **tecnología** technology / computers (2A)
la clase de — technology / computer class (2A)
la **telenovela** soap opera (9A)
el **televisor** television set (6A)
el **templo** temple; Protestant church (4A)
temprano early (8A)
el **tenedor** fork (5B)
tener to have (5A)
(yo) tengo I have (2A)
(tú) tienes you have (2A)
¿Cuántos años tiene(n) . . . ? How old is / are . . . ? (5A)
— calor to be warm (5B)
— frío to be cold (5B)
— miedo (de) to be scared (of), to be afraid (of) (9B)
— razón to be correct (7A)
— sueño to be sleepy (5B)
Tengo hambre. I'm hungry. (3B)
Tengo que . . . I have to . . . (4B)
Tengo sed. I'm thirsty. (3B)
Tiene(n) . . . años. He / She is / They are . . . (years old). (5A)
el **tenis: jugar al —** to play tennis (4B)
tercer (tercero), -a third (2A)
terminar to finish, to end (9A)
ti you *fam. after prep.*
¿Y a —? And you? (1A)
para — in your opinion, for you (6A)
el **tiempo:**
el — libre free time (4A)
pasar — con amigos to spend time with friends (1A)
¿Qué — hace? What's the weather like? (P)
la **tienda** store (7A)
la — de descuentos discount store (7B)
la — de electrodomésticos household appliance store (7B)
la — de ropa clothing store (7A)
Tiene(n) . . . años. He / She is / They are . . . (years old). (5A)
el **tío, la tía** uncle, aunt (5A)
los **tíos** uncles; aunt(s) and uncle(s) (5A)
tocar la guitarra to play the guitar (1A)
el **tocino** bacon (3A)
todos, -as all (3B)
— los días every day (3A)
tomar:
— el sol to sunbathe (8A)
— un curso to take a course (9B)
los **tomates** tomatoes (3B)
tonto, -a silly, stupid (9A)
trabajador, -ora hardworking (1B)
trabajar to work (1A)
el **trabajo** work, job (4A)
el — voluntario volunteer work (8B)
traer:
Le traigo . . . I will bring you . . . (5B)
¿Me trae . . . ? Will you bring me . . . ? (5B)
el **traje** suit (7A)
el — de baño swimsuit (7A)
trece thirteen (P)

treinta thirty (P)

treinta y uno thirty-one (P)

tremendo, -a tremendous (8A)

el **tren** train (8A)

tres three (P)

trescientos, as three hundred (7A)

triste sad (4B)

tu, tus your (2B, 5A)

tú you *fam.* (2A)

U

Ud. (usted) you *formal sing.* (2A)

Uds. (ustedes) you *formal pl.* (2A)

¡Uf! Ugh!, Yuck! (7B)

un, una a, an (1B)

un poco (de) a little (4B)

la **una: a la —** at one o'clock (4B)

uno one (P)

unos, -as some (2B)

usado, -a used (8B)

usar la computadora to use the computer (1A)

usted (Ud.) you *formal sing.* (2A)

ustedes (Uds.) you *formal pl.* (2A)

las **uvas** grapes (3B)

V

las **vacaciones: ir de —** to go on vacation (8A)

¡Vamos! Let's go! (7A)

el **vaso** glass (5B)

veinte twenty (P)

veintiuno (veintiún) twenty-one (P)

vender to sell (7B)

venir to come (5B)

la **ventana** window (2B)

ver to see (8A)

a — . . . Let's see (2A)

¡Nos vemos! See you later! (P)

— la tele to watch television (1A)

— una película to see a movie (4A)

vi I saw (8A)

¿Viste? Did you see? (8A)

el **verano** summer (P)

veras: ¿De —? Right? (9A)

¿Verdad? Right? (3A)

verde green (6A)

el **vestido** dress (7A)

la **vez,** *pl.* **las veces:**

a veces sometimes (1B)

otra — again (8B)

viajar to travel (8A)

el **viaje** trip (8A)

el **video** video (5A), videocassette (6A)

la **videocasetera** VCR (6A)

los **videojuegos: jugar —** to play video games (1A)

el **vidrio** glass (8B)

viejo, -a old (5B)

viernes Friday (P)

violento, -a violent (9A)

visitar to visit (8A)

— salones de chat to visit chat rooms (9B)

vivir to live (6B)

el **vóleibol: jugar al —** to play volleyball (4B)

el **voluntario, la voluntaria** volunteer (8B)

vosotros, -as you *pl.* (2A)

vuestro(s), -a(s) your (5A)

Y

y and (1A)

¿— a ti? And you? (1A)

— cuarto quarter past *(in telling time)* (P)

— media thirty, half past *(in telling time)* (P)

¿— tú? And you? *fam.* (P)

¿— usted (Ud.)? And you? *formal* (P)

ya already (9A)

yo I (1B)

el **yogur** yogurt (3A)

Z

las **zanahorias** carrots (3B)

la **zapatería** shoe store (7B)

los **zapatos** shoes (7A)

el **zoológico** zoo (8A)

English-Spanish Vocabulary

The *English-Spanish Vocabulary* contains all active vocabulary from the text, including vocabulary presented in the grammar sections.

A dash (—) represents the main entry word. For example, **to play —** after **baseball** means **to play baseball.**

The number following each entry indicates the chapter in which the word or expression is presented. Remember that Temas 1–4 appeared in Level A. The letter *P* following an entry refers to the *Para empezar* section of Level A.

The following abbreviations are used in this list: *adj.* (adjective), *dir. obj.* (direct object), *f.* (feminine), *fam.*(familiar), *ind. obj.* (indirect object), *inf.* (infinitive), *m.* (masculine), *pl.* (plural), *prep.* (preposition), *pron.* (pronoun), *sing.* (singular).

A

a, an un, una (1B)
a little un poco (de) (4B)
a lot mucho, -a (2A)
a thousand mil (7A)
able: to be — poder (o → ue) (6A)
about sobre (9A)
according to según (1B)
— my family según mi familia (1B)
acquainted: to be — with conocer (9B)
actor el actor (9A)
actress la actriz, *pl.* las actrices (9A)
address: e-mail — la dirección electrónica (9B)
afraid: to be — (of) tener miedo (de) (9B)
after después (de) (4A)
afternoon:
at one (o'clock) in the afternoon a la una de la tarde (4B)
Good —. Buenas tardes. (P)
in the — de la tarde (4B)
this — esta tarde (4B)
afterwards después (4A)
again otra vez (8B)
ago hace + *time expression* (7B)
agree:
I —. Estoy de acuerdo. (3B)
I don't —. No estoy de acuerdo. (3B)
airplane el avión, *pl.* los aviones (8A)
alarm clock el despertador (6A)
all todos, -as (3B)
almost casi (9A)
alone solo, -a (4A)
already ya (9A)
also también (1A)
always siempre (3A)
am:
I — (yo) soy (1B)
I — not (yo) no soy (1B)
amusement park el parque de diversiones (8A)
amusing divertido, -a (2A)
and y (1A)
¿— you? ¿Y a ti? *fam.* (1A); ¿Y tú? *fam.* (P); ¿Y usted (Ud.)? *formal* (P)
animal el animal (8A)
another otro, -a (5B)
Anything else? ¿Algo más? (5B)
apartment el apartamento (6B)
apple la manzana (3A)
— juice el jugo de manzana (3A)
April abril (P)
Are you . . . ? ¿Eres . . . ? (1B)
arm el brazo (P)
art class la clase de arte (2A)
artistic artístico, -a (1B)
as como (8A)
— a main dish de plato principal (5B)
to **ask for** pedir (e → i) (9B)
at:
— eight (o'clock) a las ocho (4B)
— eight (o'clock) at night a las ocho de la noche (4B)
— eight (o'clock) in the evening a las ocho de la noche (4B)
— eight (o'clock) in the morning a las ocho de la mañana (4B)
— home en casa (4A)
— one (o'clock) a la una (4B)
— one (o'clock) in the afternoon a la una de la tarde (4B)
— what time? ¿A qué hora? (4B)
athletic deportista (1B)
attraction(s) la atracción, *pl.* las atracciones (8A)
August agosto (P)
aunt la tía (5A)
aunt(s) and uncle(s) los tíos (5A)
autumn el otoño (P)

B

backpack la mochila (2B)
bacon el tocino (3A)
bad malo, -a (3B); mal (4B)
badly mal (4B)
bag la bolsa (8B)
balloon el globo (5A)
banana el plátano (3A)
baseball: to play — jugar al béisbol (4B)
basement el sótano (6B)
basketball: to play — jugar al básquetbol (4B)
bathroom el baño (6B)
to **be** ser (3B); estar (2B)
He / She is / They are . . . (years old). Tiene(n) . . . años. (5A)
How old is / are . . . ? ¿Cuántos años tiene(n) . . . ? (5A)
to — + *present participle* estar + *present participle* (6B)
to — able poder (o → ue) (6A)
to — acquainted with conocer (9B)
to — afraid (of) tener miedo (de) (9B)
to — cold tener frío (5B)
to — correct tener razón (7A)

to — **going to** + *verb* ir a + *inf.* (4B)
to — **online** estar en línea (9B)
to — **scared (of)** tener miedo (de) (9B)
to — **sleepy** tener sueño (5B)
to — **useful** servir (e → i) (9B)
to — **warm** tener calor (5B)
beach la playa (4A)
bear el oso (8A)
because porque (3B)
bed la cama (6A)
to make the — hacer la cama (6B)
bedroom el dormitorio (6A)
beefsteak el bistec (3B)
before antes de (9A)
to **begin** empezar (e → ie) (9A)
behind detrás de (2B)
best: the — el / la mejor, los / las mejores (6A)
better than mejor(es) que (6A)
beverages las bebidas (3B)
bicycle: to ride a — montar en bicicleta (1A)
bill la cuenta (5B)
binder: three-ring — la carpeta de argollas (2A)
bird el pájaro (8A)
birthday el cumpleaños (5A)
Happy —! ¡Feliz cumpleaños! (5A)
black hair el pelo negro (5B)
blond hair el pelo rubio (5B)
blouse la blusa (7A)
blue azul (6A)
boat el barco (8A)
boating: to go — pasear en bote (8A)
book el libro (P)
bookbag la mochila (2B)
bookshelf el estante (6A)
bookstore la librería (7B)
boots las botas (7A)
to **bore** aburrir (9A)
it / they —(s) me me aburre(n) (9A)
boring aburrido, -a (2A)
both los dos, las dos (7A)
bottle la botella (8B)
box la caja (8B)
boy el chico (1B)
—friend el novio (7B)
young — el niño (8B)
bracelet la pulsera (7B)
bread el pan (3A)
to **break** romper (5A)
breakfast el desayuno (3A)
for — en el desayuno (3A)
to **bring** traer (5B); llevar (8B)
I will — you . . . Le traigo . . . (5B)
Will you — me . . . ? ¿Me trae . . . ? (5B)
brother el hermano (5A)
brothers; brother(s) and sister(s) los hermanos (5A)
brown marrón, *pl.* marrones (6A)
— (chestnut) hair el pelo castaño (5B)
to **burn a CD** grabar un disco compacto (9B)
bus el autobús, *pl.* los autobuses (8A)
busy ocupado, -a (4B)
but pero (1B)
butter la mantequilla (3B)
to **buy** comprar (7A)
to — souvenirs comprar recuerdos (8A)
by + *vehicle* en + *vehicle* (8A)

C

café el café (4A)
cake el pastel (5A)
calculator la calculadora (2A)
camera la cámara (5A)
digital — la cámara digital (9B)
camp el campamento (8B)
can la lata (8B)
can:
I — (yo) puedo (4B)
you — (tú) puedes (4B)
candy los dulces (5A)
cap la gorra (7A)
car el coche (6B)
card la tarjeta (9B)
cardboard el cartón (8B)
carrots las zanahorias (3B)
to **carry** llevar (8B)
cartoon el programa de dibujos animados (9A)
cat el gato (5A)
CD: to burn a — grabar un disco compacto (9B)
to **celebrate** celebrar (5A)
cereal el cereal (3A)
chain la cadena (7B)
chair la silla (2B)
channel (TV) el canal (9A)
cheap barato, -a (7B)
chicken el pollo (3B)
childish infantil (9A)
children los hijos (5A); los niños (8B)
chores: household — los quehaceres (de la casa) (6B)
church la iglesia (4A)
Protestant — el templo (4A)
city la ciudad (8A)
class la clase (2A)
classroom la sala de clases (P)
clean limpio, -a (6B)
to **clean the bathroom** limpiar el baño (6B)
clock el reloj (2B)
close (to) cerca (de) (6B)
closet el armario (6A)
clothing store la tienda de ropa (7A)
coat el abrigo (7A)
coffee el café (3A)
cold:
It's —. Hace frío. (P)
to be — tener frío (5B)
to **collect** recoger (g → j) (8B)
color:
What — . . . ? ¿De qué color . . . ? (6A)
—s los colores (6A)
to **come** venir (5B)

comedy la comedia (9A)
comical cómico, -a (9A)
to communicate comunicarse (9B)
I — (yo) me comunico (9B)
you — (tú) te comunicas (9B)
community la comunidad (8B)
compact disc el disco compacto (6A)
to burn a — grabar un disco compacto (9B)
complicated complicado, -a (9B)
composition la composición, *pl.* las composiciones (9B)
computer la computadora (2B)
— graphics los gráficos (9B)
— keyboard el teclado (2B)
— mouse el ratón (2B)
— screen la pantalla (2B)
—s / technology la tecnología (2B)
laptop — la computadora portátil (9B)
to use the — usar la computadora (1A)
concert el concierto (4B)
construction project el proyecto de construcción (8B)
to cook cocinar (6B)
cookie la galleta (3A)
correct: to be — tener razón (7A)
to cost costar (o → ue) (7A)
How much does (do) . . . —? ¿Cuánto cuesta(n)? (7A)
country el país (8A)
countryside el campo (4A)
course: to take a course tomar un curso (9B)
cousin el primo, la prima (5A)
—s los primos (5A)
to create crear (9B)
crime movie la película policíaca (9A)
cup la taza (5B)
curtains las cortinas (6A)
to cut the lawn cortar el césped (6B)
cut-paper decorations el papel picado (5A)

D

dance el baile (4B)
to dance bailar (1A)
daring atrevido, -a (1B)
date: What is the —? ¿Cuál es la fecha? (P)
daughter la hija (5A)
day el día (P)
every — todos los días (3A); cada día (3B)
What — is today? ¿Qué día es hoy? (P)
December diciembre (P)
to decide decidir (8B)
to decorate decorar (5A)
decorations las decoraciones (5A)
delicious delicioso, -a (5B)
delighted encantado, -a (P)
department store el almacén, *pl.* los almacenes (7B)
desk el pupitre (P); el escritorio (2B)
dessert el postre (5B)
for — de postre (5B)
dictionary el diccionario (2A)
Did you like it? ¿Te gustó? (8A)
difficult difícil (2A)
digital camera la cámara digital (9B)
dining room el comedor (6B)
dinner la cena (3B)
dirty sucio, -a (6B)
disaster: It was a —. Fue un desastre. (8A)
discount store la tienda de descuentos (7B)
dish el plato (5B)
as a main — de plato principal (5B)
main — el plato principal (5B)
diskette el disquete (2B)
to do hacer (3B)
— *(command)* haz (6B)
— you like to . . . ? ¿Te gusta . . . ? (1A)
I — (yo) hago (3B)
What are you doing? ¿Qué estás haciendo? (6B)
What did you —? ¿Qué hiciste? (8A)
you — (tú) haces (3B)
document el documento (9B)
dog el perro (5A)
to feed the — dar de comer al perro (6B)
door la puerta (2B)
to download bajar (información) (9B)
drama el drama (9A)
to draw dibujar (1A)
dress el vestido (7A)
dresser la cómoda (6A)
to drink beber (3A)
during durante (8A)
to dust quitar el polvo (6B)
DVD player el lector DVD (6A)

E

e-mail:
— address la dirección electrónica (9B)
to write an — message escribir por correo electrónico (9B)
early temprano (8A)
earrings los aretes (7B)
easy fácil (2A)
to eat comer (3A)
educational program el programa educativo (9A)
eggs los huevos (3A)
eight ocho (P)
eight hundred ochocientos, -as (7A)
eighteen dieciocho (P)
eighth octavo, -a (2A)
eighty ochenta (P)
either tampoco (1A)
I don't (like to) — a mí tampoco (1A)
eleven once (P)
else:
Anything —? ¿Algo más? (5B)
What —? ¿Qué más? (8B)
to end terminar (9A)
English class la clase de inglés (2A)

enough bastante (6B)
to **enter** entrar (7A)
especially especialmente (9A)
evening:
Good —. Buenas noches. (P)
in the — de la noche (4B)
this — esta noche (4B)
every day cada día (3B); todos los días (3A)
Excuse me. Perdón. (7A)
to **exercise** hacer ejercicio (3B)
expensive caro, -a (7B)
experience la experiencia (8B)
eye el ojo (P)

F

face-to-face cara a cara (9B)
fall el otoño (P)
fantastic fantástico, -a (8A)
far (from) lejos (de) (6B)
fascinating fascinante (9A)
fast rápidamente (9B)
father el padre (papá) (5A)
favorite favorito, -a (2A)
February febrero (P)
to **feed the dog** dar de comer al perro (6B)
fewer:
— . . . than menos . . . que (6A)
— than . . . menos de . . . (9A)
fifteen quince (P)
fifth quinto, -a (2A)
fifty cincuenta (P)
film la película (9A)
finger el dedo (P)
to **finish** terminar (9A)
first primer (primero), -a (2A)
fish el pescado (3B)
to go —ing ir de pesca (4B)
to **fit: It / They —(s) me well / poorly.** Me queda(n) bien / mal. (7A)
five cinco (P)
five hundred quinientos, -as (7A)
flag la bandera (2B)
flavorful sabroso, -a (3B)
floor el piso (6B)
ground — la planta baja (6B)
second — el primer piso (6B)
third — el segundo piso (6B)
flower la flor, *pl.* las flores (5A)
folder la carpeta (P)
food la comida (3A)
foot el pie (P)
football: to play — jugar al fútbol americano (4B)
for para (2A)
— breakfast en el desayuno (3A)
— lunch en el almuerzo (3A)
— me para mí (6A)
— that reason por eso (9A)
— you para ti (6A)
fork el tenedor (5B)
forty cuarenta (P)
four cuatro (P)
four hundred cuatrocientos, -as (7A)
fourteen catorce (P)
fourth cuarto, -a (2A)
free time el tiempo libre (4A)
French fries las papas fritas (3A)
Friday viernes (P)
friend el amigo, la amiga (1B)
friendly simpático, -a (1B)
from de (4A)
Where are you —? ¿De dónde eres? (4A)
fruit salad la ensalada de frutas (3A)
fun divertido, -a (2A)
funny gracioso, -a (1B); cómico, -a (9A)

G

game el partido (4B)
— show el programa de concursos (9A)
garage el garaje (6B)
garden el jardín, *pl.* los jardines (8B)
to **gather** recoger (g → j) (8B)
generally generalmente (4A)
gift el regalo (5A)
girl la chica (1B)
—friend la novia (7B)
young — la niña (8B)
to **give** dar (6B)
glass el vaso (5B); el vidrio (8B)
gloves los guantes (7B)
to **go** ir (4A)
Let's —! ¡Vamos! (7A)
to be —ing to + *verb* ir a + *inf.* (4B)
to — boating pasear en bote (8A)
to — camping ir de cámping (4B)
to — fishing ir de pesca (4B)
to — on vacation ir de vacaciones (8A)
to — shopping ir de compras (4A)
to — to school ir a la escuela (1A)
to — out salir (8A)
golf: to play — jugar al golf (4B)
good bueno (buen), -a (1B)
— afternoon. Buenas tardes. (P)
— evening. Buenas noches. (P)
— morning. Buenos días. (P)
Good-bye! ¡Adiós! (P)
good-looking guapo, -a (5B)
grandfather el abuelo (5A)
grandmother la abuela (5A)
grandparents los abuelos (5A)
grapes las uvas (3B)
gray gris (6A)
— hair el pelo canoso (5B)
Great! ¡Genial! (4B)
green verde (6A)
— beans las judías verdes (3B)
ground floor la planta baja (6B)
guitar: to play the — tocar la guitarra (1A)
gym el gimnasio (4A)

H

hair el pelo (5B)
black — el pelo negro (5B)
blond — el pelo rubio (5B)

brown (chestnut) — el pelo castaño (5B)

gray — el pelo canoso (5B)

half media, -o (P)

— past y media *(in telling time)* (P)

ham and cheese sandwich el sándwich de jamón y queso (3A)

hamburger la hamburguesa (3A)

hand la mano (P)

happy contento, -a (4B)

— birthday! ¡Feliz cumpleaños! (5A)

hardworking trabajador, -ora (1B)

to **have** tener (5A)

to — just . . . acabar de + *inf.* (9A)

I — to . . . tengo que + *inf.* (4B)

he él (1B)

he / she is es (1B)

He / She is / They are . . . years old). Tiene(n) . . . años. (5A)

head la cabeza (P)

health:

for one's — para la salud (3B)

to maintain one's — para mantener la salud (3B)

Hello! ¡Hola! (P)

to **help** ayudar (6B)

How can I — you? ¿En qué puedo servirle? (7A)

her su, sus *possessive adj.* (5A); la *dir. obj. pron.* (7B); le *ind. obj. pron.* (8B)

here aquí (2B)

Hey! ¡Oye! (4B)

him lo *dir. obj. pron.* (7B); le *ind. obj. pron.* (8B)

his su, sus (5A)

home la casa (4A)

at — en casa (4A)

— office el despacho (6B)

(to) — a casa (4A)

homework la tarea (2A)

horrible horrible (3B)

horror movie la película de horror (9A)

horseback: to ride — montar a caballo (8A)

hospital el hospital (8B)

hot:

— dog el perrito caliente (3A)

It's —. Hace calor. (P)

hotel el hotel (8A)

hour: in the . . . — en la . . . hora (class period) (2A)

house la casa (4A)

household:

— chores los quehaceres (de la casa) (6B)

— appliance store la tienda de electrodomésticos (7B)

how:

— + *adj.*! ¡Qué + *adj.*! (5B)

— awful! ¡Qué asco! (3A)

How? ¿Cómo? (P)

— are you? ¿Cómo está Ud.? *formal* (P); ¿Cómo estás? *fam.* (P); ¿Qué tal? *fam.* (P)

— can I help you? ¿En qué puedo servirle? (7A)

— do you say . . . ? ¿Cómo se dice . . . ? (P)

— does it (do they) fit (you)? ¿Cómo te queda(n)? (7A)

— is . . . spelled? ¿Cómo se escribe . . . ? (P)

— many? ¿cuántos, -as? (P)

— much does (do) . . . cost? ¿Cuánto cuesta(n) . . . ? (7A)

— old is / are . . . ? ¿Cuántos años tiene(n) . . . ? (5A)

— was it (for you)? ¿Cómo lo pasaste? (8A)

hundred: one — cien (P)

hungry: I'm —. Tengo hambre. (3B)

to **hurt** doler (o → ue) (9A)

husband el esposo (5A)

I

I yo (1B)

— am soy (1B)

— am not no soy (1B)

— do too a mí también (1A)

— don't either a mí tampoco (1A)

— don't think so. Creo que no. (3B)

— stay at home. Me quedo en casa. (4A)

— think . . . Creo que . . . (3B)

— think so. Creo que sí. (3B)

— will bring you . . . Le traigo . . . (5B)

— would like Me gustaría (4B); quisiera (5B)

—'m hungry. Tengo hambre. (3B)

—'m sorry. Lo siento. (4B)

—'m thirsty. Tengo sed. (3B)

ice cream el helado (3B)

iced tea el té helado (3A)

if si (6B)

impatient impaciente (1B)

important importante (6A)

impressive impresionante (8A)

in en (2B)

— front of delante de (2B)

— my opinion para mí (6A)

— order to para + *inf.* (4A)

— the . . . hour en la . . . hora (class period) (2A)

— your opinion para ti (6A)

incredible increíble (8B)

inexpensive barato, -a (7B)

information la información (9B)

intelligent inteligente (1B)

to **interest** interesar (9A)

it / they interest(s) me me interesa(n) (9A)

interesting interesante (2A)

interview program el programa de entrevistas (9A)

is es (P)

he / she — es (1B)

it la, lo *dir. obj. pron.* (7B)

— fits (they fit) me well / poorly. Me queda(n) bien / mal. (7A)

— is . . . Son las *(in telling time)* (P)

— is one o'clock. Es la una. (P)
— is the . . . of . . . Es el *(number)* de *(month) (in telling the date)* (P)
— is the first of . . . Es el primero de *(month).* (P)
— was fue (8A)
— was a disaster. Fue un desastre. (8A)
—'s a . . . es un / una . . . (2B)
—'s cold. Hace frío. (P)
—'s hot. Hace calor. (P)
—'s necessary. Es necesario. (8B)
—'s raining. Llueve. (P)
—'s snowing. Nieva. (P)
—'s sunny. Hace sol. (P)

J

jacket la chaqueta (7A)
January enero (P)
jeans los jeans (7A)
jewelry store la joyería (7B)
job el trabajo (4A)
juice:
apple — el jugo de manzana (3A)
orange — el jugo de naranja (3A)
July julio (P)
June junio (P)
just: to have — *(done something)* acabar de + *inf.* (9A)

K

key chain el llavero (7B)
keyboard (computer) el teclado (2B)
kind: What — of . . . ? ¿Qué clase de . . . ? (9A)
kitchen la cocina (6B)
knife el cuchillo (5B)
to **know** saber (4B, 9B); conocer (9B)
I — (yo) conozco (9B)
I — (how to) (yo) sé (4B)
you — (tú) conoces (9B)
you — (how to) (tú) sabes (4B)

L

laboratory el laboratorio (9B)
lake el lago (8A)
lamp la lámpara (6A)
laptop computer la computadora portátil (9B)
large grande (6A)
last:
— night anoche (7B)
— week la semana pasada (7B)
— year el año pasado (7B)
to **last** durar (9A)
late tarde (8A)
later: See you —! ¡Hasta luego!, ¡Nos vemos! (P)
lazy perezoso, -a (1B)
to **learn** aprender (a) (8A)
to **leave** salir (8A)
left: to the — (of) a la izquierda (de) (6A)
leg la pierna (P)
lemonade la limonada (3A)
less:
— . . . than menos . . . que (6A)
— than menos de (9A)
Let's go! ¡Vamos! (7A)
Let's see A ver . . . (2A)
letter la carta (9B)
lettuce la lechuga (3B)
library la biblioteca (4A)
to **lift weights** levantar pesas (3B)
light la luz, *pl.* las luces (5A)
like como (8A)
to **like:**
Did you — it? ¿Te gustó? (8A)
Do you — to . . . ? ¿Te gusta . . . ? (1A)
He / She doesn't — . . . No le gusta . . . (1B)
He / She —s . . . Le gusta . . . (1B); A él / ella le gusta(n) . . .(5A)
I don't — to . . . (A mí) no me gusta . . . (1A)
I don't — to . . . at all. (A mí) no me gusta nada . . . (1A)
I — . . . Me gusta . . . (3A)
I — to . . . (A mí) me gusta . . . (1A)
I — to . . . a lot (A mí) me gusta mucho . . . (1A)
I — to . . . better (A mí) me gusta más . . . (1A)
I —d it. Me gustó. (8A)
I would — Me gustaría (4B); quisiera (5B)
What do you — better (prefer) to do? ¿Qué te gusta hacer más? (1A)
What do you — to do? ¿Qué te gusta hacer? (1A)
What would you —? ¿Qué desean (Uds.)? (5B)
Would you —? ¿Te gustaría? (4B)
You — . . . Te gusta . . . (3A)
likewise igualmente (P)
to **listen to music** escuchar música (1A)
little: a — un poco (de) (4B)
to **live** vivir (6B)
living room la sala (6B)
long largo, -a (5B)
to **look:**
to — (at) mirar (7B)
to — for buscar (7A)
lot: a — mucho, -a (2A)
to **love** encantar (9A)
He / She —s . . . A él / ella le encanta(n) . . . (5A)
I / You — . . . Me / Te encanta(n) . . . (3A)
lunch el almuerzo (2A)
for — en el almuerzo (3A)

M

madam (la) señora (Sra.) (P)
main dish el plato principal (5B)
as a — de plato principal (5B)
to **maintain one's health** para mantener la salud (3B)
make *(command)* haz (6B)

to **make the bed** hacer la cama (6B)
mall el centro comercial (4A)
man el hombre (5B)
older — el anciano (8B)
many muchos, -as (3B)
how — ¿cuántos, -as? (P)
March marzo (P)
match el partido (4B)
mathematics class la clase de matemáticas (2A)
May mayo (P)
maybe quizás (7A)
me me *ind. obj. pron* (8B)
for — para mí (6A), me (8B)
— too a mí también (1A)
to — me (8B)
with — conmigo (4B)
meal la comida (3A)
to **mean:**
It —s . . . Quiere decir . . . (P)
What does . . . — ? ¿Qué quiere decir . . . ? (P)
meat la carne (3B)
menu el menú (5B)
messy desordenado, -a (1B)
milk la leche (3A)
mirror el espejo (6A)
miss, Miss (la) señorita (Srta.) (P)
missing: to be — faltar (9A)
moment: a — un momento (6B)
Monday lunes (P)
on Mondays los lunes (4A)
money el dinero (6B)
monkey el mono (8A)
month el mes (P)
monument el monumento (8A)
more:
— . . . than más . . . que (2A)
— or less más o menos (3A)
— than más de (9A)
morning:
Good —. Buenos días. (P)
in the — de la mañana (4B)
mosque la mezquita (4A)
mother la madre (mamá) (5A)
mountains las montañas (4A)
mouse (computer) el ratón (2B)
mouth la boca (P)
movie la película (9A)
to see a — ver una película (4A)
— theater el cine (4A)
to **mow the lawn** cortar el césped (6B)
Mr. (el) señor (Sr.) (P)
Mrs. (la) señora (Sra.) (P)
much: so — tanto (7A)
museum el museo (8A)
music:
to listen to — escuchar música (1A)
—al program el programa musical (9A)
must deber (3B)
one — hay que (8B)
my mi (2B); mis (5A)
— name is . . . Me llamo . . . (P)
mystery la película policíaca (9A)

N

name:
My — is . . . Me llamo . . . (P)
What is your —? ¿Cómo te llamas? (P)
What's his / her —? ¿Cómo se llama? (1B)
napkin la servilleta (5B)
national park el parque nacional (8A)
near cerca (de) (6B)
neat ordenado, -a (1B)
necessary: It's —. Es necesario. (8B)
necklace el collar (7B)
to **need**
I — necesito (2A)
I — . . . Me falta(n) . . . (5B)
you — necesitas (2A)
neighborhood el barrio (8B)
neither . . . nor ni . . . ni (1A)
never nunca (3A)
new nuevo, -a (7A)
news program el programa de noticias (9A)
newspaper el periódico (8B)
next to al lado de (2B)
nice simpático, -a (1B)
night:
at — de la noche (4B)
last — anoche (7B)
night table la mesita (6A)
nine nueve (P)
nine hundred novecientos, -as (7A)
nineteen diecinueve (P)
ninety noventa (P)
ninth noveno, -a (2A)
nose la nariz, *pl.* las narices (P)
not . . . or ni . . . ni (1A)
notebook el cuaderno (P)
nothing nada (P)
November noviembre (P)
now ahora (5B)

O

o'clock:
at eight — a las ocho (4B)
at one — a la una (4B)
October octubre (P)
of de (2B)
— course por supuesto (3A)
office (home) el despacho (6B)
often a menudo (8B)
Oh! What a shame / pity! ¡Ay! ¡Qué pena! (4B)
okay regular (P)
old viejo, -a (5B)
He / She is / They are . . . years —. Tiene(n) . . . años. (5A)
How — is / are . . . ? ¿Cuántos años tiene(n) . . . ? (5A)
—er mayor (5A)
—er man el anciano (8B)
—er people los ancianos (8B)
—er woman la anciana (8B)
on en (2B)
— Mondays, on Tuesdays . . . los lunes, los martes . . . (4A)

— **top of** encima de (2B)
— **weekends** los fines de semana (4A)
one uno (un), -a (P)
at — (o'clock) a la una (4B)
one hundred cien (P)
one must hay que (8B)
onion la cebolla (3B)
online en la Red (7B)
to be — estar en línea (9B)
only sólo (5A)
to **open** abrir (5A)
opinion:
in my — para mí (6A)
in your — para ti (6A)
or o (1A)
orange anaranjado, -a (6A)
— juice el jugo de naranja (3A)
to **order** pedir (e → i) (5B)
other otro, -a (5B)
others los / las demás (8B)
our nuestro(s), -a(s) (5A)
own propio, -a (6A)

P

painting el cuadro (6A)
pants los pantalones (7A)
paper: sheet of — la hoja de papel (P)
parents los padres (5A)
park el parque (4A)
amusement — el parque de diversiones (8A)
national — el parque nacional (8A)
party la fiesta (4B)
pastries los pasteles (3B)
patient paciente (1B)
to **pay (for)** pagar (por) (7B)
peas los guisantes (3B)
pen el bolígrafo (P)
pencil el lápiz, *pl.* los lápices (P)
— sharpener el sacapuntas, *pl.* los sacapuntas (2B)
people la gente (8B)
older — los ancianos (8B)
pepper la pimienta (5B)
perfume el perfume (7B)
person la persona (5A)
phone: to talk on the — hablar por teléfono (1A)
photo la foto (5A)
to take —s sacar fotos (5A)
physical education class la clase de educación física (2A)
piano lesson (class) la lección, *pl.* las lecciones de piano (4A)
pink rosado, -a (6A)
piñata la piñata (5A)
pizza la pizza (3A)
place el lugar (8A)
to **place** poner (6B)
to **plan** pensar (e → ie) (7A)
plastic el plástico (8B)
plate el plato (5B)
play la obra de teatro (8A)
to **play** jugar (a) (u → ue) *(games, sports)* (4B); tocar *(an instrument)* (1A)
to — baseball jugar al béisbol (4B)
to — basketball jugar al básquetbol (4B)
to — football jugar al fútbol americano (4B)
to — golf jugar al golf (4B)
to — soccer jugar al fútbol (4B)
to — sports practicar deportes (1A)
to — tennis jugar al tenis (4B)
to — the guitar tocar la guitarra (1A)
to — video games jugar videojuegos (1A)
to — volleyball jugar al vóleibol (4B)
please por favor (P)
to **please very much** encantar (9A)
pleased to meet you mucho gusto (P)
pool la piscina (4A)
poor pobre (8B)
possession la posesión, *pl.* las posesiones (6A)
poster el cartel (2B)
potatoes las papas (3B)
practical práctico, -a (2A)
to **prefer** preferir (e → ie) (7A)
I — (yo) prefiero (3B)
I — to . . . (a mí) me gusta más . . . (1A)
you — (tú) prefieres (3B)
to **prepare** preparar (5A)
present el regalo (5A)
presentation la presentación, *pl.* las presentaciones (9B)
pretty bonito, -a (6A)
price el precio (7A)
primary school la escuela primaria (8B)
problem el problema (8B)
program el programa (9A)
purple morado, -a (6A)
purse el bolso (7B)
to **put** poner (6B)
I — (yo) pongo (6B)
— *(command)* pon (6B)
you — (tú) pones (6B)

Q

quarter past y cuarto *(in telling time)* (P)
quickly rápidamente (9B)

R

rain: It's —ing. Llueve. (P)
rather bastante (6B)
to **read magazines** leer revistas (1A)
realistic realista (9A)
reality program el programa de la vida real (9A)
Really? ¿De veras? (9A)
to **receive** recibir (6B)
to **recycle** reciclar (8B)
recycling center el centro de reciclaje (8B)
red rojo, -a (6A)
—-haired pelirrojo, -a (5B)
to **relax** descansar (8A)

report el informe (9B)
reserved reservado, -a (1B)
to **rest** descansar (8A)
restaurant el restaurante (4A)
to **return** regresar (8A)
rice el arroz (3B)
rich rico, -a (5B)
to **ride:**
  to — a bicycle montar en bicicleta (1A)
  to — horseback montar a caballo (8A)
right: to the — (of) a la derecha (de) (6A)
Right? ¿Verdad? (3A)
ring el anillo (7B)
river el río (8B)
road la calle (8B)
romantic movie la película romántica (9A)
room el cuarto (6B)
  to straighten up the — arreglar el cuarto (6B)
rug la alfombra (6A)
to **run** correr (1A)

S

sack la bolsa (8B)
sad triste (4B)
salad la ensalada (3A)
  fruit — la ensalada de frutas (3A)
salesperson el dependiente, la dependienta (7A)
salt la sal (5B)
same mismo, -a (6A)
sandwich: ham and cheese — el sándwich de jamón y queso (3A)
Saturday sábado (P)
sausage la salchicha (3A)
to **say** decir (8B)
  How do you —? ¿Cómo se dice? (P)
  You — . . . Se dice . . . (P)
  You don't —! ¡No me digas! (4A)
scared: to be — (of) tener miedo (de) (9B)
schedule el horario (2A)
science:
  — class la clase de ciencias naturales (2A)
  — fiction movie la película de ciencia ficción (9A)
screen: computer — la pantalla (2B)
to **scuba dive** bucear (8A)
sea el mar (8A)
to **search (for)** buscar (9B)
season la estación, *pl.* las estaciones (P)
second segundo, -a (2A)
  — floor el primer piso (6B)
to **see** ver (8A)
  Let's — A ver . . . (2A)
  — you later! ¡Nos vemos!, Hasta luego. (P)
  — you tomorrow. Hasta mañana. (P)
  to — a movie ver una película (4A)
to **sell** vender (7B)
to **send** enviar (i → í) (9B)
to **separate** separar (8B)
September septiembre (P)
serious serio, -a (1B)
to **serve** servir (e → i) (9B)
to **set the table** poner la mesa (6B)
seven siete (P)
seven hundred setecientos, -as (7A)
seventeen diecisiete (P)
seventh séptimo, -a (2A)
seventy setenta (P)
to **share** compartir (3A)
she ella (1B)
sheet of paper la hoja de papel (P)
shelf el estante (6A)
ship el barco (8A)
shirt la camisa (7A)
  T- — la camiseta (7A)
shoe store la zapatería (7B)
shoes los zapatos (7A)
short bajo, -a *(stature)*; corto, -a *(length)* (5B)
shorts los pantalones cortos (7A)
should deber (3B)
show el programa (9A)
to **show** + *movie or TV program* dar (9A)
shy reservado, -a (1B)
sick enfermo, -a (4B)
silly tonto, -a (9A)
to **sing** cantar (1A)
sir (el) señor (Sr.) (P)
sister la hermana (5A)
site: Web — el sitio Web (9B)
six seis (P)
six hundred seiscientos, -as (7A)
sixteen dieciséis (P)
sixth sexto, -a (2A)
sixty sesenta (P)
to **skate** patinar (1A)
to **skateboard** montar en monopatín (1A)
to **ski** esquiar (i → í) (1A)
skirt la falda (7A)
to **sleep** dormir (o → ue) (6A)
sleepy: to be — tener sueño (5B)
slide la diapositiva (9B)
small pequeño, -a (6A)
to **snorkel** bucear (8A)
snow: It's —ing. Nieva. (P)
so much tanto (7A)
so-so regular (P)
soap opera la telenovela (9A)
soccer: to play — jugar al fútbol (4B)
sociable sociable (1B)
social studies class la clase de ciencias sociales (2A)
socks los calcetines (7A)
soft drink el refresco (3A)
software el software (7B)
some unos, -as (2B)
something algo (3B)
sometimes a veces (1B)
son el hijo (5A)
  —s; —(s) and daughter(s) los hijos (5A)

song la canción, *pl.* las canciones (9B)

sorry: I'm —. Lo siento. (4B)

sound (stereo) system el equipo de sonido (6A)

soup: vegetable — la sopa de verduras (3A)

souvenirs los recuerdos (8A)

to buy — comprar recuerdos (8A)

spaghetti los espaguetis (3B)

Spanish class la clase de español (2A)

to **spell:**

How is . . . spelled? ¿Cómo se escribe . . . ? (P)

It's spelled . . . Se escribe . . . (P)

to **spend time with friends** pasar tiempo con amigos (1A)

spoon la cuchara (5B)

sports:

to play — practicar deportes (1A)

— -minded deportista (1B)

— program el programa deportivo (9A)

spring la primavera (P)

stadium el estadio (8A)

stairs, stairway la escalera (6B)

to **start** empezar (e → ie) (9A)

to **stay: I — at home.** Me quedo en casa. (4A)

stepbrother el hermanastro (5A)

stepfather el padrastro (5A)

stepmother la madrastra (5A)

stepsister la hermanastra (5A)

stereo system el equipo de sonido (6A)

stomach el estómago (P)

store la tienda (7A)

book— la librería (7B)

clothing — la tienda de ropa (7A)

department — el almacén, *pl.* los almacenes (7B)

discount — la tienda de descuentos (7B)

household appliance — la tienda de electrodomésticos (7B)

jewelry — la joyería (7B)

shoe — la zapatería (7B)

story el piso (6B)

stories: to write — escribir cuentos (1A)

to **straighten up the room** arreglar el cuarto (6B)

strawberries las fresas (3A)

street la calle (8B)

student el / la estudiante (P)

studious estudioso, -a (1B)

to **study** estudiar (2A)

stupid tonto, -a (9A)

sugar el azúcar (5B)

suit el traje (7A)

summer el verano (P)

to **sunbathe** tomar el sol (8A)

Sunday domingo (P)

sunglasses los anteojos de sol (7B)

sunny: It's —. Hace sol. (P)

to **surf the Web** navegar en la Red (9B)

sweater el suéter (7A)

sweatshirt la sudadera (7A)

to **swim** nadar (1A)

swimsuit el traje de baño (7A)

synagogue la sinagoga (4A)

T

T-shirt la camiseta (7A)

table la mesa (2B)

to set the — poner la mesa (6B)

to **take** llevar (8B)

to — a course tomar un curso (9B)

to — out the trash sacar la basura (6B)

to — photos sacar fotos (5A)

talented talentoso, -a (1B)

to **talk** hablar (2A)

to — on the phone hablar por teléfono (1A)

tall alto, -a (5B)

tasty sabroso, -a (3B); rico, -a (5B)

tea el té (3A)

iced — el té helado (3A)

to **teach** enseñar (2A)

teacher el profesor, la profesora (P)

technology / computers la tecnología (2A)

technology / computer class la clase de tecnología (2A)

television: to watch — ver la tele (1A)

television set el televisor (6A)

to **tell** decir (8B)

— me *(command)* dime (8A)

temple el templo (4A)

ten diez (P)

tennis: to play — jugar al tenis (4B)

tenth décimo, -a (2A)

thank you gracias (P)

that que (5A); ese, esa (7A)

—'s why por eso (9A)

the el, la (1B); los, las (2B)

— best el / la mejor, los / las mejores (6A)

— worst el / la peor, los / las peores (6A)

theater el teatro (8A)

movie — el cine (4A)

their su, sus (5A)

them las, los *dir. obj. pron.* (7B); les *ind. obj. pron.* (8B)

then entonces (4B)

there allí (2B)

— is / are hay (P, 2B)

therefore por eso (9A)

these estos, estas (7A)

they ellos, ellas (2A)

thing la cosa (6A)

to **think** pensar (e → ie) (7A)

I don't — so. Creo que no. (3B)

I — . . . Creo que . . . (3B)

I — so. Creo que sí. (3B)

What do you — (about it)? ¿Qué te parece? (9B)

third tercer (tercero), -a (2A)

third floor el segundo piso (6B)

thirsty: I'm —. Tengo sed. (3B)

thirteen trece (P)

thirty treinta (P); y media *(in telling time)* (P)

thirty-one treinta y uno (P)
this este, esta (7A)
  — afternoon esta tarde (4B)
  — evening esta noche (4B)
  — weekend este fin de semana (4B)
  What is —? ¿Qué es esto? (2B)
those esos, esas (7A)
thousand: a — mil (7A)
three tres (P)
three hundred trescientos, -as (7A)
three-ring binder la carpeta de argollas (2A)
Thursday jueves (P)
ticket el boleto (8A)
tie la corbata (7B)
time:
  At what —? ¿A qué hora? (4B)
  free — el tiempo libre (4A)
  to spend — with friends pasar tiempo con amigos (1A)
  What — is it? ¿Qué hora es? (P)
tired cansado, -a (4B)
to a *(prep.)* (4A)
  in order — para + *inf.* (4A)
  — the a la, al (4A)
  — the left (of) a la izquierda (de) (6A)
  — the right (of) a la derecha (de) (6A)
toast el pan tostado (3A)
today hoy (P)
tomatoes los tomates (3B)
tomorrow mañana (P)
  See you —. Hasta mañana. (P)
too también (1A); demasiado (4B)
  I do (like to) — a mí también (1A)
  me — a mí también (1A)
top: on — of encima de (2B)
touching emocionante (9A)
toy el juguete (8B)
train el tren (8A)
to **travel** viajar (8A)
tree el árbol (8A)
tremendous tremendo, -a (8A)
trip el viaje (8A)
Tuesday martes (P)
  on —s los martes (4A)
TV channel el canal (9A)
twelve doce (P)
twenty veinte (P)
twenty-one veintiuno (veintiún) (P)
two dos (P)
two hundred doscientos, -as (7A)

U

Ugh! ¡Uf! (7B)
ugly feo, -a (6A)
uncle el tío (5A)
uncles; uncle(s) and aunt(s) los tíos (5A)
underneath debajo de (2B)
to **understand** comprender (3A)
unforgettable inolvidable (8B)
us: (to / for) — nos *ind. obj. pron.* (8B)
to **use:**
  It's —d for . . . Sirve para . . . (9B)
  to — the computer usar la computadora (1A)
  What's it —d for? ¿Para qué sirve? (9B)
used usado, -a (8B)
useful:
  to be — servir (9B)
  is — for sirve para (9B)

V

vacation: to go on — ir de vacaciones (8A)
to **vacuum** pasar la aspiradora (6B)
VCR la videocasetera (6A)
vegetable soup la sopa de verduras (3A)
very muy (1B)
  — well muy bien (P)
video el video (5A)
video games: to play — jugar videojuegos (1A)
videocassette el video (6A)
to **videotape** hacer un video (5A)
violent violento, -a (9A)
to **visit** visitar (8A)
  to — chat rooms visitar salones de chat (9B)
volleyball: to play — jugar al vóleibol (4B)
volunteer el voluntario, la voluntaria (8B)
  — work el trabajo voluntario (8B)

W

waiter, waitress el camarero, la camarera (5B)
to **walk** caminar (3B)
wall la pared (6A)
wallet la cartera (7B)
to **want** querer (e → ie) (7A); desear (5B)
  I — (yo) quiero (4B)
  you — (tú) quieres (4B)
warm: to be — tener calor (5B)
was fue (8B)
to **wash** lavar (6B)
  to — the car lavar el coche (6B)
  to — the clothes lavar la ropa (6B)
  to — the dishes lavar los platos (6B)
wastepaper basket la papelera (2B)
watch el reloj pulsera (7B)
to **watch television** ver la tele (1A)
water el agua *f.* (3A)
we nosotros, -as (2A)
to **wear** llevar (7A)
weather: What's the — like? ¿Qué tiempo hace? (P)
Web:
  to surf the — navegar en la Red (9B)
  — page la página Web (9B)
  — site el sitio Web (9B)
Wednesday miércoles (P)
week la semana (P)
  last — la semana pasada (7B)

weekend:

on —s los fines de semana (4A)

this — este fin de semana (4B)

welcome: You're —. De nada. (5B)

well bien (P); pues *(to indicate pause)* (1A)

very — muy bien (P)

What? ¿Qué?, ¿Cuál? (3A)

— are you doing? ¿Qué estás haciendo? (6B)

— are you like? ¿Cómo eres? (1B)

(At) — time? ¿A qué hora? (4B)

— color . . . ? ¿De qué color . . . ? (6A)

— day is today? ¿Qué día es hoy? (P)

— did you do? ¿Qué hiciste? (8A)

— do you like better (prefer) to do? ¿Qué te gusta hacer más? (1A)

— do you like to do? ¿Qué te gusta hacer? (1A)

— do you think (about it)? ¿Qué te parece? (9B)

— does . . . mean? ¿Qué quiere decir . . . ? (P)

— else? ¿Qué más? (8B)

— happened to you? ¿Qué te pasó? (8A)

— is she / he like? ¿Cómo es? (1B)

— is the date? ¿Cuál es la fecha? (P)

— is this? ¿Qué es esto? (2B)

— is your name? ¿Cómo te llamas? (P)

— kind of . . . ? ¿Qué clase de . . . ? (9A)

— time is it? ¿Qué hora es? (P)

— would you like? ¿Qué desean (Uds.)? (5B)

—'s happening? ¿Qué pasa? (P)

—'s his / her name? ¿Cómo se llama? (1B)

—'s it (used) for? ¿Para qué sirve? (9B)

—'s the weather like? ¿Qué tiempo hace? (P)

What!:

— a good / nice idea! ¡Qué buena idea! (4B)

— a shame / pity! ¡Qué pena! (4B)

When? ¿Cuándo? (4A)

Where? ¿Dónde? (2B)

— are you from? ¿De dónde eres? (4A)

(To) —? ¿Adónde? (4A)

whether si (6B)

Which? ¿Cuál? (3A)

— ones? ¿Cuáles? (6B)

white blanco, -a (6A)

who que (5A)

Who? ¿Quién? (2A)

Why? ¿Por qué? (3B)

wife la esposa (5A)

Will you bring me . . . ? ¿Me trae . . . ? (5B)

window la ventana (2B)

winter el invierno (P)

with con (3A)

— me conmigo (4B)

— my / your friends con mis / tus amigos (4A)

— whom? ¿Con quién? (4A)

— you contigo (4B)

without sin (3A)

woman la mujer (5B)

older woman la anciana (8B)

work el trabajo (4A)

volunteer — el trabajo voluntario (8B)

to **work** trabajar (1A)

worse than peor(es) que (6A)

worst: the — el / la peor, los / las peores (6A)

Would you like . . . ? ¿Te gustaría . . . ? (4B)

to **write:**

to — e-mail escribir por correo electrónico (9B)

to — stories escribir cuentos (1A)

Y

yard el jardín, *pl.* los jardines (8B)

year el año (P)

He / She is / They are . . . —s old. Tiene(n) . . . años. (5A)

last — el año pasado (7B)

yellow amarillo, -a (6A)

yes sí (1A)

yesterday ayer (7B)

yogurt el yogur (3A)

you *fam. sing.* tú (2A); *formal sing.* usted (Ud.) (2A); *fam. pl.* vosotros, -as (2A); *formal pl.* ustedes (Uds.) (2A); *fam. after prep.* ti (1A); *sing. ind. obj. pron.* te (8B); *pl. fam. ind. obj. pron.* os (8B); *ind. obj. pron.* le, les (8B)

And — ? ¿Y a ti? (1A)

for — para ti (6A)

to / for — *fam. pl.* os (8B)

to / for — *fam. sing.* te (8B)

with — contigo (4B)

— don't say! ¡No me digas! (4A)

— say . . . Se dice . . . (P)

young joven (5B)

— boy / girl el niño, la niña (8B)

— man el joven (5B)

— woman la joven (5B)

—er menor (5A)

your *fam.* tu (2B); *fam.* tus, vuestro(s), -a(s) (5A); *formal* su, sus (5A)

Yuck! ¡Uf! (7B)

Z

zero cero (P)

zoo el zoológico (8A)

Grammar Index

Structures are most often presented first in *A primera vista*, where they are practiced lexically. They are then explained later in a *Gramática* section or a *Nota*. Lightface numbers refer to the pages where structures are initially presented or, after explanation, where student reminders occur. **Boldface numbers** refer to pages where structures are explained or are otherwise highlighted.

Acknowledgments

Cover Design Tamada Brown & Associates

Program Graphic Development Herman Adler Design

Maps Mapping Specialists

Technical Illustration/Additional Graphics Herman Adler Design; New England Typographic Services; Publicom; John Reece

Illustrations Wilkinson Studios; Bob Brugger: pp. 80, 109, 113, 136, 137; Donna Catanese: p. 52; Dennis Dzielak: pp. 11, 15, 157, 226; Seitu Hayden: pp. 4, 9, 14, 22, 23, 27, 134, 136, 140, 143, 167, 169, 171, 197, 289, 299, 310; Reggie Holladay: pp. 65, 76, 77, 110, 230, 321; Tim Jones: pp. 4, 5, 8, 9, 14, 71, 73, 79, 107, 127, 141, 143, 144, 156, 162, 164, 165, 319, 325; Jonathan Massie: pp.126, 133, 251, 257, 325; Tom McKee: pp. 5, 8, 9, 19, 20, 64, 65, 99, 146, 147, 172, 173, 175, 194, 282, 283; Donna Perrone: pp. 17, 94; Judy Stead: pp. 95, 102, 191, 196, 204, 311; Nicole Wong: pp. 187, 327

Photography Front and back covers: El Morro Fortress, San Juan, Puerto Rico, Robert Frerck/Odyssey/Chicago; (front cover inset) Visitors in the Caribbean National Forest (El Yunque), Puerto Rico, Andrea Booher/Getty Images; Photographers who contributed to the studio/location photography: Bill Burlingham, Burlingham Photography and John Morrison, Morrison Photography.

xii-xiii, José Fuste Raga/CORBIS; xii inset, Danny Lehman/CORBIS, xiii inset, www.corbis.com/Phil Schermeister; xiv-xv, Danny Lehman/CORBIS; xvi-xvii, David Zimmerman/CORBIS; xvi inset, Stuart Westmorland/CORBIS; xviii-xix, Jim Erickson/CORBIS; xx-xxi ©Galen Rowell/CORBIS; xxii-xxiii background Paul Hardy/CORBIS, xxii inset, Mark L. Stephenson, xxiii br, ©José Fuste Raga/CORBIS; xxiv-xxv ©Craig Tuttle/CORBIS, xxiv inset, © Bob Daemmrich/The Image Works, Inc.; xxv br inset, Ron Watts/CORBIS, xxv bl Corbis Royalty Free; xxvi b, Jim Zuckerman/CORBIS; xxvi t, Jimmy Dorantes/LF

1 LWA Stephen Welstea/CORBIS; 2d, © Nicholas Eveleigh/ SuperStock; 2 t, Jimmy Dorantes/LF; 2 b, Peter Chartrand/DDB; 3, Craig Lovell/The Viesti Collection, Inc.; Bob Daemmrich/ Stock Boston; Bob Daemmrich/ Stock Boston;13, Pete Saloutos/CORBIS; 26, The Stock Market; 28 t, Steve Vidler/eStock Photography LLC; 28 m, Jeff Greenberg/Photo Edit; 28 b, ©Robert Frerck/OP/Chicago; 29 m, The Stock Market; 30 inset, M. Lee Fatherree. Collection of Federal Reserve Bank of Dallas.; 30–31, Rob Lewine/Corbis; 37 (2), Courtesy of Sony Electronics, Inc.; 37 (5), PhotoDisc/GettyImages; 39 t, Dick Luria/Taxi/GettyImages; 39 b, Carmen Lomas Garza; 43 bl, Dorling Kindersley Media Library; 44, Rivera, Diego (1886–1957). The grinder (La molendera). 1924. Oil on canvas, 35 7/16 x 46 1/16 in. Museo Nacional de Arte Moderno, Instituto Nacional de Bellas Artes, Mexico City, D.F., Mexico./ Art Resource, N.Y.;45 b, © Tony Freeman/PhotoEdit; 45 t, ©Jimmy Dorantes/LatinFocus.com; 46 t, ©CORBIS/Sygma; 47 r, Goya, Francisco (1746–1828). Ritratto della famiglia di Carlo IV. Prado Madrid./Art Resource, N.Y.; 47 l, The Bridgeman Art Library International, Ltd.; 52 t, Steve Shott/Dorling Kindersley Media Library; 54, Courtesy of Ana Sofía Villaveces; 55 t, Courtesy of Ana Sofía Villaveces; Robert Fried Photography; 56 t, David Seawell/CORBIS; 57 t, Robert Frerck/OP; 57 m, Lou Bopp; 57 b, Jimmy Dorantes/LF; 62, Lawrence Migdale/ Stock Boston; 62–63, Robert Fried/Stock Boston; 63 inset, Silva, Simón. Orgullo de la familia. 1997. Simón Silva; 72, Carlos Goldin/DDB; 73, David R. Frazier/ Photolibrary/Alamy; 75, Ilene Perlman/Stock Boston; 76 b, Joe Viesti/VC; 79, David Young-Wolffe/PhotoEdit; 81 m, Jimmy Dorantes/LF; 81 b, U.S. Department of Agriculture; 82, HIRB/Index Stock Imagery, Inc.; 82 b, Jimmy Dorantes/LF; 82 t, PhotoDisc/GettyImages; 84, Megan Bowers/LF; 85 t, ©Buddy Mays/CORBIS; 85 m, ©Danny Lehman/CORBIS; 86 t, Robert Frerck/OP; 86 m, Ulrike Welsch/PhotoEdit; 87, Robert Fried Photography; 92a, m, Courtesy of El Fenix Restaurants; 92–93, Robert Fried/Stock Boston; 92 inset, Dalí, Salvador (1904–89), Young Girl looking out of the window. Museo Español de Arte Contemporáneo, Madrid, Spain. The Bridgeman Art Library International Ltd.; 103, HIRB/Index Stock Imagery, Inc.; 108, Hector Mata/AFP/PhotoEdit; 111, Rhoda Sidney/Stock Boston; Robert Frerck/Odyssey Productions, Inc.; 112 b, Jimmy Dorantes/LatinFocus.com; 114, Bob Daemmrich/Stock Boston; 115, Patti McConville/IS; 118, Jeff Greenberg/Stock Boston; 119 t, Rhoda Sidney/Stock Boston; 119 m, Bonnie Kamin/PhotoEdit; 124, Ulrike Welsch/Stock Boston; 124–125, Rob Crandall/Stock Boston; 135, Robert Frerck/WC; 148 b, Rob Crandall/Stock Boston; 148 m, Bob Krist/eStock Photography, LLC; 148 t, Kim Newton/WC; 149 t, Kal Muller/WC; 149 b, Robert Fried Photography; 154 Manuello Paganelli/WC; inset, Miró, Joan (1893-1983). Self-portrait, 1919. Oil on canvas. © ARS, NY. Photo: J.G. Berizzi. Musée Picasso, Paris, France./Art Resource, N.Y.; 154–155, Owen Franklin/Stock Boston; 162, Marlborough Gallery, Inc.; 163, Robert Fried Photography; Robert Frerck/WC; 164, Michael Newman/PhotoEdit; 165 money, Jimmy Dorantes/LatinFocus.com; 170, © David Young-Wolff/PhotoEdit;175, ©Mitchell Gerber/CORBIS; 176 bl, t, Joe Viesti/VC; 176 m, IFA Bilderteam/eStock Photography LLC; 177 tl, IFA Bilderteam/eStock Photography; 177 b, Joe Viesti/VC; 178, Wolfgang Kaehler Photography; 179, Robert Frerck/WC; Robert Fried/Robert Fried Photography; 184 inset, Englebert Photography, Inc.; 184–185, (background) Ulrike Welsch Photography; 192–193, ©2004 Ulrike Welsch Photography; 195 t, bl, Robert Fried Photography; 195 br, Bonnie Kamin/PhotoEdit; 195 m, H. Huntly Hersch/D. Donne Bryant Stock Photography; 198 b, Robert Frerck/WC; 199 m, Thomas R. Fletcher/ Stock Boston; 201 l, SuperStock, Inc.; 201 m, San Diego Historical Society; 201 r, Richard Pasley/Stock Boston; 205, Joe Viesti/VC; 206, ©Robert Frerck/OP; 208 t, Spencer Grant/ PhotoEdit; 208 m, Leslye Borden/PhotoEdit; 209 tl, Peter Bennett/Ambient Images; 209 tr, Joe Viesti/VC; 210, Walter Bibikow/Stock Boston; 211 t, David Young-Wolff/PhotoEdit; 216 inset, View of Toledo, El Greco, Metropolitan Museum of Art, New York/Index/Bridgeman Art Library, London/New York; 216–217, Royalty-Free/CORBIS; 221 bl, Michael Sewell/Peter Arnold, Inc.; 224, ©Wolfgang Kaehler/CORBIS; 226, Robert Fried/DDB; 227, Art Womack/IS; 228 t, ©Danny Lehman/CORBIS; 228 (1), Salatiel Barragan/LatinFocus.com; 228 (2), Ulrike Welsch/PhotoEdit; 228 (3), Robert Fried Photography; 228 (4), Salatiel Barragan/LatinFocus.com; 228 (5), Russell Gordon/Danita Delimont, Agent; 229 r, Galen Rowell/ CORBIS; 229 l, Suzanne Murphy Larronde/DDB; 229, br, ACE STOCK LIMITED/Alamy; 231, M.Paganelli/WC; 235 b, Mireille Vautier/WC; 235 t, Caroline Woodham/Image State/International Stock Photography Ltd.; 236, Robert Frerck/OP; 237, Jimmy Dorantes/LatinFocus.com; 238, Paul Harris/Stone/GettyImages; 239 b, ©Robert Frerck/OP; 239 tr, Richard Cummins/Corbis; 240 m, Gisela Damm/eStock Photography, LCC; 240 t, Michele Burgess/Stock Boston; 240 b, ©Robert Frerck/OP; 241 tr, Gavin Hellier/Getty Images, Inc.; 241 b, ©Robert Frerck/OP; 242 t, tr, Gavin Hellier/Getty Images, Inc.; 243 t, © Lake County Museum/Corbis; 243 b, DDB; 248–249, Courtesy of the Peace Corps; 256, AGE Fotostock America, Inc.; 257, ©2004 Ulrike Welsch Photography; 258 (1), Myrleen Cate Ferguson/PhotoEdit; 258 (2, 3), Michael Newman/PhotoEdit; (4), David Young-Wolff/PhotoEdit; 259 b, Courtesy of Interplast; 259 t, Inga Spence/DDB; 261 b, Jimmy Dorantes/LatinFocus.com; 262 b, Jonathan Nourok/PhotoEdit; t, © David-/young Wolff/Photo Edit – All rights reserved.; 264, ©Chris Hamilton/CORBIS; 267 t, ©Fernando Alda/CORBIS; 267 b, Steve Raymer/NGS Image Collection; 268 all, PhotoDisc/GettyImages; 269 t, Courtesy of the Mobility Project Organization, www.mobilityproject.org; 269 b, Marcelo Salinas/LatinFocus.com; 270, SuperStock, Inc; 271 br, Puerto Rican Foundation For Conservation; 271 t, Ro De La Harpe/ Animals Animals/Earth Scenes; 271 b, Bob Daemmrich/Photo Edit; 272 b, A. Ramey/PhotoEdit; 273 t, Mary Kate Denny/PhotoEdit; b, SuperStock, Inc.; 274 t, Bob Daemmrich/Stock Boston; 274 b, Bruce Farnsworth/Chuck Place Photography; 275, Jonathan Nourok/PhotoEdit; 275 b, Peter Chartrand/DDB; 280 inset, Dalí, Salvador. Portrait of Luis Buñuel, 1924. Oil on canvas, .70 x .60 m. Coll. Luis Buñuel, Mexico City, D.F., Mexico./Art Resource, N.Y.; 280–281, Primer Impacto © Univisión Communications Inc. 2002, All rights reserved.; 289, Reuters NewMedia Inc./CORBIS; 290 t, Courtesy El Juego de la Vida/©Televisa 2002/All rights reserved.; 291 l, David Young-Wolff/PhotoEdit; 291 r, Michael Newman/PhotoEdit; 293, Bob Daemmrich/Stock Boston; Ulrike Welsch/ PhotoEdit; 294 b, Leroy Jean Marie/CORBIS SYGMA; 296 b, Steve Chenn/CORBIS; 297, t, David Young-Wolff/Photo Edit, 297 b, Jeremy Horner/CORBIS; 298 b, Noticiero Univisión, © The Univisión Network Limited Partnership 2002, All rights reserved.; 300 t, Scott Barrow/IS; 300 b, Tony Freeman/PhotoEdit; 301 l, DD Gordon; 301 r, ©Robert Frerck/OP; 303 t, ©Robert Frerck/OP; 303 m, David Young-Wolff/PhotoEdit; 303 b, Robert Fried/Stock Boston; 308–309, Roberto M. Arakaki, IS.; 308 inset, Picasso, Pablo (1881–1973). Reading the Letter, 1921. Oil on canvas, 184 x 105 cm. Photo: J.G. Berizzi. © ARS, NY. Musée Picasso, Paris, France./Art Resource, N.Y.; 316, Candida Höfer/Biblioteca de la Real Academia de la Lengua Madrid IV; 319, ©Robert Frerck/OP; 322, t, Robert Frerck/OP; 325 t, © J. Griffis Smith/Texas Department of Transportation; 327 tl, ©John Vachon/CORBIS; 327 tr, ©Robert Frerck/OP; 327 b, Jeff Greenberg/IS; 330 t, Ulrike Welsch Photography; 330 b, Najlah Feanny/Stock Boston; 331 t, James Davis/IS; 331 b, ©Robert Frerck/OP; 336, LatinFocus.com; ©Royalty-Free/CORBIS; Robert Fried Photography; 337, Mireille Vautier/WC; David Young-Wolff/Photo Edit; Ulrike Welsch/Stock Boston.

Video *¿Eres tú, María?* is based on the novel *¿Eres tú, María?* (from the "Lola Lago, Detective" series) by Lourdes Miguel and Neus Sans, Difusión Centro de Investigación y Publicaciones de Idiomas, S. L. Barcelona, Spain, 1989.

Key D. Donne Bryant Stock Photography = DDB; ImageState/International Stock Photography, Ltd. = IS; Latin Focus Photo Agency = LF; Odyssey Productions, Inc. = OP; The Viesti Collection, Inc. = VC; Woodfin Camp & Associates = WC

Text Chapter 6B, p. 137: "¿Quién hace las tareas?" by Matilde de la Vara from *Muy Interesante*. Marzo 2002, No. 250. Published by G Y J España Ediciones, S.L., S. en C. Chapter 8B, p. 261: "Reduce-Reusa-Recicla" from La Fundación Puertorriqueña de Conservación & Logo of Fundación Puertorriqueña de Conservación. Copyright © 2001. Used by permission of Fundación Puertorriqueña de Conservación. Chapter 9A, p. 297: Cable Mágico Guía de Programación Mensual. Abril 2002, No. 107. Chapter 9A, p. 300: Adapted from ¡Apágala! from *Time For Kids*. April 12, 2002, Vol. 7, No. 22. Copyright 2002 Time Inc. All rights reserved. Chapter 9B, p. 318: Adapted from "A sus teclados, listos...¡a navegar!" from *Image Doc*. Marzo 2002, No. 159, p. 48.

Note: Every effort has been made to locate the copyright owner of material used in this textbook. Omissions brought to our attention will be corrected in subsequent editions.